THEOCHARIS E. DETORAKIS
PROFESSOR AT UNIVERSITY OF CRETE

HISTORY OF CRETE

TRANSLATED BY JOHN C. DAVIS

IRAKLION 1994

Translated into English by J. C. Davis 1994

To my children
Stathis and Marina

‘Since most of those who have written on Crete are not in accord with one another, it should be no wonder if some may disagree with what we are about to relate’
(Diodorus Sikeliotes V, 80,4)

PREFACE

to the English edition

In the middle of the Mediterranean basin, located in a position almost equidistant from Europe, Asia and Africa, lies the island of Crete. Its privileged position is linked with a rare -perhaps unique- combination of geographical and climatic conditions. The length of the island, from the headland of Sidero in the east to Cape Grambousa in the west, is 260 km (156 miles), and at its widest point the island measures 56 km (34 miles) from north to south between the headlands of Stavros and Lithinon, while at the isthmus of Ierapetra it is just 12 km.

Crete generally impresses for being a mountainous island, and it does indeed resemble a huge extended rock rising out of the sea. Mt. Ida, or Psiloritis, dominates the centre of the island, towering to a height of 2456 m. (8058 ft.), while to the west the peaks of the Lefka Ori, or Madares, compete for attention (2452 m.). The mountain range of Diktys in the east is slightly lower reaching a height of 2148m. Linking these three main groups of mountains are smaller mountains and hills separated by beautiful green valleys and slopes covered in vineyards and olive groves, and intersected by rivulets and dry streams that turn into torrents in winter, and a number of plains of which the largest is Mesara Plain in the south of the province of Herakleion.

These geographical features give Crete a remarkable natural character combining elements of the North and of the South, of Europe and of Africa. Variations of landscape and of weather conditions in Crete can be so great that within the space of a few miles one's impression of the island changes completely. Its unique natural beauty both enchants and captivates the onlooker. Few places on Earth have a comparable wealth and variety of flora and fauna.

On Crete the cedar and the mountain cypress exist side by side with the olive, the palm and banana trees, while in many parts of the southern coastal region the winter is so mild that the swallows do not fly further south. A huge variety of crops and agricultural products ensures the rich self-sufficiency of the island despite its apparent mountainous character.

Crete appears to turn its face towards Europe, and its south side towards Africa. The north coast is indented with deep natural harbours and hospitable bays, while the south coast is rugged and harsh with few bays and virtually no decent harbour apart from that of Ierapetra. This difference explains the development and precedence of the north side of Crete over the south.

Crete is famous, however, chiefly for its long and eventful history and its contribution to world civilisation. Its history is daunting for its variety and wealth of events and achievements. It is not an exaggeration to say that nowhere in Greece can boast such a long and rich historical and cultural tradition as Crete, stamped as it is by such a distinct character.

In my *History of Crete,* originally published in Athens in 1986 and reprinted in Herakleion (1990), I have attempted to give an accurate overview of the tumultuous events and cultural features of the island. I was very grateful for the enthusiasm with which the book was received by the Greek reading public and for the flattering reviews from specialists in the field. The book, which has been described as 'the best history of Crete', gives a clear and full account of the history and culture of the island from neolithic times (ca. 6000 B.C.) right up to the Nazi invasion of Crete in 1941 with the legendary Battle of Crete. Written in a plain and simple style and as a continuous narrative without chronological gaps, the *History* is a synthesis of the vast international bibliography that has grown up around the field of Cretan studies.

The translation of the book into English seeks to fill a large gap that had existed till now in the bibliography. The international reading public is now able to become acquainted with the rich history of Crete in its entirety, with the turbulent events affecting the life of its people, as well as the incalculable contribution it has made to world civilisation, within the pages of one volume, based as it is on the available documentation and containing all the main components of the island's long historical experience without declining into tiresome detail.

The English translation is based on the second Greek edition and was not altered in any significant way. A few oversights that had remained in the Greek text were corrected and a very few extracts from documents and records were left out of the English version simply because it was thought that they were not of especial interest to the non-Greek reader. At the end is appended a short bibliography, arranged according to subject and historical period. A full bibliography for those who are interested in pursuing a branch of Cretan history further has been compiled by myself in the Greek periodical *Palimpseston,* vol. III (Herakleion, Crete 1986), pp. 161-237.

In presenting my work to the foreign reading public, and the Anglophone reading public in particular, I would like to take this opportunity to thank John Davis, an English philologist and Byzantinist conducting research at the National Hellenic Research Foundation in Athens, for his careful and elegant translation. I should also like to express my gratitude to the directors of the Regional Administration of Crete, George Senetakis and Stavros Kambelis, for their recognition of my work and the financial support they have secured for the publication through European Community funding.

Theocharis E. Detorakis

PREFACE

to the Greek edition

Spyridon Lambros, in his preface to the *Short History of Crete* (1909) by Stephanos Xanthoudidis, remarked that 'the time for the writing of an accurate history of Crete has not yet arrived.' Today, over eighty years later, this observation still holds true. The history of Crete is daunting, both in length and in the variety and number of events it includes. Nowhere in Greece can boast such a long and rich historical and cultural tradition as Crete, stamped as it is by such a distinct character. Consequently, despite the archaeological and historical research that has been carried out this century, along with the publication of books and articles and the holding of international colloquia that have Crete as their subject and whose proceedings are then published in large and lavish volumes, there is still much about which we are either ignorant or unsure in Cretan history. Of course our knowledge has increased greatly, but this increase has in turn given rise to other difficulties, as the scholar is faced with the problem of availing himself of, and assimilating, the vast bibliography that expands daily with studies published in practically every language of the world. The historian who has chosen Crete as his object of research must be acquainted with all this, as well as being familiar with specialist fields that are not always directly related to his subject.

Bearing all this in mind one might be excused for seeing the attempt at writing a general history of Crete as a somewhat hazardous enterprise. The writer exposes himself all too easily to censure from his fellow scholars who may criticise his mistakes and oversights or his failure to exploit the formidably large bibliography to the full. To this we should add the excessive sensitivity of Cretans to subjects concerning their local history: the writer may find himself accused by his fellow islanders of giving a biased account or for unwittingly concealing facts, especially concerning people and events of recent history.

I was well aware of all these difficulties and my misgivings about the whole endeavour were great. But the alternative was that we would run the risk of never writing a general history of Crete which may serve the contemporary reader and which may inform him of the history and events of the island through the ages. Today there is still no authoritative and readily available history for the general reader or scholar who wishes to acquaint himself easily with Cretan history. The large works of the older historians of Crete (those of Psilakis, Xanthoudidis, Kriaris and Mourellos), though undoubtedly important in their day, bear all too clearly the weaknesses of their age. They reflect the demands of both readers and academics of a different epoch and they can no longer serve as manuals of Cretan history. While they have not necessarily lost all their usefulness, they have lost their authoritativeness.

I have therefore sought to fill a gap in the bibliography. My long professional concern with the eventful history of Crete led me to write the present work, and the persistent incitement and moral support of many good friends helped me to overcome my initial misgivings. The *History of Crete* which I now present to the public has been written entirely anew, on the basis of the modern bibliography, and endeavours to assemble the findings of modern historical research. Following the example of that great doyen of Cretan studies in Greece, Stephanos Xanthoudidis, I have written in a popularizing style, giving a continuous narrative without the cumbersome clutter of footnotes and bibliographical references. I have also tried to focus on the key features of Crete's history without burdening my account with great detail, and to give equal weight to all the historical periods, from neolithic times (ca. 6000 B.C.) right up to the Nazi invasion of Crete in 1941. The reader should therefore be availed of a concise yet broad-sweeping overview of the entire course of Cretan history. I have paid particular attention to certain subjects, such as the Byzantine period and the early years of Ottoman rule on the island, which have not to date been examined in great depth by scholars.

For those, whether specialists in the field of Cretan studies or the general reader, who may be interested in exploring the subject further a bibliography is appended at the end of the book arranged according to the sections and chapters of the text. A full index of subjects, names and places follows the bibliography.

I would like here to express my gratitude to all those who in one way or another helped me in the realization of this work, and to the curators and staff of the various museums, archives and libraries at home and abroad where I worked. I especially thank my good friends Stylianos Alexiou and Nikos Panayiotakis for their kind advice and suggestions. Finally it remains for me to thank my dear wife for her undivided support and for the interest she has always shown in the progress of this work. Without her help this book may never have been written.

Theocharis E. Detorakis

CONTENTS

PART ONE

PREHISTORIC CRETE

CHAPTER I

THE DAWN OF CIVILISATION

Neolithic Crete

Evidence of human habitation in Crete during the Palaeolithic period has not as yet been uncovered. A few finds, such as the rock-paintings on the floor of a cave in the village of Asphendou near Sphakia in southern Crete, were initially believed to be Palaeolithic but were later dated to the Bronze Age (c. 2000 B.C.). Some tools made from antler that were found in Kalo Horafi (Rethymnon) have been dated to the interglacial period but, again, do not offer secure evidence. It seems quite likely, however, that the archaeologist's spade will one day reveal Palaeolithic remains and evidence for the existence of man on the island during this period. Indeed it would be strange if man had not reached Crete at this time.

The oldest evidence of human habitation in Crete dates to the so-called pre-Pottery period (6100-5700 B.C.) and was found in the lowest levels at Knossos, thus distinguishing it as the oldest known settlement in Crete. Pottery was not found among the artifacts of this period, although the working of clay does not seem to have been totally unknown, and it is for this reason that this period has been termed pre-Pottery. The few small artifacts found at this site, such as wooden and stone tools, jewellery, burnt seeds (wheat, barley and lentils) and the bones of domesticated animals (goats, sheep, cattle and pigs) give us an idea of the life of its inhabitants. Everything points to a civilisation at a 'developed productive level,' since evidence for a way of life based exclusively on hunting or fishing is absent. Another feature that has been brought to light in excavations at Knossos is the custom of burying the dead in shallow shaft-graves and in rock-cut chamber tombs close to the settlements, as well as evidence for worship of the dead.

The Neolithic period proper in Crete covers the years 5700 to 2800 B.C. and is divided into early (5700-3800), middle (3800-3500) and late (3500-2800). Besides Knossos and its harbour Katsambas, other Neolithic centres have been identified in Crete, including habitation of caves such as at the caves of Miamou, Eileithuia, Trapeza and Akrotiri at Chania. Neolithic houses were constructed of rough clay bricks, stone and wood. They were often built on a stone socle and consisted of several rectangular rooms. Tools such as axes, hammers, clubs and daggers were generally made from river pebbles, bone or wood. Obsidian from Milos was widely used for weapon heads.

Pottery to begin with was crude and without decoration, but with the passing of time it became more sophisticated with incised decoration or markings, and sometimes with a red and black colour from the uneven baking. The potter's wheel and kiln still lay in the future. The pots were simply baked in the fire.

The first figurines, made of clay or stone, appeared during this period and they represent upright human forms, usually female. One of the oldest figurines represents a fat woman, sitting in the 'eastern' fashion. It was found in Kato Ierapetra and is now in the Archaeological Museum in Herakleion. These figurines may be our earliest evidence for worship of a female deity, symbol of fertility throughout the entire east Mediterranean. It is thought that this deity, which became dominant in Crete, was of eastern origin. On a smaller scale we have votive figurines representing animals and birds.

We know virtually nothing about the inhabitants of Crete during the Neolithic period. We do not know whether they came as colonisers from the Cycladic islands or from the Dodecanese and neighbouring Asia Minor, and it is impossible to say what the racial origin of these people may have been. Many believe that already in the fourth millenium B.C. the Cretan population was composed of peoples of differing origins.

In the most advanced stages of the Neolithic period we have clear evidence of both trade and cultural relations between Crete and the Cyclades, Egypt and the East. After about 3000 B.C. copper starts to appear in Crete, most probably brought by settlers from Asia Minor. Civilisation now enters a phase of rapid development.

CHAPTER II

MINOAN CIVILISATION

1. Archaeological excavations

The Minoan civilisation is surely the greatest achievement of Crete, and the most important of the bronze age cultures within the Greek world as a whole. For thousands of years it was buried in the ground and right until the end of the nineteenth century our knowledge of prehistoric Crete was very meagre indeed. There were abundant mythical accounts by ancient Greek and Latin authors that kept alive the memory of an illustrious local ruler, Minos, son and disciple of Zeus the king of the gods who also happened to have been born in Crete. His land enjoyed prosperity and the rule of law and was admired for its hundred cities of which Knossos was the most renowned. The lofty pride of Minos and the artistic genius of Daedalus produced unique and incomparable works of art in this city. The sea-kingdom of Minos extended to the islands and even as far as Attica which was compelled to pay a woeful tribute in blood to the Cretan Minotaur, until the hero king of Athens, Theseus, was to deliver his city from the Minotaur's tyranny. All this obscure web of myth seemed to echo a golden age that had been lost forever.

Archaeological excavation then appeared to bring these myths to life and to prove the factual core behind the myths. Foreign travellers and antiquarians on their visits to Crete had pointed out and described various remains, and especially inscriptions, that were still visible above the ground. The first person to discover the palace of Knossos and to carry out a small excavation of a part of it was the merchant and antiquarian Minos Kalokairinos from nearby Herakleion. A short while later in 1884 Joseph Hadzidakis, chairman of the Educational Association of Herakleion, working with the Italian archaeologist Halbherr, dug at various caves (Idaion Andron, Spcos Eileithuias), while in the same year the Law Code inscription was discovered at Gortyn.

The last twenty years of the nineteenth century saw an increase in the number of foreign archaeologists who were interested in conducting excavations in Crete, especially following the impressive discoveries at Mycenae on the Greek mainland. Heinrich Schliemann, the director of the dig at Mycenae, himself attempted to negotiate with the Turkish landowners in the area of Knossos, but his efforts were unsuccessful. In 1894 the Englishman Arthur Evans (1851-1941), curator of the Ashmolean Museum in Oxford, arrived in Crete. Evans believed that the solution to the enigma surrounding Mycenean civilisation would be found in Crete. Having carried out a brief investigation at Hagios Onouphrios in the Mesara plain, he decided to concentrate his archaeological work on Knossos. However, historical events in Crete between 1895 and 1898 prevented Evans from proceeding until in 1898 Crete was granted autonomy by the Ottoman State thus now creating favourable conditions for systematic excavations. After negotiations with the Turkish landowners Evans bought an extensive piece of land on the hill of "Kephala" (the name of the area where the Knossos palace was situated) and started excavating in March 1990. The results quickly proved to be impressive. The excavation proceeded rapidly and revealed the Minoan palace and a mass of finds such as vases, seals, writing tablets and figurines. Evans had secured his name for posterity as the father of Minoan archaeology. He moved into his villa, named Ariadne, built next to the site of Knossos and, with a select band of fellow workers, directed the excavations and studied the finds. The results were later published in his monumental work *The Palace of Minos at Knossos* (1921-1936), a study which has been described as a brilliant and imaginative attempt at the historical reconstruction of Minoan civilisation. Today, over fifty years since its publication, Evans work is still considered essential to the subject and unsurpassed in its scholarship.

Naturally Evans did not limit himself just to a study of the findings from his excavations. He also made impressive restorations both of the palace and of the wall-paintings, for which he obtained the assistance of talented artists. His methods of restoration do not find many sympathizers among modern archaeologists who criticise Evans for his arbitrariness in restoring much of the palace and for the weak basis of his artistic views. Yet so far there has not been a single theory that has overturned the basic conclusions of the first great archaeologist in Crete. Thus rose the palace of Minos from out of the depths of the Cretan land, brought back to life by the convictions of a man whose life's ambition was to establish the historical truth lying behind the enchanting myths of antiquity.

At the same time as Evans was excavating at Knossos other archaeologists, both Greek and foreign, were investigating other centres of Minoan civilisation. Joseph Hadzidakis, Curator of Antiquities in Crete and a founding member of the Archaeological Museum of Herakleion, discovered the palace of Mallia in north-eastern Crete and the Minoan site of Tylissos, while the archaeologist and leading figure of Cretan studies, Stephanos Xanthoudidis (1864-1928), investigated the vaulted tombs in the Mesara plain. The Italian Archaeological School excavated the palace of Phaistos (1900-1909, 1950 and later), the French Archaeological School excavated at the palace of Mallia (1922-1929) and American archaeologists excavated at the Gournia settlement on the northern edge of the isthmus at Ierapetra (1904).

It would take up much space to describe in detail all the excavations that have been carried out in Crete. It is worth mentioning, however, that a highly productive phase of excavations began again after the Second World War. Experts and scholars from foreign archaeological schools have continued their excavations at the above-mentioned Minoan centres and at new sites, in caves and on mountain top shrines, in settlements, palaces and country houses, all with interesting finds. Greek archaeologists have also played an important role in Cretan archaeology: Marinatos, Sakellarakis,

Davaras, Platon, Alexiou (the latter two have published works in English) and many others who by their excavations have brought to light new evidence for Minoan culture and who have helped solve various problems associated with Minoan studies. The archaeological dig (1960) conducted under the direction of N. Platon at the palace of Zakros in eastern Crete, the largest palace site after Knossos, was of major importance and uncovered many interesting artifacts. It is very likely that continued excavation in western Crete and the further analysis of finds will help us form a more complete and accurate picture of Minoan civilisation and may also mean that we will have to revise older opinions and theories.

2. The sites of Minoan Crete

The largest and most important of the Minoan sites in Crete are to be found in the central and eastern parts of the island, and generally on, or close to, the northern coast. The main centre, and the heart of Minoan Crete, was Knossos, close to the present day town of Herakleion. Another important centre, that overlooks the plain of Mesara, was Phaistos. Tradition holds that the king of Phaistos was Rhadamanthos, the brother of Minos. A third brother, Sarpedon, was king at Mallia about 40 km east of Knossos. The ancient name of this centre, however, is not known to us. Zakros, on the eastern edge of Crete, was also a wealthy and powerful Minoan centre, situated conveniently for links with Egypt and the rest of the Near East. All these sites are noteworthy for their large, imposing palace complexes.

Besides these main centres, many smaller Minoan settlements, dwellings, farms, cave sanctuaries and mountain shrines, tombs and cemeteries have also been identified and excavated. The map of Minoan archaeological sites in Crete shows dense settlement in the central and eastern parts of the island, and particularly along the northern coast. The southern coast was then, as now, rugged and not easily approachable, and without large harbours or beaches. Also in western Crete, as far as we can tell, there are only a few Minoan sites. Recent research, however, has started to uncover more finds from the western part of Crete.

3. Dating Minoan civilisation

We owe the dating of Minoan civilisation to its first great scholar, Sir Arthur Evans. Basing his calculations on the pottery found in Crete and on the study of Egyptian and eastern finds on the island, as well as the Cretan works that had been discovered in Egypt, Evans attempted to link Cretan chronology to Egyptian, the latter being already known to us from the Pharaoh dynasties. He thus proposed a rough chronology that was divided into three main periods: Early Minoan (3400-2100 B.C.), Middle Minoan (1580-1200 B.C.) and Late Minoan (1580-1200 B.C.). Each of these was in turn divided into three smaller phases. The high point of Minoan civilisation was dated by Evans to Middle Minoan III and Late Minoan I (1700-1450 B.C.).

New dating was proposed by Professor Platon in 1958 at the Eighth International Symposium on Prehistory and Protohistory held in Hamburg. This dating was based on totally new criteria, namely: the main phases in the life of the palace complex at Knossos. Platon believed that the first palace complex had been constructed around 2000 B.C. and was destroyed around 1700 B.C. It was then rebuilt on a much grander scale but was finally destroyed in about 1400 B.C., most probably by a massive volcanic eruption at Thera (Santorini) to the north of Crete. This new dating method, which seems to have been widely adopted, has brought with it new terminology and periods. It is thought that the Neolithic period ends in Crete in about 2600 B.C., and that this was succeeded by the following: Pre-Palace (2600-2000 B.C.), Proto-Palace (2000-1700 B.C.), Neo-Palace (1700-1400 B.C.) and Post Palace (1400-1100 BC).

In the table below are presented the two dating systems and how they correspond to each other, as well as their relationship with the Pharaoh dynasties of Egypt:

EVANS' DATING	B.C.	EGYPTIAN DATING	PLATON'S DATING	B.C.
Neolithic	-2700	Dynasties II-III	Neolithic	-2600
Early Minoan I	2600-2400	Dynasty IV	Pre-Palace I	2600-2400
Early Minoan I	2400-2200	Dynasties V-VI	Pre-Palace II	2400-2100
Early Minoan III	2200-2000	Dynasties VI-X	Pre-Palace III	2100-1900
Middle Minoan I	2000-1900	Dynasty XI	Proto-Palace I	1900-1850
Middle Minoan II	1900-1700	Dynasty XII	Proto-Palace II	1850-1800
Middle Minoan III	1700-1600	Dynastyies XIII-XVII	Proto-Palace III	1800-1700
Late Minoan I	1600-1450	Dynasty XVIII	Neo-Palace I	1700-1600
Late Minoan II	1450-1400	Dynasties XVIII-XX	Neo-Palace II	1600-1500
Late Minoan III	1400-1100	Dynasty XX-XXI	Neo-Palace III	1500-1450
			Post-Palace I	1450-1320
			Post-Palace II	1320-1260
			Post-Palace III	1260-1150
Sub-Minoan	1150-1000			

4. The main phases of Minoan civilisation

a) The Prepalatial period (2600-2000 B.C.)

Minoan civilisation is the earliest European civilisation to reach such a high degree of sophistication. It was also the most important Bronze Age civilisation within the Greek world. The theory that Egyptian settlers brought bronze with them to the island no longer has many supporters. It is currently thought that the entire Aegean area was inhabited at this time by a race of people who are usually termed Prehellenes or Aegeans. These were the Pelasgoi recorded by classical writers, thought also to be identical with the Leleges from Karia in south-west Asia Minor. Their existence is attested by archaeological, historical and linguistic evidence. Common place-names with the endings -nthos, -ndos, -s(s)os, and -t(t)os (recalling the many place-names ending in -sa and -nda in Karia) such as Labyrinthos, Knossos, Hymettos, Parnasos, Corinth, Tiryns (accusative Tiryntha), Lindos in Rhodes and many others, as well as common nouns such as hyacinth, narcissus, plinth and cypress are considered to be the linguistic remains of the Pelasgoi. These people, who belonged to the so-called Mediterranean type, being narrow-skulled, short in stature and with dark hair and eyes, bore no resemblance to the Semitic peoples of the east or the Egyptians and other peoples of the north coast of Africa. They were the people who introduced the use of bronze to the region of mainland Greek, the Cyclades and Crete.

The spread of the use of copper and bronze in the Aegean area has been linked to a widespread movement of populations from the coastal region of Asia Minor to Crete, the Cyclades and southern Greece in the middle of the third millenium B.C. These areas enter a phase of rapid social and cultural development, marked chiefly by advances in seafaring and trade relations with the east, Cyprus and Egypt. Copper was imported from Cyprus, gold from Egypt and silver and obsidian from the Cyclades. The east coast of Crete (Mallia, Zakros and Palaikastro) developed rapidly, being well placed for trade with the commercial centres of the east Mediterranean. The role of these centres, which were open to influence from the east, was of fundamental importance for the formation and development of Minoan civilisation. It was during this period that prosperous communities of farmers and shepherds grew up in the fertile plain of Mesara; and towards the end of this period commercial centres started to develop in central Crete and appear to have been linked to one another by a network of roads, such as that between Phaistos and Knossos. Knowledge of bronze manufacture brought changes to the life of the time. Boat design was perfected and communication with other Mediterranean coastal areas to east and west became both safer and efficient.

The quality of life was still low, however. Some caves were still inhabited during the prepalatial period, such as at Miamou, Eileithuia, Trapeza and Arkalokhori. Houses were built according to a specific design. The most interesting of these were discovered at Vasiliki near Ierapetra. Almost all the houses show a combination of stone and mud brick work with interior plastering. We even seem to discern traces of town planning in the settlements of the time.

Cave burial was still practised, but vaulted tombs have also been found (in the Mesara plain) which are thought to be the forerunners of the 'beehive' burial chambers found later in Mycenae and Crete. Each community usually had a communal burial ground, and worship of the dead, with votive vases, jewellery, ribbons and so on, was clearly common practice. At Hagia Photia near Siteia an extensive cemetery was discovered with small rock-cut tombs.

With the passing of time life moved on apace. It is possible for us to distinguish development from the beginning of the first phase where we can still see survivals of Neolithic features, such as at Pyrgos and Hagios Onouphrios, up to the more sophisticated and varied forms found at Koumasa and Vasiliki A and B. The Cretans appear to have learnt stone-working techniques from the Egyptians and managed to produce fine stone artifacts, chiefly vessels used as votive bowls for the dead. Finds from Mokhlos near Siteia and from the Mesara tombs demonstrate the extent of their knowledge concerning stone-working. Cretan rock types, such as steatite, gypsum, stalactite, limestone, and serpentine were all widely used. Obsidian was still imported from Milos, flakes of which were used for shaving. It seems that a shaved face was the preferred fashion throughout the entire Minoan period.

The potter's wheel had been in use for some time and pottery of the period is impressive for its artistry, and each region had its own distinct style: Pyrgos pottery, distinguishable for its black, mottled colour, and Hagios Onouphrios pottery with red lines incised around the base of the vessels. Towards the end of the period we find polychrome pottery, forerunner of the famous Kamares ware of the next period. The spiral shape, the dominant decorative motif of the Minoan period, is first encountered at this time.

There are also artifacts of fine workmanship in gold, silver and bronze. Men's and women's jewellery, daggers and seals in various forms and of the most delicate craftsmanship all indicate the potential of Minoan art during the prepalatial period and foreshadow the peak that was to come in the following age.

Stylianos Alexiou has given us an eloquent description of what life in Crete in 2000 B.C. must have been like: 'Around the end of the prepalatial period, namely ca. 2000 B.C., Crete seems to have offered an advanced way of life, prosperity and impressive signs of progress. It still had thick woods and many streams; and the inhabitants, dark-eyed, swift, vivacious and lightly dressed, lived in the crowded villages, not very different to today, near the streams and on the coast, and close to the groups of vaulted tombs where their forefathers lay. Its seas were traversed by fleets of trading vessels sailing to the Cyclades, Egypt and the coast of Asia Minor in order to buy obsidian, gold, copper, silver and ivory in exchange for Cretan products (Egyptian scarabs found in Crete attest to these trading relations). The olive was already cultivated, cattle, goats, sheep and pigs were reared and the island as a whole was densely inhabited, even in the south. At their festivals they played at bull-vaulting, and their religion seems to have been based on the worship of a Mother Goddess. Life on the island continued in this fashion, awaiting the rapid developments that were to mark the next period: developments that were to give Crete the distinction of being the birthplace of European civilisation.'

b) The Protopalatial period (2000-1700 B.C.)

After a long and creative formative period Crete embarked on a new and perceptibly more advanced phase of cultural evolution. The characteristic feature of this new period is the development of urban life, with all its concomitants, such as monumental architecture and a more refined lifestyle. At the dawn of the second millenium (ca. 1950 B.C.) large palace complexes were built at Knossos, Phaistos, Mallia and Zakros. Excavation has identified smaller palaces at Monastiraki near Amarion and in the district of the town of Chania. These palaces develop in parallel, and they lasted in this form for about two centuries.

This new and unprecedented cultural high point for Crete probably arose under the following historical conditions:

i) Powerful local rulers, the descendents of ancient lords, appear in the towns of central Crete.

ii) The relations between these local kings must have been peaceful during this period. Only peace and cooperation could have enabled long term, dynamic cultural creativity. This state of peace must have prevailed after a long period of internal unrest and civil war. There is evidence from mythology of internal strife, and this has been confirmed by the discoveries of archaeology. Alexiou identified a number of prepalatial citadels on various naturally fortified sites on the island. It seems, then, that the much discussed *Pax minoica* was founded after internal feuds and tension between the Cretan rulers.

iii) Peace and cooperation between the Cretan rulers may have been the result of threat from abroad. The migration and settlement of new peoples in the Aegean and on the coast of Asia Minor may have alarmed the leaders of the Cretan cities and led them to form some kind of Pan-Cretan political union capable of withstanding possible invasion and colonisation of the island.

iv) We cannot tell whether the rulers of the Cretan cities were vassals of the king of Knossos, undoubtedly the largest and most powerful of the cities. But it is quite probable that the king of Knossos was *primus inter pares*.

v) There is much evidence to suggest that there was already an organized social hierarchy, with distinctions in social class, in these Cretan cities. It is also certain that there were many slaves. Slavery was a cornerstone of Egyptian society and of the east in general. It should be no surprise that this institution also appeared in Crete. The execution of the large and ambitious architectural projects in the towns of Crete surely presupposes the existence of a sizeable slave class.

vi) The Cretan economy of the time was flourishing. Cretan trade was quite probably the most prosperous of the east Mediterranean and even outclassed Cypriot trade. The bases for the Minoan sea-kingdom, about which classical writers inform us, had already been laid down. Thucydides (*The Peloponnesian Wars,* Book 1, ch. iv) knew of Minos, the earliest of the kings in the Greek world, and how he built up a powerful naval fleet with which he was able to dominate the islands, found colonies and subdue piracy so that he might reap in the benefits of taxation.

The foundation of the first Minoan palaces, whose precise design we are unable to accurately reconstruct, was linked to a more general cultural advance. Pottery became much more developed, and the potter's wheel and kiln were widely used. The earliest type of Minoan pottery is represented by so-called *barbotine* ware (with relief decoration covering the whole surface of the vases, attached while the clay is still wet). The most impressive pottery of the period, however, is the so-called Kamares ware, produced at the workshops of Knossos and Phaistos. It is called Kamares after the cave at Kamares in Mesara where pots of this style were first recovered. They are impressive for the subtle workmanship and elegance they display and their attractive decoration in unfaded colours. The main decorative patterns are spiral or curve shapes in a great variety of forms. The decoration is in red or white on a black background. The so-called eggshell ware constitutes a special category of vases, finely worked with incredibly thin walls, hence the name eggshell. These pots were made either for ceremonial use (as libation vessels or drinking cups) or for the home. It is characteristic that, for the first time in the history of art, we have in Cretan pottery of this period a combination of the aesthetic and the practical. Even the largest of the vases, such as the pithoi of the royal stores, are decorated with particular care. There are even stone vessels of exquisite artistry, such as oil lamps, circular tables, jugs, and flower-shaped bowls.

The development of sealstone carving followed a similar course. Besides the use of soft material (clay) they now used hard semi-precious stones (such as agate, haematite, jasper, sard, chalcedony and rock-crystal) to produce superb works of miniature art. Many of the sealstones have hieroglyphic letters carved on them, such as often appear in Crete during this period.

Metalwork of the period produced mostly daggers, double axes and everyday implements. Jewellery also reached a high level of artistry. A very fine piece is a gold pendant that consists of two conjoined bees sucking honey from the same honeycomb found at the Chrysolakkos cemetery at Mallia. It is a unique work, both in respect of its subject as well as its execution.

Society of the prepalatial period was more developed. Idols of the time give us a good idea of their dress, as well as associated moral attitudes of the Minoans. The men always wear a girdle around the waist, and the women wear long, broad skirts.

Religious notions do not appear to have changed substantially from the previous period. Personified nature was worshipped in the form of the great Mother Goddess; and the natural cycle of the seasons was worshipped in the form of a young god who died and was reborn each year. There were no temples and the sanctuaries were in caves or on mountain tops.

Burial practice is of especial interest in this period. The communal burial of earlier times was gradually abandoned and individual burial in larnakes (clay burial chests) or pythoi became the practice. This change has been interpreted (by the scholar Glotz) as reflecting a decline in ancestor worship. Older vaulted tombs were reused, and some new ones were also built. Ossuaries were found at Palaikastro and at Mokhlos near Siteia, while at Mallia an entire graveyard was discovered.

In about 1700 there appears to have occurred a sudden destruction of the Minoan palaces. Scholars do not agree on the causes of this destruction and the theories conflict. Some believe that it was due to incursions by Indo-European peoples, and the Proto-Indo-European Luwians in particular, who arrived in the region from Anatolia in Asia Minor, some attribute the destruction to attacks by the Hyksos tribes of Egypt, others to internal crisis and the outbreak of civil war, and others still to natural causes such as earthquake. The older theory of Palmer and Huxley that claimed there had been an invasion of Crete by Luwians and the Hyksos people no longer finds adherents. The composition of the population did not change substantially until after 1450 B.C. when the Mycenaeans established themselves on the island. Before this date there is no evidence for invasion and settlement of other peoples in Crete. The most likely explanation for the disaster of ca. 1700 B.C., which brought an end to the Protopalatial period, is the occurrence of a massive volcanic eruption on Thera (Santorini) that was probably accompanied by a severe earthquake.

c) The Neopalatial period (1700-1400 B.C.)

The disaster of 1700 B.C., however, did not put an end to the creative energy of Minoan civilisation. Within a few decades new grandiose palaces were built on the ruins of the old, and Cretan civilisation entered its golden age.

The Neopalatial period is divided into three phases: the first (1700-1600 B.C.) was a period of reconstruction and preparation, the second (1600-1500 B.C.) was the age of the greatest achievements and the peak of the entire Minoan epoch, and the third (1500-1400 B.C.) was the period of the extension of Minoan influence on other peoples of the Mediterranean, especially the Mycenaeans in the Peloponnese.

Perhaps the greatest achievement of Minoan Crete was its architecture, by which we are also able to guage its wider potential. Magnificent palace complexes, consisting of two or more floors and with intricate internal design, were built in all the main centres of Crete. The palace of Knossos, the largest and most impressive achievement of Minoan architecture, covered altogether an area of 22,000 square metres, originally rose to a height of three or four floors and contained about 1,400 rooms. Its highly complicated structure gave to Greeks of a later period the mythical image of the Cretan Labyrinth. Today we know that the word 'labyrinth' (which the Greeks preserved with the meaning of a maze) originates from the Lydian or Karian word 'labrys' which meant double axe, and presumably in Minoan Crete it meant something like Place of the Double Axe. At Phaistos and Mallia the palaces were smaller and covered an area of about 9,000 square metres, while the palace at Zakros was slightly smaller (7-8,000 square metres) though no less magnificent.

It is interesting that all the palace complexes of Crete are of very similar design. They are constructed around a large central court and comprise a complex and intricate mass of buildings. They have a large entrance passage, imposing columned porticos, monumental staircases joining the floors and royal apartments, light wells for the lighting of internal parts of the buildings, rooms with many windows, and a water supply and sewage system. There were large store rooms, repositries, archive rooms, treasuries, reception rooms, shrines, artists' and craftsmen's workshops and school class rooms. The flooring was of green slate paving slabs and the walls were of limestone and gypsum masonry in ashlar construction. An exceptionally rich interior decoration, with frescoes, a variety of pictorial representations and coloured plastering gave a brilliance to the palaces, and turned them into places of fairy-tale enchantment. The palace of Knossos, as reconstructed from the finds by the creative imagination of Sir Arthur Evans, helps us to appreciate the true extent of the Minoan architectural achievement. The most reliable picture we can form of the function and use of the royal apartments was best preserved for us at the palace of Zakros, the only palace not to have been plundered and with all its artifacts still in their place.

Close examination of the Minoan palaces proves that they were not created simply by the adding of one building onto another, or by what has been termed by archaeologists as an 'agglutinative' process. Rather, the palace construction was the result of a uniform and deliberate design by experienced architects. The whole palace was planned and executed with care and professionalism right down to the last detail. As N. Platon remarked, 'few building projects from ancient times were conducted with such thorough and comprehensive expertise.' Today they astound us with the advanced technical knowledge and engineering capabilities which they display for their time. The designers were able to solve various technical difficulties such as lighting, ventilation, water supply and sewage disposal, besides the basic requirements of structural mechanics.

There can be little doubt that these large palace complexes also answered the demands of the dual role of their royal occupants as political and religious leaders. The archaeological remains enable us to reconstruct to some extent the life of the Minoans in relation to the palaces. The towns developed around the palaces and were quite populous. Evans estimated the population of Knossos to be about eighty to one hundred thousand.

Besides the large palace complexes of the towns smaller luxury villas were also built for use as summer retreats, generally of the same basic design as the large palaces but on a smaller scale. The summer mansions of the king of Knossos at Archanai, of the king of Phaistos at Hagia Triada and of the king of Zakros at Epano Zakros have been identified. In various parts of Crete there have also been found luxury country houses and even farmsteads, similar in appearance to the later Mycenaean megara, which most probably belonged to high-ranking officials of the time or to powerful local lords and landowners (at Sklavokambos, Tylissos, Nirou Khani, Mitropoli at Mesara, Apodoulou near Rethymnon, Platy in the Lasithi plain, Achladia near Siteia, Prophitis Ilias and Ayios Konstantinos at Praisos, and elsewhere). At some of these farmsteads we have clear evidence of the kind of farming activity that was taking place, such as at Vathypetro near Archanai, where farming and handicraft facilities were found (olive press, wine press, store rooms, the remains of a potter's kiln, etc.). An extensive and well-organized road network linked these small centres with the main towns.

Alongside the palatial architecture of the period we also have interesting examples of tomb architecture from around 1600 B.C. The royal tomb at Isopata to the south of Knossos constitutes an impressive tomb construction, suitable for the burial and worship of the deified king. In this period they also used shallow chamber-like tombs in various forms, in some cases comprising a cemetery, cut out of soft rock. These cemeteries were used without interruption right through the Post Palace years. Vaulted tombs of the neopalatial period have also been excavated. The most important were found at Kamilari (near Phaistos) and at Knossos. The artifacts in the vaulted tomb at Kamilari attest clearly to the existence of worship of the dead, even from the beginning of the neopalatial period.

As always happens at such high points in the history of civilisations, the art of the period in all its manifestations presents us with impressive works. Besides architecture, Minoan painting reaches its zenith, whether in the frescoes which complement the architecture, or vase painting. At the Knossos palace we have relief decoration on walls and ceilings as well. It is the large frescoes, however, which are the outstanding achievement of Minoan art. They are dated to about 1600 B.C. The few patches that survived all that time cannot allow us a complete reconstruction of these monumental works, and much of their composition is still debated. Nevertheless they are examples of the trends and potential of art during this great period. The subjects depicted are social (banquets, dance, festivals), religious (bull-vaulting, and representations of deities such as the well-known 'La Parisienne') or purely naturalistic subjects (landscapes with flowers and leaves, animals and birds, and marine subjects with fish, octopus and sea-urchins). It is notable that there is no picture with war as its theme.

Neopalatial pottery displays new tastes. The polychrome Kamares ware with its abstract decorative motifs gradually gives way to the so-called flower vases and shortly later (after 1500), Marine ware. The decorative motifs are taken from nature (plants, branches, flowers and leaves) and the sea (octopus, star-fish, dolphins, argonauts and coral). There is also a change in the shape of the vases. Three-handled stirrup jars become common. Impressive also is a range of libation vessels which imitate animals' heads (lion or bull) and shell-fish.

Stonework and sculpture reached its height during this period. Polychrome and veined rocks (such as marble, basalt, obsidian, alabaster, steatite and porphyrite) were transformed in the hands of the great Minoan artists into an infinite variety of libation vessels and household utensils. The finest examples of this kind were found at the palace of Knossos and the villa of Hagia Triada. A rhyton made of rock crystal, with a gold-leafed twisted ring on its neck and with a handle made of crystal beads, found in the treasury at Zakros, is an unparalleled masterpiece.

Sealstone carving was also notable during this period: the seals gave Minoan artisits the opportunity to display their skill in the art of miniature sculpture. Naturalistic subjects or themes taken from the ritual life of the times are carved with incredible attention to detail on the hardest of precious stones. The shapes of the seals are usually lentoid or amygdaloid (almond shape). Many of them were used as amulets and magical charms to protect the wearer from evil spirits.

The plastic arts also flourished during this period, chiefly in the form of idols. Faience, gold, ivory, bronze and, to a lesser extent, stone were all used; and clay was one of the most common materials. Among the finest examples of sculpture from these times are the idols of the Serpent Goddess in faience, and the bull-vaulter of Knossos, an exquisite model of an acrobat portrayed at the moment when he is executing his dangerous vault over the bull. As has already been remarked, this is an important moment in the history of art: the human form is free and poised in space, performing a formidable and magnificent act.

This great civilisation was most likely destroyed by earthquake following a powerful volcanic eruption on Thera (Santorini). Specialists believe that two large earthquakes took place between 1500 and 1450 B.C. destroying the Minaon centres and thereby creating the conditions in which the Mycenaeans could intervene in Crete. Professor Platon described the events as follows: 'It has been shown that the destruction was the result of two successive eruptions of the volcano on Thera between 1500 and 1450 B.C. The second of these eruptions was so powerful and its effects were so devastating that the Mycenaeans were able to establish themselves on the island.' Marinatos, who first proposed the theory of the volcanic explosion and the consequent destruction it caused to the Minoan sites, compared its force with that of Krakatoa in 1887, the largest volcanic eruption recorded in historic times.

Public life in Minoan Crete

1. Political power. The political system that prevailed in Minoan Crete was the centralised power of the monarchy. This system was above all theocratic, by which the king derived his power from the gods. The king, therefore, was not simply a bearer of political power, but was also high-priest exercising supreme religious power. He was the representative of god on earth and was most probably held to be a god himself. The symbols of his power were a crown with lilies and peacock feathers, and a necklace with lilies and the mythical bird, the griffin.

2. Minos. The most important figure in Cretan culture in prehistoric times was Minos, king of Knossos and son of Zeus and Europe. It was from his name that Evans coined the term Minoan for this long period of Cretan civilisation. Classical Greek tradition speaks of two kings with the name Minos, one more ancient than the other. Historians today believe that the name Minos is probably just a royal title similar to that of the Pharaoh of Egypt. Numerous legends arose from the personage of Minos. He was the son and

disciple of the great god Zeus and it was from Zeus, according to Homer, that he obtained the laws and advice for the good government of his land *(Odyssey* 19, 178-79):

> *'Among their cities is the great city of Knossos,*
> *where Minos reigned from when nine years old,*
> *he that held converse with great Zeus...'*

For this reason the justice of Minos was legendary amongst the ancient Greeks who believed that Minos was the judge of the dead along with his brother Rhadamanthus, and Ajax. According to another tradition Minos had two brothers, Rhadamanthus and Sarpedon. Professor Marinatos related the first brother with Phaistos, because he is referred to as the son of Phaistos, and the second with Mallia. Minos fought with his brothers for control of the island, and succeeded in expelling them from Crete and securing power for himself alone. Rhadamanthus fled to Boeotia in mainland Greece where he established a colony, while Sarpedon fled to the coast of Asia Minor. If there is some core of truth in these legends then the so-called *Pax minoica* must have been imposed on Crete after a hard fought struggle on the part of the central power of Knossos, as we mentioned above.

Minos' wife was Pasiphae who bore him many children: Katreus, Deucalion, Glaucus, Androgeos, Akalle, Xenodike, Ariadne and Phaedra. He was also said to have had numerous children by nymphs.

In his pursuit of Daedalus he arrived in Sicily with his army where he came to a tragic end. The daughters of king Kokalos, who were hiding Daedalus, drowned Minos in the bath at Daedalus' instigation. For many years his tomb was pointed out at Agrigentum in Sicily, until the tyrant of the city, Thyron, returned Minos' bones to the Cretans according to an account by Diodorus Sikeliotes (IV, 79,4).

3. The Minoan Thalassocracy. The Minoan state was

founded on domination of the sea. From 1700 B.C. onwards more and more harbour settlements developed, thus promoting naval activity and trade relations, especially with the eastern Mediterranean. Kato Zakros, situated midway down the eastern coast of Crete, appears to have been the most important site, linking Crete with Egypt, Cyprus and Syria. The bronze Cypriot scales and the Syrian ivories which were recovered here, are confirmation of the trade links with the east. Alexiou believed that it was from Zakros that the Cretan embassies of the Keftiu (Minoans) embarked for Egypt, bearing tribute to the Pharaoh. Other Cretan ports were Palaikastro, the isle of Pseira, Mokhlos in east Crete, Gournia, Amnissos and Katsambas (the ports of Knossos), and Kommos and Matalla (the ports of Phaistos). According to tradition Kydonia was founded by Minos, while the large port of Suda was also used for trade with the towns of the western Mediterranean.

The naval activity of the Cretans seems to be the subject of the well known myth of the Minotaur and Theseus. Ancient Greek historians often mention the sea kingdom of Minos, on which the Minoan economy depended. Thucydides wrote, 'Minos is the earliest of all those known to us by tradition who acquired a navy. He made himself master of a very great part of what is now called the Hellenic Sea, and became lord of the Cyclades islands and first coloniser of most of them, driving out the Karians and establishing his own sons in them as governors. Piracy, too, he naturally tried to clear from the sea, as far as he could, desiring that his revenues should come to him more readily.'

4. Minoan colonies. Cretan naval activity was linked to the organization of the Minoan colonies at various well-placed sites in the Mediterranean, which constituted ports of call and control points on the sea routes of the time. Minoan sites have been identified on Aegean islands and on the coast of Asia Minor (Kythera, Milos, Kea, Thera, Skopelos, Rhodes, Karpathos, Miletus and elsewhere). Many coastal towns in ancient times were called Minos and linked their foundation to the period of expansion of Minoan

power. A small island close to Megara in Attica was known as Minos, and the most important of the three towns on Amorgos was also called Minos. Towns called Minos existed on Siphnos, Paros, Corfu, Monemvasia, Sicily, Gaza in Palestine and even as far away as the Arabian peninsula. Two towns in Crete, one close to the headland of Drepanon and the other at Kamara in Merabello, also had the name Minos. The name may also be echoed in the present day village of Minothiana near Kolymbari. The ancient legends of the campaigns and inglorious end of Minos in Sicily perhaps contain an element of truth about Minoan expansionism.

5. S o c i a l o r g a n i z a t i o n. Minoan society was based around the great families who were subject to the local lords. From 1700 B.C. onwards the old families started to lose influence, while the lords, who had accrued more and more power for themselves, became kings.

Farming and pasturing were the main occupations of the people. The inhabitants of the coastal communities were sailors and traders. The easier acquisition of wealth after 1700 B.C. must have created a new gentry class, whose rights were based on their private fortunes. This can be deduced from the rich decoration of the Minoan country villas along the coast and on the islets, such as Pseira, around Crete. The slaves, of course, constituted another large class.

6. T h e e c o n o m y a n d t r a d e . The Minoan thalassocracy (sea kingdom) secured large sources of wealth for Crete. But Cretan products in the field of pottery, textile manufacture, woollen goods, embroidery and metalwork, and the exploitation of the medicinal and aromatic herbs and plants of the island as well as its rich agricultural produce all contributed to the prosperity of the Cretan economy. Ethereal oils and medicinal herbs, extracted from the plants on the island, always played an important part in Cretan trade; and, in fact, many of these are still used today and are still called by their ancient names: minthe (mint), eleliphaskos (sage) and diktamon (dittany) to name just three.

It should be remembered that Crete in Minoan times was still thickly wooded with cedar, pine and cypress. The sweet smelling wood of the cypress of Crete was highly prized even in much later historical times.

Minoan trade was probably not wholly in the hands of private merchants, but was also carried out under the supervision of the central power. Alexiou has convincingly argued that perhaps all Minoan trade was state run and that the merchants were in essence functionaries of the Minoan royal service.

Private life. The role of women

It is hard for us to give a complete picture of life in Minoan Crete. The silent finds from the excavations are not always secure evidence for the archaeologists' hypotheses, and their interpretation often leads to disagreement amongst researchers. We should not forget that Minoan civilisation extends across a vast period of time. More than twelve hundred years separate the end of the Neolithic period (ca. 2600 B.C.) from the date of the final destruction of the palace sites in ca. 1400 B.C. It is only natural that internal and external events and developments that occurred during this long period should have influenced both the way of life and its material and aesthetic manifestations as the years passed. We therefore have to be content with just a few indications that arise from the study of the finds and from a combination of theoretical evaluations of similar evidence from other civilisations of the Aegean and the peoples of the east of this period. It is possible, however, to see some survivals of an ancient way of life in contemporary life and customs of the island, a knowledge of which can often help in the interpretation of the archaeological finds.

Everything seems to indicate that the Cretans were (and are today) a people with a strong feeling for nature and life, full of optimism and a creative temperament. Professor Platon made the following observation: 'The Minoan's especially close bond with life makes him feel and produce only those things that are related to life's positive side. It is as if a poem of joy and vivacity is resounding everywhere. This is why there seems to be little concern for the unknown future or for death. Since the Minoans are not worried about the future they tend not to dwell on the past as the Mesopotamians did, nor to crystallize the present for eternity as was the case with the Egyptians. Minoan creativity always seems to be infused with a sense of well-being and contentment.'

Most of the population was involved in farming and pasturing. Consequently there were many peasant festivals that were related to the worship of natural forces and spirits of fertility, as was the case in most ancient cultures. The famous Harvester Vase from Hagia Triada shows us a scene from a peasant ritual or festival. Harvesters with implements on their shoulders sing a hymn to the deity, accompanied by musicians and a priest who is shaking a rattle of some sort as was done in the ancient Egyptian worship of Isis. The singers, who are depicted in the middle of the picture, have been dubbed the first quartet in European history.

Features of rural life are well represented in Minoan art. But higher cultural forms presuppose the existence of urban life. At the larger sites in Crete there seems to have arisen an aristocracy with greater demands for a more refined lifestyle. We are astonished today by the refinement and grace of women's dress of the period, and by other embellishments: the wealth of jewellery, the cut of the cloth, and the hairstyles in all their splendid luxury. We can only assume that there must have been similar attitudes to cleanliness, the use of perfumes and cosmetics, and lipstick for women. The frescoes in the Minoan palaces are revealing and the figure of the 'Parisienne' is typical. Even the men, whose dress is very simple (a girdle around their middle), are always shaved and wear jewellery.

Minoan civilisation also impresses us today for the apparent freedom that women enjoyed and the existence of a female aristocratic class. In contrast to other ancient cultures in which women in appear to live in the shadow of male domination, women Minoan Crete participate actively and on an equal footing with men in all aspects of social life. They had a prominent place at religious festivals and public occasions where, indeed, they are shown as being carried in litters born by servants, and they took part in dangerous games, religious ceremonies, and even went hunting alongside men. This does not automatically mean that society was matriarchal in Crete, though some scholars have found evidence in Minoan civilisation of the remains of a matriarchal society from a much earlier period. Certainly equality for women in Minoan Crete indicates a much more advanced notion of life, which is all the more impressive if we take into account the fact that in later cultures, such as that of Athens in the time of Pericles, women were condemned to a dull domestic existence dominated totally by men.

The prosperous life of the Minoans is evident from their depictions of public occasions, their games and their religious ceremonies and festivals. The Minoan palaces had an area for performances. At Knossos and Phaistos we have the oldest theatrical venues in Europe. Both sites have open-air, paved arenas with rising rows of stone seats for the audience which could number several hundred. The theatres at both sites are situated on the western wing of the palace. At Phaistos the theatre area comprises the entire court.

The Minoans were particularly fond of dancing. This can be seen in the frescoes and in other pictures and is confirmation of the reputation that Cretans enjoyed throughout the whole of antiquity as talented dancers. Homer gives us a wonderful description of Cretan dance in the Iliad (18, 590-606). He describes the Knossos dance, as illustrated by Hephaestus on the shield of Achilles:

'Therein furthermore the famed god of the two strong arms cunningly wrought a dancing-floor like unto that which in wide Knossos Daidalos fashioned of old for fair-tressed Ariadne. There were youths dancing and maidens of the price of many cattle, holding their hands upon the wrists one of the other. Of these the maidens were clad in fine linen, while the youths wore well-woven tunics faintly glistening with oil; and the maidens had fair chaplets,

and the youths had daggers of gold hanging from silver baldrics. Now they would run round with skilful feet exceeding lightly... and now again they would run in rows toward each other. And a great company stood around the lovely dance, taking joy therein; and two tumblers whirled up and down through the midst of them as leaders in the dance.

Homer's description recalls faithfully the Minoan dance as portrayed in the Cretan frescoes showing banquets and festivals, and it recalls Cretan dance as still performed today. It is at one and the same time an ancient and a contemporary theme, as with so many other things in Cretan culture.

Athletics games, religious processions, hunting and acrobatics were all greatly admired by the Minoans. They particularly enjoyed acrobatics and the more dangerous games, of which bull-vaulting was the most highly esteemed. It must have been not only an impressive spectacle but also extremely dangerous: the vaulter had to show the greatest of skill in leaping over the back of a frenzied bull, as is portrayed quite clearly in the frescoes and other pictures on seals and reliefs. This game, according to scholars, was almost certainly part of a religious ceremony. Similar games were held later in Mycenae, and even until more recently in Thessaly and several cities in Asia Minor such as Smyrna, Sinope and Ancyra. Alexiou believes that young men and women from all over Greece probably took part in the bull-vaulting games in Crete. This may be the substance behind the well known myth of the man-eating Minotaur, to which Athens had to send seven youths and seven maidens as tribute each year. Needless to say, these Cretan bull contests had nothing to do with the bull-fighting of present day Spain.

Contests such as boxing and wrestling were also popular in Minoan Crete. The contestants in these sports are shown in pictures as wearing helmets and holding nets so that they might avoid the blows of their opponent. A cup from Hagia Triada is revealing: it is considered to be the earliest evidence of a 'stadium' sport in the Greek world.

All these are manifestations, therefore, of 'the emotional world and love of life of a glorious people which, besides being advanced in the rational organization of social life, nevertheless maintained the power of imagination and the youthful vitality of the senses,' as Alexiou aptly remarked.

Minoan religion

The precise form and nature of the religion of the Cretans during the Minoan period is very hard to determine. In contrast to other contemporary civilisations such as those of Egypt and Mesopotamia which left behind monumental religious works, temples and sculpture, Crete presents us with an almost inexplicable silence. 'Only Minoan civilisation appears to be without temples, statuary, reliefs, or any kind of monumental representation of the divinity, apart from a few questionable cases,' wrote Marinatos.

Needless to say, this does not mean that there was no religion or religious life in Minoan Crete. It was merely of a different character, and scholars struggle to interpret the mute finds from excavations and to formulate some possible explanations. Here we shall present the more important conclusions reached by researchers.

Fundamental to Minoan religion, as to almost all ancient religions, was the annual cycle of the seasons and the death and rebirth of vegetation. The succession of emotions experienced by primitive man before the mystery of the continuously alternating world of nature led to the deification of the natural powers and to their worship. The greatest deity in Minoan Crete was Nature herself, the Mother Goddess. Her representation is varied. At times she is depicted as standing between lions on the summit of a mountain as 'Mountain Mother' and 'Queen of the Beasts,' or elsewhere as 'Serpent Goddess' or 'Goddess of the Sacred Tree,' or of the birds or flowers. At other times she is represented as a war goddess holding a shield and sword, or as a sea goddess who sails in a sacred ship. In all these representations we clearly have a mingling of religious and magical beliefs. The personification of vegetation is expressed in the form of a young baby or young god.

It is characteristic that many of the elements and symbols of Minoan religion survive later into the religion of the Greeks: for example, the worship of Zeus and of Athene. In the Doric Crete of the years to come the young fertility god was identified with Zeus and was worshipped as 'Kouros' (youth), and who, each year, died and was reborn. The 'Hymn to Zeus Kouros' that was found at Palaikastro near Siteia, engraved on a stone plaque of the third century B.C., is clear evidence of this survival.

Besides these anthropomorphized deities, various animals (usually monkeys) or fantastic creatures, often with a human body and the head of an animal or bird, appear in religious representations in Minoan Crete. The most common mythical bird of Minoan religion appears to have been the griffin, which decorated the Throne Room at Knossos. It has the body of a lion, wings and the head of a bird. All these creatures most probably represent fertility gods.

Minoan religious rites took place in the open-air, on mountain-top sanctuaries and in caves, as well as in household shrines and specially designated areas of the palaces. The crypt of the palace of Knossos is one such place, with a central square pillar. Cave san ctuaries from this period are at the Idaian cave, the Dictaean cave, and the caves at Eileithuia, Kamares, Patsos and elsewhere.

Many symbols were used in Minoan religious worship: the sacred tree, which was usually the olive, the sacred horns, the double-axe (which in the ancient Lydian language was called 'labrys', and most probably also in the Minoan language, from which originated the word 'labyrinth' known to the later Greeks), the sacred ship and even the cross in various forms (unrelated, of course, to the Christian cross). The sacred symbols of the Minoan religion, however, are frequently difficult to interpret and have proved to be quite enigmatic for modern scholars.

The act of religious worship in Minoan Crete took place in a variety of ways: stance for prayer, religious dance, sacrifice, fires on hill tops at certain times of the year, diverse competitions and acrobatic displays. To the deity they generally offered the first fruits of the harvest, conches, models of men and animals, sacrifices of domestic animals or game. G. Sakellarakis, on the basis of the finds at Archanai, recently advanced the controversial theory that the Minoans conducted human sacrifice.

Besides the worship of their gods the Minoans also seem to have worshipped the dead. Although our knowledge is very limited we can probably assume that the Cretans, even from Neolithic times, believed in some form of afterlife. They buried their dead in graves, and often in organized cemeteries. Cremation was not practised in Minoan Crete, and was to arrive in Crete later with the Mycenaean Greeks.

The most interesting find, with respect to worship of the dead, is the famous sarcophagus found at Hagia Triada, in which two worship cycles can be distinguished: that of the deity, and that of the dead person. It has been suggested that the degree of worship accorded to the dead corresponded to the rank the person enjoyed while living.

Minoan writing

Around 2000 B.C. the first written symbols appear in Crete. They closely resemble, though do not seem to be dependent on, Egyptian hieroglyphs. Altogether 135 pictorial signs have been identified so far, representing the shape or head of animals, human forms, implements and various symbols (such as plants and the double-axe). In his book *Scripta Minoa* Evans arranged these hieroglyphic signs into two categories: the first had 91 symbols, and the second had 95. The most important example of hieroglyphic writing in Crete is the famous Phaistos Disk, discovered in 1903 by L. Pernier in the north-east part of the Phaistos palace complex, near to the archive room. This disk, which has been dated to around 1700 B.C., has caused much debate about its origin, use and content. Evans believed that it had been brought to Crete from south-west Asia, but its relation to other finds in Crete suggests rather that it was a local product. Its symbols are arranged in a spiral pattern around the disk, and they were stamped in the clay while it was still wet. For this reason it has been dubbed the earliest specimen of the art of printing. No one has yet succeeded in deciphering the meaning of the symbols.

Apart from the hieroglyphs, another system of writing was used in Crete consisting of 70 linear signs, and which was named Linear A by Evans, who first recognised this as a separate type of Cretan script. Linear A is dated to before 1500 B.C. and has been found on clay tablets at Knossos, Phaistos, Mallia, Tylissos, Palaikastro and Zakros. This script has also defeated attempts at decipherment. Georgiev believes that the script may well contain Greek elements, while Gordon believes that it is probably a Semitic language, such as that spoken by the inhabitants of Palestine and Phoenicia. Others suggest that the particular inscriptions are statistical records of men, vases and produce. The numbering is decimal and also indicates fractions.

In the fifteenth century B.C. yet another script, related to Linear A, made its appearance in Crete. This script, which has been termed Linear B, was used by the Myceaean Greeks who occupied Crete at some time between 1450 and 1400 B.C. It is well known, not only from the thousands of clay tablets which have been recovered in Crete, but also from tablets found in Pylos, Mycenae, Tiryns, Orchomenos and Eleusis in mainland Greece. The decipherment of Linear B was achieved by two English scholars, Michael Ventris and John Chadwick, in 1952. This achievement, despite the objections and reservations of many others working in the field, has been described as the greatest archaeological event of the twentieth century. The important thing to be noted about this script is that it is clearly an early form of the Greek language, a fact that it is of paramount significance for Greek history in general.

The content of the Linear B tablets appears to be accounts. They are records of the king's property, slaves, livestock, crops, weapon supplies etc. Other tablets record offerings to deities, deployment of soldiers, titles of high-ranking officials, and the names of gods and men. All this evidence, although fragmentary and limited, is of the greatest value to historians who try to understand the structure of Minoan society and the way of life of this period.

CHAPTER III

THE POSTPALATIAL OR MYCENAEAN PERIOD
(1400 - 1100 B.C.)

The massive eruption of the volcano on Thera (Santorini) that occurred around 1400 B.C. brought the final blow to the Minoan 'Empire.' The destruction of the Minoan sites in Crete was swiftly followed by incursions of Mycenaeans from the Peloponnese. The earthquake had created favourable conditions for the invaders and within a short time the Minoan sites were in the hands of new lords. The island became a Mycenaean colony. There is clear evidence that Mycenaean settlements on the land of Minos were on a large scale, especially after 1380 B.C.

The Cretan population underwent much suffering in its attempt to resist the invaders. Many fled to the mountainous and more remote parts of the island, particularly the eastern end, where they managed to preserve the Minoan language and culture for many centuries to come. They were the so-called 'Eteocretans', or True Cretans mentioned by Homer. In Praisos and in Dreros inscriptions have been found dating from the sixth to the third century B.C. written in the Greek alphabet, but in a Prehellenic and as yet uninterpreted language. It is thought a large number of Cretans abandoned the island and moved to other Aegean islands, the coast of Asia Minor and even as far as Italy. It has been claimed (perhaps exaggeratedly) that a Cretan diaspora was created.

The Mycenaean colonisation of Crete is attested in later legendary accounts and place names. Agamemnon, king of Mycenae, according to tradition, founded the cities of Lappa, Tegea and Pergamos, and settlers from Messene and Mycenae are also mentioned. Various Peloponnesian place names, such as Arcadia and

Gortyn, can also be found in Crete and are most probably survivals from the time of the Mycenaean occupation.

After 1400 B.C. palace construction no longer took place in Knossos, and the site seems to have lost first place among the Cretan cities. The new ruler probably moved his capital to another part of the island. It is interesting that centres in the west, which had been unknown in the earlier Minoan period, now started to develop, such as at Pergamos, Polyrrhenia, Kydonia, Kolymbari and Stylos near Apokoronas. This must have been due to the increase in trade relations of this area with the Mycenaean Peloponnese.

It is probably safe to assume that the ruling house of Knossos was now subordinate to the proud house of Atreus of the Peloponnese. The participation of Idomeneus and other Cretan lords in the Trojan war under the general leadership of Agamemnon, son of Atreus, should perhaps be seen in this light. Homer, in Book II (ll. 645-652) of the Iliad, mentions seven Cretan cities which took part in the Trojan war: Knossos, Gortyn, Lyttos, Miletos, Lykastos (perhaps close to modern Kanli Kastelli), Phaistos and Rhytion (Rotasi). He relates:

And the Cretans had as leader Idomeneus, famed for his spear,
even they that held Knossos and Gortyn, famed for its walls,
Lyttos and Miletos and Lykastos, white with chalk,
and Phaistos and Rhytion, well-peopled cities;
and all they beside that dwelt in Crete of the hundred cities.
Of all these was Idomeneus, famed for his spear, captain,
and Meriones, the peer of Enyalios, slayer of men.
And with these there followed eighty black ships.

The style of the civilisation in Crete at this time is distinctly Mycenaean. Evans himself discerned Mycenaean influences in Knossos, and more recent archaeological evidence has confirmed this view. Mycenaean buildings of the megaron type have been found at Tylissos and Hagia Triada, and many Mycenaean settlements have been identified at various strategically well-placed sites. As already mentioned, Mycenaean centres began to develop in the east of the island as well.

The administration of Crete during this period was altered and adapted to the Mycenaean model. On the clay tablets found at Knossos, just as at Pylos in the Peloponnese, we often read the word 'wanax', an early form of the Greek word meaning 'king'. The island seems to have been divided into small states, or city-states, whose rulers were subordinate to the new ruler of Knossos and successor to the illustrious dynasty of Minos.

The Mycenaeans also brought their customs to Crete: their long beards and dress, the short tunic, and burial practice. Mycenaean beehive tombs (at Archanai and Stylos Apokoronou) became common, as well as chamber tombs cut out of rock. Tub-shaped larnakes (clay burial chests) have been found in many parts of Crete such as at Sellopoulo, Gypsades at Knossos, Amnisos, Gournes, Mesara, Miletos (modern Milatos), Kritsa, Palaikastro, Stavromenos at Rethymnon, Chania and elsewhere. Towards the end of the period cremation also seems to have been practised.

Mycenaean religion also arrived in the island. The new gods were Greek gods: Zeus, Hera, Poseidon, Athene. They gradually replaced the worship of the Great Goddess of the Minoan religion. The names of the new gods often appear on the clay tablets written in the Linear B script. There is evidence for the existence of a 'Priestess of the Winds' and of a 'Mistress of the Labyrinth.' It is reasonable to assume that elements of the Mycenaean religion mingled with elements of the Minoan religion and ceremony and that a local polytheism existed on the island. Many of these features survived through the Myceaean period into the Doric age in Crete. The names Diktynna and Britomartis (meaning Sweet Virgin), as well as the worship of the Child-Zeus until late in antiquity are all considered to be Minoan survivals.

The economy of this period, despite the decline it suffered, was still based on the same activities: the export of choice Cretan products such as olive oil, honey, wine, aromatic herbs and dried fruits. It maintained relations with the East: Cyprus, Syria and Egypt. Cretan shipping, which had once been so active, was now in the service of the Mycenaeans. In the period of the great raids of the 'sea-peoples' of the twelfth century the Mycenaeans of Crete appear to have been the strongest in resistance. It is known that the Cretans were in contact with the kingdom of Rameses III and that the Philistines (Keftiu) of Palestine were Cretans too. Evidence also suggests that Cretans settled in Rhodes.

Copper-work and the manufacture of weapons seem to have been the only crafts that were flourishing. The fine arts, including pottery, the plastic arts, sealstone carving and jewellery making, which demand different concerns and highly developed skills, were all in decline.

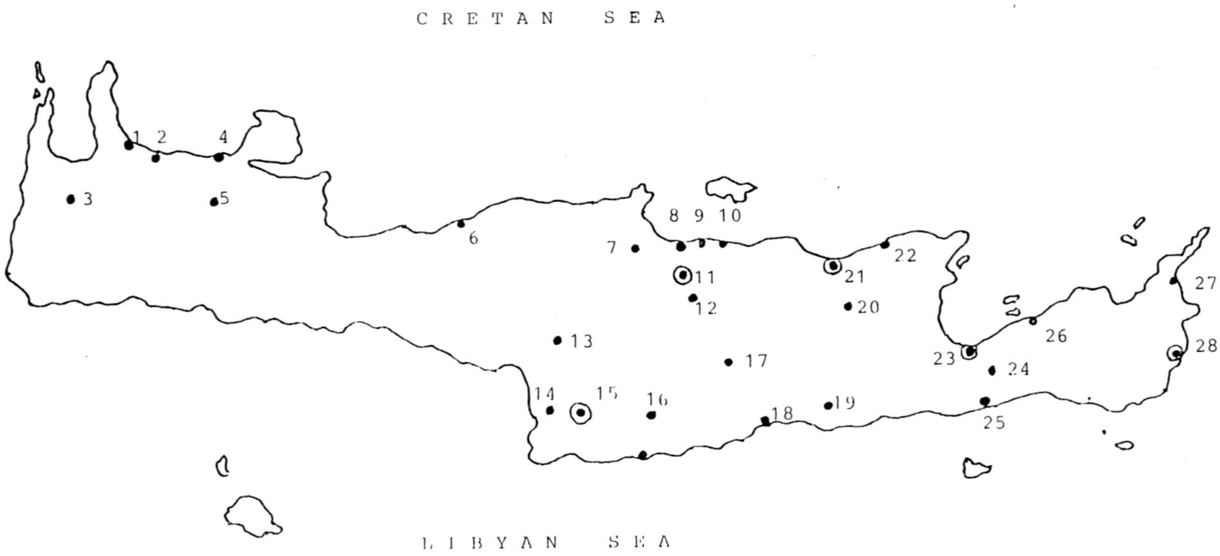

1. Map of Minoan Crete.
Legend.

1. Kolymbari, 2. Maleme, 3. Polyrrhenia, 4. Cydonia, 5. Stylos, 6. Rethymnon, 7. Tylissos, 8. Port of Cnossos (= Iraklion), 9. Amnissos, 10. Nirou Hani, 11. Knossos, 12. Archanes, 13. Kamares, 14. Hagia Triada, 15. Festos, 16. Gortyna, 17. Arkalochori, 18. Inatos, 19. Viannos, 20. Karfi, 21. Malia, 22. Milatos, 23. Gournia, 24. Vassiliki (of Hierapetra), 25. Hierapetra, 26. Mochlos, 27. Palaecastro, 28. Zarkos

PART TWO

DORIAN CRETE (1100 - 69 B.C.)

CHAPTER I

THE DORIAN CONQUEST

The Trojan War was the ultimate expression of the power of the Mycenaeans, but it also marked a turning point in their fortunes. A few years later the old Achaean world ('Achaean' is the word Homer used to describe the Mycenaean Greeks) was shaken by the incursions of the Dorians, reckoned by Thucydides to have taken place eighty years after the sack of Troy. The Mycenaean kingdoms, weakened by prolonged internicine disputes and civil strife were unable to present any serious resistance to the new, aggressively adventurous Greek tribes who now descended from the north. Within a few years the Mycenaean sites were destroyed and their inhabitants put to flight. The destruction of Mycenae has been dated to around 1125-1120 B.C. Groups of fugitives migrated to Crete and Cyprus from the Greek mainland, witnessed by the vases of the so-called "Granary jar" style found in central Crete. Trade was at a low ebb and passed into the hands of the Phoenicians; and civilisation seems to retreat. The new lords of the Greek world imposed a new code of conduct, the use of iron, cremation of the dead, and a new manner of dress. The more powerful weapons enabled them to conquer and expand rapidly. Continual migration meant that their burial practice spread widely and cemeteries of the period are full of cremation urns and funerary offerings. However, it has been claimed by many that the custom of cremation is not necessarily related to the Dorians, but may rather be of eastern origin. Early evidence for cremation has been found in Rhodes, Kos and Cyprus. During the early Dorian centuries, otherwise known as the Geometric period (1100-800 B.C.), cremation was widely practised in Crete as well. The short tunic of the Mycenaean age and the many-pleated dress of the Minoans were now replaced by a simpler form of dress, a seamless piece of cloth fastened over the shoulders with a clasp. It is clear that civilisation was undergoing a transformation on every level.

The Dorian invasion of Crete must have had even more destructive consequences. Many believe that the Dorians first took control of Crete, and then moved on to the Peloponnese. Whatever the case, archeaological evidence suggests that the Cretans put up fierce resistance at the major sites, and at Knossos in particular which, for yet another time, was put to the torch. There is evidence that many of the inhabitants fled to the coast of Asia Minor. Within a few years the austere martial life of the Dorians succeeded the more refined world of the Minoans and Mycenaeans.

Minoans, Mycenaeans and Dorians in Crete now merged together into a new ethnic and cultural entity. The genuinely Greek element of the island, the Mycenaeans, was now reinforced with new Greek blood, that of the Dorians, while the few remaining descendants of the Minoans, known as Eteocretans ('True Cretans'), were marginalised to the eastern end of the island. Homer was familiar with this local mixture of inhabitants and languages on the island of Minos (*Odyssey*, XIX. 175-77):

They have not all the same speech, but their tongues are mixed.
There dwell Achaeans, there great-hearted native Cretans,
there Kydonians, and Dorians of waving plumes,
and goodly Pelasgians.

Recent research into the place-names of ancient Crete indicates that Greek place-names account for 70% of the total, Pelasgian 20%, and Eteocretan 10%.

Greek place-names include Mt Aigaion, Ampelos, Anopolis,

Axos, Aptara, Araden, Arkades, Gortyn, Dia, Dion, Dreros, Erythraion Akron, Herakleion, Thenai, Hieron, Kairatos, Kale Akte, Kaloi Limenes, Kriou Metopon, Kydonia, Lamon, Lappa, Leuka Mounts, Leuke, Lithaios, Lissos, Holous, Panormos, Polichne, Rithymna, Rhytion, Stelai, Chersonesos, Hydramos, Phalanna, Phaistos and Holeros etc .

Pelasgian (pre-Greek) place-names include Amnisos, Arbion, Beukasos, Berekynthos, Ide, Knossos, Labyrinthos, Larisa, Pergamos, Pyrhanthos, Syrinthos, Tylissos, Hyrtakina, etc.

Eteocretan place-names include the following: Inatos, Karneso(polis), Kytaion, Leto, Minoa and Myrin(n)a .

The entire Dorian period can be broadly divided into the following periods:

I. Sub-Minoan (1100-1000 B.C.)

II. Geometric (1000-725 B.C.)

- a) Early Geometric (1000-900 B.C.)
- b) Middle Geometric (900-800 B.C.)
- c) Late Geometric (800-725 B.C.)

III. Orientalising (Daedalic) (725-600 B.C.)

IV. Archaic (600-500 B.C.)

V. Classical (500-323 B.C.)

VI. Hellenistic (323-67 B.C.)

CHAPTER II

DORIAN CRETE : THE FIRST CENTURIES (11th-9th CENTURIES B.C.)

1. The Dorian settlement of Crete

In order to firmly establish their rule, the new lords of Crete organized extensive settlements throughout the island. Myth recounts how Teutamos (or Tektamos), the son of Doros, king of the Dorians, established the first dynasty in Crete just one generation after the foundation of the Dorian sites in the Peloponnese. Ancient tradition also preserves the memory of two Dorian settlements in Crete: Pollis and Delphos from Sparta and Althaimenes from Argos are cited as being the first settlers, the two former settling in central Crete, and the latter in western Crete. At some time in the 10th century Dorians from the Argolis came to settle in Crete, and, much later, there were Cretan towns that still preserved the memory of their Dorian descent. Lyttos and Gortyn must have been among the earliest Dorian colonies. Herodotos believed that Lyttos was older than Gortyn because it had preserved its pre-Greek name. Colonisation continued into the 9th century as well, when settlers (Magnetes) from Pelion and Ossa established a settlement between Gortyn and Phaistos.

Strong evidence for the Dorianization of Crete is the presence on the island of three Dorian tribes -the Hylleis, Dymanes, and Pamphyloi. Later Cretan inscriptions inform us of yet other Dorian tribes, the Echanoreis, the Aischeis and the Aithaleis. Another Dorian tribe, the Kamiris, is mentioned on an inscription at Ierapetra, and the Pharkaris on inscriptions at Praisos. The precise origin and date of arrival in Crete of the Kydonians has not yet been determined with certainty. It is possible, however, that the tribes mentioned in the inscriptions were not in fact the Dorian tribes themselves, but rather local, indigenous nobility who had recognised their Dorian overlords, or who achieved recognition from them as equals within the new society of the Cretan cities. Whatever the case, Crete became thoroughly Dorian and, right up to the end of antiquity, it was to remain a bastion of the Dorian Greek world.

2. Life in Dorian Crete

The first centuries of Dorian Crete are a dark age for us. We have no sources for this period, and later accounts are confused and obscure. It is reasonable to assume from the few archaeological remains for this period that the lifestyle became rudimentary. There were no major works of art, and writing disappeared altogether. The invaders entrenched their position in strongly fortified citadels at Gortyn, Prinias, Axos and Hyrtakina. These years were also a period of intense struggle with the native Cretans, both Mycenaean and Minoan. A new warlike order was established in Crete after an age of radical transformation and reorganization.

One of the immediate consequences of the Dorian invasion must have been the abandonment of the traditional patriarchical kingdom as we recognise it in the earliest phases of history. It is characteristic that after the Dorian conquest we hear of only one king in Crete: Etearchos of Oaxos (modern Axos Milopotamou). Herodotos tells us (*Histories,* IV. 154), 'There is a town in Crete called Oaxos, of which one Etearchos became ruler.' It is very doubtful, however, if Etearchos was in fact a genuine king in the ancient sense of the word.

Evidence of artistic activity is very meagre indeed. The basic change to be seen is the presence, in pottery, of the Geometric style (1100-800 B.C.). Vases are decorated in geometrical patterns: triangles, squares, diamond shapes, concentric circles and semi-circles, crosses etc. Scholars disagree as to the origins of this new style and they discount, at least in the case of Crete, its relationship with the Dorians. Many support the view that this style came from the East. Knossos was still the most active centre and developed its own polychrome geometric style. Recent research has brought to light the existence of various Geometric settlements in north-west Crete.

More favourable living conditions seem to have developed during the 9th century and new centres began to appear, such as at Arkades, Dreros, Lato, Lyttos, Axos, Eleutherna, Aptera, Lappa, Kydonia and Polyrrhenia. Western Crete also flourished in this period, perhaps due to the settlement of people from mainland Greece. Many important finds show that Crete maintained strong economic links with the East (Syria), Cyprus (perhaps Crete's most important trading partner), the Aegean islands and even Athens.

The Dorians were also responsible for the construction of the first temples. Recent archaeological research conducted by a Canadian team led by Professor Joseph Shaw uncovered a temple dated to the 10th century at the site of Kommos, near the village of Pitsidia in the Mesara plain. This is thought to be the oldest temple of its kind in Greek lands.

CHAPTER III

A BRIEF RENAISSANCE
THE ORIENTALISING AND DAEDALIC PERIOD
(8th-7th CENTURIES)

The eighth century B.C. was a critical time in the history of the ancient Greek world. Trade and shipping activity revived and a wave of colonial expansion began. During the first phase of Greek colonialism Crete became active once more. After nearly three centuries, it turned to the sea and merchant shipping, and even established its own colonies. Modern research has shown that Cretans were most likely in the forefront of the great colonial expansion of the Greeks. From 735 B.C. onwards Cretans are seen to have established colonies in Sicily, Etruria and the coast of France around Marseille, where they arrived about a hundred years before the Phokaians. Shortly later (in the early 7th century) they participated in a joint expedition with the Rhodians to set up colonies in Gela and Agrigento in Sicily, and they joined with Sparta and Argos in founding other colonies. Koroibos from Itanos acted in league with Thera in establishing a colony in Kyrene in 631 B.C. From that time onwards relations between Crete and Kyrene were very friendly. Crete was again in the vanguard of the shipping and mercantile activities of the day.

Art also revived during this period. Cretan art flourished in the 8th and 7th centuries B.C., though unfortunately it did not last beyond this time. Eastern features were subsumed within the dictates of Greek aesthetics, thus creating a new distinct art style in Crete. Bronze shields found in the Idaian Cave are a good example of Eastern influences on Cretan art. The art of this period has been termed 'Dedalic', not because of the Daidalos of Minoan times, but because of a brilliant artist of the same name to whom tradition attributes the invention of the sculptor's implements, as well as the creation of the first monumental statues in marble and fired earthenware. He is also attributed with the invention of the technique of making statues in hammered bronze. These early examples of the sculptor's art have their eyes wide open and their limbs are in motion. Daedalos' pupils included Cheirisophos, Dipoinos and Skyllis, who came to be known as the 'Daedalids.' They went to work in the Peloponnese, where they set up their workshop, and became the first masters of this school of art in Archaic Greece.

Our evidence for Daedalos the sculptor is very scant, and many doubt his actual historical existence. Yet the undisputed careers of his 'pupils' and the impressive works recovered in Crete from this period tend to confirm the veracity of the account. Indeed archaeologists have brought to light the remains of various temples (at Prinias, Gortyn and Dreros) of the 8th and 7th centuries B.C. with their own distinctive features and rich sculpted decoration, all still unheard of in mainland Greece. Three small bronze figures (80-40 cm) that were discovered at Dreros and most probably portray the gods Apollo, Artemis and Leto, are the first examples yet found of hammered bronze sculpture. Close study of these works and various others, such as the Cretan head in the New York Museum and the so-called 'Lady of Auxerre' in the Louvre, have led many to believe that Crete in the 7th century B.C. was the most vigorous part of the Greek world and that it was responsible for 'passing on the invigorating spirit of art from the East to mainland Greece.' There is, besides, ample proof of the presence of Cretan artists in Athens and elsewhere in Greece during this period.

Unfortunately, this impressive and promising revival was short-lived. It was abruptly cut off in the 6th century, without having reached its peak. From the end of the 7th century Crete enters a period of decline again. Trade declined and the sea no longer seemed to stir the passions of the fearless seafarers of the previous centuries. The island became isolated and cut off from the rest of the Greek world. This isolation and decline, which was to last right the way up to the time of the Roman domination of the island, appears to be due to two factors: on the one hand, there was the rapid development of the Ionian city-states, such as Athens and Miletus, which took over control of Mediterranean trade; and on the other, the political and social system of the Cretan cities which, as with other Dorian centres, was immobile and inflexible in the face of the new conditions and did little to encourage a robust response to challenge in the sphere of trade and seafare.

Besides all this, it seems that internal disputes had broken out in Crete. The island was paralysed by an almost permanent state of civil crisis that was to mar its fortunes throughout the years of antiquity, until the Roman conquest. Two accounts testify to the situation in Crete in antiquity: Herodotos mentions that Syrian adventurers, having failed to overthrow Polykrates, sailed to Crete with some Samian fugitives and established Kydonia (Chania) in 519 B.C. without meeting any resistance from the islanders; Pindar in his ode to Ergoteles the Himerian (*Olympian,* XII, 16), mentions the rebellion in Knossos which drove Ergoteles to abandon his home city and flee to Himera in Sicily where he became a citizen with the name Himeraios 'formerly of Knossos'.

CHAPTER IV

SOCIAL AND POLITICAL LIFE IN THE CRETAN CITIES

1. Dorian society in Crete

Our knowledge of the organization of Dorian society in Crete is based chiefly on accounts given by authors writing later in the period under discussion (Plato, Aristotle, Ephor and others). Moreover, publication of Cretan inscriptions has thrown much light on many aspects of society at this time.

Society in Crete was organized on lines very similar to those in Sparta and the other Dorian centres in Greece. The population of the cities was divided into three classes: free citizens, *perioeci* (free inhabitants, but without the right to political liberty), and slaves. The first class was composed chiefly of the Dorians who constituted the ruling élite of the city-states, and who had exclusive control over military and political matters, as well as controlling the land allotments worked by the numerous slaves. In order to enforce and maintain their power the Dorians organized a strict military system, of which the best example was Sparta. A short poem, known as the 'Skolion,' dating from a later period (probably 4th century B.C.) by the Cretan poet Hybrias, gives an idea of the weapon-wielding Dorian order.

The free citizens were organized into 'clubs' of professional warriors known as *hetaireiai.* According to an account by a man called Dosias, preserved for us in Athenaios' writings, 'the citizens are distributed in clubs which are called "andreia" ('halls of men').' (*Deipnosophistae,* IV, 143b). And the lexicographer Hesychios explains that in Crete they worshipped Zeus 'the Hetaireios,' in other words, the protector of the *hetaireiai.* These 'clubs' were composed of the great Dorian families of the island. All those who did not have political rights were called *apetairoi* (lit. 'non-companions').

The original inhabitants of Crete who, it seems, had come to recognise Dorian rule were termed *hypekooi* or *perioeci.* They were mostly peasants who maintained ownership of a part of their property and payed taxes to their Dorian masters. To the *peroeci* class also belonged the seamen and merchants, as well as the craftsmen. All of these groups came to have a vested interest in the Dorian order and it is worth recalling that there never seems to have been a rebellion against the Dorians in Crete.

The slaves formed a large class in Crete, composed not only of native Cretans but also of captives from military campaigns. They farmed on the nobles' estates and enjoyed only a very meagre income. The slaves in Crete are referred to in the sources as *klarotai, mnoitai, aphamiotai* and *oikeis.* According to an account by the historian Sosikrates, preserved in Athenaios, 'the Cretans call common labour *mnoian,* and private labour *aphamiotas.'* Slaves, therefore, were divided into two categories: public and private, and were named *mnoitai* and *aphamiotai* respectively. They were also generally termed *klarotai* since they worked the *kleroi* (land allotments) owned by the nobles.

The precise legal status of the slaves is unknown to us, although the inscriptions are explicit about the distinction between free citizens and slaves. It is clear, however, that each city had its regulations protecting the slaves, and stipulating their obligations and rights.

2. Political organization

A direct consequence of the Dorian conquest of Crete was the abandonment of the patriarchal royal system and the organization of oligarchical political regimes. The great Dorian families that we come across in other parts of Greece (the Hylleis, Dymanes and Pamphyloi), undertake the administration of the island. The political system in Crete was centred around the aristocracy, and varied only slightly in its organization from city to city.

There were three main political organs:

i) The kosmoi. This was the name given to the members of the ruling 'committees' of the Cretan cities. Their number varied from four to eleven. They were otherwise known as *archontes, kosmetores* or *damiourgoi.* They were elected by the great Cretan families and their tenure of office lasted one year. Reelection to the same office was forbidden for a certain length of time ranging from three to ten years. The council of the *kosmoi* was called the *eunomia.* The functions of the *kosmoi* were broad-ranging and similar to those of the five Ephors of Sparta. They were the military leaders in time of war and the highest functionaries in peacetime. In the Lexikon of Hesychios the word *kosmos* is synonymous with the word for general. Inscriptions inform us that there were *kosmoi* for special affairs and offices, such as the *xenios kosmos,* who was responsible for alien citizens, and the *kosmos hierourgos* who was in charge of religious matters. The Kosmoi were empowered to summon the people to assembly (known as *ekklesia*) in order to ratify their decisions. And at the end of their term of office they had to give an account of their policies. In instances where they were found to have overstepped their privileges or failed in their duties they were liable to the heaviest of penalties.

The 'Prime Minister' of the *kosmoi* was called the *protokosmos* or *kosmopolis* (attested in an inscription at Lyktos). His name was given to the year of his premiership (providing a system for the reckoning of years), just as with the Archon in Athens.

ii) The Council of Elders. This was an advisory body composed of *kosmoi* who had been particularly noteworthy in the conduct of their office. The elders, armed with their experience and prestige, guided the *kosmoi* in decision-making. It is likely that they also had judicial powers. Only on occasions when the *kosmoi* were dismissed from office on account of discreditable or cowardly conduct did the elders undertake the administration of the city until new *kosmoi* were elected.

iii) T h e A s s e m b l y. The Assembly (Ekklesia) was attended by free citizens on set days or on emergency sessions. According to Aristotle, the Assembly's only function was to ratify the decisions taken by the *kosmoi* and the elders.

Ancient writers acknowledged the fact that the political system in the Cretan cities was not as rigid as in Sparta. It was a system based on the rule of an aristocratic class, though with a certain veneer of democratic procedure, as Polybius, the Greek historian of the second century B.C., observed.

CHAPTER V

THE INSTITUTIONS IN THE CRETAN CITIES

1. The public mess-tables

The public mess-tables were an ancient Doric institution and survived in Sparta and Crete right through to the years of late Antiquity. Strabo (I,481) mentions that Sparta adopted the institution from Crete and held on to it with almost religious fervour, while in its native Crete the public mess-tables gradually became obsolete with the passing of time. Aristotle described the Cretan mess-tables as being better organized than the Spartan.

According to the ancient sources the Cretan mess-tables functioned in roughly the following manner. Every city had a special building called an *andreion* ('hall of men') that was designed for festive gatherings of the citizens. The citizens (male adults) participated in the mess-table life organized in groups (*hetaireiai*). The ruling body of the city was responsible for the organization of the mess-table, and the financial resources of the mess were derived from income earned from public properties and tax paid by the *perioeci*. The citizens themselves also contributed a tenth of their income to support the mess-table. Aristotle describes the Cretan public mess-tables as being the most important public expression of the political system: 'Now the Cretan arrangements for the public mess-tables are better than the Spartan; for at Sparta each citizen pays a fixed poll-tax, failing which he is prevented by law from taking part in the government . . . but in Crete the system is more communal, for out of all the crops and cattle produced from the public lands, and the tributes paid by the serfs, one part is assigned for the worship of the gods and the maintenance of the public services, and the other for the public mess-tables, so that all the citizens are maintained from the common funds, women and children as well as men.' (Politics, 1272a, 12-21.)

The mess was a simple place. Each *hetaireia* had its own table and there were special tables set aside for guests, just as there were also special hostels or dormitories in each city to accommodate visitors.

Women, helped by slaves, were responsible for preparing the mess-table. Food was served in a specific manner. The ruling dignitaries had quadruple portions, while male children were served a quantity that was half an adult male's portion. Women and girls had no place at the men's mess, though it seems that a part of the food was distributed to homes. An inscription in Gortyn mentions the 'distributors of food' which most probably referred to those who shared out the food to houses from the public mess-table.

The public mess-tables were not simply a social and economic institution. They were a fundamental part of the functioning of the state. The men, when gathered at the mess-table, discussed their city's affairs, sang paeans and battle songs, and honoured praiseworthy citizens with tales and songs. The young men watched the life of their elders and were thus initiated into the ideals of Dorian society.

2. Upbringing and education

The way in which youths were brought up and educated in Cretan towns was similar to the Spartan system. It was designed to produce brave warriors, to serve the military ideal of the Dorians. Again Aristotle tells us, 'In Sparta and Crete both education and the laws are almost exclusively framed to serve warfare' (Politics, 1324b, 8-9). The main features of this education were strict discipline, austerity and gruelling exercise. Until the child was eighteen the family had total responsibility for his education. The sources tell us that in these years the youths learnt to read and write, and they learnt hymns to the gods, eulogies on great men, the laws, war dances and martial games. Learning the laws was considered one of the most important lessons. They learnt the laws in verse and accompanied by music so that they might be more easily remembered. Education from an early age was of an overtly political orientation. Ailianos gives the following account: 'In Crete the children of free citizens were firstly taught the laws by means of song, so that they might more easily retain them in the memory, and so that if they were ever to infringe the laws they could not plead ignorance of them. Secondly, they had to learn hymns to the gods. And thirdly, they learnt eulogies on great men.'

Ephor is also reported to have given a similar account (preserved in Strabo's *Geographies,* X,480): 'In order that courage, and not cowardice, might prevail, from boyhood they had to grow up accustomed to arms and toils, so as to scorn heat, cold, marches over rugged and steep roads, and blows received in gymnasiums or regular battles; and they had to practice, not only archery, but also the war-dance, which was invented and made known by the Kouretes at first, and later, also, by the man who arranged the dance that was named after him, I mean the Pyrrhic dance, so that not even their sports were without a share in activities that were useful for warfare; and likewise that they should use in their songs the Cretan rhythms, which were very high-pitched, and were invented by Thales, to whom they ascribe, not only their Paeans and other local songs, but also many of their institutions; and that they should use military dress and shoes; and that arms should be to them the most valuable gifts.'

Once the youths had reached the age of eighteen they were put in groups called *agelai* (sg. *agele*) where they began their military education proper, until they reached the age of marriage. The members of the *agelai* were called *agelastoi* or *dromeis,* while those who were still too young to be in these groups were referred to as *apageloi* (ie. non-*agele* members) or *apodromoi.* Each *agele* had its own leader, a father of one of the youths. He would lead the youths in their daily exercise –an exhausting programme of physical training both on the track and in hunting, in the handling of weapons, in defence and in attack. He would punish severely anyone who showed disobedience, and would reward the diligent and obedient with moral support. The young men thus became accustomed to hardship and discomfort, and learnt to view their weapons as precious objects. And of all the weapons, the Cretans were particularly fond of the bow and the javelin.

Strong bonds of friendship and cooperation developed between the young men. They tended to be paired off, and the older and more experienced of the two undertook to train the younger in the art of war and living.

Strabo describes (X,483) how on certain days the *agelai* organized war games in imitation of real combat: 'on certain appointed days "Troop" contends with "Troop", marching rhythmically into battle, to the tune of a flute and lyre, as it is their custom in actual war; and they actually bear marks of the blows received, some inflicted by the hand, others by iron weapons.' Perhaps the poem by Hybrias, mentioned earlier, was one such song that accompanied the armed competitions of the youths.

The youths' training also included productive occupation. An inscription at Dreros mentions that the members of the *agelai* were obliged to plant an olive tree and to cultivate it until it had grown to a certain size. Whoever failed to carry out this obligation was fined 50 gold stateres.

Once their education was completed the young men swore an oath of allegiance to their homeland and the *agele* was disbanded. We do not know the exact wording of the oath, but there is an inscription which tells us that the oath was sworn before the Kosmoi of the city. Elsewhere we are told that the young men were obliged to marry on the completion of their studies (Strabo, X,482). If this was indeed the case they probably held mass weddings. This was another aspect of the state's involvement in the life of the community, controlling thereby the rate of birth and the increase in the population. As Thomson claimed, marriage was subject to state control and constituted a public ceremony for all the young men of the same age.

This course of education remained practically unchanged until well into the Hellenistic age. Inscriptions of the second century B.C. from east Crete (Dreros and Mallia) still mention the existence of agelai.

CHAPTER VI

LEGISLATION AND THE GORTYN LAW CODE

Historians have noted that the Cretan towns before the fifth century B.C., isolated as they were from the rest of the Greek world and embroiled in constant internal disputes, found their finest mode of expression in legislative procedure. We can form a good picture of judicial notions in the Cretan towns in this period from the Law Code inscription discovered at Gortyn at the end of the nineteenth century (it was recovered in sections in 1857, 1879 and 1884 by various archeaeologists - Thénon, B. Haussoulier and Fr. Halbherr). Its complete discovery was achieved in 1884 by Fr. Halbherr. It is in fact the largest surviving Greek inscription and for that reason it has been dubbed the Queen of Inscriptions. The largest part of this inscription can be seen today inscribed on a wall on the northwest side of the Odeon of Gortyn, now under a covered shelter. A small part of the Law Code is in the Louvre and other smaller segments are now lost. The Code was inscribed on twelve large stone tablets 68cm wide by 172cm high, and was located almost entirely along the length of a semi-circular wall construction 8.75m in length, in four equal-length sets of hewn limestone.

The inscription is written in an ancient form of the Dorian dialect as spoken in Crete, which consisted of an alphabet of eighteen letters. The 17,000 letters are written boustrophedon (ie. one line from left to right and the next line right to left and so on alternately). Altogether it contains 637 lines over the twelve tablets. It has been dated to the late 6th/early 5th century B.C. (latest studies date it to the years 480-460 B.C.). Nevertheless, it seems highly likely that this legislative text represents ancient precepts of Gortyn law, which must have been similar to that of the other Cretan towns of the period. We thus have the original text of the oldest and most important law code of Greek antiquity. Lambros wrote that, 'The Gortyn Law Code is the earliest such surviving code by man: a code truly remarkable for its many provisions, of which some are considerably more liberal than those of Attic or Roman law. At the same time it is the oldest surviving written prose text of the Greeks, somewhat archaic and rough in its Cretan dialect, as is also the form of the letters in which it is written.'

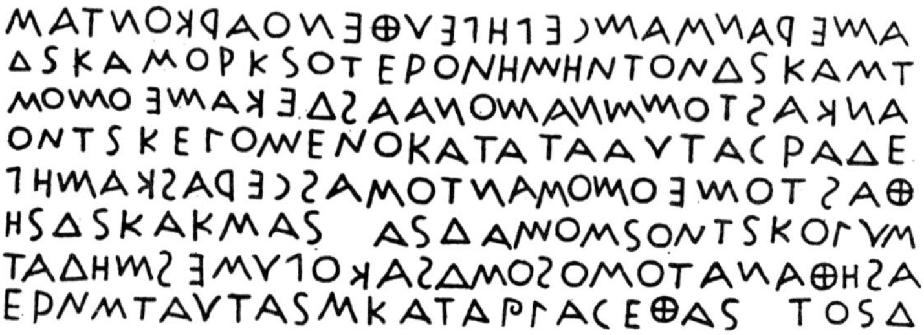

2. Part of the Gortyn Law Code (*IC* IV, Tituli Gortynii, 98-99).

The inscription is of paramount importance. Historians believe that it gives us a typical example of legislation in the Dorian towns of Crete, and it acquires even more significance in the light of the fact that we have very little information on this subject from elsewhere. Of course this is not a Law Code with a tight structure or a systematic record of legal procedure. Various issues are addressed without any obvious logical sequence or inherent connection. Nonetheless, in the form which it has it still remains an immensely important monument. Its main provisions are concerned with the personal freedom of the citizens, the clear and legally binding distinction between the classes of free citizens and slaves, civil and criminal offences (including rape and adultery), family law (divorce, distribution of paternal property, legal recognition of offspring, relations between parents and children, adoption etc.), business matters and many other issues. It is interesting that the legislation does not appear to demand any particularly severe punishment and it always requires a court decision in order to enforce the punishment, with clear guidelines for each case. It makes various provisions for women, though without appearing to grant any special privileges. The death penalty is not mentioned in the Gortyn Law Code.

The Law Code does not just have significance for the history of law. It gives an insight into the economic and social organization of the Dorian communities of Crete in the sixth century B.C. It also has considerable linguistic value. Thanks to the Gortyn Law Code we have access to the Dorian dialect of ancient Greek as spoken in Crete during these early historical years. In the absence of other literary texts surviving intact from this period the linguistic value of the Law Code cannot be overestimated.

Here is an extract from the Code:

If a man and his wife separate, (then) the wife should take back all that belonged to her when she married, plus half of the produce (income) if this produce is from her own land; and she shall keep half of all cloth she has woven, plus five gold stateres if the husband is the cause of the divorce. If, however, the husband maintains that he is not responsible for causing the divorce, the judge will decide on the matter after making the husband give oath.

CHAPTER VII

CRETE IN THE CLASSICAL AGE
(500 - 323 B.C.)

1. Introduction

During the two centuries of the golden age of Greece, the so-called Classical period of the fifth and fourth centuries B.C., Crete seems to be on the margin of Greek history. Both literary sources and inscriptions reveal very little about relations between the Cretan towns and other Greek centres. In around 450 B.C. we hear of the treaty of Knossos and Tylissos with Argos. At the same time Knossos struck up an alliance with Rhodes, and Lyttos with Lindos. Corfu and Athens maintained trade relations with the Cretan cities. The Athenian comic writer Hermippos, in recounting in his work *Phormophoroi* (The Porters), which was performed before 425 B.C., the goods imported into Athens from other parts of the Greek world, mentions also that 'fair Crete' sent valuable cypress wood for sacred use.

During this time Crete was plagued with inter-city warfare. There seems to have been a wide gulf between the larger and more developed commercial centres (such as Knossos) and those (Gortyn and Lyttos, for example) which insisted on adhering to tradition and refused to adapt to new conditions. The geography of the island, with its large mountainous areas and difficult communications between one region and another, tended to accelerate its political fragmentation and to aggravate internal disputes, thus draining it of its strength. Plato has left an account for us of the internicine hostility among Cretans, in the words of the Cretan Kleinias: 'That which most men term peace is simply a word; in practice, all the cities are in a constant state of undeclared warfare with one another.' The cities were all at war with one another, or striking up countless alliances and pacts: 'Everyone is permanently at war with all the other cities.' We hear of rebellions in various cities and the overthrow of political leaders. The case of Ergoteles, who was compelled to leave Knossos during the uprising of 476 B.C., and flee to Himera in Sicily, is characteristic of this period.

Nevertheless, despite the internal disputes between the Cretan cities, there survived a sense of community. The relations and common features shared by their law codes are evidence of an underlying unity in Crete. And it is also significant that when the great writers of antiquity (Plato, Aristotle, Ephoros, Xenophon and others) talk of Crete they consider it as a single political and social entity.

Another feature of this period was the poor state of the economy of the island. This meant that many Cretans were forced by necessity to sign up as mercenaries in foreign armies, especially after the Peloponnesian Wars (431-404 B.C.). Thucydides frequently mentions the Cretan archers who served in the Athenian army. Later, Cretan archers were among those in the expedition of the Ten Thousand led by Cyrus (401 B.C.). From then onwards we find Cretan mercenaries in practically all the armies of antiquity, including the army of Julius Caesar (Cretenses sagitarii). Professor Spyridakis who recently compiled a comprehensive list of Cretan mercenaries in antiquity, using names found in our sources, remarked that 'Trapped in a vicious circle of poverty, the Cretans were often compelled to tread the tragic road of self-imposed exile in order to survive, despite the fact that the Cretan's love of his homeland was legendary in antiquity.' This was the opinion of all the ancient historians: Diodoros Sikeliotes (37,18) has preserved for us the cynical answer of a Cretan mercenary to the Roman consul L. Julius Caesar, 'We use our bow for profit, and our every arrow serves for silver, as we are scattered throughout every land and sea.'

2. Crete and the Persian Wars

During the period of the Persian Wars Crete remained unwaveringly neutral. Herodotos mentions (VII, 169) that shortly before the congress at Corinth (481 B.C.) where the Greeks discussed their strategy for confronting the Persian enemy, they sent envoys to Crete, inviting the Cretan cities to help in the common struggle against Xerxes. Before sending their reply, the Cretan cities consulted the Delphic oracle. The oracle reminded the Cretans of the sufferings caused them by their involvement in the Trojan War and thus discouraged them from participating, despite their readiness to do so.

Modern historians interpret the negative response of the Cretans differently: the internal politics and social conditons of the island did not enable them to join in the common cause. The disputes among the social classes and cities, and the general climate of political instability made it virtually impossible for the Cretans to become involved in overseas campaigns. Likewise, the geographical position of Crete, its distance from other Greek areas and its weak economy all inclined to increase her fears of what might happen in the event of a Persian invasion of the island. And so the Delphic oracle was the ideal excuse for Crete to stay neutral. We should also remember that the Cretans' refusal to stand by their fellow Greeks can be partly explained by the Dorian psychology which was above all conservative and viewed any bold military venture, such as that now proposed by Athens, with great scepticism.

3. Crete and the Peloponnesian War (431-404 B.C.)

Similarly, the Cretan cities maintained neutrality in the case of the Peloponnesian Wars. The words used by Thucydides for Corfu apply also to Crete (I,31): 'They allied with none of the other Hellenes, neither striking up agreements with Athens nor with Sparta.'

An attack against Kydonia in 429 B.C. by an Athenian naval squadron, with Phormion at the command, did not lead to further hostilites. Thucydides wrote that this action was taken at the instigation of Nikias, the Gortyn consul in Athens, with the intention of supporting Athens' ally Polichne, a town close to Kydonia. It is likely, however, that this attack in fact had totally different aims. Some fugitives from the island of Aegina, which was a trading partner of Kydonia, had fled to Kydonia in 431 B.C. following their expulsion from Aegina by the Athenians on account of their friendship with Sparta. Since that time the Athenians were bent on hunting down the Aeginetans wherever they had sought refuge. Phormion's expedition therefore was aimed rather at the Aeginetans than at Kydonia itself. Nonetheless, the incident rekindled old hatreds within Crete. The inhabitants of Polichne had collaborated with the Gortynians and the Athenians in the attack on Kydonia.

4. Crete in the fourth century B.C.

From the mid-fourth century onwards we begin to follow the course of Cretan history with greater confidence in our knowledge. The island gradually emerged from the isolation and self-dependence into which it had withdrawn and reappears again on the stage of the major events of the day, frequently finding itself at the centre of international attention both strategically and politically, as the field of contention between the great powers of the age. Crete also becomes an object of interest to the great philosophers and the authors of works on the constitutions of the Greek city-states. Both Plato and Aristotle, for differing reasons, described Crete. We know that the last great historian of the classical period, Ephoros, devoted a special study to Crete, though unfortunately it has not survived. For this period, therefore, we have reliable accounts which help us to form a clearer picture of Cretan history during the later period of antiquity. This led the historian Wilamowitz (and more recently, Kirsten) to claim, with some exaggeration of course, that Crete was 'rediscovered in the fourth century, after a "total eclipse" from the Greek scene in the previous centuries.' It has been said that Cretan history begins at the moment when the history of the ancient Greek world comes to an end.

P l a t o a n d C r e t e. Plato mentions Crete in five of his dialogues: *Crito, Protagoras, Phaedo,* the *Republic* and the *Laws*. The pseudo-Platonic dialogue *Minos* also refers to Crete. Plato praises the good order of Cretan society and the education of its youths. His last dialogue, the *Laws,* is of especial interest for Cretan history, and is in fact set in Crete. The conversants in the dialogue are the Cretan Kleinias, member of a committee which has been assigned the task of organizing a new city which is in the process of being built, the Spartan Megillos and an unnamed Athenian who is obviously Plato himself in old age. The dialogue takes place on the occasion of the foundation of the new Cretan city, and its subject is the nature of the laws that are to be adopted.

This work has been dated to the last years of Plato's life and is believed to have been written around 347 B.C. It gives us information chiefly of a human-geographical and political nature. The nature of the country and its customs and institutions attract Plato's interest. The central issue of the dialogue, however, is education and legislation. Plato examines the character of both the Cretan and Spartan systems and criticises their one-sidedness, since all their laws are designed merely to foster military virtues and bravery. According to the Cretan, Kleinias, all public and private institutions are designed to encourage the attainment of military prowess. And this is in harmony with the nature of Cretan society since here life is an endless war waged by all. The philosopher's intention here, of course, is to project his own ideas on the 'good ordering' *(eunomia)* and prosperity of cities. This prosperity, as Plato would have it, does not depend on a one-sided fostering of military virtues; rather, it requires a balanced and harmonious development of all the virtues: of wisdom, prudence, justice and valour. However, Plato's draws largely on features of the Cretan system in order to develop his description of the organization of his ideal political system.

A r i s t o t l e a n d C r e t e. In contrast to Plato, who was always attempting to pursue ideal models, Aristotle examines closely the organization of the Cretan system and its institutions, and identifies its weaknesses. Unfortunately we only have a few surviving extracts from his work *Cretan Republic.* In his *Politics,* though, he discusses at length the organization of the Cretan political system. He observes from the outset how well-placed Crete is geographically. He attributes Crete's ancient hegemony of the seas in the time of Minos to this position, and that in his own days the island was safe from external intervention. This isolation, Aristotle goes on to observe, discouraged the *perioeci* from rebelling and compelled them to accept the yoke of their Dorian masters, unlike Sparta where the *peroeci* and the *helots* (serfs) often revolted against their lords. He comments on the close links between the Cretan and the Spartan systems and, in comparing their corresponding institutions, concludes that the Cretan system is the more ancient, as, for example, in the case of the public mess-tables. But he believed the institution of the Kosmoi in Crete to be less efficient than that of the Ephors in Sparta. The Cretan political system, according to Aristotle, was of an aristocratic type since the Kosmoi were elected by only a select group of families and, moreover, they were often mere organs of these powerful families. The inability of the Kosmoi to effectively govern the cities tended to nurture the desire for power in various strong personalities who then sought to win the allegiance of the people, instill rebellion, and ultimately war among themselves and create anarchy. It was for this reason, so Aristotle asserted, that 'the political system in Crete resembled something like a political order, but in fact was not a true system; rather it was an arbitrary regime that tended to lead to tyranny.'

5. The beginning of foreign intervention in Crete. The ' Foreign War '

The so-called 'Foreign War' gives us an idea of what the situation in Crete was like in the middle of the fourth century B.C. At this time Knossos, which was still a large city with a strong influence over the other towns of central Crete, was demanding first place among the Cretan cities. As Diodoros Sikeliotes remarked (XXXIII, 10) : 'Knossos laid claim to supremacy; for in the past the city had had the honour of being the ruling power.' The main obstacle to the expansionist policies of Knossos was Lyttos, a strong Dorian centre to the east of modern Herakleion, near the villages Xeidas and Kastamonitsa. Lyttos, according to tradition, was a Spartan colony, and it was true that the local institutions shared many features with those of Sparta. Tension between Knossos and Sparta increased until a fierce war broke out in 346 B.C. The unbridled ambition of Knossos to maintain first place on the island led, for the first time in the recorded history of Crete, to the invitation for help from outside forces. Knossos, offering a handsome wage, employed mercenaries hired from the ousted ruler of the Phokians, Phalaikos. For the mercenaries it was an opportunist venture which quickly turned into straightforward pillaging. Phalaikos was in a position to seize control of Lyttos, but, at the crucial hour, the city sought the assistance of its founding city Sparta. The Spartan king, Archidamos, rushed to Crete and swiftly crushed Phalaikos and relieved Lyttos of the seige. Phailakos, however, escaped with his men and turned on Kydonia, but without success: during the seige of the town he was killed and his army routed.

The episode of Phalaikos and his troops in Crete is evidence both of the extent of the crisis in relations between the cities of the island and, more generally, of their declining power. These events, besides their local significance, should be seen in terms of Crete's relations with outside powers during this period. Aristotle made the astute observation: 'The Cretans do not even share in foreign affairs, and also the island has only lately been invaded by warfare from abroad, rendering manifest the weakness of their laws.'

6. Crete in the time of Alexander the Great (336-323 B.C.)

We know that many Cretan mercenaries served in Alexander the Great's troops, and we also know that his admiral Nearchos was a Cretan, perhaps from the city of Lato. The position of the Cretan cities towards the Macedonian kingdom was not united. Certain cities such as Knossos, Gortyn, and Kydonia were strongly in favour of the Macedonians; others, led by Lyttos, preferred the Spartans. Sparta tried to cultivate anti-Macedonian sentiment in Crete through the pro-Spartan towns of the island. Indeed, immediately following Alexander's expedition through Asia (334 B.C) the Spartan king Agis gave the order to his brother Agesilaos to hasten to Crete in order to organise anti-Macedonian elements. Most probably the idea was to incite the Cretan cities to piracy, thereby cutting off Alexander's contact with the rest of Greece. This led Alexander to turn his attention to Crete. Very shortly after 332 B.C. he sent one of his commanders, Amphoteros, to Crete in order to dispel the Spartan presence there and to anticipate any possible disruption.

Unfortunately we do not possess information on developments in Crete at this time. Indirect evidence can be gained from an inscription in Kyrene, known as the Stela de Cereali. Crete and the rest of Greece were hit by massive crop failures in the years 330-326 B.C. The inscription lists the towns which, with Alexander's assent, received their grain from Kyrene. The five Cretan cities mentioned in the list are Knossos, Gortyn, Kydonia, Hyrtakina and Elyros. It is probably safe to assume that these were the cities which had showed support for Alexander, otherwise it is unlikely that they would have been entitled to allocations of grain at reduced prices.

CHAPTER VIII

CRETE AND HELLENISTIC GREECE
(323 - 69 B.C.)

After the death of Alexander the Great (323 B.C) and the foundation of the Greek kingdoms in the East, Crete became a centre of attention for the various new Greek states that had been created and who now sought to forge relations with the Cretan cities. External pressure and intervention led to an intensification of the existing internal differences in the island and to an incessant state of civil war that sapped the island of whatever strength it may have had and left it vulnerable to the later designs of the Romans. During the Hellenistic years these conflicts reached their height.

1. Leagues of Cretan cities.

The friendly or hostile relations within Crete, and relations between the Cretan cities and the Hellenistic kingdoms and the powers of Greece proper, led to the formation of alliances and leagues of the Cretan towns around the strongest cities of the island. The nature and aims of these unions are still not fully understood and it is hard to tell whether they were political, economic or religious. Inscriptions and historical accounts, however, inform us of the existence of four main leagues already at the beginning of the third century B.C.

a) The Knossos League

This was a broad-based, powerful union of twenty cities. These cities are named in an agreement of 293/292 B.C. between Knossos and Miletos in Asia Minor: Knossos, Tylissos, Rhaukos, Chersonesos, Milatos, Eltynia, Herakleion, Priansos, Apollonia, Petraia,

Itanos, Praisos, Istron, Holous, Dreros, Lato, Eleutherna, Axos, Kydonia and Phalasarna. This was the most important league in Crete and extended to much of the island.

b) The Gortyn League

Inscriptions inform us of the member cities of this league: (the cities are referred to by the names of their citizens) the city of the Gortynians, of the Lyttians, of the Arkades, the Ariaioi, and the Hyrtaioi. We know nothing about the city of the Ariaioi. The Hyrtaioi must be the citizens of Hyrtakina in south-west Crete (modern Selino), although it appears to have been a member of another league as well.

c) The Mountain League

This league is first mentioned in the sources in the early third century (293/292 B.C.). *Oreia* (meaning 'mountainous') was the name given to the area of the modern-day district of Selino. Four cities of the area were the main members of this league: Lisos, Elyros, Hyrtakina and Tarra, the religious centre being at Lisos. Coins with a goat's head or with a bee found at these sites are presumed to have been minted by the Mountain League. An inscription found at Lisos mentions an alliance between the king of Kyrene, Magas, and the Mountain League (IC II, XVII,1).

d) The Phaistos League

This League was comprised of three cities: Phaistos, Matala and Polyrrhenia in west Crete.

It should be noted that, despite the existence of the above four leagues, Crete in the Hellenistic years was essentially composed of two main powers who contended for domination, both political and military, of the rest of the island. These two cities were Knossos and

Gortyn. Knossos had distinctly imperialist designs, while Gortyn sought rather to be master of a federation. Whatever the case, both sides proved incapable of realising their ambitions. Two other cities, Lyttos in east Crete and Kydonia in the west, were strong centres in the third century, and were sometimes in alliance and sometimes in conflict with Gortyn and Knossos.

2. Sparta and Crete

At the beginning of the third century many Cretan cities were still closely associated with Sparta. Inscriptions and historical writings indicate that Lyttos and Gortyn in east Crete and Polyrrhenia in west Crete were the main channels of Spartan influence in the island. It is known that the king of Sparta, Areus, went to Crete in 273 B.C. in order to support Gortyn in her struggle against Knossos. It seems also that Polyrrhenia erected a statue of Areus in his honour. Plutarch relates that the Spartans planned to send their women and children to friendly Cretan cities at the time of Pyrrhos' invasion of Sparta.

3. Crete and Ptolemy's Egypt

After 270 B.C. many Cretan cities, especially in the east of the island, were under the influence of the Ptolemies of Egypt. The need to control the sea routes of the east Mediterranean gave Crete especial importance in the foreign policy of the ambitious and dynamic Ptolemy II (285-147 B.C.). A military force under the leadership of the commander Patroklos was installed at Itanos in the east of the island. It seems that the Itanians themselves requested the presence of the Egyptians in the area in order to counter more effectively the raids from neighbouring Praisos. For the two cities were constantly at odds with one another, since both sought to control the sanctuary of Diktaian Zeus in nearby Palaikastro. A later inscription at Itanos, dated to 164-145 B.C., tells us the following: 'The Itanians dwell in a coastal city and rule an ancestral land near to the sanctuary of Diktaian Zeus, and they also rule islands which include the island of Leuke; but being afflicted from time to time by the neighbouring Praisians they succeeded in winning the help and protection —for their city, land and islands— of king Ptolemy of Egypt...' (*IC* III, 9A, p. 36 and II,37). Also an honorary resolution passed by the Itanians refers to the honours that the city accorded to Ptolemy's commander Patroklos in recognition of the great services he performed for their city: 'By decision of the Itanians at their council and assembly: since Patroklos the son of Patron the Macedonian, commander sent by king Ptolemy to Crete, showed himself to be a great and just man towards the city of the Itanians and contributed so much for them, so that the citizens of Itanos might have a secure city, administered by the laws, and so that they might live in safety in the land, they saw fit to make Patroklos a state guest and benefactor and citizen and native participant in all their worldly and sacred affairs' (*IC* ,III,IV,2-3).

Crete thus became a protectorate of the Ptolemies, a situation which lasted for roughly two centuries. The influence of the Ptolemies spread to other cities, even in the west of Crete. Stephanos Byzantios mentions that a Cretan city (perhaps Chersonesos) was renamed Arsinoe, in honour of the Queen of Egypt, the sister and wife of Ptolemy II. Between 246 and 228 B.C. many inscriptions were set up announcing the honorary resolutions passed by the cities for Ptolemy III and his family. Similar honorary inscriptions were set up in Gortyn, Eleutherna, Lappa and Phalasarna. The inscriptions also inform us of the fact that other cities such as Rhithymna, Aptera, Dreros and Olous had become allies of Egypt. Moreover, it is known that many Cretan cities had taken part as allies of Egypt in the Chremonid War (267-261 B.C.) waged against Antigonos, king of Macedonia. Strabo talks of the close relations between Gortyn and Ptolemy IV who helped with the fortification of the city (221 B.C.).

However, it was not only the Ptolemies of Egypt who sought to win over the loyalty and allegiance of the Cretan cities. The kings of other Hellenistic states attempted to do much the same thing. Crete became a permanent feature of their foreign policy. Again the inscriptions give us an idea of the complexity of the various inter-state relations and alternating alliances. Lyttos, for example, maintained friendly relations with the Seleucid kingdom. In 249 B.C. Antioch II renewed the treaty with the city of the Lyttians which his father had first signed. Eleutherna honoured the Ptolemies, but later signed a friendship treaty with Antigonos, king of Macedonia (some time between 227 and 224 B.C.); and Hierapytna did the same.

4. The war against Lyttos (220 B.C.)

Crete was afflicted by deep crisis at the end of the third century B.C., and passions ran so high that the result was a terrible tragedy with the city of Lyttos playing the role of victim. Events evolved in a curious manner. The two main cities, Knossos and Gortyn, which in previous times had been in a constant state of animosity, now struck up an alliance and, according to the second century historian Polybius (53,7), they agreed to share control of the entire island apart from the city of Lyttos. Knossos, however, benefited from an internal crisis in Gortyn; for Gortyn at this time was troubled by fierce political disputes between its two 'parties,' the party of the 'Elders' and the party of the 'Young Ones.' The Elders of Gortyn supported the policies of Knossos, while the Young Ones supported the independent policy of the small but proud city of Lyttos. Various towns in the west of Crete, such as Lappa and Polyrrhenia, also followed the independent policy of Lyttos. Knossos and Gortyn suddenly became alarmed: they feared that a general rebellion might break out among the Cretan cities, so they decided to punish Lyttos severely as an example to the others.

Knossos, which was unable to impose its will on its own, looked to foreign assistance for yet another time. Indeed a thousand Aetolian mercenaries arrived on the island in the pay of Knossos. Having helped the Elders secure their power in Gortyn, they then turned on Lyttos. The sack and destruction of Lyttos which took place in 220 B.C. gives us an idea of the savagery of Cretan civil wars. The attackers seized their opportunity when the Lyttian men were all absent from the city on campaign in Hierapytna. The city was put to the torch and the women and children taken back to Knossos as prisoners. When the Lyttians returned to their city and discovered the catastrophe that had befallen them they could not face the idea of staying in the same place. They took refuge in Lappa from where they tried to continue their hopeless struggle against Knossos. Polybius gives a dramatic description of the destruction of Lyttos (IV, 54):

'At about the same time the Lyttians having left with their whole force for an expedition into the enemy's country, the Knossians getting word of it seized on Lyttos which was left without defenders, and having sent off the women and children to Knossos, and burnt, demolished, and in every way they could wrecked the town, returned home. When the Lyttians came back to their city from the expedition and saw what had happened, they were so much affected that none of them had the heart to enter his native town, but one and all after marching round it and many times bewailing and lamenting the fate of their country and themselves, turned their backs on it and retired to Lappa. The Lappaeans received them with the utmost kindness and cordiality; and thus having become in one day cityless aliens instead of citizens they went on fighting against Knossos with the other allies. Thus was Lyttos, a colony of the Spartans and allied to them by blood, the most ancient city in Crete, and ever, as all acknowledged, the breeding place of her bravest men, utterly and unexpectedly made away with.'

Resistance to Knossos, which continued for some years in west Crete with its centre at Polyrrhenia and Lappa, eventually led to further intervention from outside. This time, Polyrrhenia and Lappa requested the help of Philip V of Macedonia. This ambitious monarch, who saw Crete as a permanent and abundant source of mercenary soldiers, as well as an ideal base for the control of the rest of the Aegean, responded immediately to the request of the Cretans and sent 500 troops (400 Illyrians and 100 Phokians). At the same time the Achaeans of the Peloponnese sent 200 men under the command of Philopoimen. The outcome of this campaign was that at least three other cities —Eleutherna, Aptera and Kydonia— broke away from the control of Knossos. Within a very short time Philip V succeeded in securing control of a large part of west Crete. A Macedonian protectorate was established on the island in 217/216 B.C. and Philip was recognised as 'Protector' of Crete.

5. A period of respite for the Cretan cities

Following the destruction of Lyttos there was a respite in Cretan feuding. There was talk of peace and this was achieved thanks to the intervention of outside factors. Polybius considered this 'concord of mind' of the Cretans as a major political achievement of Philip V of Macedonia, for which he was deemed 'Protector' of the island. Other Greek centres also seem to have contributed; an inscription in Magnesia in Asia Minor set up on the occasion of the recognition of the sanctuary of Artemis of Leukophryene and the sanctity of the city, mentions the contribution of the Magnesians to the cessation of civil war in Crete.

This peace and unity, however, was superficial and short-lasting. The old loyalties and alliances with outside powers were maintained with the result that Crete continued to be an arena for conflicting interests. While west Crete was under the political control of Philip V, east Crete continued to be influenced by the Ptolemies of Egypt. Various isolated cases of smaller alliances of cities still existed: Polyrrhenia with Melos, Aptera with Miletos, and Allaria with Paros. Crete also kept in contact with the major sanctuaries of the Greek world, such as at Delphi and Delos.

6. The Koinon of Crete

The *Koinon* (which could be loosely translated as the 'House of Commons') was a political institution that first appeared in Greece during the age of the successors (the so-called *diadochoi*) of Alexander the Great. Inscriptions of the late third century B.C. indicate that in Crete they had the 'Koinon of the Cretans' (IC I,2,1, Priansos). The early stages of the Cretan *Koinon* are not fully understood. Van Effenterre believes (on the basis of an account by Diodoros Sikeliotes which mentions the return of the bones of Minos, by the Theran tyrant of Agrigento in Sicily, to the Cretans in general and not to any one particular city) that already in the fifth century B.C. there was a *Koinon* of the Cretans. Most historians, however, date the organization of the *Koinon* to the late third century, and to 221 B.C. in particular, when the two largest Cretan cities, Knossos and Gortyn, signed an agreement with each other in order to impose their power over the rest of the island. These two cities played a leading role in the organization and running of the Cretan *Koinon,* although all the cities suppposedly participated on a basis of equality.

The function and political jurisdiction of the Koinon of the Cretans is only partially known. There was a council whose members were called *synhedroi* (delegates), and a general assembly that was called the *Koinon* or *Plethos* (meaning 'congregation' or 'throng') of the Cretans. The assemblies were held in Knossos and other cities, including Axos, Priansos and Lappa. There is also evidence of common legislative organization. The inscriptions talk of the Cretan *diagramma* which most likely was the basic legislation code and regulated relations between the Cretan cities and aimed to maintain the peace. There is also mention of a common (federal) court known as the *koinodikaion* which was responsible for settling disputes between member cities of the *Koinon*. However, many scholars believe that the *koinodikaion* was not in fact a court as such, but rather the term given to the system of common legislative procedure of the Cretan cities. After the Roman conquest of Crete the Cretan *Koinon* was preserved as a local institution whose head was called the Cretarch. Powerful Cretan families, such as the Kydantes in the first century B.C., rivalled for the office of head of the Cretan *Koinon*. It is also likely that the *Koinon* had its own currency.

It is generally thought that the term 'syncretism,' which originally meant the unity and concord of the Cretan cities in the face of common enemies, had its beginnings in the institution of the *Koinon*. Plutarch refers to this phenomenon in his work *On fraternity* (19.17,20) where he says that the Cretans 'often clashed and warred with each other, but in the face of an outside enemy they put aside their differences and united; and this is what they call syncretism.'

7. The 'Cretan War' (205-201 B.C.)

The Aegean policy of Philip V of Macedonia brought more turmoil to Crete. Philip V was an ambitious monarch who strove to dominate the entire Greek world of the time. An alliance with Crete would help him realise his expansionist ambitions. The only power which posed a serious obstacle to his plans was the island of Rhodes which, however, was supposedly his friend and ally. The large naval fleet of Rhodes controlled all the sea routes to the East and sea trade was almost exclusively in the hands of the Rhodians. The naval power of Rhodes could be shaken in two ways: by piracy or by war. Philip V used both these methods. To begin with he turned the Cretans, who were old timers at piracy, against Rhodes. Alongside the Cretans, Aetolians also took part in the pirate raids, led by Dikaiarchos, and Spartans led by their guileful king Nabis. After 205 B.C. piracy had become a real menace to Rhodes' trade and the time was ripe for parallel military action. Philip incited some of the Cretan cities to declare war on Rhodes. We do not know the details of this war, which is referred to in the sources as the Cretan War. What we can say is that Hierapytna and Olous (modern Elounda) seem to have been the first to respond to Philip's call to war.

Rhodes first reaction was diplomatic. It turned to Rome and condemned Philip's schemes. Thus, when the Romans waged war on

Philip V (in 201 B.C.), Rhodes was in a position to take on Hierapytna and Olous with its own forces. Rhodes managed to secure Knossos as a partner in the campaign against Hierapytna (200 B.C.), and many cities of central Crete came in on the side of Knossos. Hierapytna could not wage war on two fronts. The 'Cretan War' ended favourably for Rhodes. A treaty which has survived (IC III,III,3A) contains the terms of the truce, terms that were especially onerous for Hierapytna. Hierapytna was compelled to revoke all its alliances with other powers and to place all its harbours and bases at Rhodes' disposal. A similar inscription in Olous confirms the total imposition of Rhodian power over the city. Now the greater part of east Crete was controlled by Rhodes, and its naval bases were well-placed to stamp out any pirate activity in the region.

8. Crete in the second century B.C.

The rise to power of Rhodes put an end to piracy stemming from the cities of east Crete. Knossos was dominant throughout central Crete and was on friendly terms with Rhodes. The piracy that remained was confined to west Crete and, in particular, to those cities that supported Nabis, the king of Sparta. This cunning and unscrupulous ruler, whom the ancient historians describe in the blackest of terms, controlled a wide network of piracy which, from as early as 198 B.C., included many cities in west Crete that provided him with bases for his fleet. In the war between the Romans and Philip V, Nabis supported the Romans and provided them with 600 Cretan mercenaries, most of whom were from Gortyn.

Following their victory at Kynos Kephalai in 197 B.C. and having successfully worked the subjugation of Philip V, the Romans turned against their supposed ally Nabis. The Roman historian, Titus Libius, records the text of the treaty signed by Nabis with the Romans (196 B.C.). By this treaty the Spartan king was obliged to break off all relations with the Cretan cities and to cede all the bases and ports that were nominally under his control to the Romans. This event was a turning point in the history of Crete, for it marked the beginning of Roman involvement in the island. In the future the Romans were to intervene on various pretexts and would exert decisive control over the affairs of Crete.

Piracy, however, does not seem to have been drastically reduced; on the contrary, it reached new heights. Just a few years after the victory of the Romans against Antioch III of Syria and Galatia (189 B.C.) Quintus Favius Laveon, commander of the Roman fleet in the Aegean, sailed to Crete in order to free thousands of Roman prisoners held by Cretan pirates. It is worth noting that the Cretan cities refused to hand over the prisoners, with the exception of Gortyn. Throughout the entire period that followed, right up to the time when Crete became a part of the Roman empire, Gortyn was the centre for pro-Roman sentiment on the island, while Knossos and Kydonia represented the policy of resistance to Roman intervention.

The pro-Roman position held by Gortyn was dictated by two crucial problems it was facing at this time: the war with Knossos and the flight of Hannibal to their city. The Romans were very anxious to apprehend the Carthaginian commander who had caused so much trouble for them. This is why there were so many illustrious Roman representatives, such as Scipio, in Crete at this time. They were there under the pretext of mediating for peace between the Cretan cities during the latest Cretan war.

During the same period there was also a reorientation of Cretan foreign policy in support of Eumenes II of Pergamum. An inscription of 183 B.C. refers to an alliance that was formed between thirty-one member cities of the *Koinon* of Crete and the ambitious ruler of the eastern kingdom of Pergamum. This inscription gives us the largest number of known Cretan cities to have participated in the *Koinon:* Gortyn, Knossos, Phaistos, Lyttos, Rhaukos, Hierapytna, Eleutherna, Aptera, Polyrrhenia, Sybrita, Lappa, Axos, Priansos, Allaria, Arkades, Keraia, Praisos, Lato, Biannos, Mala, Eronos, Chersonesos, Apollonia, Elyros, Hyrtakina, Eltynia, Anopolis, Heraden, Istron and

Tarra. The first in this list was Gortyn. Cretan mercenaries under the command of the Gortynian Kydas also served in the army of Eumenes.

Polybius informs us of the outbreak of new internal crisis on the island in about 180 B.C. Although we are lacking any basic evidence that enables us to form a clear picture of this crisis we may conjecture that it was another civil war that developed into a particularly savage affair. He mentions the destruction and decimation of various cities, such as Miletos and Dreros at the hands of Lyttos, Rhaukos at the hands of Knossos and Gortyn, and Apollonia at the hands of Kydonia. Polybius makes special mention of the destruction of Apollonia, which he describes as 'a terrible and lawless deed.' In 171 B.C. the powerful city of Kydonia, which had grown strong and prosperous through trade, attacked its former friend and ally Apollonia. We are ignorant of the reasons for this hostile act, but the eloquently restrained description by Polybius of the destruction is dramatic (27.16,3-4): 'They slew the men, they seized all goods and property, and the women and the city were shared out and taken possession of.' This incident caused further complications. Gortyn, which at this time was the most powerful of the Cretan cities and had undertaken to ensure internal security and peace, turned against Kydonia. This put Kydonia in great danger, but a temporary truce was agreed thanks to the mediation of the Romans who sent Quintus Minucius to the island with ten ships in 170 B.C.

The situation, however, remained far from stable both in internal affairs and in foreign relations. An example of the continually changing relations of the period is provided by the occasion when Eumenes II of Pergamum responded to a request for assistance by Kydonia, and sent 300 troops to Crete in order to combat the Gortynian attack, who also happened to be an ally of Pergamum.

Just a few years later (155-153 B.C.) Crete was again at war with Rhodes. This was the so-called second 'Cretan War.' And once again the *causus belli* was the continued pirate raids conducted by the Cretans to the cost of Rhodian trade. The war ceased after the mediation of the Romans, whose intervention was requested by Rhodes.

CHAPTER IX

ARTS AND LETTERS IN DORIAN CRETE

1. Cretan writers

The austere and closed system of Dorian Crete did not exactly foster in its citizens the intellectual and artistic aspirations that we witness elsewhere in the Greek world. An extreme conservatism was probably the main cause for the poverty of literary production in Crete at this time. In Plato's *Laws* the Cretan, Kleinias, admits that 'We Cretans don't much practise foreign letters' *(Laws,* III 680c). There are very few Cretan names that enjoyed wide recognition associated with the ancient literary tradition.

A prophet and purifier who enjoyed a wide reputation was Epimenides of Knossos (or perhaps of Gortyn), a figure who has become largely lost in the mist of the Cretan past. He became famous when, in 612 B.C., he was invited to Athens to purify the city from the taint of the murder of Kylon. Ancient sources rank him among the seven sages of ancient Greece and consider him a contemporary and close friend of Solon. His life was linked to various strange and perplexing myths, such as his fifty-seven year sleep in the Diktaian cave, and his invention of a secret foodstuff that staves off hunger. Epimenides is also attributed with the organization of religious affairs and festivals in Crete, which is why after his death he was worshipped by the Cretans as a god. There is also a well-known verse said to be by Epimenides which mentions the character of the Cretans and is preserved for us in St Paul's *Epistle to Titus* (I, xii): 'The Cretans are always liars, evil beasts, slothful bellies.'

An important Cretan poet, Thaletas of Gortyn, is believed to have lived in the seventh century. Ancient tradition refers to him as the teacher of Lykourgos of Sparta. He was a poet and musician, and is said to have introduced music for the flute, paeans, *gymnopaidiai* (festivals at which boys danced and performed gymnastic exercises naked) and *hyporchemata* (songs accompanied by dancing and pantomimic action) into Sparta. According to Strabo, Thaletas devised a special kind of poetry for musical accompaniment known as the 'Cretan metre.'

In some lists of the seven sages of antiquity mention is made of Myson the Cheneus of Siteia, although little else is known about him. Another figure, Diogenes Apolloniates, from Apollonia in Crete, was a pre-Socratic philosopher and contemporary of Anaxagoras and pupil of Anaximenes. He developed his theories in a work known as *On Nature,* of which only a few fragments have survived. He believed, as did his teacher Anaximenes, that the principle element of the world was air from which all other matter was formed. According to an account by Diogenes Laertios, Diogenes Apolloniates was condemned for impiety in Athens in 405 B.C.

Rhianos from the town of Bene near Gortyn (or, according to another tradition, from Keraia in west Crete) was a notable epic poet of the third century B.C. He was a grammarian and scholar of the Homeric epics and he himself composed a long epic poem with the title *Herakleiad* in fourteen books on the subject of the twelve labours of Herakles. In another epic, the *Messeniaca,* he related in verse the history of the second Messenian war. Other works by Rhianos, which were later used extensively by Pausanias, were the *Achaïca,* the *Eliaca,* the *Thessalica,* as well as a curious work with the title *Pheme* ('Rumour' or 'Repute'). In addition, in the Palatine Anthology there are ten love poems attributed to Rhianos. Of this vast output, which was highly praised by the ancient grammarians, only forty-four verses and a few place-names in the lexicon of Stephanos of Byzantium have survived.

Another poet, Sotades of Maroneia, was most probably from Maroneia in Crete (and not from the like-named city in Thrace) and was active in the years of Ptolemy II (first half of the third century B.C.). He wrote coarse poetry in an unbridled crude tone and in a cutting satirical vein. It is for this reason that he is held to be the leading figure among ancient obscene writers. He wrote in a peculiar metre of his own which bears his name. In one of his poems he boldly attacks Ptolemy II for his incestuous marriage with his sister Arsinoe. He paid a heavy price, however, for his outspokenness, and met with a violent death. Athenaios gives us an account of the episode (XIV,621 a-b): 'Patroklos, the commander of Ptolemy, seized him (Sotades) in the island of Kaunos and, sealing him in a lead pot, drowned him in the sea.'

An example of the kind of lyric poetry popular in Dorian Crete is provided by the *skolion* of Hybrias, which we discussed earlier. It should probably be dated to the third century B.C. since the form of the Dorian dialect in which it is written is already quite simplified.

Finally Pausanias (Attica 34.4) mentions a man called Iophon of Knossos, an interpreter of oracular sayings in hexameter verse at the temple of Amphiaraos at Oropos.

In the first century B.C. the sceptic philosopher Ainesidemos of Knossos lived in Alexandria in Egypt. He is held to be the reviver of the ancient sceptic philosophy of Pyrrhon and the master of the new sceptic school of thought. Of his works, the *Eight Books on the Pyrrhonian Discourses,* the *Outline of the Pyrrhonian philosophy, Against wisdom, On Inquiry,* and *First Introduction* have all survived only in fragments.

2. The arts

Most of the Cretan artists (chiefly sculptors and architects) of the archaic, classical and hellenistic periods lived and worked outside Crete where they could find better conditions and opportunities. Pausanias mentions Aristokles of Kydonia (late sixth century) who was well-known as a bronze-smith. One of his works which represents Herakles fighting with the Amazon Hippolyta, was erected at Olympia as a dedicatory offering from Euagoras of Sicily. Another famous sculptor, contemporary with Aristokles, was Cheirisophos. Pausanias saw a large statue of Apollo in Tegea which had been fashioned by Cheirisophos, as well as a 'self-portrait' statue of Cheirisophos himself.

Another sculptor who worked in bronze was Kresilas of Kydonia, a contemporary of the greatest ancient sculptor, Pheidias. Pliny relates how he saw four of Kresilas' works of which the finest was a sculpture of the great Athenian statesman Perikles at Olympia.

Two other famous architects, Chersiphron of Knossos and his son Metagenes, began construction of the famous temple of Artemis at Ephesus in Asia Minor in the first half of the sixth century. They also wrote, according to an account by the Roman historian Vitruvius, a treatise on the temple. In recent years Marinatos put forward the view that these two great architects, having worked in the heart of the Ionian Greek lands of Asia Minor, returned to Crete bringing with them the new Ionic architectural order. Two decorated pediments found at Amnisos have been attributed to these two artists.

Interesting monuments of this period in Crete include the Asclepeion of Lebena, which was founded by the Gortynians in the fourth century B.C. and later developed into a major religious centre of Asclepius, the Delphinium of Knossos, dedicated to the god Apollo, the Pythium of Gortyn, again dedicated to Apollo, and the temple of Athene at Lyttos.

Recent archaeological excavations have uncovered important evidence, chiefly of the Hellenistic period. Superb decorated mosaic floors were found near Chania.

PART THREE

THE ROMAN PERIOD

CHAPTER I

ROMAN CONQUEST AND ADMINISTRATION

Following the subjugation of southern Greece by the Romans in 146 B.C. it was only to be expected that Crete would come to occupy a central place in Rome's East Mediterranean policy. The occupation of Crete was to provide Rome with a unique opportunity to control the main sea routes, to reduce pirate activity and to protect naval commerce more effectively. Besides, Crete was well-placed to act as a bridgehead for Rome's imperialist ambitions further east in the Mediterranean. The Roman historian Florus states Rome's ambitions more bluntly: 'If the truth be known, we conducted the Cretan war from the simple desire to conquer and enslave this important island.'

Rome's interest in Crete started from an early date. As far back as the third century B.C. Roman garrison commanders were present in Itanos, which at that time was a protectorate of the Ptolemies of Egypt. Cretan inscriptions of the period mention the worship of the Roman deity Fortuna Primigenia. Open conflict, however, was not to occur until much later.

It was the so-called second Mithridatic war (74-64 B.C.) which gave the Romans a pretext for intervention in Crete. Mithridates VI, the ambitious king of the Pontus, rose up in rebellion against the Romans, accompanied by other discontented leaders. In 85 B.C. Mithridates sent his commander Dorylaos to Crete in order to recruit a select corp of Cretan mercenaries who were then used in the struggle against the Romans. Besides their links with Mithridates the

Cretans were accused (and not unjustly) of collaborating with the imfamous pirates of Kilikia who used the bays and harbours of Crete as hideouts. There are many historians today who doubt that Crete was actively involved in piracy, but the evidence in ancient sources cannot be ignored.

In 74 B.C. the Roman senate appointed Marcus Antonius, father of Mark Antony the famous general of the second triumvirate, as commander of the Mediterranean fleet whose task it was to conquer Crete. To begin with Marcus Antonius was apparently reluctant to undertake such a risky naval operation. In 71 B.C. he sent envoys to Crete seeking the annulment of the Cretan alliance with Kilikia. The negative response of the Cretan *Koinon* compelled the Roman commander to use force. However, this first campaign failed miserably. The Cretan commanders Panares of Kydonia and Lasthenes of Knossos took the intitiative by attacking the Roman fleet in the sea between modern Herakleion and the island of Dia and defeated it. Many Roman ships were sunk and others were captured along with their crews. Many of the Roman prisoners were hung from the masts of the ships and Marcus Antonius was forced to sign a humiliating treaty with the Cretans. The Roman senate, however, refused to ratify the treaty and, shamed, Marcus Antonius died having been dubbed with the ignoble and ironic title 'the Cretan'.

Following this episode the Cretans became afraid of Roman reprisals and they tried to dispel the crisis by negotiation. Immediately after Marcus Antonius' defeat an embassy of thirty eminent Cretans arrived in Rome with proposals for an alliance. But the Roman senate, already determined that Crete should be conquered, gave a very cool reception to the Cretan envoys and set forth the harshest terms: the release of the prisoners of war, submission of the entire Cretan fleet, the deliverance to Rome of 400 Cretan hostages from the most illustrious families of the island including the commanders Panares and Lasthenes, and, finally, the payment of reparations amounting to 4000 silver talents. At a general assembly of the Koinon in Crete it was unanimously decided to reject all the

Roman terms and to prepare the island's defences for the expected Roman reprisals. The Cretan cities, in the face of a common enemy, now presented a united front in spite of their differences. They managed to amass a force of some 26,000 men from all over Crete, and Panares and Lasthenes were appointed as commanders-in-chief.

Rome appointed consul Quintus Caecilius Metellus with the task of subjugating Crete. The campaign began in 69 B.C. with the landing of Roman legions in west Crete. The first major military encounter took place near Kydonia, where the Cretan defence had been organized. The Cretans were forced to retreat before the superior forces of the Romans. Subsequently the war became a succession of sieges of the Cretan fortresses as the Romans made their way from one end of the island to the other, thus purging the island of all pockets of resistance. The cities of Eleutherna, Lappa and Lyttos that had always been on good terms with one another put up stout resistance, but were eventually forced to submit.

The Cretan struggle reached its finale at Knossos. Lasthenes fortified his home city for the siege, but, despite a brave defence, this city too succumbed to the might of the Roman legions. It is said that when all hope of repelling the Romans was lost Lasthenes gathered all the treasures of Knossos in his home and burnt them so that they would not fall into Roman hands. Lasthenes and his men retreated to Hierapytna where Aristios was commander. With the capture of this last city in 67 B.C. the Romans achieved the total subjugation of Crete. Consul Quintus Caecilius Metellus was given the honorary title 'the Cretan' and he was received in Rome by a triumphal welcome. Crete now followed the same course as the rest of the Greek world. The Roman historian Dio Cassius remarked that the Cretans had been made subjects of another people for the first time in their history.

Consequences of the Roman conquest

With its subjugation to the Romans Crete was annihilated as a political and military power. Its major centres were all destroyed and the various alliances, both foreign and internal, were annulled. Civil war, however, and the constant bloodshed on the island were also brought to an end. Now subject to the general Roman political climate and the *Pax Romana* the Cretan cities entered a long period of peace such as they had not seen for centuries. Throughout the entire period of Roman domination not a single Cretan conflict is mentioned in the sources. A local dispute which broke out in the early second century A.D. between Kisamos and Polyrrhenia did not develop into a significant conflict and was quickly resolved with the intervention of the Romans.

The Romans never attempted to Latinise the island. In any case this would have been a vain undertaking, both because of the nature of the land and of the inhabitants. For this reason we do not observe any ethnic or demographic changes in Crete during this period. The population remained Greek with a relatively high level of lifestyle. The main Cretan characteristic of its Greek dialect also remained unchanged.

Nor did the Cretans oppose their Roman overlords. The Romans were never compelled to station a large force on Crete and they limited their rule to the spheres of political administration and economic exploitation. Rebellions, a common feature of the later Venetian and Turkish periods in Crete, do not appear to have taken place under Roman rule. Only during the final phase of the Roman civil wars does there seem to have been political unrest in Crete when various Cretans considered the time to be ripe for shaking off the Roman yoke. But again the Cretan cities were divided on the issue. Some of the cities supported Antony, while others supported Octavian. Antony, under whose jurisdiction Crete came, viewed the island as a suitable strategic centre for his ambitious designs on the Roman empire. In 36 B.C. he garrisoned his forces in Crete and turned on all the cities that had resisted him, such as Lappa, while other cities which he considered friendly were granted tax concessions. He also granted the right to Roman citizenship to a number of eminent Cretan families. However, following his victory in 31 B.C. at Actium, Octavian punished the cities which had supported Antony (such as Knossos) and, in his turn, granted favours and privileges to those cities, such as Lappa and Kydonia, which had been opposed to Antony.

With the passing of time and during the period of peace and stability Crete no longer occupied an important place in Roman affairs. It became a remote outpost where the Romans would exile various undesirable political or military figures.

The political organization of Crete

Following the Roman conquest of Crete it became a part of the *provincia* of Cyrene, with the aim (according to Cicero) of making Roman control of Egypt more efficient. The political and military centre of this dual province was Gortyn which had always been loyal to Rome. Crete was administered by a proconsul accompanied by a *quaestor* (paymaster), a *legatus* (staff officer) and commissioners. The Roman officials stayed in Gortyn where there is also evidence for the existence of a special Roman assembly *(conventus)*.

During the early years of Roman rule the political organization and administration of Crete was not fully developed. Julius Caesar arranged the administrative separation of Crete from Cyrene and after his death (44 B.C.) the Roman senate issued a curious order whereby Crete was no longer to be considered a Roman province. In 43 B.C. Brutus was given the task of running the Cretan administration, while Cassius was appointed as controller of Cyrene. In 38 B.C. Mark Antony gave a part of east Crete to his friend and ally Cleopatra of Egypt. And later Octavian decided to strengthen the Roman presence by installing veteran soldiers and officials in the island to whom large areas of fertile land were granted. Territory around Knossos was given to Capua of Campania in exchange for land which Capua had given to veterans of Octavian. Knossos was settled by Roman soldiers and transformed into a Roman colony with the name Colonia Julia Nobilis.

In 27 B.C., by decree of the emperor Octavian Augustus, Crete was reunited with Cyrene in Africa as a single province, with Gortyn as the administrative capital. This situation remained unaltered until the end of the third century A.D. when Diocletian added Crete to the province of Mysia (Asia Minor).

The Romans, as was their custom, encouraged local administrative control in the Cretan cities. The Cretan *Koinon* continued to function just as it had done during Hellenistic times. The master of the *Koinon* in the Roman period was the high priest, who was perhaps the equivalent of the Cretarch of earlier times. The Koinon organized musical and athletic games that were held in Gortyn every five years and it had the right to mint its own brass coinage. Inscriptions also indicate that other local centres had their own mints during the Roman period (at Kydonia, Hierapytna, Axos, Eleutherna, Lappa, Lyttos and Polyrrhenia).

The role of the *Koinon* was not confined to these proceedings alone. It frequently developed its own political activity, for example in the case where it appealed to the Roman senate about the arbitrary behaviour of the local Roman administrators towards the islanders. The *Koinon* also displayed its proud independence on occasions when it refused to extend public commendation to unworthy Roman officials. The account by Tacitus (*Annales,* 15,20) of the trial of the haughty Cretan governor Claudius Timarchus in 62 A.D. is one such case.

CHAPTER II

THE CENTRES

1. The centres - buildings - technical achievements

Throughout the period of Roman domination the chief city and capital of Crete was Gortyn. It saw a rapid increase in its prestige since it served both as home to the leaders of the island and as the commercial centre. It was a populous centre and, according to Strabo, measured some 50 stades (6 miles) in diameter. The Romans adorned the city with large public monuments, such as temples, theatres, amphitheatres, public baths, columns and statues. Excavations have uncovered a number of these monuments: the Praetorium (residence of the proconsul), the temple of Pythian Apollo, the Iseium (temple of the Egyptian deity Isis), the Nymphaeum (temple of the Nymphs), the Odeon, the Forum (the Roman market-place), and others. The traveller Christopher Buondelmonti, who toured the island in the 15th century (1415-1417), mentions counting over 2,000 statues and other archaeological remains in the district of Gortyn.

Knossos, which had initially been designated capital of the island by the Romans was obliged to take second place. It failed to develop into a military centre and Roman buildings have not as yet come to light, although the forum has been identified.

An important centre in west Crete was Kydonia. It is mentioned as being one of the cities which had a theatre during the Roman period. This theatre, which was still standing in 1583 according to the account by the Italian traveller Onorio Belli, was destroyed by the Venetians and its materials were used to repair the walls of the city.

Lyttos, too, one of the oldest of the Cretan cities, was an

important centre during the Roman period. A huge theatre -the largest in Crete- was located here. Archaeological excavations which began in the summer of 1983 brought to light the Roman council chamber and other interesting finds.

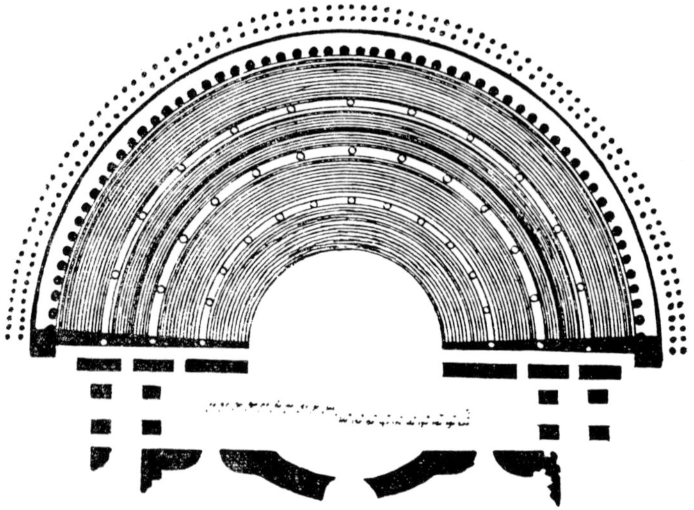

Figure 3
The Roman theatre at Lyttos. Plan by Onorio Belli (1586). (S. Spanakis, To theatro sti Romaiki Kriti, *Proceedings of the Second International Conference on Cretan Studies, vol. II, p. 158, Plate 23.*)

Other centres of importance during the Roman period were Hierapytna, which also had a large theatre and amphitheatre, Phaistos, Eleutherna, Lappa and Phalasarna. Smaller centres started to appear on the south coast of Crete serving as harbours for the Roman galleys on their way to the East. The sources mention Kaloi Limenes, Matalla and Lebena (modern Lenta). At the latter there was a large temple dedicated to Asclepius, which was destroyed in the earthquake of 46 B.C.

During the imperial years Crete enjoyed the favour of a number of Roman emperors and above all Trajan (98-117) and Hadrian (117-138). Inscriptions and statues of these emperors that have been found in many parts of Crete attest to the gratitude of the Cretans towards their benefactors. As was their practice, the Romans undertook large construction projects such as roads, bridges and aquaducts for the public benefit. The remains of such works can still be seen: the huge aquaducts at Lyttos and Chersonesos are impressive even today.

2. The Roman lifestyle in Crete.

It was only natural, considering the length of the Roman period, that elements of the Roman lifestyle should have left their mark on Crete and its inhabitants. Public spectacles, animal contests and gladiatorial contests are all attested in the Cretan cities. The mere presence of amphitheatres in various Cretan cities (Kisamos, Gortyn, Chersonesos and Hierapetra) confirms that such events, of clearly Roman origin, were organized as part of daily life. There is also evidence for the existence and functioning of public baths. An inscription from Ini in Monofatsi mentions the public baths at Arkades, with separate times for men and women. Mention is also made of the *oikonomos* (manager) of the public baths. We can safely assume that such amenities were common in other Cretan cities.

Roman influence was even greater in the sphere of religion and worship. The ancient gods of the Greek pantheon continued to be revered even in the first centuries of the Christian era, but at the same time the worship of other gods from the East, and Egypt in particular, became more common. It is known that Kybele and Ephesian Artemis were worshipped in Crete. Festivals that were of purely Roman origin, such as the worship of the deified emperors and members of the imperial family, of the senate, and even of Rome itself all passed into Cretan life as official state sponsored occasions.

These influences, however, did not change the underlying Greek character of the Cretan people. Their influence was limited chiefly to the governing classes in the urban centres, while the majority of the Cretan people remained true to its older Greek customs and traditions.

3. Letters and the arts

Cultural life in Crete during the Roman period left little of interest behind. Just one notable poet, Mesomedes, is mentioned as being a freedman of the emperor Hadrian. Eleven lyric verses have survived in his name, and two of them are particularly noteworthy: *In the Adriatic,* a description of a journey to the Adriatic Sea, and *Ekphrasis Spongou,* a love poem about a sponge which the poet gives to his beloved. Mesomedes' poetry was later to influence Synesius of Cyrene.

The main objects of artistic interest from the period are sculpture and decorated mosaic floors. A mosaic floor design has been uncovered in Knossos (now in the Herakleion Museum), along with the signature of its artist, who has a Roman name but signs in Greek letters: ΑΠΟΛΙΝΑΡΙΣ ΕΠΟΙΕΙ (executed by Apolinaris). A Roman building of the third century A.D. at Chania contained fine mosaics, one of which depicts the mythical subject of the carrying off of the nymph Amymone by a satyr and her rescue by the god Poseidon. Its colours are still intense and bright and the composition is of the highest artistry, thus making it a prime example of the workmanship in the medium at this time.

CHAPTER III

RELIGION AND WORSHIP IN ANCIENT CRETE

The religious practice of the Cretans from Dorian times through to the later Roman period did not differ substantially from the rest of Greece. The Greek deities, brought to the island by the Mycenaeans and the Dorians, were mingled with the deities of the Minoans, thus leading to a new religious compound wherein many characteristic elements of the Minoan religion survived below the surface of the Greek pantheon. There are many deities which are to be found only in Crete, and not elsewhere in the Greek world, such as the Cretan Britomartis, Mistress of Animals, and Diktynna, which are generally thought to be remnants of the earlier faith. The same occurs in the case of the epithets and qualities, again only met in Crete, attributed to the various gods.

According to myth that was kept alive until late Antique times Crete was the birthplace of Zeus, who was thus dubbed 'born of Crete'. He occupied a special place in Cretan worship and was referred to by a number of epithets: Agoraios, Hekatombaios, Asterios, Kretagenes (Cretan born), Tallaios, Eleutherios, Belchanios, Horatios, Skylios, Diktaios, Soter, Epopsios, Thenatas, and so on. Apollo also received especial reverence, and had the epithets Delphinios, Pythios, Leschanorios, Dekataphoros and Karneios. In a few cities, such as at Lyttos, the goddess Athene was worshipped with the epithet Polias.

Worship was conducted in temples and cave sanctuaries. The most important temples, which later developed into major religious centres, were the Delphinian temple at Knossos and the Pythian temple at Gortyn, both dedicated to Apollo. Other important centres were the Asclepian temple at Lebena, the Diktynnaion temple on the headland at Spatha west of Kydonia, and the Samonian temple at Itanos, dedicated to the goddess Athene. One of the major centres for the worship of Zeus was the sanctuary of Dyktaion Zeus at Palaikastro near Siteia, where the god was worshipped in the form of a *kouros* (young man) and who was reborn and died each year, a characteristic survival of the deified cycle of the seasons of the Minoan faith. The excavations conducted by the British Archaeological School at Palaikastro in 1904 brought to light an inscription dating from the third or second century B.C., inscribed on hard black stone and bearing the famous hymn to Zeus Cretagenes (now in the Herakleion Museum). In the hymn the god is eulogised as 'greatest *kouros*' who comes with the chorus of the other gods in order to be honoured with dance and song. He is praised for his divine might and for the good things he has brought to mankind. Finally, he is beseeched to bring happiness to his people, to bless all men and animals, to bring forth abundant fruit, to send favourable winds, to protect the ships that sail on the seas, and to guide the Cretans' armies and leaders.

A major religious centre for the worship of Zeus was the Idaion Cave, mentioned by nearly all the ancient Greek and Latin historians. The important finds recovered by G. Sakellarakis in his archaeological excavations have demonstrated clearly that the cave was a religious sanctuary without interruption from prehistoric times up to the close of Antiquity.

The cave of Eileithuia, known to us from the Homeric epics, was the sanctuary of the goddess of childbirth. Here again a number of interesting finds have been recovered.

During the Hellenistic period the custom of worshipping Egyptian deities such as Isis and Serapis was introduced into Crete, as well as to other Greek regions. Gortyn had temples dedicated to both these gods, known as the Iseium and the Serapeium. In the Roman period other deities were added to the list, such as Fortuna, whose temple is also mentioned as being in Gortyn. Ancient historians also mention various religious festivals, the number of which must have been very great.

A subject which has been only partially investigated is that of the ancient Cretan calendar. H. M. Guarducci has established a list of the names of the months as attested in Cretan inscriptions. At Knossos, for example, the following months are mentioned: Audouchaios, Heraios, Karneios, Koroneios, Nekysios and Spermios. At Aptera the months Diktynnaios and Phthinoporios are attested; at Hiera-pytna we have Theodaisios and Imalios; at Praisos, Dionysios; at Gortyn, Belchanios, Leschanorios and Thermoloios. The month names suggest a connection with the worship of local deities. For the time being, however, litlle else is known about the relationship between the ancient months and our modern calendar.

From the age of the emperor Augustus Crete appears to have adopted a more widely used calendar, practically identical with that of Cyprus and Bithynia. Sources for the years 6-9 A.D. inform us of the Cretan calendar, which, according to the scholar V. Grummel, corresponds to the modern calendar as follows:

1	Thesmophorios	from 23	September	31days
2	Hermaios	24	October	30
3	Imanios	23	November	31
4	Metarchios	24	December	31
5	Agyeios	24	January	28
6	Dioscorios	21	February	31
7	Theodosios	24	March	30
8	Pontios	23	April	31
9	Hyakinthos	24	May	30
10	Hyperberetaios	23	June	31
11	Nekysios	24	July	30
12	Basileios	23	August	31

CHAPTER IV

THE CITIES OF ANCIENT CRETE (FROM ARCHAIC TO ROMAN TIMES)

Ancient writers described Crete as being 'the land of a hundred cities' *(hekatompolis).* It is doubtful whether a hundred cities within the confined space of an island the size of Crete really did achieve any notable size. Most of them were more like large villages, many of which still exist today. Below is a list of the ancient Cretan cities based on the geographical studies carried out by P. Faure, Stylianos Alexiou, N. Platon and Stergios Spanakis. The second column indicates the modern place-name (where this is known) and district.

1	Acharna	Archanes, Temeni
2	Aeros	?
3	Agneion	Agios Sostis, Kisamos
4	Aipeia	?
5	Alas	See Lasaia
6	Alassa	See Lasaia
7	Albe	?
8	Allaria	Stavromenos, Milopotamos
9	Ampelos	Xerokambos, Siteia
10	Amphimala (-malion)	Georgioupoli, Apokoronas
11	Amyklaion	Kokkinos Pyrgos, Pyrgiotissa
12	Anopolis	Anopoli, Sphakia
13	Aoros	Eleftherna, Milopotamos
14	Apollonia	Agia Pelagia, Malevizio
15	Apollonia	Eleftherna, Milopotamos
16	Apollonias	Argoules, Sphakia ?
17	Aptara (Aptera)	Palaiokastro, Apokoronas

18	Araden (Eraden)	Aradaina, Sphakia
19	Arbis	Arvi, Viannos
20	Ariaioi	?
21	Arkades (Arkadia)	Profitis Ilias, near the village of Afrati, Pediada
22	Arsinoe	Lyttos harbour (probably at Malia)
23	Asos	?
24	Astale	Bali, Milopotamos
25	Atrikos	?
26	Axos (or Oaxos)	Axos, Milopotamos
27	Bene	district of Gortyn
28	Biannos	Ano Viannos, Viannos
29	Biennos	between Phalasarna and Krio Metopo
30	Bionnos	Kerame, Agios Vasileios
31	Boiai	?
32	Boibe	near Gortyn
33	Chersonesos	Chersonesos, Pediada
34	Chersonesos	Akrotiri Sphinari, Kisamos (?)
35	Daidala	?
36	Dion	in the bay at Fodele
37	Doulopolis	?
38	Dragmos	eastern edge of Crete, between Itanos and Praisos, near Diktaion Ieron (Palaikastro Siteia)
39	Dreros	hill of Agios Antonios, east of Neapoli, Merabello
40	Einatos	Tsoutsouros, Monofatsi. The harbour of ancient Priansos
41	Elaia	Grambousa, Kisamos
42	Eleutherna	NW of the village Prines, Milopotamos. See also Apollonia
43	Eltynia	Kounavi, Pediada

44	Elyros	500 metres east of the village Rodovani, Selino, on the hill of Kefala.
45	Eronos (or Erranos)	Papoura, Lasithi
46	Eteia (or Etis)	in the neighbourhood of Petra, Siteia
47	Glenos	?
48	Gortys	Gortyna, Mesara
49	Grammion	?
50	Herakleion	Iraklio, Temeni
51	Hierapolis	Levin
52	Hierapytna	Ierapetra
53	Holopyxos	?
54	Hydramia (or Hydramon)	Dramia, Apokoronas
55	Hyrtaioi	?
56	Hyrtakos (or Hyrtakinos or Hyrtakina)	Temenia, Selino
57	Illatia	between Illaria and Sivrita
58	Inachorion	Innachorion, Kisamos
59	Istoi	?
60	Istron (Istros)	Pyrgos-Kalo Chorio, Ierapetra
61	Itanos	Erimoupoli, Siteia, NE of the Toplos monastery
62	Kalamyde	Kastelli, Selino (modern Palaiochora)
63	Kaloi Limenes	near the town of Lasaia
64	Kantanos	Kantanos, Selino
65	Karnessopolis	Lyttos
66	Katre	Kadros, Selino (?)
67	Kaudos (or Kaunos)	the island of Gavdos
68	Keraia	Rokka, Kisamos
69	Kisamos	Kastelli, Kisamos. The harbour of Polyrrhenia
70	Kisamos	Kalami, Apokoronas

71	Knossos	Knossos
72	Korykos	at the headland of Grambousa, Kisamos
73	Kydonia	Chania
74	Kytaion	Palaiokastro, Rogdia (Malevizio)
75	Lamon	Plakia, Agios Vasileios
76	Lappa (or Lampe)	Argyroupoli, Rethymnon
77	Larisa	Kalamafka, Ierapetra
78	Lasaia	Kali Limenes, Kenourio
79	Lasos	Lappa (?)
80	Lato (or Hetera)	3km N. of Kritsa
81	Lato at Kamara	Agios Nikolaos
82	Leben	Lenda, Kenourio
83	Lipara	an islet near Kydonia (?)
84	Lissos (or Lissa)	Ai-Kyrkos, Selino
85	Lykastos	Vitsalia, at the village of Profiti Ilias (Kanli Kastelli), Temeni
86	Lyttos	between the villages of Xidia, Aski and Kastamonitsa, Pediada
87	Malla	Malles, Ierapetra
88	Marathousa	Lappa ?
89	Maroneia	?
90	Matallon (Matalla)	Matalla, Pyrgiotissa
91	Milatos	Milatos, Merambello
92	Minoa	Marathi, Kydonia. Port of Aptera
93	Minoa	Pacheia Ammos, Ierapetra
94	Mykenai	?
95	Myrina	Mykene (or Syvritos) ?
96	Modaioi	Modi (?), Kydonia
97	Oios	?
98	Oleros	Meseleri, Ierapetra
99	Olous	Elounda, Merambello
100	Osmida	Ornithe, at the site of the village of Oros, Rethymnon (?)

101	Pannona	Agios Thomas, Monofatsi
102	Panormos	Agia Pelagia, Malevizi
103	Pantomatrion	village of Panormon, near Kastelli, Milopotamos
104	Pelkin (Pelkis)	Kastraki-Pelekanes, Selino
105	Pergamos	Troulli, SW of the village Grimbilliana, Kisamos
106	Petra	?
107	Phaistos	Phaistos, Pyrgiotissa
108	Phalanna(i)	Veni, Amari (?)
109	Phalannaia	?
110	Phalasarna	Akrotiri Koutri, Kisamos
111	Pharai	?
112	Phoinikous	Loutro, Sphakia
113	Phoinix Lampaion	Plakias, Agios Vasileios
114	Poikilasos (Poikilasion)	small coastal town at the site of Voukilasi or Voukoliasi, Sphakia, on the headland of Tripiti between Souyia and Agia-Roumeli
115	Polichne	near ancient Kydonia
116	Polyrrhenia	at the site of the modern village of Polyrrhenia, Kisamos
117	Praisos	Vaveli - Nea Praisos, Siteia
118	Prespidai	between Dreros and Milatos
119	Priansos	Kastelliana, Monofatsi
120	Pronos	?
121	Psychion	Akrotiri Melissa, Agios Vasileios
122	Pyloros	Apesokari - Plora, Kenourio
123	Pyranthos	Pyrathi, Monofatsi
124	Rhamnous	Stomion, Kisamos
125	Rhaukos	Agios Myron, Malevizi
126	Rhithymna	Rethymnon
127	Rhizenia	Krousonas? Prinias, Malevizi?
128	Rhytion (Rhytiassos)	Rotasi, Monofatsi

129	Sipilen	between Eleftherna and Kydonia
130	Soulia	Agia Galini, Agios Vasileios
131	Stalai	Dasonari, Siteia
132	Strenos	?
133	Suia	Souyia, Selino
134	Syba	Syia (Souyia)
135	Sybrita	Thronos, Amari
136	Syrinthos	Makris Yialos, Siteia
137	Tanos	near Kydonia
138	Tarra	Agia Roumeli, Sphakia
139	Tegea	near Polyrrhenia
140	Thebe	?
141	Thenai	Palaiochora at Kartero, Pediada
142	Therapnai	between Eleftherna and Kydonia
143	Trita	Astritsi, Pediada
144	Tylissos	Tylissos, Malevizi

Figure 4.
Map of the main towns of Crete during the Classical, Hellenistic and Roman periods *(see key on p. 105)*

1. Agneion
2. Phalasarna
3. Kisamos
4. Polyrrhenia
5. Viennos
6. Hyrtakina
7. Kantanos
8. Elyros
9. Lissos
10. Suia
11. Tarra
12. Anopolis
13. Phoinix
14. Pergamos
15. Polichne
16. Modaioi
17. Kydonia
18. Minoa
19. Aptara
20. Amphimala
21. Hydramia
22. Lappa
23. Rhithymna
24. Pantomatrion
25. Astale
26. Eleutherna
27. Sybrita
28. Axos
29. Soulia
30. Phaistos
31. Matallon
32. Lasaia
33. Leben
34. Pyloros
35. Gortyn
36. Rhaukos
37. Tylissos
38. Dion
39. Apollonia, Panormos
40. Kytaion
41. Herakleion
42. Knossos
43. Acharna
44. Eltynia
45. Pyranthos
46. Rhytion
47. Arbis
48. Priansos
49. Arkades
50. Lyttos
51. Chersonesos
52. Biannos
53. Milatos
54. Dreros
55. Olous
56. Lato, near Kamara
57. Lato, other
58. Istron
59. Malla
60. Hierapytna
61. Siteia
62. Itanos
63. Praisos
64. Ampelos
65. Oleros
66. Kaunos

CHAPTER V

THE ARRIVAL OF CHRISTIANITY IN CRETE

The arrival of Christianity in Crete was an event of immense significance for the future course of the island's history. The first nucleus of the Cretan Church was established very early, most probably by the Jewish community of the island, and by those who had witnessed the sermon of St. Peter in Jerusalem on Pentecost (cf. *Acts of the Apostles* 2, xi). Systematic conversion of the island and the organization of the church was undertaken by St. Paul during his second mission, after his release from obligations in Rome (62-63 A.D.). Paul's visit to Crete was short and he assigned the task of organizing the first Christian church to his follower and disciple Titus to whom he wrote: 'For this cause left I thee in Crete, that thou shouldst set in order the things that are wanting, and ordain elders in every city, as I had appointed thee' (Titus, 1 v.).

We know very little about how much Titus accomplished in Crete since no official or reliable source of evidence for Crete has survived from this the earliest period in the history of the apostolic church. In later years a rich tradition of legend developed around Titus, the first bishop and patron of the Cretan church. The tradition claims that Titus himself was Cretan, born of a noble family and related to Rustillus, proconsul of the island. He founded nine dioceses in Crete "in Knossos and in Hierapytna, in Kydonia and in Chersonesos, in Eleutherine and in Lampe, in Kisamos and Kantanos, so that altogether there were nine dioceses along with Gortyn". This source, however, dates to the sixth century and probably echoes the organization of the Cretan of later times. Titus' death has been dated very tentatively to the year 105 A.D. He has always held a special place in the church in Crete.

Tradition, however, has not preserved the names of Titus' successors. At the end of the second century A.D. (ca. 170-190) an active bishop of Gortyn was Philip who is today held as a saint in the Roman Catholic Church. He was a contemporary of Dionysius, the celebrated bishop of Corinth with whom he was in correspondence, and he was a staunch defender of the Christian church in Crete in the face of the early Church heresies such as Gnosticism, Marcionism and Montanism.

A contemporary of Philip and a highly learned hierarch of the early Church was the bishop of Knossos, Pinytus, also held to be a saint in the Roman church. Pinytus too kept up correspondence with Dionysius of Corinth and worked tirelessly in defence of the Church against heresies.

The total lack of evidence for the early Christian period in Crete unfortunately prevents us from being able to form a more complete picture of these times. It is not until we reach the mid-third century of our era that we start to have a few meagre pieces of information. The persecution of the emperor Decius (250 A.D.) seems to have been especially harsh in Crete. The victims of this persecution were the first known martyrs of the Cretan Church, the so-called Ten Saints (Agioi Deka), who, according to tradition, were martyred at the site of Aulonion (the present day village of Agioi Deka) near Gortyn on 23rd December 250 A.D. These saints were the following: Theodoulos, Satornilos, Euporos, Gelasios, Eunikianos, Zotikos, Pompios, Agathopous, Basileides and Euarestos. According to the oldest legends these saints came from different parts of the island: "Five were from the metropolis of Gortyn, namely Theodoulos, Satornilos, Euporos, Gelasios and Eunikianos, of the higher part of the same town which is known as Hermaios, while Zotikos was from Knossos, Pompios from Leobene, Agathopous from Panormos, Basileides from Kydonia and Euarestos from Herakleion". It is worth noting that all these saints were from the central or western part of the island, perhaps indicating that still in the mid-third century A.D. Christianity had not penetrated the east part of Crete.

These ten martyrs continued to be highly regarded by the chroniclers of the Byzantine Empire in later years.

During the period of the persecution of the emperors Marcian and Diocletian, Cyril the bishop of Gortyn was martyred on 9th July 304, but it is unknown in which year the Cretan St. Theophilos (whose feast day is celebrated on 31st March) and the so-called Twelve Cretan soldier martyrs (celebrated on 12th August) were martyred.

PART FOUR

BYZANTINE CRETE

(330-1204)

CHAPTER I

THE EARLY BYZANTINE PERIOD

(330-824)

The history of Byzantine Crete is generally divided into three periods. The first period covers the first Byzantine centuries up to the time of the Arab conquest of the island (324-824), the second covers the Dark Age of Arab rule (824-961) and the third covers the so-called second Byzantine period of Crete up to the time of the Venetian conquest of the island in 1204.

1. Outline

The sources for the first Byzantine period are wholly inadequate to form a clear picture of historical events in Crete at this time. The English historian J. B. Bury commented that for many years Crete lived in 'blissful obscurity' until it was to once again become depressingly infamous in the early 9th century with the Arab conquest. Byzantine interests were centred chiefly on the East during this early period and this is the main reason why Crete, along with many other of the western provinces of the Byzantine Empire, only rarely and sporadically attracted the interest of Byzantine historians and chroniclers.

A d m i n i s t r a t i o n. Up to the time of the emperor Diocletian (284-305) Crete and Cyrenaica constituted a single Roman province. With the administrative reforms of Diocletian, however, Crete was joined for a short period with Mysia in Asia Minor. Constantine the Great (the first Christian emperor and founder of the new East Roman capital of Constantinople in 330) later linked Crete to the larger imperial administrative unit of Illyricum, as the southern part of the Balkan peninsula was then known. With the definitive division of the Roman state into two parts (East and West) in 395 under the emperor Theodosius, Crete remained in the eastern half of the Empire.

It seems that various institutions of local administration, such as that of the Cretan Koinon, were maintained until the end of the fourth century. Inscriptions in Gortyn confirm the fact that the Koinon was still functioning in this period, though naturally it had adapted itself to new political circumstances.

Right up until the time of Justinian in the sixth century of our era the old Roman imperial administrative system, ie. the separation of political and military power, was still intact. Justinian brought to the administrative system of the Byzantine state radical reforms which gradually led to the development of the institution of the "themes". Provinces which presented specific problems were administered by a governor who wielded political and military power simultaneously. The attractive position of Crete both militarily and commercially led the Byzantine state to implement the new administrative institutions here as well. In a work known as the *Synekdemos,* a valuable source for the period (published in 535), by Hierokles Grammatikos mention is made of the administrative organisation of the Byzantine state and of the situation in Crete. Crete is described as comprising a self-governing province which occupied eleventh place in the total of sixty-four provinces of the Empire. It was ruled by a governor bearing the title Consularius whose residence was in Gortyn.

Later, when the administrative units of the themes came into being in the Byzantine Empire, Crete constituted a separate theme. Earlier historians believed that Crete never in fact constituted a separate theme or independent administrative unit, but this view needs to be revised. The scholar G. Spyridakis has argued convincingly that already by the beginning of the eighth century (that is, a century before the Arab conquest) Crete was a distinct Byzantine theme administered by a governor. A lead seal dated by Stylianos Xanthoudides to the late seventh or early eighth century bears the words "Stephanou strategou" (under the administration of the governor Stephanos), while in the time of the emperor Constantine V (740-775) the historian Theophanes refers to "Lardotyros, the arch-satrap of the island". Furthermore, in the so-called Uspenskij Taktikon (first published in 1898, but dated to the mid-ninth century) reference is made to "the patrician and governor of Crete", "the archon of Crete", and the "domestici, excuvitores, drungarii and archontes of Chaldia and Crete". The governor of Crete, who bore the title "Archon" and who held the office of the "spatharius" or "protospatharius", occupied an envious place among the Byzantine dignitaries. Research has brought to light the names of several of the governors of Crete, preserved chiefly on the inscriptions on seals, for example, "the consul Nikolaos, royal spatharius and archon of Crete", "Petronas, royal spatharius and archon of Crete", and "Constantine, royal spatharius and archon of Crete".

The main centres and population. The administrative and military centre of Crete and the residence of the head of the Cretan church was Gortyn during the first Byzantine period. The *Synekdemos* of Hierokles mentions twenty-two towns and centres in Crete: "The province of Crete under a consularius has 22 cities: Metropolis Gortyn, Inatos, Bienna, Hierapetra, Kamara, Alyngos, Chersonesos, Lyttus, Arkadia, Knossos, Soubritos, Oaxios, Eleutherna, Lampai, Aptera, Kydonia, Kisamos, Kantania, Elyros, Lissos, Phoinike or Aradena, and the island of Klados". These were most probably not towns or cities in the modern sense of the terms, but they must have been large local centres which have survived down to our own times. It is interesting that the island of Klados (today Gavdos) is mentioned: it was evidently populated then and may even have had its own diocese.

We can only make a rough estimation of the population of Crete in the first Byzantine period. If we take into account the fact that in the years immediately following the Arab conquest the island had twenty-one dioceses and that each diocese corresponded roughly to twelve hundred souls, the total population may have been around 250,000. This population was purely Greek and, as far as religious faith is concerned, Christian. There were a just a few Jews in the main centres.

E c o n o m y. The Cretan economy in these years was chiefly agricultural and pastoral. We do not have any evidence for significant commercial activity, although many believe that the capital Gortyn, situated as it was near the ports of the south coast of the island, would have favoured trade with the East. There is some reason to believe, however, that the island prospered. The large number of early Christian churches that have been identified by archaeologists are strong evidence for the existence of peace and considerable wealth on the island. In fact most have been found at the coastal sites which would suggest that piracy was not a common phenomenon in the region at this time. Cretan agricultural products were widely sought. The Roman Plinius expressed his admiration for Cretan agricultural products, while, later, Arab poets and historians praised the fertility of the Cretan soil. The Byzantine historian Theophanes, who wrote in the early ninth century, tells us that in the year 732 the Emperor Leo III enforced extremely harsh taxation on Crete and Sicily in order to balance the state budget. He may have been motivated by revenge. For Crete, which remained fiercely attached to the Orthodox tradition, was against the iconoclastic policies of the emperors of the time and joined the active resistance of the other mainland Greeks against the Byzantine emperor in 727.

M a i n h i s t o r i c a l e v e n t s . (Incursions, famine, plague and earthquakes). Throughout this period Crete was afflicted by incessant incursions and disasters. A severe earthquake accompanied by a tidal wave is recorded for 9th July 365 during the reign of the Emperor Gratian. Many Cretan towns were destroyed and, as Theophanes goes on to describe, "Calamity hundredfold or more befell

Crete". Another earthquake occurred in the year 415 which destroyed the town of Gortyn. The Emperor Theodosius II furnished generous help for the reconstruction of the Cretan capital. Yet another earthquake struck Gortyn in 448. The chronicler Malalas wrote that "In this year the state building - unusual for having 12 rotundas- of the metropolis of Gortyn collapsed". Other strong earthquakes occurred in 531 and 7th April 795.

The plague seems to have afflicted the island frequently. Although we do not possess any certain evidence for the period under discussion we can speculate on the nature of such epidemics from the regularity with which they occurred in later times. It is known that a major outbreak of the plague occurred in 542, which originated in Egypt and then spread across the entire Mediterranean, as recorded by the sixth century historian Procopius. Another major epidemic is recorded later for the year 746 "when pestilent death fed on the entire world", as the Emperor Constantine Porphyrogenitus wrote.

It is enemy incursions into the island that are of the greatest interest for this period. It is recorded that in 623 bands of Slavs invaded the island. The source for this information is the Syrian Thomas the Elder who is dated to the seventh century and whose history has only been preserved in a medieval Latin translation. He mentions the Slav incursions thus: "Slavi Cretam ceterasque insulas invasere, atque illic pii viri Kenesrinesque comprehensi sunt, quorum fere viginti interfecti".

From the mid-seventh century the Arab threat starts to loom. The Arab fleet carried out attacks on the islands and coastline of the Christian world and Crete was often the victim of these attacks. Moavia plundered the Cretan coast with his fleet and in 656 a major attack was launched by the Arab commander Abd Allah bn.Sa'd (Abdullah, son of Saïd). The Arabic sources for the period relate how his wife, Qayla bint Umar, accompanied him on his raiding expeditions. A Christian inscription from Herakleion mentions another Arab raid in 671, and, a short while later in 674, two Arab commanders, Abdella, son of Caïs, and Faidal, wintered in Crete, according to Theophanes' account. At the beginning of the eighth century, in the time of the caliph Walid (705-715), repeated raids are mentioned throughout all the following years. A valuable source for the period is the Life of St. Andrew of Crete, head of the Cretan Church from 712 to 740, in which an account is given of a raid by the Arabs and how Andrew managed to boost the morale of his fellow islanders at the fortress of Drimeos. St. Andrew of Crete's orations also frequently mention the Arab raids. The severity of his remarks is evidence of the scale of the threat and the fear of the islanders.

There is another source, whose reliability, however, is not certain, which describes how when the Arabs, along with the Slavs, attacked Patra in 805, they had come from a raid on Crete. The Arab attacks were relentless and ever more persistent until the time when they eventually took control of the entire island in about 824. The Byzantine imperial fleet seems to have offered no resistance and failed utterly to protect the island which was such an important part of its domain. And Crete, too, does not seem to have been able to defend itself effectively in these critical times.

CHAPTER II

THE CHRISTIAN CHURCH IN CRETE DURING THE FIRST BYZANTINE PERIOD

During the early centuries of the Byzantine Empire Crete constituted one of the twelve archdioceses of Illyricum (the south Balkans) and was subject administratively to the control of the see of Rome. After 476, when Rome fell to the Visigoths, the Church of Crete was brought for a short period under the control of the Patriarchate of Constantinople, and then, following the reconquest of Italy by the Emperor Justinian, it returned to the jurisdiction of the Pope. This dependence of the Cretan Church on the see of Rome was maintained until the mid-eighth century, when Constantine V (740-775) removed the entire theme of Illyricum from papal jurisdiction and brought it finally under the control of the Church of Constantinople in about 754. This move by the iconoclast emperor was obviously related to the political line of the day in the East Roman Empire which had put a ban on the veneration of holy icons. It is known that Pope Gregory III was opposed to the iconoclast decrees of the eastern Byzantine emperors of the time and it was only to be expected that the attitude of Rome would not go unpunished by the Byzantine emperors. More recent views on the subject link the administrative changes in ecclesiastical affairs with the collapse of Byzantine power in Italy, after which control of the Roman Church passed into the hands of the early medieval Frankish rulers. It would have been totally unacceptable for the Byzantine state to allow any of its provinces to fall under the ecclesiastical control of a foreign political power.

The subject of the relationship between the Cretan Church and Rome has not yet been fully explored. We do possess some interesting evidence, however. In 668 the Council of the Cretan Church, presided by archbishop Paul, brought a conviction against bishop Ioannes of Lampe, though it is not known why. Pope Vitalian objected to the Cretan decision and strongly supported bishop Ioannes.

The head of the Cretan Church at this time bore the title of archbishop. The dioceses that were subject to his ecclesiastical jurisdiction ranged from eight to ten according to the period. During the first Byzantine period the Cretan bishops participated in the Ecumenical Church Councils from the time of the Council of Serdica (342/3). It is from the proceedings of these Councils, and from inscriptions, seals and the so-called "Taktika" (the official lists of titles known as Notitiae Dignitatum) that appear after 731, as well as from other literary and historical sources that we learn the names of the heads and bishops of the Cretan Church and the organisation of the local bishops. In the Taktikon of the Emperors Leo III and Constantine V (731-746) Crete is reported as having twelve dioceses, a fact that is confirmed by other texts that describe Crete as being *dodekathronos* (twelve-throned). These dioceses in order of importance were Gortyn, Arkadia, Knossos, Chersonesos, Siteia, Hierapetra, Sybrita, Lampe, Kantanos, Kisamos, Kydonia and Eleutherna. Ten bishops from Crete were present at the Seventh Ecumenical Council (787) and they were headed by archbishop Elias I who also signed the proceedings of the Council. From the proceedings it also appears that Crete occupied eleventh place in the hierarchy of dioceses of the Ecumenical Patriarchate.

A critical period for the Cretan Church was that of Iconoclasm. Crete was generally in favour of the worship of icons and this meant that it suffered various political consequences. Professor Papadopoulos has remarked that "Crete, inhabited almost exclusively by Greeks, and fiercely attached to tradition, took part, along with other islands, in the so-called Helladic uprising which broke out in 727, soon after the issue of the decree of Leo III that banned the worship of icons". One source also states that Kosmas, one of the leaders of the uprising, was Cretan. Whatever the case, it is known that following the suppression of the revolt and the reassertion of the central power, the iconoclast emperors unleashed a wave of persecution against all dissidents. This iconoclast persecution also reached Crete where it was enforced with particular harshness. The imperial governor of Crete at this time (mid-eighth century) was Theophanes Lardotyros, later described as "the most impious governor of the impious emperor". Lardotyros punished the abbot Paul, whose feast day is celebrated on 21st October, at the praetorium in Herakleion in 765. The phrase "in the so-called praetorium of Herakleion" (in the Greek text the name Herakleion is in the genitive, which can be confused with the personal name Herakleios) contained in the hagiographical text of the martyrdom of the abbot has created a literary and historical problem for scholars. For some, the word Herakleiou (the genitive ending in Greek is -ou) is a place name and therefore comprises our first witness to the name of the modern day capital of the island, Iraklion, before even the time of Arab domination in Crete, while others believe that the phrase refers to the praetorium in Gortyn of the emperor Heraclius (610-641).

Another Cretan martyr for the iconodule cause was Andronikos (ca. 767). The most celebrated Cretan martyr of the period, however, was Andrew *en Krisei* (in Judgement). Andrew was born in Herakleion - "in the so-called Castle of Crete" - as the sources record, in the early eighth century. In around 762 he went to Constantinople where he suffered a terrible death on 20th October 767 on account of his adherence to the worship of icons and his refusal to obey the imperial iconoclast decrees. Iconodules revered the martyr and his tomb at the monastery of the Judgement in Constantinople and it became a place of pilgrimage. Recent historians (including Paparrigopoulos and Lambros) attribute the death of St. Andrew more to political than religious reasons. Paparrigopoulos has written that "the death of St. Andrew *en Krisei* was more likely a punishment for some political crime than an instance of religious persecution".

Figure 5
Drawing of the church of St. Titus, Gortyn. By G. Gerola, *Monumenti Veneti. II, 14*

During the more tranquil period preceding the outbreak of Iconoclasm several powerful ecclesiastical personalities lived and worked in Crete. These included Myron, the bishop of Gortyn and all Crete (second quarter of the fourth century), and Eumenios, also bishop of Gortyn, both canonised by the Church. A certain St. Kosmas the Hermit (died 658) is recorded as having lived in the seventh century whose relics were translated to Venice in 1058 by merchants, and who was revered there as a local saint.

The greatest figure of the Cretan Church during these formative centuries was undoubtedly Andrew Ierosolymites, archbishop of Crete (712-740) and celebrated orator and hymnographer. He was perhaps the greatest figure ever in the ecclesiastical history of Crete and was possessed of keen intellectual and administrative abilities, astonishing rhetorical skill and a highly developed poetic sense. The orations of Andrew Ierosolymites, which were most probably delivered in Crete, attest to the strong bond of affection that existed between the archbishop and his spiritual flock which he defended and exhorted during the difficult times of the Arab raids and other hardships.

Cretan saints who lived outside Crete included Gregorios, who lived and died in the monastery of Akritas in Constantinople, and Nikolaos of Kydonia, abbot of the monastery of Studiou, a famous zealot, and friend and fellow martyr of Theodore the Studite during the second period of Iconoclasm (813-843). Nikolaos died in 868.

During the long period of peace and stability in the Church from 313 to the outbreak of Iconoclasm in 730, many churches were built in Crete. The archaeologist's spade has to date uncovered over forty early Christian wooden-roofed churches. The three-aisled early Christian church (with transept) at Panormos near Mylopotamos is dated to the fifth century and is the largest early Christian basilica in Crete and one of the largest in Greece as a whole. St. Titus' church in Gortyn, a magnificent wooden-roofed basilica, is dated to the sixth century, and became an important place of pilgrimage for Cretans to worship the Apostle and patron saint of the island up to the time of the Arab conquest. Tradition has it that the Apostle's relics are preserved somewhere in the church. Another fine example of early Christian architecture is the basilica of Souyia near Selino, which has splendid mosaic floors.

Monastic remains from the first Byzantine period have not survived. However, literary and historical sources must leave us to assume that there were a number of monasteries in Crete.

CHAPTER III

THE PERIOD OF ARAB RULE
(ca. 824 - 961)

The Arab conquest of Crete is one of the most important events in Byzantine history. There are many questions surrounding this event that have still not been answered and which are still debated by scholars since many of the sources, both Greek and Arabic, are either silent on the matter of the conquest of Crete or they contain information that is contradictory or conflicts with other sources. Such questions include the precise date of the Arab invasion and conquest of Crete, the landing place of the Arab forces and the circumstances surrounding their installation on the island, the extent of resistance or lack of it on the part of the Christian population, the extent of forced or voluntary Islamicisation, ethnic compositon and changes on the island in this period, the state of the Christian Church, and so on. Here we shall present an outline of the main events and attempt to offer some answers to the above questions in the light of recent research.

1. The origins of the Arab conquerors

The history of Arab rule in Crete begins in far off Spain, where there was a multitude of small Arab states in the early ninth century. Internal crisis between the Moslem rulers of Andalusia forced the leader of Cordoba, Abu Hafs, to abandon his city and look for a new home elsewhere with his people. It is not known exactly how many people left with Abu Hafs. Greek sources mention forty ships, while the Arab historian Himrayi says that the crews and civilians amounted to 10,000.

These adventurers landed in Egypt in about 813, at the beginning of the caliphate of Ma'mun, and, exploiting the political chaos that they found there, they captured Alexandria in 818 only to be expelled again immediately afterwards. Desperately seeking somewhere to settle they set their course for Crete. The recent view suggests that the choice of Crete for the Arabs was not one of chance. On the contrary, it seems that the Egyptians, who had always had half an eye on Crete and had raided it in the past, directed these Cordoban adventurers to the island. Several Arab sources indicate that this was a deliberate policy on the part of the Egyptian Arabs, as has been pointed recently by the scholar Christidis.

2. Invasion and conquest

It is a curious fact that so few hardened warriors should have been able to capture Crete and establish their power on the island for almost 140 years. Greek sources attribute the capture of Crete to the general decline in Byzantine vigilance caused by the revolt of Thomas the Slav in 821-823. Internal crisis marked these years in Byzantium and resulted in neglect of the coastal regions and islands, a neglect that was immediately seized on and exploited by the Arabs. The Byzantine historian Genesios gives the following account: "In the same year in which the revolt of Thomas broke out, Agarenes (Arabs) from Spain fearlessly laid waste the Roman land . . . and Apohapsis (Abu Hafs) committed outrages on the well-clad people of Crete and took many captives and seized much plunder, and, having learnt precisely the layout of the land, he departed again. In the next season he fitted out forty ships and descended on the island again..."

As is evident from the sources the Agarene leader first conducted a reconaissance mission before deciding on the final settlement of his people here. This, of course, was only to be expected. The question remains, however, of when the final invasion took place and where exactly the Arab forces landed. Scholars used to think that the landing probably took place in the modern day bay of Almyros, a few miles west of Herakleion, or perhaps even in the larger Suda Bay near Chania. Both these places are today considered highly unlikely. It is far more likely that the Arabs in fact landed somewhere on the south coast, not only because this is where Arab raids were usually carried out, but also because the Byzantine fleet was less able to respond quickly and effectively in this area. The sources mention that the landing took place at a headland known as "Charax". Professor Panayiotakis argued that this should be identified with the present day Lithinon, east of the bay of Mesara, a view which many scholars share today. The fact that a large number of Arab coins have been discovered in the area of the bay of Mesara gives further support to this hypothesis.

Scholars are equally uncertain of the precise date of the final invasion of Crete by the Arabs. It has to be dated to after the revolt of Thomas the Slav (823), but the proposed dates range from 823 to 828. The year 824 is perhaps closest to the truth. Disagreement arises because of the large gap which seems to separate the first raid from the final conquest. Undoubtedly Crete was conquered gradually, step by step; it could not have been otherwise. The Arab historian Baladuri (died 892) wrote that "There was an invasion of Crete during the caliphate of Ma'mun (813-833) carried out by Abu Hafs Umar Aysi the Andalusian, who became known as 'the Cretan'. To start with he captured one fortress and stayed there. Later he began to conquer the rest of the island, step by step, until nothing remained in Byzantine hands, and he demolished all their forts". Byzantine sources, however, state that there was one city -either Kydonia or Gortyn- which never fell into Arab hands.

All the sources agree on one thing, however, and that is the foundation of the first Arab fortress in Crete. This fortress was Chandax, modern day Herakleion. According to tradition a monk pointed out the strategic importance of the place to the Arabs. Modern historians, simply following the opinion of Byzantine chroniclers and historians, used to believe that the town was established at the time of the Arab conquest and attributed the name

Chandax (in Greek) to the deep moat or trench that the invaders dug around the fortress (Rabdh el Khandak, The Fortress of the Trench): "They dug out a deep trench, and then embedded stakes into it, from which it now has the name Chandax". A town must have existed on the site before the arrival of the Arabs and perhaps even the name Chandax predates their arrival. It was from Chandax that the Arab conquest of the entire island was organised.

It is surprising that the sources do not say a word about Cretan resistance to the Arab invasion. Only Genesios and later historians who based their accounts on his work mention that Gortyn was besieged and sacked. His account also gives great importance to the martyrdom of the bishop Cyril, a piece of information that led to the adding of a second Cyril and martyr to the episcopal registers for Crete. It has been demonstrated, however, that Cyril probably never existed and that he entered the historical tradition as a result of some confusion. The Arabic sources do not mention the subject at all.

Many historians have tried to explain the fact that there does not appear to have been any kind of resistance on the part of the Cretan population. One theory suggests that the political climate produced by the Iconoclast controversy may have been the cause of the islanders' indifference. Since the Cretans had been fanatically in favour of icon worship and had resisted the imperial iconoclast decrees they may have felt some sympathy for the Arabs, simply by way of reaction to the hated policies of Constantinople. This theory, however, has no factual basis and seems somewhat far fetched, especially if we judge by the Cretan stance in previous and following centuries towards foreign invasion. If, as is claimed, the Cretans had 'welcomed' the Arabs, surely Arab historians would have referred to the fact with some satisfaction? And in any case the same historians speak of the steady conquest of the island "step by step". There is some evidence to suggest that several years after the Arab invasion many parts of the island were still not under Arab domination, and some isolated regions, such as Sphakia, may never indeed have experienced Arab rule. The scholar Christidis has argued convincingly that Arab rule in Crete may have been limited to just the present day nome of Herakleion and a few other villages of north Crete. The concentration of Arab coins found in these parts tends to support this view.

3. Consequences of the Arab conquest

The installation of the Arabs in Crete and the consolidation of their power on the island was an event of immense significance and it created considerable problems in the already turbulent East Mediterranean. The Arabs of Crete, who were also known as Mosarabs or Saracens or Afri, organised a special kind of emirate on the island which was only very loosely dependent on the other overseas Arab centres. Its survival and livelihood were based on piracy and the economic oppression of the native population. For 140 years the Saracens of Crete earned the dubious reputation of being the scourge of the seas. Chandax, which was walled and fortified with much care and expense was the base and centre for the gathering of the treasure and plunder reaped from piracy. Accounts of the period echo the fear and terrror which the pirates of Crete inspired in the inhabitants of the islands and coastal regions round about. They were described as the "Godless Cretans" in Byzantine texts, and Crete was the "God-forsaken island".

Some of the Cretan Saracen raids are of wider interest for Byzantine history since they can be viewed within the context of the main Arab-Byzantine conflicts of the ninth and tenth centuries. In 862 they attacked Mytilene on Lesbos and then moved on to raid the peninsula of Mount Athos. In 866 they again went north to the coast of Chalkidike. In 872 they plundered the coast of the Adriatic and the city of Brac, and in the following year (873) Sa'id, the son of Abu Hafs the conqueror of Crete, along with a Cretan Moslem convert called Photios, organised a massive plundering expedition in the Aegean. Sailing in twenty-seven ships they reached as far as the Hellespont, looting islands and coastal centres. Eressos in Lesbos suffered particularly at their hands, and many of its residents fled to Chalkidike where they established a new settlement of the same name. In the end the Cretan Arabs were repulsed from the coast of Thrace by the able Byzantine commander Niketas Oöryphas. They then headed south to the Peloponnese and raided Methone, Pylos and Patra. Oöryphas, in pursuit, had his ships pulled over the Isthmus of Corinth across to the Gulf of Corinth and then defeated the Arab pirates in the Gulf of Patrai. But later the Arab pirates returned. In 902 they plundered Demetrias and Attica, and in 904 they collaborated with the Moslem convert Leo of Tripoli in the sack of Thessalonica.

The Arab presence was even more severe for the native inhabitants of Crete who were plunged into a long period of harsh servitude. Crete became detached from the Byzantine Empire and disappeared from the civilised world. With the demise of the economy and the loss of contact with the other Byzantine centres Cretan civilisation reverted to a very rudimentary form of lifestyle. Many today believe that it is mistaken to view Crete of this period as simply a nest of piracy. Yet not a single cultural monument from these times has survived, and not a single literary work or learned figure can be boasted by Crete for the period of Arab rule. In recent years archaeological research has only succeeded in bringing to light various coins minted by the Cretan emirs; these have enabled scholars, however, to compile a genealogical list (though with some lacunae) of the emirs of Crete. Of these emirs only Shuaib, a son of Abu Hafs, is mentioned as being a man of intellect and learning. We do not know whether the Saracens respected the Christian churches, monasteries, and other places of worship of the island, as seems to have been the case in other Arab-dominated areas of the East. It has been claimed that the church of St. Titus in Gortyn, the most important centre for worship of the Apostle on Crete, did not suffer destruction at the hands of the Arabs, contrary to what earlier historians had asserted.

Older historians tended to exaggerate the extent of the Arab presence and penetration into the population of Crete and the number of conversions to the faith of Islam. More recent opinion suggests that the Arab influence was probably much more limited. Professor Tomadakis has convincingly demonstrated that the make up of the population changed very little indeed during this period, and what changes did take place were chiefly in the urban centres. The agricultural and pastoral population was virtually unaffected, both in respect to language, religion and customs. Indeed it is quite likely that, as regards the latter, the Cretans influenced their new rulers, just as happened in the later but much longer periods of Venetian and Turkish rule. The same seems apply in the case of the Moslems of the island. The number of conversions to Islam following the subjugation of the island was probably limited and not compulsory, since mass conversion of the conquered subjects was financially not in the Arabs' interests. The Arab sources moreover make no mention of forced conversion to Islam on the island. The language also remained intact and only a very few Arabic words entered the local speech. Such words include amiras, azapes, zagari, fari, kanaki, neraji, gazi, aziganya. Some Arab place names have also survived: Katsabas, Mastabas, Suda, Aposelemis (=Abu Selim), Siba, Humeri, Roukaka, Misiri, Sarakenos and Sarakena.

4. Byzantine attempts at recovering Crete

The loss of Crete was a serious blow to Byzantium. It not only lost one of its major administrative districts -a theme- but it also lost control and supervision of the sea routes in this volatile area of the East Mediterranean. The recovery of Crete was therefore a matter of top priority, not only with respect to prestige, but also with respect to the security of the trade routes in the region.

Unfortunately for Byzantium, it was in no fit state to conduct a major sea campaign. Crete was a considerable distance from the Byzantine capital, and the sea held many dangers. The Byzantines were faced by enemy fronts on all sides during this period and this was the main obstacle to undertaking a major campaign to liberate Crete. Nonetheless, various attempts were made. Immediately following the capture of the island by the Arabs, the emperor Michael II (820-829) appointed Photeinos (who was already *strategos* of the large theme of Anatolikon) governor and military commander of Crete. He was charged with the task of preventing the Arabs from making a permanent settlement on the island; but this expedition, which has been dated to 825-826, ended in failure.

Another commander, Krateros, governor of the theme of Kibyrraioton, attempted to recover Crete immediately after the unsuccessful effort of Photeinos (ca. 829). Krateros managed to land his forces on the island and achieve some success in the beginning. But the Byzantine force was defeated at the River Amnisos, about four miles east of Herakleion, and Krateros, who fled in panic, was routed by the Saracens. He seems eventually to have been taken captive near the island of Kos, where he was put to death by impaling. The modern place name of Karteros which is used for the area of ancient Amnisos, is most probably an echo of the Byzantine general's unsuccessful presence and action in Crete.

Michael II then launched a third campaign, this time led by the commander Oöryphas. The soldiers who took part in this campaign were called the *tessarakontarioi* (the Forties) because each of them was paid forty gold pieces for taking part. The campaign, however, was a failure and Oöryphas restricted himself to just a few smaller confrontations in other parts of the Aegean.

A few years later the Empress Theodora appointed the powerful logothete Theoktistos as head of a large naval force. The sources say that he managed to win back a sizeable part of Crete and reestablish Byzantine authority (843/844). A commander, Sergios Magistros Niketiates, and an archon are mentioned as exercising Byzantine authority on the island during this period. According to a later account by the historian Michael Attaleiates, Sergios founded a monastery on Crete dedicated to the Virgin, known as the monastery Magistrou, where, tradition has it, he was buried. This Byzantine success, however, was short-lived and hopes were soon dashed of recovering the island completely. Byzantium was still not strong enough to tame the Saracens of Crete.

There was one more attempt at recovering the island in 865. The Emperor Michael III and the Caesar Vardas organised a new campaign. The sources generally reveal that the Cretan problem had concerned Vardas for a long time. However, he was murdered while the fleet was still off the Thracian coast (21 April 865) and so the expedition was called off.

In the following years the imperial fleet continually tried to strike at the Cretan Saracens with various bold expeditions. The commanders Niketas Oöryphas and Nasar frequently pursued the Saracens as far as the Cretan coast, but never attempted a fully organised campaign to actually retake Crete.

In the early tenth century the Arab raids became even more intense, culminating in the sack of Thessalonica on 31 July 904, led by the Moslem convert Leo of Tripoli. Saracens from Crete took part in this attack -one of the greatest tragedies to befall Byzantium. Byzantium had to act with greater determination. As part of his campaign against piracy, the *logothete tou dromou* Imerios carried out a more concerted effort to recover Crete. A large force was gathered: the sources speak of 8740 soldiers from the themes, 15,293 soldiers from the imperial battalions, and 14,000 rowers. This impressive force headed for the Cretan coast, but was recalled in 912 after a lengthy and inconclusive conflict. The expedition ended in tragedy when a strong pirate force attacked the imperial fleet in the sea off Chios and literally devastated the entire Byzantine force. Yet another crushing defeat was added to the list of Byzantine failures.

In 949, during the reign of Constantine Porphyrogenitus, another unsuccessful campaign was organised. A mediocre and foolish general, Gongyles, was entrusted with commanding the expedition which he swiftly led into utter disaster, much like that of 912.

5. Nikephoros Phokas and the recovery of Crete

Fortune was to smile, however, on Nikephoros Phokas, a commander with great experience of the Arab enemy. It was thanks to his undoubted genius as a military commander that Crete was finally liberated. The campaign was organised by Romanos II's top minister Joseph Bringas, a capable planner, who supported the expedition right up to its successful conclusion. Nikephoros Phokas' military plan was based on massive superiority of numbers and the superior strength of the Byzantine navy. In this way contact could be maintained with the centre and a secure supply line be ensured for the provision of the imperial forces. It had become obvious that only by massive naval superiority could the Arab fleet, which was the main buttress of Arab domination on Crete, be defeated.

The figures given in the sources for the force amassed by Phokas are contradictory, however. According to those who continued the chronicle of Theophanes, the Byzantine force consisted of 3307 ships: 2000 warships (armed with Greek Fire) with 250 soldiers on each, 1000 transport ships and 307 supply ships. Arab sources, however, talk of 700 ships with 72,000 foot soldiers and 5000 cavalry. Other sources talk of just 250 ships.

Nikephoros Phokas gathered his forces at Phygela, Asia Minor, in the summer of 960. They then headed for the island of Ios from where they dispatched scout vessels to gather intelligence. In July of 960 he reached the coast of Crete and landed with his army at the beach of Almyros a few miles west of Herakleion. The sources say that he set up a fortified camp near Phoinikia, three miles southwest of Chandax, and then began the difficult siege of the fortress of Chandax. The siege lasted for the second half of 960 through to March 961. The Arabs held out bravely against the Byzantine stranglehold, avoiding forays out of the walls and other such risky encounters. On just one occasion they managed a surprise attack and inflicted great damage on the Thracian force commanded by Pastilas. Perhaps the derisory expression 'Pastelas' in east Crete for someone who is lazy and indolent is a memory of this military defeat preserved in the name of the general. It is also mentioned that the discontent of the Byzantine army because of inadequate supplies and provisions during the harsh winter of 960-961 was appeased just in time by the swift dispatch of extra supplies by the minister Joseph Bringas.

The fortress of Chandax finally yielded to the Byzantines on 7 March 961. They massacred the Arabs and looted the town. The long siege and accumulated hatred did nothing to make the Byzantine soldiers more merciful in their treatment of the defeated city and its population, despite Nikephoros Phokas' instructions that they leave the Moslem women unharmed.

It is impossible to calculate the number of Arabs who died in the siege, although the number of 200,000 given by Arabic sources must surely be an exaggeration. Many were taken captive in order to add lustre to Phokas' triumphal entry into Constantinople. Amongst these prisoners were the old emir of Crete, Abdul Aziz Qurtubi (ie. of Cordoba), who is referred to as Kurupen in the Byzantine sources, and his son Nu'man. The Byzantines in fact conferred honours on the defeated emir of Crete, and later his son Anemas embraced the Christian faith and served the Byzantine emperor, dying later in battle against the Russians.

The Arab treasure that the Byzantines found in Crete was vast. It is said that 300 transport ships were required to bring the load back to the Byzantine capital. Phokas sent a part of the treasure to his confessor Athanasios the Athonite, the founder of the monastery of Lavra on mount Athos, so that Athanasios might build and organise the monastery in which Nikephoros intended to spend his last years. The foundation of the first monastery of the great monastic community of Mount Athos is thus linked to the reconquest of Crete.

Phokas, with his well organised military campaign, succeeded in releasing Crete from its 140-year servitude to the Arabs, and brought it back within the realm of the Byzantine state. It is said that a prophesy made at this time claimed that the liberator of Crete would later become emperor. It was for this reason that the triumphal entry of Phokas into the city of Constantinople (an honour frequently bestowed on victorious Byzantine generals) was postponed for almost two years. After the untimely death of the Emperor Romanos II (963) the patriarch Polyeuktos crowned Phokas emperor, marrying him at the same time to Romanos' widow, Theophano.

CHAPTER IV

THE SECOND BYZANTINE PERIOD IN CRETE (961-1204)

With the recovery of Crete and its return to the Byzantine Empire a new period of Cretan history begins that was to last some 250 years, until its capture by the Venetians. Little evidence exists for this period and there are many questions that remain unanswered or whose answers are obscure. Given the present state of our knowledge therefore it is only possible to give a brief outline of events on Crete at this time.

1. Fortifications and other defensive works

A top priority for the Byzantines after the recapture of Crete was the full restoration and consolidation of Byzantine power on the island. They not only had to eradicate all remaining traces of Arab power, but also to organise the effective defense of the island against possible Arab attempts to regain their lost kingdom. It was therefore necessary to ensure the constant vigilance of the Byzantine navy and to construct strong fortifications along key points of the Cretan coast. Nikephoros himself founded the castle 'Temenos' on the present day site of Roka near Kanli Kastelli (Prophitis Ilias). It is thought that the name of the castle was extended to the entire district known today as Temenos. Recent archaeological research at Herakleion has uncovered part of the Byzantine walls. The so-called 'Arabic' wall, therefore, that Xanthoudidis believed belonged to the period of Arab rule in Crete, was in fact constructed in the second Byzantine period. This wall was subsequently covered by the later wall built by the Venetians (15th century). Similar fortifications were also built in other parts of Crete but they have so far not attracted archaeologists' attention.

The Byzantines also tried to create a strong political base on the island by establishing centres that were especially loyal to imperial power. Nikephoros Phokas established a settlement of war veterans, as was the Byzantine custom after a successful territorial campaign, in agriculturally fertile districts. Even today some place names which echo this settlement policy still survive: Armenoi, Varvaroi, Varvaro, Tsakono, Sklaverochori, Sklavediako, and others. Some scholars also believe that the place name Mouchtaroi (a village in Pediada) derives from the medieval Greek word 'mourtarioi', meaning 'rebels', and not from the Arabic word Moatar, meaning 'garden', as was previously claimed.

2. Administrative organization

Immediately after the recovery of Crete by the Byzantine state, it was restored as a Byzantine administrative province ('theme') with its own governor. In the so-called 'Escorial Taktikon', which is dated to the years 975-979, mention is made of the '*strategos* (commander and governor) of Crete', amongst a list of other *strategoi* of Greece and Cyprus. The strategoi of Crete appear also in documents, inscriptions and seals up to the early eleventh century. In the will of the Cretan minor saint, Ioannes Xenos, dated 20 September 1027 -a source text of great historical interest- two *strategoi* sign their names: 'Philaretos Bracheon, protospatharios and strategos of Crete' and 'Eumathios, protospatharios and strategos of Crete'. It seems that the one came to succeed the other. Another figure, referred to as Michael 'disypatos (bi-consul) and strategos of Crete' is known from his seal. All these stategoi resided in Chandax, which had now become the administrative and military centre of Crete. The old capital, Gortyn, had now lost its primacy and fell into decline and obscurity.

Some decades later, with the administrative reforms carried out by Alexios Komnenos (1081-1118), the governor of Crete was given the title Doukas (Duke) or Katepano, a title that implied even higher status than that of strategos. This apparent change of status suggests that the theme of Crete had been promoted in the hierarchy of provinces. The Byzantine title of duke was kept also by the Venetians for their governor on Crete when they later took control of the island. Several names of dukes are known to us, chiefly from their seals, as well as from various literary texts and inscriptions. Their family names and titles show that they were descended from some of the most illustrious Byzantine families. For example, the duke of Crete between 1088 and 1089 Michael Karantinos, was descended from one of the greatest aristocratic families of Constantinople. Nikephoros Diogenes, another duke of Crete, was the son of the Emperor Romanos IV, as we are informed by Anna Komnene in her history *The Alexiad*: 'The governorship of the island of Crete was entrusted to the care of Nikephoros himself'. Finally, Nikephoros Kontostephanos, a later duke of Crete, was brother-in-law of the Emperor Alexios III Angelou.

We do not know of other important historical events from this period in Crete. A rebellion aimed against the Emperor Alexios I Komnenos is mentioned as taking place in 1092-1093 organised by Karykes, duke of Crete. It was swiftly crushed, however, and Karykes was killed. The Cretans then remained loyal to the imperial power. The old view that Karykes' rebellion was linked with the rebellion of Rhapsomates in Crete and that it was just a part of a wider insurrectionary movement against imperial power is no longer held to be correct. A source which should probably be considered unreliable is a hagiographical text in which mention is made of Norman control of Crete in the late twelfth century.

We also possess very little information on the economic state of Crete during this period. It is notable, however, that Venetian merchants were interested in the island already from the early twelfth century. A document has survived from the year 1111 referring to trade in agricultural products and livestock, and other documents that refer generally to Venetian commercial links with Crete. According to later Latin saints' lives, Venetian merchants discovered the relics of the Cretan saint Kosmas the Hermit and took them over to Venice (20 April 1058), where they are still kept in the church of S. Giorgio Maggiore.

3. The tradition of the twelve archontopoula.

One of the most discussed problems of this period is the credibility of the historical truth behind the tradition of the twelve *archontopoula* (which can be loosely translated as 'leaders') who settled in Crete with the imperial sanction of Alexios I Komnenos in order to consolidate imperial authority on the island. These Byzantine archons were the forebears of the great aristocratic families of Crete who later backed almost continual resistance to the Venetian authorities during the long period of Venetian rule. The twelve archons, according to tradition, were as follows: the house of the Phokades, the Skordiledes, the Gavalades, the Kalaphatoi, the Arkoleoi, the Chortatzedes, the Mousouroi, the Varouches, the Melissenoi, the Litinoi, the Argyropouloi (or Agiostephanites) and the Vlastoi. The branches of these families were many; for example, the Kallergides were descended from the Phokades, and the Pateroi, the Kapsokalyves, the Psaromelingoi, the Marapharades, the Papadopouloi, the Kontes, the Foumides, the Loumbinoi (Longinoi), the Trachinoi, the Nomikoi and the Vasilopouloi from the Skordiledes, and so on. Many of these family names have survived intact down to our own day, or with minor variations. Many place names in Crete are also associated with these families: Mousouro, Kallergo, Nomikiana, Foumiana, and others.

Although the document which forms the basis of the tradition of the settlement in Crete of these twelve aristocratic families is old, it does not appear to be authentic. The whole 'tradition' may in fact be a later creation, perhaps of the early Venetian years. What we do know is that during the Comnenian period (1081-1185) large areas of landed property were granted to native aristocratic figures in Crete. By the late twelfth century a powerful landowning class that had benefited from imperial grants of land was in existence in Crete. This class was generally composed of personages who had provided outstanding military or political services to the Byzantine Empire. They were termed ‘pronoiarioi’ or ‘episkeptitai’. These powerful families later (during the period of Venetian rule) struggled to secure their privileges and to maintain their aristocratic status, invoking the fact that they were descended from the major Cretan families of Byzantine times. It is quite likely that the tradition of the twelve *archontopoula* of Crete was created during these early years of Venetian rule in order to secure a place for the aristocratic Cretan families within the new political status quo. This is perhaps the best explanation for the much debated issue of the phenomenon of the legendary medieval *archontopoula* of Crete.

CHAPTER V

THE CHURCH OF CRETE DURING THE SECOND BYZANTINE PERIOD

The long period of servitude to the Arabs and the complete isolation of the Cretans from the main body of the official Church naturally led to a weakening in Orthodox Christian religious practice. Leo the Deacon, a Byzantine historian of the late tenth century, mentioned the deviations of the Cretan Church from generally approved practice: "It is reported that the Cretans are practitioners of divination and ribaldry and other errors, having long been inclined to the Manichaeans and Muhammadans" (Bonn edition, p. 25). This source does not indicate of course that the Cretans had been converted to Islam *en masse* as historians used to believe. If this was the case, a whole new missionary campaign would have been organised by the Ecumenical Patriarchate when Byzantium regained control of the island, in order to convert the Cretans back to Christianity. No such missionary work has been claimed for Crete. The career St. Nikon Repent, who came to Crete and stayed for seven years (962-969) seems to have been a matter of personal initiative. The preaching of this famous religious figure had a wide impact and contributed significantly to the revival of Christianity in Crete. In order to consolidate the Church's authority on the island Nikon established many new churches. Particular mention is made of the church of Agia Photini, built by Nikon on a site three days' walking distance from Gortyn. Unfortunately this reference has not been confirmed by archaeology. The historian B. Psilakis found that at Vyzari, near Amari, are the ruined remains of a large church that seemed to correspond with the tradition of the church founded by Nikon. However, recent archaeological research has proved that it is in fact an early Christian basilica of the fifth century.

We can talk with more certainty about the activity of the Cretan saint Ioannes Xenos. Ioannes was born in the village of Siva, near Pyrgiotissa, in the mid-tenth century. He was a learned and highly active monk who worked chiefly in west Crete, preaching and organising monastic communities on the island. He founded many monasteries of which the most important is the monastery of Myriokephala at Rethymnon, he brought icons from Constantinople, built churches and secured, by means of the issue of an imperial chrysobull, their financial support from the state. The life and testament (20 September 1027) of the saint provide us with an impressive picture of his career.

The organisation of the Cretan Church followed roughly the same pattern that it had before the Arab conquest. The archdiocese of Crete was reestablished, with its seat at Chandax where a magnificent new church was founded dedicated to the patron saint of the island, the Apostle Titus, on the site of the present day church in Herakleion. The following twelve dioceses belong to the archdiocese of Crete, as documented in the Taktikon of the Emperor Basil II the Bulgarslayer (dated 980): Gortyn, Arkadia, Knossos, Chersonesos, Aulopotamos, Siteia, Agrio, Iera, Petra, Lampe, Kisamos and Kydonia. The titles and extent of jurisdiction of the dioceses do not always correspond exactly with the situation before the Arab conquest. Many changed, and many cities and sees from early Christian times were deserted or had disappeared. The bishops now kept their old titles, but resided in large villages that were called Dioceses (in Greek, Episkope) and have kept that historical name ever since. This is to be seen chiefly in west Crete. Thus, the bishop of Kisamos resided at the village Episkope, near Kisamos, the bishop of Eleutherna now had the title 'bishop of Ario' (or Agrio) and resided at the village of Viran Episkope, near Rethymnon, the bishop of Kydonia was now termed 'bishop of Agia Episkope' and resided at Agia, near Chania. Likewise the bishop of Lampe had jurisdiction over Ano and Kato Syvrito (Suaret, during the period of Arab rule) and resided at the village of Thronos (Thronokklesidia) near Amari.

Twelfth century sources also mention the diocese of Kalamon, near Rethymnon, although the precise place where the bishop resided is not known. This diocese was still in existence in the early Venetian period.

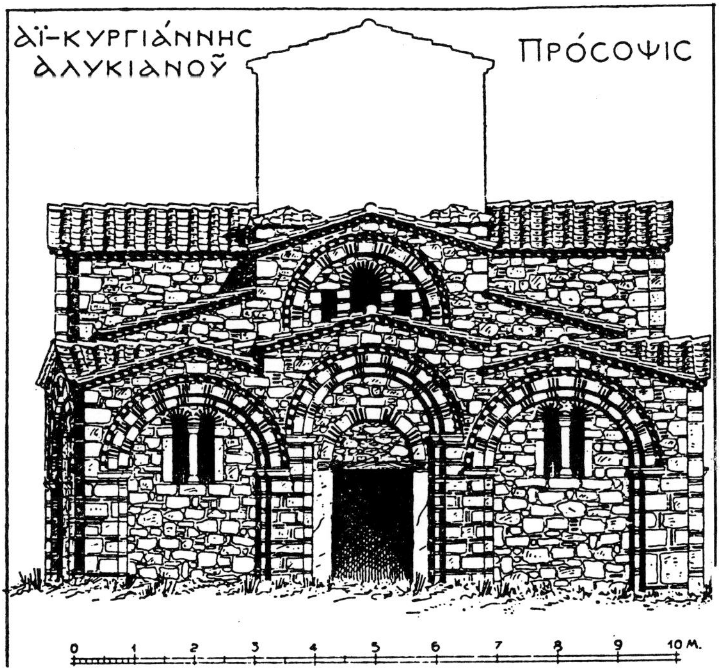

Figure 6
Cruciform church of the eleventh century (G. Antourakis, *Christianiki Archaiologia,* vol. II, Athens 1984, figure IV 12a.)

We know the names of many bishops and other ecclesiastical figures of this period, chiefly from the Synodikon of the diocese of Sybrita and from seals. We know the dates for some of them. For example, we have the seals of Stephanos, metropolitan bishop in the early eleventh century and a certain Manuel Limas from the late twelfth century. We also have the seals of bishop Ioannes of Gortyn (10th-11th century), Konstantinos and Nikephoros of Knossos (10th century) and George of Arkadia (late 10th century). A noteworthy figure of the period was Elias, metropolitan of Crete, scholar and writer (he wrote *Exegeseis on the orations of St. Gregory* and *Answers to various questions*). He seems to have been active towards the end of the eleventh and the beginning of the twelfth century. Finally, in a document of the year 1196, mention is made of the diocese of Kalamon and the monastery of St. Niketas at Sphakia (known as Frangokastello during the period of Venetian rule).

The last metropolitan bishop of Crete of the second Byzantine period was Nikolaos. After the sack of Constantinople by the Fourth Crusade (1204) and the dramatic events that followed, Nikolaos left Crete and went to Nicaea in Bithynia, the new centre of the Greek Nicaean Empire. He was accompanied by the bishops Gregory of Petra and Ioannes of Arkadia. Paul, the bishop of Knossos remained in Crete, as did the bishops of Chersonesos and Agrio, whose names, however, have not survived.

M a n u s c r i p t s. A number of manuscripts, written in Crete by monastic scribes, have survived from the second Byzantine period. The oldest known Cretan manuscript is now held in the monastic library of Lavra on Mount Athos (Ms. 451* Δ 75) and is dated to the tenth century. It contains orations of St. John Chrysostom and was written, according to a note in the manuscript, "by the hand of the worthless monk Ioannes, and finished by the grace of God on the 6th of September 986". The illustrated Gospels, now held in the library of the monastery of Sinai (no. 114), which were donated to the monastery of Eleoussa at Chandax (the monastery is in fact at Kitharida of Malevizi), are of especial interest. According to the note in this manuscript, which is the earliest evidence we have for the existence of this monastery, "This holy and divine book of the Gospels was donated to the convent of Eleousa in Crete, outside the walls of Chandax, newly built and dedicated to the Virgin Mother, in February 1175 A.D. ".

The scholar Voreadis from Herakleion, and publisher of the paper *Herakleion* (1893), recorded that the monastery of Kremaston, near Neapoli (in Merabello district), contained a parchment manuscript of the Gospels of the tenth or eleventh century. This manuscript was later transferred to Demogerontia on the Lasithi plain, but since then it has disappeared.

Generally speaking, identified Cretan manuscripts dating to the time before the Fourth Crusade amount to nine in all and are held in manuscript collections abroad. Just one has survived in Crete itself and it is dated to the 11th or 12th century. It is written on parchment and contains the orations of St. Gregory of Nazianzus. It is owned by the Archaeological Museum of Herakleion and is today held in the collection of the Historical Museum of Crete (Ms. Herakleion 2 [2.IMK 666]).

PART FIVE

THE PERIOD OF VENETIAN RULE
(1204-1669)

CHAPTER I

THE VENETIAN CONQUEST OF CRETE

1. Crete and the Fourth Crusade

The unprecedented turn of events during the course of the Fourth Crusade was to have a dramatic influence on the fate of the Byzantine Empire. When the crusaders turned their attention from the Holy Land and decided to sack the Christian city of Constantinople in 1204 the Byzantine state was effectively dissolved. The Greek mainland now became host to a score of small kingdoms and fiefs ruled by Frankish lords. The age of Frankish rule in Greece had begun.

Already by May of 1203 Crete had been caught up in the tide of these dramatic events. The Byzantine prince Alexios, son of the deposed emperor Isaac II Angelos, entered into negotiations with the leaders of the Fourth Crusade in order to secure his restoration to the Byzantine throne. He made many tempting offers to the crusaders, and one of these included Crete as a gift to Boniface of Montferrat. After the sack of Constantinople the crusaders recognised Boniface's right to take possession of Crete. This concession, however, was more of a burden than a benefit to Boniface: he lacked the means to take control of the island and he was quite unprepared for and inexperienced in naval ventures.

Enrico Dandolo, the wily doge of Venice, seized this unexpected opportunity and used it to his advantage. His representatives offered

Boniface financial and political incentives to concede Crete to the Serenissima of the Republic of Venice. The agreement, which was kept secret, was signed in Adrianople on 12 August 1204. Crete thereby became a Venetian dominion for the meagre price of 1000 silver marks (about 5000 gold ducats).

2. Genoese and Venetians in Crete

Dandolo's plan was a stroke of genius. By taking possession of Crete, Venice had sealed its control of a chain of islands in the south that would serve as a bridge for its trade in Egypt and the East. Crete's ideal position at the crossroads of the Mediterranean was to give Venice supreme mastery of the seas.

However, Venice was still chiefly preoccupied with consolidating its new conquests elsewhere in the Peloponnese and the Aegean, and was not sufficiently prepared to take full control of Crete from this date. It was to pay heavily for this delay: the audacious Genoese pirate and Count of Malta, Enrico Pescatore, arch rival of the Venetians, seized control of a large part of central Crete with the help of his friend Alamanno da Costa. It is impressive that this Genoese adventurer met with no resistance from the local population and that he was able to refortify the castles at Chandax, Siteia and Rethymnon and build other smaller fortifications at various strategic sites in order to make his foothold stronger on the island.

The Venetians were outraged by the actions of the Genoese in Crete and immediately dispatched a fleet with a force (1206). The commanders of this first campaign were Ranieri Dandolo and Ruggiero Premarino. The campaign ended in utter failure. Another expedition was then organised in 1208, led this time by Giacomo Longo. In the spring of 1209 the Venetians managed to seize control of the castle of Palaikastro, northwest of Chandax. Venice appeared to be prepared to extract Crete from Genoese hands at any cost, while the Genoese were in no position to give assistance to Pescatore. The conflict dragged on until 1212. Giacomo Tiepolo, the first Venetian duke of Crete, managed to prevail and compelled his Genoese rival to come to terms and leave the island. A few Genoese enclaves held out until 1217. The final surrender, however, of Alammano da Costa to the Venetians on 11 May 1217 marked the end of the Veneto-Genoese struggle for possession of the island. Another final effort by the Genoese to regain control of Crete at the end of the century (1294) led to nothing. Venice was now undisputed lord of Crete. The island was now to enter upon another long period of irksome oppression, that was to last until 1669. Venice, however, was to confront persistent and fierce resistance on the part of the Cretan population and was to expend vast amounts of blood and money for over two centuries, in order to maintain its authority.

CHAPTER II

THE CONSOLIDATION OF VENETIAN RULE IN CRETE

1. Venetian settlements

Venice's most pressing and urgent concern was to achieve absolute control of this large and far-off dominion whose population remained stubbornly and unremittingly hostile to its presence. The dispatch to the island of the first Venetian duke of Crete, Giacomo Tiepolo, in 1209 was a prudent political move. Tiepolo was charged with removing all remaining Genoese enclaves and with creating strong Venetian centres, as well as stamping out any resistance on the part of the local population and establishing a base for the administration and economic exploitation of the island. Tiepolo correctly perceived that the only way to assert Venetian authority was to organise and establish a strong, permanent Venetian community on the island. The new dominion was a long way from Venice and its ships needed nearly a month to cover the distance with the difficulties and dangers of the time. At Tiepolo's suggestion and request, it was decided to establish communities of noble families from Venice on Crete, thus implementing a kind of military settlement plan that would assist in the swift and secure movement of forces to combat any resistance and acting as a kind of police supervision of the island. The Venetian settlers were to be granted fiefs in the form of the most fertile areas of land, and they would offer their military services and dedication to the Venetian capital in return. The order for the first mission was signed in Venice on 10 September 1211. It is known as the Carta Concessionis, and constituted an agreement between the metropolis and its colonial subjects.

The first colonials departed from Venice on 20 March 1212.

They consisted of 132 nobles, or knights (*milites, cavalieri*), and 48 infantrymen (*pedites* and *sergentes*). A second wave of colonising began in 1222 and other emigrations to Crete took place in 1233 and 1252. The settlers who came in 1252 built the town of Chania, on the site of ancient Kydonia. Further settlers came sporadically in later times. Roughly 10,000 Venetian settlers came to Crete altogether during the first century of Venetian rule. If one takes into account the fact that this number represents about one sixth of the total population of Venice at that time, one can appreciate the importance that Venice attached to its new possession.

2. The administrative system

Venice had no intention of establishing in Crete a purely feudal system such as existed in western Europe at this time. For political and military reasons it preferred to set up a mixed system much like its own. Chandax, now called Candia in the Venetian dialect, thus became the Venice of the East. The entire island constituted a single administrative region, which they proudly called the Kingdom of Crete (Regno di Candia). The islands of Tinos (Tine) and Kythera (Cerigo) also belonged to the administrative district of Crete.

In 1211, immediately following its final subjugation, the island was divided by the Venetian authorities into six provinces, called *sexteria,* as follows:

1. The sexterio of Agioi Apostoloi (S. Apostoli, Cannaregio). This included the districts of Siteia, Ierapetra, Lasithi and Merabello, all of which today comprise the region of Lasithi.

2. The sexterio of Agios Markos (S. Marco). This included the areas around Rizokastro (Belvedere), Pediada and Pezokounava.

3. The sexterio of Stavros (S. Croce). This included the areas of Monofatsi (Bonifacio), Kainourio (Castelnuovo) and Pyrgiotissa.

4. The sexterio of Castello. This included the areas of Mylopotamos, Ario and Apano Sybritos

5. The sexterio of Agios Pavlos (S. Paolo). This included the

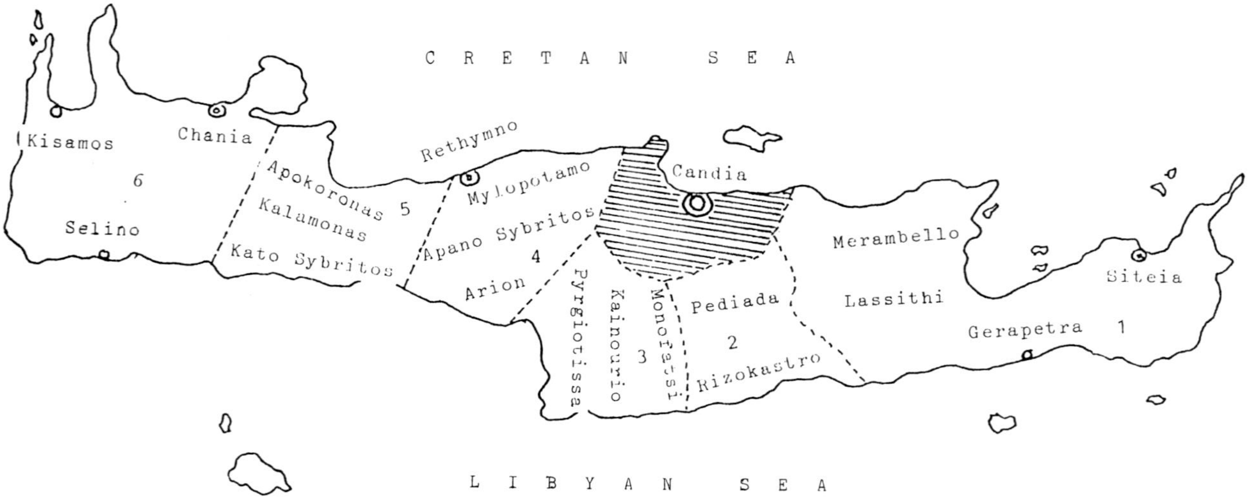

Figure 7
Map showing the six provinces (sexteria) of Crete during the 13th century. The shaded area around Candia comprised the Parte di Commune of Venice.

areas of Kalamonas (Rethymnon), Kato Syvritos (Agios Vasileios) and Psychro (Akrokoronas, Bicorno).

6. The sexterio of Dorsoduro. This included the areas of Chania, Kisamos and Selino (Orna, Arna).

This pattern was kept for about a hundred years. In the early 14th century Crete was divided into just four large regions (territoria) which correspond roughly to the present day administrative districts ('nomes' in Greek):

1. The territoria of Candia. This was the largest territoria and included the present day nome with its seven subdistricts and the province of Merabello and the mountain plain of Lasithi.

2. The territoria of Rethymnon (Rettimo). This included the four present day provinces of the nome.

3. The territoria of Chania (Canea). This included the the present day provinces of Kydonia, Apokoronas (Psychro), Kisamos and Selino (Orina).

4. The territoria of Siteia (Sitia). This included the present day provinces of Siteia and Ierapetra.

Sphakia was the only part of Crete which Venice never managed to fully subjugate. The shadowy authority of Venice was here exercised by a Superviser who was answerable either to Chania or to Candia, according to the period.

The administrative organisation of Crete was a replica of that of Venice. The highest political office was held by the duke (Duca di Candia) who was elected by the nobility of Venice. He resided in Candia and his term of office lasted for two years. He exercised power with the help of two advisors who also served for just two years. The duke and his two advisors constituted the Signoria of Crete. From the early 14th century onwards officials known as rectores were elected as the governing administrators in the main towns of the other regions of Crete: in Chania, Rethymnon (from 1307 onwards) and Siteia (from 1314 onwards). The rectores also had limited military power within their regions.

A large number of officials carried out the task of administrating

Crete. Most were appointed directly from Venice and served the home city with the utmost loyalty. The officials who dealt with economic affairs, the so-called *camerarii* or *camerlengi,* occupied first place in the administrative hierarchy. Each territoria had its own treasury (camera). The lowest in rank were the magistrates (giudici) and the police (justitiarii, domini de nocte). All public and official posts were occupied by Venetians and Italians. The native inhabitants were allowed only to exercise the public office of notary or lawyer. As time passed, however, and when the old feudal system started to wane, the Venetian administration became more open. After 1500 there was a steady convergence between local and Venetian elements on the island and native Cretans began to occupy important posts in the administration.

3. Military organization

Military control of Crete was secured by organising well-placed fortifications and a mobile and ready infantry and cavalry force. The Venetian lords of Crete were obliged to maintain war horses and to go out to battle themselves in the case of any uprising.

Command and responsibility for the organization of the army was in the hands of the Capitano di Candia, who resided in Candia. The navy was under the command of the Admiral of the Fleet of Venice, the Capitano General da mar, whose rank was higher than any held by the Venetians on the island. The Venetian lords of Crete were also obliged to serve in the galleys of the Serenissima as helmsmen.

In times of crisis Venice sent a Proveditor General to Crete, who was entrusted with absolute power in military matters, which included both defence and fortifications, mobilisation of forces and the conduct of war campaigns. With these unlimited powers the Providetor General took practically the entire administration of Crete into his own hands. From 1569 onwards the institution of the Providetor General became permanently established on the island, for it was then that the Turkish threat became increasingly real, and

Venice was anxious to preserve her dominions. The Providetor General was elected to his post by the nobility of Venice, and several of the Providetor Generals later became doge of Venice. Although the local authorities on Crete frequently expressed discontent at the fact that they were ignored and disregarded by the exceptional powers of the Providetor General the institution nevertheless proved highly useful and sometimes essential for the survival of the Venetian community on Crete. With very few exceptions (such as the Provvidetor Cavalli, who was particularly cruel) the Provvidetors were prudent and judicious men who helped considerably in settling serious political and military issues on Crete. Many fortification works as well as public welfare projects on Crete were carried out thanks to the enlightened management of the Providetor Generals, many of whom were remembered with admiration by later generations. Of these Giacomo Foscarini (1575-1577) was one of the most famous.

As with the Dukes of Crete, the Providetor Generals were in office for a period of just two years and at the end of their term in office they had to submit a report in Venice on the situation in Crete, making reference to their own works and making suggestions and proposals for the handling of whatever problems were affecting the island. Today these reports constitute a precious and highly reliable source of historical evidence for the period in Crete. Their study and publication has done much to throw light on various previously unknown aspects of Cretan history.

Figure 8
The winged lion of St. Mark, symbol of the Serenissima of the Republic of Venice (a sketch by M. Boschini, *Il Regno tutto di Candia,* Venice 1651)

CHAPTER III

CRETAN RESISTANCE

The Cretan people by no means accepted the loss of their national and religious freedoms without protest. The heads of the leading noble families of the island were fully conscious of their natural dependence on, and relationship with, the Byzantine Empire, and the Byzantine ideal never died in Crete. The presence of a foreign master on the island who threatened both the Cretans' national and religious freedoms immediately provoked a reaction from this irrepressible people. The resistance in Crete, which sometimes took on the character of a national and sometimes of a social movement, was a unique phenomenon in the history of Frankish rule in Greece. Twenty-seven uprisings and other local movements are recorded over a period of two centuries. Venice maintained its hold chiefly because the divisive disagreements between Cretan leaders never enabled a common coordinated resistance to develop. Here we shall examine the course of these Cretan uprisings during the era of Venetian rule.

1. The revolt of the Agiostephanites

We have very little evidence for the first recorded uprising against the Venetians which reportedly took place in 1211. The most likely cause of the revolt was probably the arrival in Crete of the first Venetian settlers who seized the property of the Church and of the leading families. The movement broke out in the region of Lasithi and was led by the family of the Agiostephanites. The rebels took control of the castles of Siteia and Merabello and then managed to become masters of the whole of east Crete. The Duke of Crete, Giacomo Tiepolo, unable to confront the insurrectionists, requested assistance from the ambitious Duke of the Aegean, Marco Sanudo. After a hard fought struggle the revolt was crushed and its leaders, the Agiostephanites, forced to leave the country or to swear an oath of allegiance to Venice.

The refusal of Tiepolo to fulfil his promises to Marco Sanudo led the two dukes into a serious dispute that was to last about four years. Marco Sanudo managed to seize control of Candia and seven other fortresses. Tiepolo withdrew to the fortress of Temenos (Roka), while the Cretans went to Sanudo's help, led by the powerful Byzantine archon Sevastos Skordiles. Reinforcements were dispatched immediately by Venice and Tiepolo was able to confront the rebels and regain Candia. Sanudo, having signed a treaty in 1212 or 1213, had to leave Crete. Twenty Cretan archons, also forced to leave, accompanied him.

2. The revolt of the Skordiledes and the Melissenoi

During the course of the next twenty years three major uprisings broke out in Crete, led by the Skordiledes and the Melissenoi. The launching point for these uprisings were the two mountainous provinces of Rethymnon: Apano Syvritos (Amari) and Kato Syvritos (Agios Vasileios). This is why these two uprisings are often called the "Revolt of the Two Syvritoi". These revolts very quickly spread across the whole of west Crete.

The pretext for the revolt was given by the rapacious behaviour of Petros Philikanevos, the castellano of the castle of Bonrepare (Monopari) near Rethymnon, who stole horses and livestock from the land of the powerful Skordiledes family. The Duke Paolo Curino who had a reputation for excess and cruelty against the Orthodox Christians either did not want or was not able to dispense justice in this case, with the result that a major revolt broke out in 1217. The leaders of the revolt were Konstantinos Sevastos Skordiles and Michael Melissenos. The Venetians were defeated in a number of engagements and within a short period almost the whole of west

Crete, from Mylopotamos south, was in the hands of the rebels. It was now clear to Venice that arms and violence were not the best way to subdue unrest on the island. It was necessary to use diplomacy and negotiation with the Cretan leaders. Indeed the new duke, Domenico Delphino, quickly came to terms with the rebels. By the treaty of 13 September 1219 the leaders of the rebellion were granted fiefs and privileges, 75 serfs were freed, various privileges were secured for the monks of the monastic dependency on Crete (at Stylos, Apokoronas) of the monastery of St. John the Divine of Patmos, and for the first time penalties were established for Venetians who abused the Cretan peasants. In turn, the Cretan archons swore an oath of fealty to the Venetian Republic. The most important achievement of this revolt, however, was the successful attainment of privileges which put the Cretan archons on an equal footing with their Venetian counterparts. A Cretan nobility, about whom we shall talk later, was steadily gaining recognition from the Venetians.

The installation of new Venetian settlers in Crete in 1222 caused a new revolt, this time led by Theodoros and Michael Melissenos. Carrying out the orders of Venice, the duke Paolo Curino signed an agreement with the leaders of the uprising, thereby granting them, in 1223, feudal fiefs.

A few years later in 1228 another more serious revolt broke out led this time by the Skordiledes and the Melissenoi. Two other archon families joined forces with the rebels: the Arkoleoi and the Drakontopouloi. The duke of Crete, Giovanni Storlado, was wholly unprepared for such a revolt and was compelled to seek the assistance of the duke Angelo Sanudo (son of Marco Sanudo) of the Aegean, who resided on Naxos. Duke Sanudo, seeing this as an opportunity to win considerable gains, came eagerly to Crete where he fought with great valour. He was responsible for the construction of the fortress at Suda.

However, the shared desire for freedom had once again revealed itself among the Cretans and Byzantine Greeks. The Cretans sought the help of the Byzantine emperor in exile, Ioannes Vatatzes, in the kingdom of Nicaea in Asia Minor. He readily responded to the Cretans' request, sending a fleet of 33 ships to Crete and a sizeable force of soldiers, which, in the event, proved to be insufficient for the task of sustaining the revolt. After a few short-lived successes which included the seizure of the fortresses of Rethymnon, Mylopotamos and Kainourio (Castel nuovo), and the siege of the castle of Monofatsi, the Byzantine fleet was forced to retreat under threat of destruction by attacks from the Venetian fleet. Just a few soldiers, the so-called Anatolikoi, who had come with the force sent by Vatatzes remained behind in Crete to carry on the struggle, but their efforts came to nothing.

Once again, the revolt was to end in the conclusion of a treaty. Three agreements were signed in all, in 1233, 1234 and 1235, by which the leaders Nikolaos Sevastos Demonoyannis and Michael Melissenos succeeded in securing fiefs and feudal privileges, while also securing the protection of their serfs. Only the Drakontopouloi refused to sign the treaty and continued to fight on for a while in east Crete along with the Anatolikoi soldiers. In the end it was agreed that they should leave the fortress of Agios Nikolaos at Merabello, and be allowed free passage to Asia Minor. After this nothing is known of the fate of the Drakontopouloi.

3. The revolt of 1262

The period from 1236 to 1260 was peaceful. A new wave of revolts of a distinctly national character began in 1262. Following the recovery of Constantinople in 1261 by the Byzantines, the Emperor Michael VIII Palaiologos had hopes of extracting Crete from Venetian control and restoring it to the fold of the Byzantine empire. To achieve this he sent a certain Stengos to Crete bearing letters for the Greek Cretan archons George Chortatzis and Michael Skordiles Psaromelingos. Revolt broke out immediately (1262) and was led by Chortatzis, Skordiles and Melissenos. The revolt was also backed by the local clergy, who recognised the young Byzantine emperor as the sole legal bearer of political power in Crete and as the only force that would be able to reunite the Church of Crete with the Ecumenical Patriarchate. The struggle lasted four years and much blood was shed. Unfortunately, the help that Michael VIII had promised never arrived and the complications that arose in his foreign policy meant that he was unable to pursue further his vision of regaining Crete. Within Crete itself the rebels became isolated when the young but powerful Cretan archon Alexios Kallergis declined to throw his support behind the rebels, keen that he should lose none of the privileges he had gained from the Venetians. By the treaty of 1265 Venice granted amnesty to all the participants in the revolt and ratified privileges that it had granted earlier to the Cretans, while it further granted two new fiefs to the leaders of the uprising. At the same time, the Venetians guaranteed Stengos safe passage from Crete, and, for his part, Michael VIII Palaiologos formally recognised Venetian rule on the island.

In the following year there was unrest in Candia which caused anxiety for the Venetian authorities. Powerful Cretans such as Alexios Kallergis and the brothers George and Theodoros Chortatzis planned a new uprising, exploiting the involvement of Venice in its war with Genoa. Kallergis eventually backed down and the resolute stand of the new duke, Giovanni Belegno, averted the present danger of another revolt.

4. The age of the major revolts (1272 - 1333)

a) The Chortatzis revolt

The first major revolt of a truly nationalist character broke out in 1272 (or 1273). The causes of the revolt still remain unclear, but it is quite possible that the oppressive and arbitrary rule of the Venetians was to blame. George and Theodoros Chortatzis of Rethymnon, both valiant men with strongly patriotic sentiments, undertook the leadership of a new struggle that began in east Crete. The base of the campaign was the mountain plateau at Lasithi. Violent battles took place on the plain of Mesara where the rebels, having killed the duke, one of his advisors and many other Venetian nobles (the flower of the Venetian society of Candia), very nearly won the day (1276). George Chortatzis laid siege to Candia and the Venetian position began to look desperate. However, personal differences and disputes between the leaders (Konstantinos Psaromelingos killed Sephes Chortatzis while they were distributing the spoils of the battle), the lack of adequate supplies and above all the treacherous connivance of Kallergis with the Venetians eventually condemned the revolt to failure. Thanks to well-planned action on the part of the Venetians and the dispatch from Venice of strong reinforcements the revolt of Chortatzis was finally stamped out in 1278. The historian Xanthoudidis wote that "The revolt of the Chortatzis brothers did not end up with compromise as had been the case with all previous uprisings, and with the satisfaction of personal or group interests and demands, such as happened in the case of Kallergis (with the granting of fiefs and other feudal privileges), because since the rebels had had an essentially nationalist programme and aimed at the liberation of the island, they had either to attain their fundamental aim or alternatively face defeat and the heavy hand of reprisals from the victor, as occurred with the Chortatzis brothers and others who were banished from Crete". The Chortatzis brothers were in fact outlawed and were compelied to flee the island in order not to be arrested by the Venetians. They fled to Asia Minor along with many other Cretan rebels. Many of them later served in the army of the ambitious commander Alexios Philanthropinos (1293-1295). In Crete, Venice implemented a programme of harsh reprisals and frightful punishments in order to set an example to other potential dissidents and to instill fear in the population. The strain on relations between the Venetians and the Cretan population had reached its height.

b) The revolt of Alexios Kallergis

In 1282 the greatest of the Cretan aristocratic revolts against the Venetians broke out. The main architect of the revolt was Alexios Kallergis, the most illustrious Cretan of the period. He was descended from the great Byzantine family of Phokas, and they were strongly conscious of their Byzantine background and had the imperial double-headed eagle on their coat of arms. It was said that the name Kallergis was given to him by the Venetians, honouring him as an agent of good.

Kallergis appears on the scene for the first time during the revolt of 1262. Pursuing an essentially opportunist line, sometimes siding with the rebels and sometimes siding with the Venetians, he managed to achieve considerable power and vast wealth, thereby becoming respected as much by the Venetians as by his own fellow Cretans. With his fief situated at Mylopotamos he was in the ideal position to control Crete. Again Xanthoudidis gives a portrait of Kallergis: "To wealth and background -both hereditary advantages- Alexios added great personal talent such as valour, martial astuteness, fine judgement, intelligence and eloquence. But he was also a product of his times: egoism, vaingloriousness and a thirst for preeminence filled his soul and only served to diminish the purity of his nationalist sentiments. Flattered by the magnificent honours and privileges that were conferred on him by his Venetian rulers, he proved incapable of sacrificing these for the higher ideal of the national restoration of his homeland, as the noble-minded Chortatzis brothers had done".

Having collaborated with the Venetians and having succeeded, by means of cunning and treachery, in removing the Chortatzis brothers from their homeland in 1278, Alexios Kallergis remained the undisputed "Cretarch".

The failure of the Venetians to honour the agreements made following previous revolts and their attempts to limit the increasing strength of Kallergis were the main factors that led to his inspiring a major revolt that was to drag on for a long seventeen years (1282-1299) and was to make the Venetian position almost untenable. Some have expressed the opinion that the revolt was in fact instigated by the Byzantine emperor Michael VIII Palaiologos who, faced by the threat of a Veneto-Angevin alliance, sought to stir up revolt in Crete in order to keep the Venetians diverted.

Whatever the case, the revolt quickly spread. The greatest Cretan families of the time came to Kallergis' side: Varouchas, Gavalas, Vlastos, and even Michael Chortatzis, nephew of the leaders of the previous revolt. Mylopotamos was the centre of the rebels' operations, but in fact the entire island rose up in support of Kallergis.

The Venetians tried to subdue the rebels from the start by a show of force and the implementation of the most draconian measures. They destroyed monasteries that had acted as rebel enclaves in earlier revolts, they killed and tortured those that they arrested and they declared the Lasithi plain off-limits and inhabited by no one, not even allowing people to graze their flocks on it (1284) because it had always been a hide-out of the rebels. They were above all concerned to arrest Kallergis himself and the other rebel leaders, but in this they were unsuccessful.

Indecisive conflicts and battles carried on for over a decade. The continual arrival of military reinforcements and supplies from Venice and the various plans devised by the dukes all proved futile.

Venice was in a critical position in 1296 when the Genoese attempted to take control of the western end of Crete. The Genoese admiral Doria captured and sacked Chania and invited Kallergis to join forces with him, tempting him with the promise that Genoa would recognise him as a hereditary governor of Crete. At this critical moment Kallergis refused to collaborate with the Genoese, and this was to lead to the first attempts at reconciliaton with Venice. The understandable war fatigue that both sides felt, the refusal of Kallergis to join in the siege of the large Venetian fortresses and the disagreements among the rebel leaders finally brought the revolt to an end.

The treaty of Alexis Kallergis (Pax Alexii Callergi). The revolt was officially ended with the signing of a treaty on 28 August 1299. This was an event of immense significance for the subsequent development of Veneto-Cretan affairs. For the first time, the rights of the Cretan people were set out in permanent and stable form. It is also significant that Kallergis always honoured the terms of the agreement and, according to one source, he obliged his successors to also abide by the terms of the treaty.

The treaty, which contained 33 articles, was signed by Michael Vitale, Duke of Crete, and was ratified immediately by the Republic of Venice. The main terms of the treaty were the following:

1. A general amnesty was granted, and property, which had been appropriated by the Venetians with the declaration of war, was returned to its former owners.

2. Kallergis was restored to the status he enjoyed before the revolt, with the addition of four fiefs west of Stroumboula. He was also given the right to grant fiefs, feudal privileges and honours himself to a third party, and to breed war horses.

3. Marriage between Venetians and Cretans was allowed.

4. Tax exemptions were granted to the rebels for their debts, with the possibility to pay off outstanding amounts within a period of two years.

5. The rulings of the courts set up by Kallergis during the revolt were recognised as valid.

6. One hundred serfs, who had been arrested for supporting the revolt, were freed.

7. Kallergis was granted control of the monasteries that lay west of the mountain Stroumboula, with the same rent as they had paid before the time of the revolt.

8. Kallergis was also granted the right to collect rent from the monasteries that belonged to the Latin Archdiocese of Crete in the same area (west of Stroumboula) on very favourable terms.

9. Of even greater interest were the articles of the treaty that dealt with ecclesiastical affairs. Kallergis was given the right to install an

Orthodox bishop in the diocese of Agrio and to collect rent from the two neighbouring dioceses of Mylopotamos and Kalamonas (Rethymnon). This article was particularly important, especially if one considers the state of the Cretan Church during these difficult times (see below). The diocese of Ario was subsequently named the diocese of Kallergiopolis. An Orthodox bishop of the name Alexander Kalliergis is recorded as being there from 1322 to 1324. Most probably the residence of this diocese was located at the present day hamlet of Agridia (near Klepsimia, Mylopotamos).

Following the settlement of the treaty Kallergis acquired vast power and came to be considered the only permanent leader of the Cretan Orthodox population. It is interesting that the scribe and scholar Michael Louloudes, a refugee from Ephesos in Asia Minor which had fallen to the Turks, noted in one of his manuscripts (now held in the library of the monastery of St. John the Divine on Patmos) that he finished writing it on 18 September 1310, "during the reign of the emperor Andronikos and the ruler of Crete, Alexios Kallergis".

Kallergis abided by all the terms of the agreement and was thought to be on such good terms with the Venetians that the name of his lineage, by a unique concession of Venice, was recorded in the Libro d'Oro of the Venetian nobility. It is no surprise therefore that he dissuaded his fellow islanders from staging a new revolt in 1303 when many Cretans saw that the chaos caused by the severe earthquake which occurred on 8 August provided them with an ideal opportunity to strike at the Venetians. A few years later on 23 May 1311 Sanudo, the Duke of Crete, sent a confidential letter to Kallergis informing him of suspicious stirrings of rebel elements in the region of Sphakia: Kapsokalyvis, the Koutis brothers, Philokalis, Lithinos, the Katzouropouloi and Sarakenopoulos. He asked Kallergis to send spies in order to gather information.

The Venetophile stance of Kallergis infuriated many of the noble Cretan families (including the Chortatzis, Melissenos and Agiostephanites families), who not only accused him of treachery and self-interest, but also made an attempt on his life at Mylopotamos. In his last years Kallergis lived at Candia, but even his enemies managed to assassinate his son, Andreas Kallergis, along with many of his followers. Alexios Kallergis died in 1321 and was buried in the monastery of St. Katherine's of the Sinaites in Candia.

c) The revolt at Sphakia

Despite the settlement that was reached between Kallergis and the Venetians, the arbitrary conduct of power by the Venetians did not come to an end. Another revolt broke out in the district of Sphakia in 1319 on the pretext that the Venetian garrison commander had offended the honour of the daughter of the house of Skordiles. Her relatives killed the garrison commander and his men and then declared open rebellion. Many Cretans from west Crete hurried to the side of the rebels of Sphakia and organised their defence in the Samaria Gorge. Duke Giustiniano sent a large force to crush the rebellion which came to an end when Alexios Kallergis intervened on behalf of the Venetians.

In the same year (1319) smaller insurrections took place led by the Varouchis and the Vlastos families. Again thanks to Kallergis' intervention they came to nothing.

d) The revolt of Margarites and Vardas Kallergis (1333)

Crete was quiet for fourteen years until 1333 when another large rebellion started. This time the cause was the decision of the new duke Vlasio Zeno to enforce an emergency tax for the construction and repair of the Venetian galleys with the intention of hunting down the pirates in the region that had become the scourge of the Cretan coasts.

The first protest occurred in the village of Margarites where 400 men swore to resist the new taxation measures. They were immediately joined by the inhabitants of the western provinces, Sphakia, Selino and Kisamos and a full-blown revolt was under way by September 1333. The revolt was led by Vardas Kallergis of the house of Kallergis, Nikolaos Prikosiridis from Kisamos and the three Syropoulos brothers. The revolt quickly spread and the leaders decided to make an attempt on Candia.

The Venetians, however, were assisted by the sons of Alexios Kallergis, and in particular by George whose conduct was especially selfish and insidious. The revolt ended in 1334 with the arrest and execution of the protagonists and the burning of the village of Margarites. It is notable that 50 Cretan serfs helped the Venetians to arrest and execute the leaders Vardas Kallergis, his son Sephes, the brothers Michael and Leo Syropoulos and Theodoros Melissenos. The Venetians also exiled the families of the rebels in 1335 and it was ruled that the children and brothers of Vardas Kallergis should remain in prison for life as an example to others who might harbour rebel sympathies. For politico-religious reasons they also banned non-Cretan Orthodox clerics from staying on the island. A measure intended to divide and rule was that of giving financial compensation to all those who remained loyal to Venice during the rebellion.

5. The revolt of Leo Kallergis and of the Psaromelingos family (1341)

In 1341, just seven years after the revolt of Vardas Kallergis, a new rebel movement appeared, initially at Apokoronas and later at Sphakia, Mylopotamos and Mesara. The revolt was instigated by Leo Kallergis, the nephew (some say the son or grandson) of Alexios Kallergis, one of the few members of the Kallergis family not to pursue a pro-Venetian policy. Leo, who had pretended to be a law-abiding friend of the Venetians managed to correspond in secret with Kostas Smyrilios and incite him and his sons, Michael and John, to rebellion at Apokoronas. They immediately responded to the call to arms along with other noble families including the Melissenoi, the Sevastoi, the Skordiledes and the Psaromelingoi. The contribution of Konstantinos Skordiles, father-in-law of Leo Kallergis, and his sons Michael and Emmanuel, was particularly important.

The grandson of the famous Alexios Kallergis, also called Alexios, took the side of the Venetians. He managed to arrest Smyrilios and his sons who in turn betrayed Leo Kallergis and revealed to the Venetians the existence of the secret correspondence between them and Kallergis when they were in Apokoronas. Smyrilios and his sons were executed and the duke, Andreas Cornaro eventually succeeded in arresting Leo for whom he had reserved a terrible death. He tied him in a sack and threw him into the sea.

Following the death of Leo Kallergis, however, the revolt took on even greater dimensions. Kapsokalyvas, father-in-law of Leo, and his two sons, who were also known as the Psaromelingoi brothers, were now fired with a spirit of revenge. Entrenched in the inaccessible mountains around Sphakia they managed to take control of the mountain regions of Rethymnon (Ano and Kato Syvritos), and they laid siege to Kastelli, near Mylopotamos, where Alexios Kallergis was based. Other rebel leaders joined forces with them, including another Alexios Kallergis or Souleas, probably from the branch of the Kallergis family of Kisamos.

The fate of the revolt was decided in the Mesara plain, where the duke managed to lure the Psaromelingi brothers into an ambush and crush their force. John was killed in battle and Michael, who had been wounded by an arrow, ordered one of his followers to cut off his head and take it to the Venetians so that he might save himself .

After the massacre of Mesara plain and the death of the valiant Psaromelingoi brothers, whose daring and courage was even admired by the Venetians, the rebellion in Rethymnon and the rest of west Crete was quelled in 1347. The Venetians, in an orgy of revenge, tore families apart, sent women and children to Venice and tortured to death all those who had been involved or who were suspected of being involved.

6. The revolt of St. Titus (1363-1366)

An event that was to shake the Republic of Venice and have severe consequences for Crete, especially with respect to the relations between the native population and their Venetian lords, was the revolt -which came to be known as the revolt of St. Titus- of the Venetian nobles on Crete against the metropolis, Venice. The Venetian feudal lords on Crete had repeatedly protested to Venice about the oppressive taxation imposed by Venice and of their lack of recognition in the metropolis. They were considered second-class aristocracy. The refusal of Venice to satisfy the just demands of the lords of Crete was a snub to their honour and it was only natural that further action would be taken by them. Gradually the idea of seceding from the jurisdiction of Venice took root. The imposition of new taxation by Venice in 1363 for the purpose of repairing and improving the port of Candia sparked off a strong reaction in Crete. The Venetian feudal lords refused to pay up and started to plot a rebellion led by the two noble families of Gradenigo and Venier. The main inspiration behind the revolt, however, was Titus Venier. Open revolt broke out on 9 August 1363. The rebels arrested the duke, Leonardo Dandolo, and his advisors and threw them into prison, declaring the end of Venetian rule on Crete and the establishment of an autonomous, independent Republic under the protection of the patron saint of Crete, the Apostle Titus. It came to be termed the Republic of St. Titus, and his flag was substituted for the flag of St. Mark. The rebels immediately elected a new duke, Mark Gradonigo, who was given the title of *Guvernator et Rector* of Crete, along with four advisors.

From the very beginning the rebels tried to secure the friendship and support of the local Cretan population, and especially of the leading Cretan noble families, and they made lavish promises to them in return for their support. They promised equal status and equal legal rights for the Orthodox and Catholic Churches on the island, they abolished the restrictions on ordination of Greek Orthodox clergy on the island and they allowed Orthodox rites and services to be conducted even in the cathedral of St. Titus, while at the same time many Venetians themselves became Orthodox. John, George and Alexios Kallergis all participated in the rebellion.

The rebellion quickly spread to other towns of the island -Siteia, Rethymnon and Chania- where the Venetian authorities were also overthrown and new rebel leaders put in their place. Titus Venier was appointed as the new governor of Chania.

News of the revolt came as a shock to Venice. Word was immediately sent to pope Urban V in Avignon and to the other European rulers, in order to secure either their support or their neutrality. At the same time Venice tried to settle the matter peacefully before being compelled to take up arms and become embroiled in a costly and risky military enterprise. An embassy of five envoys was sent to Crete to negotiate and bring about a peaceful settlement of the issue, but it failed in its aims. Resort to arms was the only solution. Venice quickly gathered a large force of Italian mercenaries and appointed Lucino dal Verme of Verona as its commander. A fleet of thirty-three galleys and twelve transport ships was equipped for the campaign with Domenico Michiele as admiral.

The rebels, who were aware of the plans and the preparations of Venice, also started to prepare for the critical encounter. However, disagreements arose in the ranks of the rebels and a number of them regretted having entered the dispute with Venice. It was only with difficulty and threats that Titus Venier managed to keep the rebels in order.

The Venetian fleet arrived at Crete on 7 May 1364 and anchored in the bay at Frascia, near the castle of Palaikastro seven miles west of Candia. The rebels rushed to block all the roads to Candia, but in the first battle which took place on 9 May, they were utterly defeated and routed. On the very same day the Venetian fleet sailed into Candia and took control of the town, which surrendered without a fight, and restored Venetian authority. The flag of St. Mark was raised once again and the Provveditors implemented without delay the strictest orders of the Venetian capital. The rebels were dubbed as traitors and the ten leading figures of the revolt were immediately beheaded. The purge lasted until August, with trials, imprisonment, exile and the hunt for all guilty or suspicious personages related to the rebellion along with the seizure of their property. On 17 August in Rethymnon a proclamation put a price on the Kallergis family: 8000 ducats for John, 3000 ducats for Alexios and 2000 ducats for George. It was also decreed that the families of Gradonigo and Venier should be broken up and the women and children be expelled from all Venetian domains in the Mediterranean. All were declared *personae non grata* for the Venetian nobility and they lost their fiefs and rights.

The same was carried out in the other Cretan towns where Venetian authority was quickly restored.

The swift and relatively easy restoration of Venetian authority in Crete had other broader consequences. The *Carta concessionis* of 1211, by which fiefs and privileges had originally been granted to the first Venetian lords of Crete, was annulled, and practically all the remaining Venetians were obliged to swear an oath of allegiance and eternal loyalty and devotion to Venice.

The victory was celebrated in Venice with unprecedented festivities, while the young duke of Crete, Petro Moresini, made 10th May an official local holiday. In the future this day was to be celebrated with spectacular displays and festivities, ceremonies and courtly contests. The most impressive of all the celebrations was the creation of an artificial garden in St. Mark's Square in Candia, through which the duke and his attendant courtiers passed for the official ceremony that was held in the cathedral of St. Titus.

7. The Kallergis Revolt (1364-1367)

The outlawed Kallergis family members, John, George and Alexios, unable to act in any other way, resorted to the desperate measure of another rebellion before the revolt of St. Titus had even been cleared up. They were backed by the outlawed Venetian lords, the brothers Titus and Teodorello Venier, Antonio and Francisco Gradonigo, Giovanni Molino, Marco Bonale and many others. The rebellion, which came to be known as the Kallergis Revolt, began in

August 1364 in west Crete (at Mylopotamos) and quickly spread to the whole island with numerous rebel groups springing up. The revolt took on a distinctly nationalist character, since the rebels fought with the Byzantine banner and with the aim of reuniting Crete with the Byzantine Empire. In order to further this pro-Byzantine nationalist policy, the Emperor John V Palaiologos persuaded Anthimos, the bishop of Athens, to transfer to Crete with the ecclesiastical title *Proedros* (First Minister) of Crete. Within a few months the whole of west Crete, apart from the coastal fortresses and the capitals of the provinces, had fallen into rebel hands.

As usual Venice responded with boldness and determination. It persuaded the pope to declare holy war on the Cretan rebels and to grant remission of sins to the Latin soldiers. His permission was also secured to recruit Turkish mercenaries from Asia Minor and to buy cavalry chargers. Soon a large force descended on Crete in company with five Provveditors, who were entrusted with absolute authority.

Despite the immense odds against them, the rebels managed to stir up revolt in east Crete and to use the inaccessible mountain plateau of Lasithi as a base for operations. In March 1365 the rebellion had taken on the character of guerilla warfare with rebel groups carrying out hit and run attacks, thereby causing considerable disruption for the Venetians. However, the Venetians were possessed of abundant supplies and virtually inexhaustible economic resources, while the rebels became ever more hemmed in. The disastrous crop failure of 1365 dealt a severe blow to rebel morale and led to a split in the leadership. The Venetians turned the situation to their advantage and managed to arrest the Venetian leaders and condemn them for treason. The Gradonigi and Venieri brothers and many others besides were tortured to death. Only Titus Venier managed to save himself by fleeing Crete. The eastern provinces, bowed by fear and deprivation, declared loyalty to Venice. Pockets of rebels continued their struggle for nearly another year in west Crete, and primarily in Sphakia where the Kallergis family had taken refuge. In April 1367 the adventurous Provveditor Giustiniani succeeded in breaking through the mountains around Sphakia and reaching Anopoli, where the rebellion was finally quelled with the arrest, thanks to his betrayal, of the Kallergis family.

Venetian revenge was fierce. The rebel leaders were all executed and the Cretan resistance given all but its final death-blow. Among those who died was Anthimos, former bishop of Athens and First Minister of Crete, who was thrown into prison and died from maltreatment in 1371. The Provveditor Giustiniani wrote in his report to the Venetian Senate that the Cretans no longer had leaders and that they would never be able to raise the banner of rebellion again. In order to wipe out every last pocket of resistance the Venetians issued an order to evacuate and destroy the three mountain refuges of the rebels at Lasithi, Eleutherna (Mylopotamos) and Anopoli (Sphakia). By the imposition of severe penalties they not only banned these mountain plains to human habitation, but even banned the grazing of livestock. These regions were to remain deserted for almost a hundred years.

With this last rebellion of the Kallergis family the period of Cretan rebellions came to an end. Venetian documents no longer speak of open war (guerra publica occurente) in Crete. The historian Stephanos Xanthoudidis wrote that "This was the last armed struggle [against the Venetians] on the island. The Cretan freedom fighters, who struggled for 157 years against the superpower of the age eventually exhausted themselves in the uneven fight and they no longer had the morale to continue, nor hope of further help from Byzantium whose situation was forever becoming worse... The Greek State of Byzantium breathed its last in 1453 with the fall of the city of Constantinople. What else could the Cretans hope for under these circumstances? If they managed to rid themselves of the Venetians they were quite aware that they would most probably fall victim to the much worse tyranny of the Turks, to which the rest of the Greeks had now succumbed. They therefore bowed to their fate. Later smaller insurrections and conspiracies of the fifteenth and sixteenth centuries were local and limited in character and easily suppressed by the authorities".

8. The plot of Sephes Vlastos (1453-1454)

After the suppression of the Venetian led revolt of 1363-1364 and the subsequent revolt of the Kallergis family a long period of peace ensued on the island. Conditions were now more favourable for the economic recovery of the island. The benefits of peace became apparent during the first half of the fifteenth century with the impressive increase in production and exports from Crete. Fr. Thiriet described it as a 'half century of contentment'.

A bold rebel group, generally known as the Plot of Sephes Vlastos, organised itself in Rethymnon just a few months after the fall of Constantinople. With the final collapse of the Byzantine state, Crete was the only part of the Greek world with a dynamic Greek presence and a vigorous awareness of its Byzantine traditions. The Byzantine ideals were bolstered by the many refugees from Constantinople who arrived on the island after the capture of the city by the Turks. Moreover, the Orthodox clergy of Crete reacted strongly to the Union (of the Orthodox and Catholic Churches) decided at the Council of Florence in 1439 and proclaimed in Constantinople in 1452 and they isolated those few Cretans that were in favour of the Union. It was within this political and religious climate that the idea gradually developed of reviving the Byzantine Empire, but this time with its centre in Crete. This utopian dream itself developed into a political plot inspired by Sephes Vlastos, a man of considerable stature and influence, and a member of the noble Byzantine family of Vlastos based in Rethymnon. His most notable supporters were the priest Manasses Arkoleos and Leondakios Troulinos from Rethymnon, and the priest Paul Kalyvas and George Kallergis from Chania. The scholar M. Manousakas has remarked that the plot 'may be considered as a protest movement against the prevailing Venetian policy which supported the enforcement of the union of the Churches in its dominion of Orthodox Crete. It can also be considered as a way of confronting the national disaster of the fall of Constantinople in

1453. It was a bold and, perhaps, over-optimistic attempt at liberating the most secure (for the circumstances of the day) and important remaining Greek territory, in which, many believed, lay the fate of the Greek nation and hope of continuing the Byzantine Empire'.

The plot of Sephes Vlastos, however, was crushed before it even had a chance to get launched. The priest John Limas and the Venetian Andrea Nigro betrayed the conspiracy and its participants to the Venetian authorities. The Venetians moved swiftly and decisively: they arrested the ringleaders and tortured them to death in August 1454. By the use of terror and the temptation of large rewards for informing on other insurgents the Venetians succeeded in disbanding the network of the conspiracy and thereby avoided the outbreak of open rebellion.

Following this plot the Venetian authorities directed much of their wrath against the Greek Orthodox clergy of Crete, whom they held responsible for stirring up hostility. Of the thirty-nine denounced for taking part in the plot, ten were members of the clergy. Venice also banned the ordination of Cretan priests for a period of five years.

Another plot that was centred on Rethymnon, in 1460, again met with failure. Many Cretans, including the priest Petros Tzangaropoulos and others from Constantinople and the Peloponnese, were involved in this plot. One refugee from Constantinople, John Argyropoulos, was a particularly sharp thorn in the Venetians' side. The plot is recorded as having been betrayed to the Venetians by David Mavrogonatos, a Cretan Jew. Others are also mentioned: John Limas, Emmanuel Limas and George Vergitsis. The Venetian authorities quickly rounded up the culprits and executed them. One of the more outstanding members of the plot who met his death at this time was John Gavalas.

These two plots were the very last manifestations of the Cretan resistance, but they were to result in the hardening of the Venetian attitude on religious policy and in increasing official support for papal propaganda on the island. By enactment of the Council of Venice it was decided that all attempts at promoting the position of the Orthodox Church on the island should be quashed at once. One product of this new religious policy in Crete was the famous 'klerodotema' of the once Greek Orthodox, now Roman Catholic, cardinal Bessarion. A papal Bull issued in September 1462 granted 300 ducats yearly, from the fiefs of the Latin patriarchate of Constantinople in Crete, to eleven pro-Union priests and a deacon in Candia. The number of pro-Union priests who were in receipt of this gift or allowance, known as the 'klerodotema', was later increased to sixteen. This material support for all those in Crete who were in favour of the union of the Orthodox and Catholic Churches was linked to other privileges and backing, both political and moral.

9. The revolt of George Cantanoleos (1527)

The final rebellion to take place in the long chain of Cretan revolts against Venetian rule took place in 1527, and is known as the revolt of George Cantanoleos, or Rabid George. The lack of reliable sources for this revolt, linked with the fact that a popular Greek novel of the nineteenth century (published 1872) known as 'The Cretan Weddings' by Zabelios served to confuse the record, means that we have little to go on for the certain identification of the causes, aims and course of events.

Recent studies have helped throw new light on the subject, chiefly by linking the movement to the response of the peasant population of west Crete to the taxation measures imposed on them and the administrative injustices meted out by the Venetian authorities. The nationalistic and autonomistic character that the movement may have been able to acquire did not in fact have time to develop.

Already from 1523 onwards at Kerameia, near Chania, an armed band of some six hundred men had taken the law into their own hands. This movement quickly spread to the Sphakia and Selinos regions and the mountains around Kydonia. At first the Venetian authorities were slow to respond, primarily because they feared intervention by the Turks, and they tried to bring the rebels to heel by means of threats. When it was realised that this method was not succeeding they had to take recourse to armed confrontation which broke out in October 1527. Geronymo Corner, the Provveditor General of Crete, managed to suppress the revolt within a month, although small pockets of resistance continued to remain active until January 1528.

Venetian reprisals were, as usual, harsh and merciless. The villages that were linked with the revolt near Chania -Kerameia, Alikambos, Meskla and Lakkoi- were destroyed. The ringleaders were executed and all those who succeeded in escaping to more remote parts of the island were outlawed. George Cantanoleos had a price of one thousand gold *hyperpyra* on his head and he was eventually betrayed to the authorities. 592 inhabitants of the rebel villages were evicted and it was forbidden for new inhabitants to settle in these villages. Certain families that were suspected of harbouring rebel sympathies were evicted, despite having sworn oaths of allegiance to Venice. Most indicative of the Venetian perception of the gravity of rebel activity was the fact that the entire Kontos clan was banished from Crete. In all, 1050 members of the clan were exiled to various Aegean islands and Cyprus. Some of them, after 1536, were allowed to return to Crete and rebuild their villages, although of course they were always regarded with the greatest suspicion by the Venetian authorities. Venice continued to regard the island with suspicion throughout the decades that were to follow. In his report to Venice in 1594 the Provvidetor General Philip Pasqualigo listed the families and clans which he believed posed a serious threat to security on the island: the Kontos clan of Alikambos, the Foumis clan of Kerameia, the Cantanoleos clan of Christogerako (Koustogerako), the Mousouros and Sgourafos clans of Omalos, and the Pateros clan (the most dangerous of all, according to the report).

CHAPTER IV

THE CHURCH OF CRETE DURING THE PERIOD OF VENETIAN RULE

The long period of Venetian rule was a time of particular hardship for the Church of Crete. The Venetians, who from the very beginning aspired to make both their presence on the island and their exploitation of its resources permanent, viewed the Orthodox Church as their strongest and most dangerous enemy. It was not only the difference in dogma that divided the Cretans and the Venetians. It is known, for example, that the Venetians were never fanatical Catholics and that they were in almost constant dispute with the pope. The guiding principle behind their political actions had always been that which was in the best interest of Venice. The Venetians themselves were accustomed to saying that they were firstly Venetians and secondly Christians (primo Veneziani, poi Christiani). They were constantly concerned about the fact that in Crete the Church was the major symbol of unity for the native Cretans; it was also the foundation for the Byzantine ideal, and the main vehicle for resistance against the foreign power.

One of the first actions therefore of the Venetians in Crete was to effect the curtailment of the Cretan Church's power by removing the Orthodox hierarchy. There were strict orders forbidding the visit to the island of Orthodox priests from elsewhere: by means such as this it was thought that the Cretan people, deprived of religious leaders, would gradually sink into religious indifference and become easy prey for the Catholic propaganda that had begun from the first moment that the Venetians settled on the island. Pope Innocent III had issued a papal Bull proclaiming that pilgrimage to the site of St. Titus at Candia in Crete was equivalent to pilgrimage to the Holy

Land, by which the pilgrim could also obtain remission for his sins. Active and fanatical monastic orders of the Roman Catholic Church founded numerous Latin monasteries chiefly in or close to the larger urban centres of the island, which then served as permanent centres for the conversion of the Cretans to Catholicism. A Latin archbishop was appointed to the archdiocese of the Cretan Church which was subordinate to the Latin patriarch of Constantinople. Indeed Venice always took care to appoint a member of one of the important families of Venice to the office of archbishop of Crete. Sometimes this even involved appointing a child to the office of archbishop who never in fact set foot in Crete. They were simply the owners of vast wealth (comprised of twenty-five fiefs) that were granted to the Latin archdiocese around Candia. Later, Latin bishops were also appointed to the other dioceses of Crete, and they formed their own local Church council, although its resposibilities were limited.

P r o t o p a p a d e s (head priests). The office of Protopapas was one of the highest in the hierarchy of the Cretan Orthodox Church in the main urban and provincial centres. The Protopapades enjoyed the full confidence of the Venetians and were paid servants of the public treasury of the Authentia (Sovereign of the island), and consequently dependent on the Venetian administration. They were obliged to conduct services alongside Catholic priests, to chant and participate in processional liturgies and to sing the praises of the pope and the Cretan archbishop. They had been ordained in the Orthodox faith, but they were Uniats (ie. in favour of the union of the Catholic and Orthodox Churches) and pro-western. Many of these priests had a reputation for corruption and moral decadence that was even cause for Venetian disgust. A well-known case was that of the protopapas of Candia, Ilarion Sotirchos, in the mid-sixteenth century who, according to a report submitted by Gaspar Viviano, a Latin vicar of the archbishop, lived with his mistress and had abandoned his family and his priestly duties; it had been twenty years since he had last performed a church service. It is clear that these Protopapades had no relationship with Orthodox patriarchates or with the Orthodox priesthood in general, and they cannot be considered as the foundation for the survival of Orthodoxy on the island. On the contrary, they provoked the disgust and contempt of the lower Cretan clergy and the Cretan people. But many of the Protopapades had enjoyed a higher education and were honoured with ecclesiastical titles, such as in the case of Ioannes Plousiadenos (1429?-1500), Protopapas of Candia, and later bishop of Modon (Methoni, in the Peloponnese), and the scribes Ioannes Rossos, George Alexandrou and Nikolaos (or Laonikos) Kavadatos.

From the year 1462 onwards, following an initiative of the cardinal Bessarion (a Greek by origin), a papal Bull was issued for the establishment of a Church bequest at Candia designed for providing support for pro-Union priests of the region. This was the so-called 'Klerodotema (Bequest) of Bessarion' which was mentioned earlier.

An ecclesiastical office similar to that of the Protopapas was the Protopsaltes (Lead Cantor), again a paid servant of the Venetian administration. Many of the Protopsaltes, besides their musical education (they both practised and taught ecclesiastical chant), were also highly educated and were distinguished as writers and scribes.

The situation of the Orthodox clergy. Cretans who wished to be ordained had first to receive permission from the Venetian authorities of the island, obtainable on payment of a large sum of money, and then they had to travel to the Peloponnese or to Asia Minor in order to find an Orthodox priest who was empowered to ordain them. Cretans generally chose to go to the Peloponnese (at Koron, Modon or Corinth), or to the Ionian islands, or to Asia Minor to be ordained. Then armed with their certificates of ordination they returned to Crete where their papers then had to undergo close scutiny by the Venetian authorities in order to confirm the validity of the ordination. In order to become a parish priest in an urban district, village or even monastery it was necessary to undergo examination by a committee, in accordance with Venetian law, and to receive the approval of the feudal lord.

The spiritual superiors of the Orthodox clergy of the island were the Protopapades. The Latin clergy did not have any jurisdiction over the Orthodox clergy apart from in cases of ecclesiastical misdemeanours whose gravity and nature were defined, however, by the political authorities of the island. Only the Latin archbishop of Crete, in order to secure greater revenue, was empowered with supreme spiritual and administrative jurisdiction over 130 priests in Candia and its surrounding districts. These priests, although they were obliged to recognise the primacy of the pope, could only be described as Uniats in a very superficial sense. Most of them were loyal Orthodox.

The religious policy of the Venetians in Crete was not unchanging throughout the long period of Venetian rule on the island. During the early decades of the Venetian period Cretan Church leaders were allowed to remain on the island, as in the case of Vasileios Varouchas who was bishop of Mylopotamos. The treaty of Kallergis also gave rise to the short-lived diocese of Kallergioupolis, where mention is made of an Orthodox bishop, Alexander, in the early fourteenth century. These, however, were isolated cases that did not have any broader ecclesiastical control on the island.

The Ecumenical Patriarch did not cease to be interested in the situation of the Cretan Church. In the turbulent period of the St. Titus revolt the Emperor of Constantinople John V Palaiologos and his patriarch Neilos persuaded archbishop Anthimos of Athens to leave his diocese and transfer to Crete as head of the Cretan Church (Proedros of Crete). Anthimos' career in Crete is dated to the period of the Kallergis revolt (1365-7). The Venetians arrested Anthimos and put him in prison. Maltreatment led to his death in 1371. Ten years later the patriarch of Constantinople sent a highly learned monk, Joseph Bryennios, to Crete, where he remained for twenty years (1381-1401). With his preaching, writings and teachings Bryennios injected new life into Orthodoxy on the island and successfully rebuffed the pro-Western theologians of the day. However, he was eventually expelled from the island by the Venetians.

From the early sixteenth century onwards the religious policy of the Venetians towards the Orthodox Christians of the island became more tolerant. The greater the Turkish threat became, the more the Venetians turned towards the Orthodox Cretans. After the Battle of Lepanto (1571) Venice decided to establish an Orthodox hierarchy in Crete, with a metropolitan bishop and four or five other bishops, in order to secure the support of the Cretans in the eventuality of a Turkish attack. This decision, however, was revoked by the fanatical Catholic Giacomo Foscarini, Proveditor General of Crete from 1575 to 1577, who considered the Orthodox priests as the main culprits behind the wave of local rebellions that had plagued Crete. He proposed that the number of Orthodox priests be reduced and that new ordinations be forbidden for a certain period because he viewed the number of Cretan priests to be excessive for the needs of the island. This persecution of the Orthodox priests came to be known as the Priest Hunt (in Greek, 'Papadokynegon').

The monasteries. It is within this context that we have to look at and examine the manifold and important role played by the monasteries of Crete during the long period of Venetian rule. The monasteries were the bastions of Byzantine Orthodoxy on the island. Whilst the Orthodox clergy was for a number of reasons under intense pressure in the urban centres, and was weakened in its Orthodox consciousness, the monks of the monasteries remained stern bastions of the Orthodox faith throughout these difficult times. Their almost fanatical adherence to the Byzantine tradition had a strong influence on the faith of the ordinary people. Monastic Orthodoxy on Crete erected a strong wall between the ruling Venetians and the oppressed people of Crete and thereby helped preserve the national characteristics and unity of the Cretans. Various zealot monks, founders of monasteries and of monastic charters such as Joseph Philagris and Neilos Damilas (late fourteenth and early fifteenth centuries) were also vociferous apologists for the Orthodox faith and polemical theologians who left us important ecclesiastical writings. They carried out successful disputations with various pro-

Western theologians of the time, such as Maximos Chrysovergis and Demetrios Kydonis, and also organised Cretan opposition to the unionist terms of the Council of Florence (1439).

In the last years of the Venetian period there was a vigorous revival of monasticism in Crete, and many new monasteries were founded and other older monasteries that had been abandoned or left to decay were restored and reopened. The reasons for this impressive revival were many: political, social and economic. Recent research at the state archives of Venice have brought scores of monasteries to light that were hitherto unknown to researchers. The larger monastic centres had particular prestige at the time, such as the Sinai monastic dependency of the monastery of St. Katherine's at Candia, the monastery of Agarathou, the monastery of Apezonon, the monastery of Vrontisiou, the monastery of Akrotiriani (Toplou), the monastery of Arkadiou, the monastery of the Holy Trinity at Tzagarolon, the monastery of the Virgin at Gonia and others. These monasteries contained schools and libraries and the monks copied manuscripts. And famous ecclesiastics of the age, such as the patriarch Cyril Loukaris, the patriarch of Alexandria Meletios Pegas, the bishop of Cythera Maximos Margounios, and the profusive writer and theologian Meletios Syrigos, were members of these monastic communities.

T h e m o r a l s t a n d i n g o f t h e c l e r g y. The absence of any ecclesiastical hierarchy that could exercise control over the moral and religious life of its clergy naturally led to a slackening of Christian ethics. Joseph Bryennios who stayed in Crete for no less than twenty years (1381-1401) inveighed against the sinful ways of the married clergy and the monks, and accused them of all kinds of immoralities: impiety, avarice, debauchery and drunkenness. In particular he castigated the old custom of the 'syneisakton', that is, the women that for supposedly spiritual and ethical reasons were brought to the homes of monks, but in fact lived with them. A stern patriarchal encyclical order was issued by the Ecumenical Patriarch Matthew I in about 1401 to the clergy of Crete concerning the matter of the ‘syneisakton’. There were Cretan monks of course who also condemned the same phenomenon. They were zealous Christians who did not wish to see disrepute fall on the Church: men such as Neilos Damilas of the early fifteenth century and Nathanael Bertos towards the end of the same century.

As time passed so the situation seems to have improved. The abbots of the Cretan monasteries started to prove themselves to be profound theologians and men of great moral standing. At the same time the patriarchate of Alexandria, chiefly on account of the fact that a number of its patriarchs such as Meletios Pegas and Gerasimos Spartaliotes were of Cretan origin, began to exercise a degree of spiritual supervision over Crete and to actively intervene by means of interpretative pronouncements on matters of doctrine and Church discipline, thereby imposing ecclesiastical order.

A highly learned Latin ecclesiastic, Gaspar Viviano, who held the offices of bishop of Siteia and vicar of the Latin archbishop of the island composed and published for the Orthodox clergy of Crete a series of teachings (1567) in which he discusses the moral life and necessity for dignified conduct by members of the clergy.

The Latin clergy was in no better state. The higher clerics rarely even visited their sees which they held onto for the sole reason of enjoying the revenues. Most of them were men of minimal education and many led moral lives wholly incompatible with their assumed role of Christian prelates. The Latin monasteries, generally concentrated in the large urban centres, often sheltered criminals and impostors who had little interest in religious affairs or the moral and religious instruction of the people.

Crete and the Reformation

A relatively unexplored though interesting aspect of the religious history of Crete has been investigated recently by Professor N. Panayiotakis. This concerns what seems to have been an attempt to disseminate the ideas of the Church reformation in Candia. The local authorities responded swiftly and efficiently in stamping out the small core of supporters of the Reformation. Gaspar Viviani, the Latin bishop of Siteia, in the faculty of vicar of the Latin archbishop of Crete and by order of the Council of Ten, conducted an inquisition into the matter in the summer of 1568. Three men were held to be responsible and they were immediately arrested: a doctor Yannis Kassimatis, Franceso Gentile, originally from the Italian city of Lucca, and then a school teacher in Candia, and Manousos Maras (the son of the distinguished notary of Candia, Michael Maras), who had recently returned from completing his degree at the University of Padua. All three were condemned to death by the local court of the Holy Inquisition, the president of which was bishop Viviani. No other such incidents connected with the Reformation were recorded after this.

CHAPTER V

CRETAN SOCIETY UNDER VENETIAN RULE

1. Population. Demographic features

The overwhelming majority of the Cretan population (about 97%) was composed of the native Greek Orthodox element. The Venetians, despite repeated waves of settlement, never amounted to more than about 10,000 individuals and they remained concentrated in the main urban centres.

Information concerning the size of the Cretan population is lacking for the first centuries of Venetian rule. Historians have calculated, perhaps with some exaggeration, that in the fourteenth century the population had fallen to a mere 50,000. The continual rebellions, hardship, privation and, above all, severe epidemics all played their part in devastating the population. After the end of the rebellions and the improvement of economic and living conditions there was a marked increase in the population, reaching as much as 300,000. After 1500 we have more detailed knowledge of the situation, furnished chiefly by the reports of the dukes and Providetors, many of which have now been published. A source (which is probably not very reliable) for 1510 puts the population figure at 300,000, while twenty years later another source for 1534 gives the drastically reduced number of 175,268. A fearful outbreak of the plague in 1523 which spread throughout the entire island clearly struck hard at the population. The eighteenth century historian Cornelius reckoned that the number of those who died in the plague was around 26,000. We have official figures from the last century of Venetian rule thanks to the detailed and carefully compiled censuses that were carried out at the time. In the report submitted by the Providetor Zuane Mocenigo (17 April 1589) Crete is said to have

1,087 villages with a total population of 208,000. The *territoria* of Candia had 486 villages with 76,000 inhabitants, while the town of Candia itself had a population of 16,000. The *territoria* of Siteia (along with Ierapetra) had 85 villages with a total population of 21,000. The town of Siteia had 1,654 inhabitants. The *territoria* of Rethymnon had 245 villages with 42,000 inhabitants, and the town of Rethymnon had just 5,500. The *territoria* of Chania had 263 villages and 36,000 inhabitants, while the town of Chania had 6,000 inhabitants. In the same report the population of Sphakia was estimated to be around 2,500.

A census was conducted by the duke Trivan in 1644, just twenty-five years before the Turkish conquest of the island. It is clear from this report that peace and prosperity had led to a dramatic increase in the population. The whole island had a total of 1,254 settlements: 496 in the *territoria* of Candia, 148 in Siteia, 296 in Rethymnon and 314 in Chania. The total population of the island was 287,165 (150,742 men and 136,423 women). Mention is also made of 3,527 clerics (both married and monks), 35,065 children over the age of eight, and 11,445 elderly and incapable of labour. The census also records the noble families, the bourgeois class and the merchants: 82 noble families of Venetian lineage and 198 noble families of Cretan lineage (nobili Cretesi), 387 bourgeois families (cittadini) and 66 merchant families (mercanti).

The Jewish community of the island was economically powerful. The Jews were generally concentrated in the main towns where they lived in their own separate neighbourhoods. By occupying themselves with trade and usury they managed to amass vast wealth with which they were then able to exercise their influence. The census of Marco Gradenigo (1627) records the number of Jews on Crete as being 1,160 out of a population of 192,725.

From time to time numbers of Greeks also fled to Crete as a place of refuge, most frequently from Asia Minor where the Turkish presence was becoming ever greater. Place names such as Trapezonta (< Trebizond), Prousa (< Bursa) at Acharnes, and Kastamonitsa are reminders of the origins of their inhabitants who were largely refugees from Asia Minor during the period of the fourteenth and fifteenth centuries. Various Cretan surnames, such as Dramyttenos (Adramyttenos, that is, of Adramyttion) also betray Asia Minor provenance. Many Byzantine families fled to Crete after the final fall of Constantinople in 1453. Some of them remained in Crete, such as the families of Apostolis, Mousouros, Kalaphatis and Vardas, while others continued northwest to the Peloponnese and the Ionian islands.

Again following the subordination of the Venetian domains in the Peloponnese to the Turks, many Greeks fled to Crete from the Mani, Monemvasia and Nauplia. Some of them were scholars or holders of high office such as the Protopapas of Nauplia, Nikolaos Malaxos, who settled in Candia. Most of the refugees from the Peloponnese settled in the Lasithi plain and at Chania.

2. Social classes

Cretan society during the early Venetian period followed the pattern of the feudal society of Europe. Its distinguishing feature was the strict division of its citizens into classes. These classes can be summarised as follows:

i) The Venetian nobility (nobili Veneti). These were the descendents of the Venetian nobles that had been sent by Venice to colonise Crete in the early period. They had been allotted the fiefs of the island and were possessed of immense wealth and social prestige, at least during the first three centuries of Venetian rule. They had a duty to rear war horses, to be available for war and to show absolute loyalty to the authority and decisions of Venice. They also had to remain Catholic since according to Venetian legislation anyone who abandoned the Catholic faith and became Orthodox had also to forfeit his titles and feudal possessions. The social gap dividing the Venetian feudal lords from their Cretan counterparts was greater than in any other part of the Frankish controlled Levant. A unique

Figure 9

Cretan coats-of arms.

1. The family of Zangarol, tombstone at the church of the Virgin in the village of Prinos, Mylopotamos (G. Gerola, *Monumenti Veneti* IV, 246, no. 297).
2. The family of Dandolo, tombstone at the church of the Saviour in the village of Karakala, Mylopotamos (ibid., 247, no. 303)
3. The family of Iakovos Cornaros, on the façade of the church of St. George, in the village of Piskokephalos, Siteia (ibid., 278, no. 449).
4. An unknown hellenised Veneto-Cretan family, with the Greek initials I. X. (Museum of Rethymnon, ibid., 233, no. 236).

exception to this state of affairs was the special concession of Venetian noble status to Alexios Kallergis and his descendents, as has already been mentioned.

ii) The Cretan nobility (nobili Cretesi). The first Cretan nobility was composed of the bourgeois families from Venice who settled in Crete with the first waves of colonialisation in the thirteenth century, and of former nobles who had at some time lost their Venetian titles. With the passing of time titles for the nobili Cretesi were granted to people of Cretan descent or even to Hellenised Italians in recognition of services which either they or their forbears had rendered to Venice. However, this class was to grow to such an extent that the titles started to lose their prestige. The vast majority of the nobili Cretesi were Orthodox and not particularly loyal to Venice. Only a small minority of them had feudal landed property. Most were possessed of only modest economic means and were usually involved in trade.

iii) The bourgeoisie (cittadini). The people that belonged to this class were generally inhabitants of the towns who did not possess noble titles, but who constituted the prosperous and wealthy class of townsmen, such as merchants, sailors, craftsmen, military and civil servants, doctors, lawyers and notaries. The poorer urban classes (plebe, populi, gente minuta) were also included in the cittadini, though not those who made their living by manual labour. The vast majority of the cittadini were Orthodox Greeks.

iv) The rural population (villani, parici, contadini). This class comprised the vast majority of the Cretan population, as well as the most wretched. The villani were bound to the land and had to cultivate the fields of their lords, serve in the Venetian galleys and carry out various compulsory unpaid works. There were some distinctions between the rural inhabitants. They were divided into peasants (contadini), freedmen and serfs or villeins (villani, parici). The latter fared the worst of all, being mere property of their lords and not having the protection of rights of any kind. Their lords could hire them out, lend them, sell them or transfer them just as with other property and equipment. The peasants cultivated the land of the lord under the system of sharecropping. In other words, the feudal lord gave land 'by third' to the peasants, which meant that the peasants farmed the land and gave a third of their income to their lord. In practice, however, the lords devised many ways by which they could levy a much greater sum from these unfortunate people. Besides this the peasants were expected to offer further services to their lords, both in farming the land, at harvest time and in transporting the products to the towns. Some of the peasants did enjoy some basic privileges and were not obliged to carry out the compulsory labour done by villeins. Other categories, such as priests and descendents of well-connected Byzantine families, were also exempted from having to perform community labour. The latter category, according to local tradition, included the descendents of the twelve archontopoula that were sent to Crete long before in Byzantine times. With their continual rebellions they forced the Venetians to recognise the privileges that were theirs by right of historical tradition. In the treaty of Alexios Kallergis (1299) a special proviso was made for the descendents of the archontopoula: 'Qui est arcondus sit arcondus et qui est arcondopulos debeat esse arcondopulos'.

This distinction survived virtually unaltered throughout the first three centuries of Venetian rule. From the early sixteenth century onwards, however, Cretan social structure had begun to change, especially in the towns, and Cretan society started to take on a new aspect. This change was effected by many factors. The Turkish threat, which was becoming more and more real, forced the Venetians to change their old colonial policy and to seek the voluntary cooperation of the Greek Orthodox of the island. In the last century or so of Venetian rule the relationship between Venice and its dominion of Crete ceased to be a relationship of colonial power and colony, and rather a connection that had more of a federal character. In addition, economic conditions had changed. The economy and trade gradually passed into the hands of the townsmen, who were almost entirely composed of Greeks. And while the old

Venetian feudal system was fast waning, the number of Cretans who were passing into the noble class by purchasing fiefs was fast increasing. This process had moved so far that by the end of the sixteenth century only 164 of the 964 feudal lords in the region of Candia were in fact Venetian. The situation was the same in the rest of Crete. In 1583 the majority of landowners in the region of Siteia had Greek names (Karantinos, Vlachos, Strategos, Moschos, Trichas, Lardeas, Syropoulos, Chandakitis, Lambropoulos, Mavraganos, and others).

This radical change in the structure of Cretan society was a source of concern to the more traditional Venetians, but they were unable to turn back the tide. Besides the other dangers that Venice was now facing, it had also passed into a phase of economic and political decline. It was in vain that the Provveditor General Giacomo Foscarini (1575) pointed out to Venice in his report the dangers that lay hidden in these developments, and he believed that the main culprits for this state of affairs were the notaries who were allegedly concocting contracts for the purchase of titles and fiefs. The old *nobili Veneti* had almost disappeared since, with their continued distribution and carving up of their fiefs, they become virtually impoverished. Only their names served to remind of their once great past. In the census carried out by Trivan in 1644, just twenty-five years before the Turkish conquest of Crete, a mere eighty-two *nobili Veneti* were recorded in the whole island (thirty-two in Candia, five in Siteia, twenty-seven in Chania and eighteen in Rethymnon). In the same census, however, 198 *nobili Cretesi* are recorded (eighty-one in Candia and Siteia, seventy in Chania and forty-seven in Rethymnon).

3. The hellenisation of the Venetians

An interesting phenomenon that was to have a significant impact on the formation of the new cultural character of Crete was the steady hellenisation of the Venetians who lived on the island. In contrast to the views of earlier historians, recent research has demonstrated that in essence the Latin element on the island could not very well avoid this process. In the first centuries of Venetian rule the differences between the two peoples were irreconcilable and Roman Catholicism had constituted the dividing line between them since this was the official dogma of the ruling class. Whoever embraced Orthodoxy automatically lost both his fiefs and feudal privileges. The situation changed with the passing of time and already by the beginning of the sixteenth century it is possible to discern the ascendancy of the Greek element. The Greek language was used even in official circles, Greek customs had given their colour to the Cretan way of life and the leaderless Cretan Church had nonetheless managed to keep Catholicism restricted to a small and insignificant minority. Marriage between Cretans and Venetians became ever more frequent, and many Venetians actually embraced Orthodoxy. By the end of the sixteenth century hellenisation had advanced to such a degree that the Provvidetor Giacomo Foscarini was alarmed by the fact that the Venetians of Crete could no longer understand the Italian language.

Those, however, who remained Catholic, began to feel more Greek than Venetian. They wrote and spoke in Greek and they admired the glorious intellectual heritage of the Greeks, which they now felt they shared. Typical examples of people such as these were the Rethymnon poet Daniel Fourlano, Thomas Trivizano and the Cornaro family. They are all distinguished by a helleno-centric admiration for their island of Crete. They felt deeply bound to the land of their birth and they were united by Cretan awareness. A new 'syncretism' had been created and it was on this that the intellectual and artistic renaissance of Venetian-ruled Crete was to be based. Horace's famous words on Greece's influence on the Roman empire could be said to apply to the case of Crete and the Venetians: Defeated Crete subordinated its conqueror!

4. Economy and trade

The foundation stone of the Cretan economy was, as it had always been, farming. During the first two centuries of Venetian rule with its continual social and political unrest the cultivation of grain fell drastically and the population of the island was frequently reduced to poverty and hunger. When the long period of rebellions ended and peace and order were allowed to prevail impressive increases in agricultural and livestock productivity led to the revival of agricultural exports. Fr. Thiriet, a historian specialising in Venetian-ruled Crete, has described the first half of the fifteenth century as 'half a century of contentment'. Economic development was to continue and reach its peak in the next century. The farmers concentrated their efforts chiefly on viniculture and the production of wine. Cretan wine 'malvazia' enjoyed a high reputation and was exported to many parts of Europe, including England. Some statistics are available to us: in 1512 wine production in Crete was estimated to be around one hundred thousand tonnes. About half of this was consumed in Crete, while the rest was exported (35,000 tonnes were exported through Candia and 15,000 tonnes through Rethymnon). In 1554 production in Chania alone reached 14,000 barrels.

The extensive cultivation of vines meant that the areas available for grain cultivation were limited. The Provvidetors, as part of the policy to try and make Crete self-sufficient in grain production, introduced measures to try and curtail vine cultivation. Cretan grain production at this time was sufficient for about eight to nine months of the island's yearly requirement. For the other months the authorities had to ensure the prompt importation of wheat and barley. If for some reason there was a shortage of grain in Crete, people generally went hungry from the month of March until the beginning of the summer when the first harvests of the new crop were ready. This is why the Venetian authorities attached so much importance to increasing local grain production.

Olive cultivation does not appear to have been particularly extensive during the first centuries of Venetian rule. A surprising piece of information is given by the traveller Christophoro Buondelmonti who visited Crete in the early fifteenth century (1415-1417): he records that he never came across an olive grove in Crete. In the next century, however, olive oil is recorded as being produced in significant quantities (240,000 litres in the district of Chania), which then went on to increase even more. In his report to Venice (1629) Francisco Moresini recorded that oil production was in the region of 500,000 mistata (1 mistato was roughly equivalent to 2 gallons).

Other Cretan agricultural products that were produced in large quantities and exported included cheese, cotton, silk, acorns (used for tanning), honey, wax, meat, timber (chiefly from the forests of the mountains around Sphakia), salt and saltpetre. Citrus fruits were also cultivated, especially in the regions around Chania and Rethymnon, and were exported in large quantities in the form of juice. There is mention in the sources that an attempt was made to start cultivation of sugar cane in the district of Chania.

The trade in Cretan exports increased greatly during the last century of Venetian rule. The Provveditor Francisco Moresini wrote the following in his report of 1629: 'Many containers of fine wine are exported from the kingdom [of Crete]. In a good year it can produce 500,000 mistata of oil and very large quantities of grape must and malvazia brusco. It produces shiploads of cheese; 80,000 raisins, 10,000 oldano (laudanum), 5,000 acorns. Honey in large quantities. As for salt, it can produce as much as anyone could want...' All these products were handled mainly by Cretan merchants, and sent direct to the European ports without the intervention or interference of Venice. There were Cretan shipowners and they constructed ships on the island from Cretan timber.

5. Professional life. The guilds

Artisans and professionally trained individuals were particularly active in the urban centres of Crete. Over fifty crafts, divided into various specialties, are recorded in the notarial registers and elsewhere: masons and wall-builders, woodmen, marble cutters, stone masons, carpenters, cobblers, barbers, tailors, saddle makers, bridle makers, hatters, cap makers, swordsmiths, bow makers, arrow makers, furriers, goldsmiths, locksmiths, ditchers, farm wall makers, chandlers, rope-yard workers, turners, pewterers, coopers, tanners, sausage makers and others. Other more unusual professions, such as that of the falconer, are recorded that were to become obsolete in the years of Ottoman rule. Doctors, perfumers, pharmacists, painters, haberdashers and sailers constituted special categories of their own.

The artisans and the workers they employed in these various trades and professions were organised into guilds or schools (scola) along the same lines as in the Italian cities, in order to secure the solidarity of their trade, the protection of their rights, improvements in living and working conditions and mutual aid for their members. Each guild had its own president and patron saint. The titles in the records are revealing: the guild of St. Ilias of the Masons, St. Joseph of the Carpenters, St. John the Baptist of the Haberdashers, and others. On religious feast days, such as the holiday of Corpus Domini, with an elaborate church procession taking place in Candia on the second Thursday after Lent, all the guilds took active part, holding their banners and flags.

The guilds also developed their own charities. In a document dated 1576 we read that the sailors' guild petitioned for the emancipation of slaves.

6. Compulsory labour

The peasants of Crete were obliged to offer their services not only to their feudal lords but also to the state, for the construction and repair of fortifications and other defence structures, the guarding of the coasts, and the manning of war-ships. Those who were obliged to carry out such works were all men between 14 and 60 years of age (huomini da fatti) and women of all ages. Of all the compulsory work that of manning the war-ships was undoubtedly the hardest. The exhausting work of rowing, the poor sustenance, the endemic illness and disease on board which usually affected the ordinary sailors, as well as the multitude of dangers that awaited them at sea (naval battles, attack from pirates and shipwreck) all provoked horror and loathing in the peasants. Compulsory naval service was for many the virtual equivalent of the death penalty. A popular demotic song of the period preserves for us, albeit in poetic form, some of the harsh reality of naval service:

A widowed mother kneaded out the bread for her son;
How she kneaded with her tears, and with laments,
How she lit the fire with the breath of a heavy sigh.
'My son, if you go to far off distant lands
and they put you at the oar...'

There were two forms of compulsory labour on the galleys: the soldiers (huomini da guerra or da spada) and the oarsmen (huomini da remo). The latter was indescribably hard work. They were chained to their benches and were obliged to row; any slacking was rewarded with the lash of a whip.

Each village had lists of those who were liable for compulsory labour. Those who were to work on the galleys were chosen by lot: they had to be between eighteen and fifty years old. We do not have precise numbers or information but some sources are revealing. In 1589 22,099 peasants were recorded in the relevant lists. In times of need the Provveditors General saw to it that as many rowers were enlisted as possible. For example, in 1570-1571 at the time of the Venetian-Turkish war the Provveditor General Marino de Cavalli managed to register thirty thousand more than the 7,000 who already served on the galleys. Most of these men (15,231) were from the *territoria* of Candia. In 1629 forty thousand 'strong men accustomed to hardship' were registered in the book of the Authentia.

The method of selection by lot is described for us in the report of the Provveditor General Philippe Pasqualigo (1594): 'On riding out to the villages the Provveditor gave the order for all those who were to be enlisted to come forward and present themselves. In this way the men of the village aged between fifteen and fifty would come along, and all those who seemed to be the most suitable for service were enlisted in the usual way. Then there was another step in the selection process according to the economic obligations that each man might have. Then they were rounded up in the barns or churches and when fifty or sometimes a hundred had been gathered they were chained up to each other in pairs so that they couldn't get away, and in the custody of the local noble and some horses they were promptly escorted to the galleys.'

The response of the villagers was only too natural and justified. Deliberate non-compliance with the authorities' decrees and escape to the mountains or to the barren islands close to Crete were common phenomena. Reference is even made to some despairing cases who committed suicide. 'At the time of this conscription (1594) some of the villages showed insubordination and the inhabitants fled to the mountains. Seven men in the village of Voriza were condemned to chains. Villagers from the villages of Pitsidia and Monochoro fled in boats to the small island of Gavdos, known as Paximadi, to the south of Crete... And this too happened: a villager from the village of Anopoli, who was selected by lot, in his despair hung himself by the neck...'

The fear and abhorrence of the villagers for serving in the galleys gradually led to an alternative system of substitutes. In other words, whoever did not want or was unable to serve in the galleys was given the option of finding a replacement who would undertake to perform his service in return for a large fee. The Greek texts of the period use the Italian term *antiscaro* for the man who acted as substitute. The modern place-name of Antiskari in the Kainourio district most probably comes from the *antiscari* of Venetian times. Bold adventurers, the *antiscari,* from both towns and villages, exploited to the full the unfortunate peasants who gave all they owned in order to avoid naval service.

The *antiscari* were not the only ones to exploit the peasants. The feudal lords also secured impunity for those villagers who were fugitives, thereby making them absolutely bound to the lord and his land. The historian Yannopoulos has written that 'Injustice, blackmail and exploitation of every kind were inflicted on the peasants when the authorities or feudal lords recruited for the navy's galleys. Many peasants, terrified at the prospect of having to carry out this dangerous service, if they had the means would sell a vineyard or a field or their animals at any price in order to pay the *antiscaro* fifteen or twenty tsekinia -a large sum for a peasant. The poorer villagers, however, unable to pay this kind of money, fled to the mountains and, once their lord had secured their impunity, returned to the village now totally subject to the power of their lord. They thus became an example to the other villagers, who by displaying the same total sumission to their lord so that he would save them from naval service ended up by being no better off than the lowest serfs.' In another duke's report, the following is related: 'The deprivation of the Cretan people confounds credibility. There must be few in the world who live in such miserable conditions. In order to buy off their services they give the little they can afford and then turn to the mountains and feed themselves on grass and weeds. And none of them hide their feelings' (ie. their hatred of the Venetians).

The phenomenon of the *antiscari* thus proved to be both detrimental to the economic standing of the peasants and to the strength of the Venetian navy. It was for this reason that many Provveditors suggested the abolition of the system of *antiscari,* though their words seem to have gone unheeded. It remained in practice until the very end of Venetian rule in Crete.

7. Other hardships of the Cretan people.

The institution of compulsory service was not the only hardship suffered by the Cretan people. Throughout the long course of the Venetian period Crete was also victim to a number of natural and human disasters, such as earthquake, crop failure, pirate raids and so on.

i) Earthquake. We are fairly well informed about the degree to which Crete suffered from earthquake. A large earthquake occurred in 1303 or 1304 and caused most damage at Candia. The walls and the harbour fortress were severely damaged. In 1353 another strong earthquake is recorded, this time hitting Rethymnon. The worst earthquake, however, to hit Crete occurred on 29 May 1508. It was described as 'the great disaster of Crete' in a verse by the Cretan poet Emmanuel Sklavos. A foreign traveller on the island estimated the victims as amounting to 30,000 souls, though this must surely be an exaggeration. Worst hit were Candia, Siteia and Ierapetra. The Duke of Crete, Geronymo Donatus stated in his report that of all the houses in Candia only four or five remained standing and inhabitable, while all the others were partly or totally destroyed. Western Crete was not so badly damaged. Chronicles and songs have preserved some of the terror provoked in people by the scale of this disaster.

Another earthquake is recorded as occurring on 27 February 1629. A simple memorandum preserves something of this dramatic experience: '1629. February 27th, Saturday of the Feast of the Cross, on the fourth hour of the day a great earthquake occurred on the whole island of Crete and houses fell and people were crushed and the belfries of the town. rang out and the earth groaned and shook and yawned wide as if it would swallow us up...'

On 29 September 1650 during the siege of Candia, there was a massive eruption of the volcano on Santorini followed by an earthquake which shook Crete. Marinos Tzane Bounialis, a poet of the town of Rethymnon described the event:

The world flared up with thunderous roars,
and Crete shook and the foamless sea did move
and for hours it did just swell and ever grew
until it razed the walls as if the foe were entering.

It swelled and swirled without help of wind
and the ships were dragged down into the abyss.
Ships and galleys were washed away by force
and swept and thrust across to Dia...

This huge earthquake has been compared with that which destroyed Minoan Crete in ca. 1500 B.C.

ii) Epidemics. More frequent and incalculably more devastating than the earthquakes were the epidemics -chiefly the plague- which seemed to have taken on almost endemic form in Crete. It is known that during the period of Venetian rule no less than twenty-two major epidemics of the plague with thousands of victims swept across the island. Entire villages were wiped out, never to recover again, and the fear of death kept the population in continual anxiety. Here we shall mention just two instances of the plague: in 1571 there was an outbreak of the disease which rapidly spread through the whole island killing thousands. A demotic poem of the period describes the disaster:

Sick became the people and sick the lords,
Danger there was that no one would remain.
So many did die that they couldn't bury them
something unprecedented in the history of man.
Death himself had not the time to fright them all
as they fell one after another.
The priest had not time to give them holy communion
and whoever fell ill was doomed to die.
Short breath became a grim sentence
and Hades wished to leave no one free...
It was not forty that died each day-
Thirty an hour were brought out on the cart...

The most devastating epidemic in the history of Crete broke out in 1592 and lasted, barring a few intervals, until 1595. The *territoria* of Candia was the worst affected. A chronicle note in a manuscript of the monastery of Apezonon presents us with a disaster of almost biblical dimensions. *'In the accursed year of 1592 a great visitation of death came to the island, death by plague and disease, as had never before been seen in Crete. A multitude died. This disaster hit Kastro (Candia) and the surrounding villages. Chania and Rethymnon did not taste of the evil... Two hundred and more died every day. They heaped up the dead unsung and without the proper rites like dogs. Fifty priests died in Candia... And many lost all their possessions because the houses were abandoned as everyone fled the town and went to dwell in caves and in holes in the ground. Many priests died, and doctors, the rich and the poor, to the number of thirty thousand or more. The lords were spared of this evil because they left the town and hid themselves in their villages in strong keeps so that no one would approach them there... We were most afraid then, for we learnt that the Turk was preparing an armada to fight Crete now that we were so few, having been killed by the plague. But God blinded him and we were saved from falling into his hands...'*

The general impression of the disaster is confirmed and intensified by a far more official source: the report of the Provveditor General Philippe Pasqualigo also gives a count of the number of dead. In Candia 8,600 of the total of 16,500 inhabitants died. In the countryside the disease struck no less than sixty villages and the victims were estimated to be about 5,300. Children under eight years old, Jews and gipsies were not included in the figures. The death toll was so high that, according to Pasqualigo, 'one saw fathers obliged to bury their sons, sisters buried their brothers, and wives their husbands'. The library of St. Mark's in Venice contains a book which has not been published in the modern period, with the title *Historia della peste nel regno di Candia, 1592* (History of the plague in the kingdom of Candia). After the disease had run its course the inhabitants of Candia built the church of St. Roccus who, according to western tradition, was the protecting saint against the plague, much like St. Charalambes in the Eastern Church.

The epidemics, however, did not stop there. Others are mentioned as occurring in 1611, in 1630 and in 1646. During the siege of Candia another epidemic was recorded for the years 1655-1661, adding still further fear and hardship to the sufferings of the inhabitants of the fortress.

iii) Crop failures. To the earthquakes and epidemics was frequently added famine, usually caused by drought, exhaustion of soil fertility, plague or war. As we have seen, Crete was never self-sufficient in grain production and, despite the policy of grain self-sufficiency that the Venetian authorities tried to implement, they never succeeded in dealing with the spectre of starvation. The situation became worse after the Kallergis revolt when the Venetians ordered the desertion of the Lasithi plain and Omalos.

The picture of hunger in a Cretan village in 1500 is provided in a letter of Gregoropoulos, where he talks of the bands of starving villagers who set out for Candia, naked and despairing, hoping to find relief.

A chronicler's note in a manuscript tells us of the great famine of 1591: 'Great famine came to Crete. The poor lived on birdseed and weeds, where not so much as a bean was to be found. The winter was harsh and followed by torrential rains that made sowing impossible'.

Another piece of information for the famine of 1655 comes from a note in a book of the monastery of Apanosephes: 'April 10th. I note this to remember that there was greater famine than ever, and people died from starvation, and dried bread and grain became astronomically expensive, if they were to be found...'

iv) Pirate raids. The Cretan coast was an age old target for the pirates who infested the Mediterranean in the Middle Ages and later times. The main perpetrators of this activity were the Arabs of North Africa, and above all the Barbary Coast. Christian priates were also active: the Maltese, the Genoese, the Pisans, the Catalans, the Spanish, the French and the Greeks all tried their hand at the art. As early as the beginning of the fourteenth century the Duke of Crete, Nikolaos Ziani, expressed his gravest concern to the Venetian Republic and recommended that the Venetian fleet be equipped and armed to deal with the problem of piracy. In 1317 pirate raids are recorded as taking place, particularly on the south coast of the island. Pirates from Algiers had made the small island of Chryse (today called Gaidouronisi) to the south of Ierapetra a base for their operations. Venice granted the island to Andrea Dandolo as a fief, on the condition that he build a tower and destroy the pirates' base. At the same time the Cretan authorities took serious measures to step up the protection of the coasts by means of enlisting the local population in guard duty. This was a compulsory duty and was conducted in watches.

In 1333 raids of Turks from Asia Minor are recorded as taking place. The Duke of Crete, Vlasios Zeno, organised the defence of the coasts with the introduction of an emergency tax for the fitting out of two galleys which would patrol the Cretan coastal waters.

The raids continued unabated throughout the following years, but from the mid-fifteenth century onwards they had become a grave problem. The pirates from the Barbary Coast were renowned for their savagery and audacity. A Cretan demotic song gives us a taste of the situation:

O Sun, you who race out and set upon the whole world
and rise upon the whole world of men,
do not, please, rise upon the the courts of Barbary,
and if you do, kind Sun, please set quickly,
for they have handsome slaves, with a mighty grudge,
and your rays will slash
wherever the slaves let their sad eyes fall.

There is some evidence to suggest that the Cretan harbours were markets for the slave trade in the fourteenth and fifteenth centuries, a phenomenon that was tolerated by the Venetian authorities. In 1522 pirates plundered the coast around Ierapetra and in 1527 they even entered the harbour of Chania and seized two ships that were anchored there.

Ten years later Barbarossa, perhaps the most infamous pirate of all time, arrived on the scene. In June 1538 with a massive fleet of eighty ships he began his raids on the Aegean islands, before turning on Crete. The activities of Barbarossa should be seen within the context of the campaigns of the fourth Venetian-Turkish war. Having failed to take Chania, Rethymnon and Candia, he turned his efforts to Siteia which was not well fortified. He succeeded in breaching the walls and plundered the town mercilessly, along with many villages in the district. Thousands of Cretans were taken captive and sold in the slave markets of the Barbary Coast.

The activity of Barbarossa was later continued by the equally feared Dragoutis who laid waste the villages around Apokoronas and Rethymnon in 1562. A devastating raid was carried out shortly afterwards by Uluç Ali, a beylerbey of Algiers. On 14 June 1571 he plundered the villages around Mylopotamos and then attacked Rethymnon whose terrified inhabitants had already deserted the town when he arrived. The looting that went on in the undefended town was indescribable. A Venetian wrote afterwards of the atrocities carried out by the raiders: they looted the churches, they burnt public and private buildings, they even opened the tombs of the dead in the hope of finding money and hidden treasure. Damage to the town was so great that the Venetian authorities decided to fortify it more strongly by constructing the castle of Fortetsa on the hill of Palaikastro. Alvise Lando, rector of Rethymnon and founder of the castle, described the destruction of his town in his report.

In the same summer the Turkish fleet descended on the region of Apokoronas. An anonymous Cretan wrote the following verse on the cover of a manuscript describing the event:

1571: *On the fifteenth of the month of June,*
on the day of Friday, before Saturday,
the fleet of the Turks came to the port of Suda
and burnt and looted the villages and towns
of the proud and lofty isle of Crete.

The Turks tried to win the support, or at least the neutrality, of the Orthodox Cretans, intensifying the terror by firing messages on arrows into the town before the attack. One such announcement that was shot into Rethymnon in the summer of 1571 said the following: 'Poor souls, do not fight, for we will not give you cause for lament, and neither will we take your possessions or approach your women; everything will remain in your hands. If, however, you fight, we will flay you alive, we will commit all manner of shame on your women and your lives will be ours to do with as we please. This is why we inform you of our intentions so that you can decide for your own good'.

A dramatic account, which most probably relates the occasion of the raid by Uluç Ali on Mylopotamos, is preserved on the founder's plaque built into the wall of the church of the Virgin in the village of Skepasti, near Mylopotamos. The inscription runs as follows: *'1592, the fifth indiction, March 3rd: the holy church of the All-holy Virgin was founded by commission of the priest Nikodimos of Tarmaros whose wife was lost to him as a slave twenty-eight years old and came in 1600, the Christian Easter, March 23rd'*. A local legend, which survives until today, preserves the account of her capture.

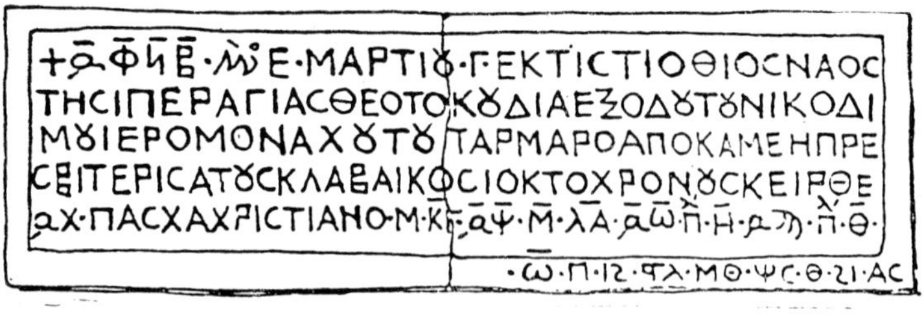

Figure 10
Founder's inscription, Skepasti, Mylopotamos. G. Gerola, *Monumenti Veneti IV*, 484, no. 12.

Slaves were a precious commodity for the pirates. The traveller Pierre Belon, who visited Crete in the mid-sixteenth century (1546-1549) mentions, among other things, the prices of the slaves in the slave markets of the East. The price of a beautiful woman was eighty to one hundred ducats, while the price of an old woman was just thirty to forty ducats. A strong man could be sold for as much as sixty ducats. A youth could fetch forty to fifty ducats. Recent research in the state archives of Venice has brought to light interesting legal documents which refer to the purchase of slaves from the Turkish pirates. They are fascinating evidence of an ever-present drama. It appears from the documents that the search for slaves and the possibility of buying them back from slavery was a family matter. The relatives of the slave, whether parents, brothers, husbands or wives sold whatever they had in order to gather the required sum of money. In the southern Peloponnese (Coron and Monemvasia) a kind of search office was set up for buying off captives, in return, of course, for a large sum of money. It was to agents such as these that the Cretans and other islanders resorted, agreeing to the most outrageous of terms, in order to try and recover their loved ones. A vivid account is preserved in a document dated 29 July 1562 contained in a notarial register of Michael Maras in Candia: 'Two years ago Turkish corsairs took captive the wife of George Tzabanis, son of Stergios, brother of me, Konstantis Tzabanis, and the aforesaid George wishes to go and find and buy back his wife; but unable to afford this enterprise he has come to you, Ioannis Papadopoulos, of Nikolas, from the village of Malia, requesting that you give him sufficient money for him to go and recover his wife from the hands of the infidel; and you, Ioannis, wishing to help as much as you can, but not having enough ready money, gave him two gold rings, which you sold to Dimiris Diplaras for the sum of eleven gold ducats... With this sum George, the brother of the aforementioned Konstantis Tabanis went and bought back his wife, but on his return to Crete, both he and his wife were captured by Turk corsairs, and we no longer know where they are to be found...' The brother of George undertook to pay off the debt that was owed by his lost brother.

We know that in the Ionian islands special funds were set up for the repurchase of captured relatives. These funds were based on the voluntary contributions of the Christians, and a special tax paid by the merchant ships. A similar office or fund does not seem to have been in operation in Crete, however. It seems to have been common, though, for wealthy and devout Christians to leave a portion of their will for this social purpose. The noble Markos Papadopoulos, who died in 1603, included the following condition in his will: 'My inheritors and successors will undertake to give every year the sum of one hundred tzikinia for the purpose of repurchasing two Christian slaves, who desire no more and no less than to be free, from the hands of the Turks...'

During the years that followed until the final capture of Crete by the Turks in 1669 the pirate raids continued and even intensified. In the Provveditors' reports of the period we read of frequent and desperate requests to Venice for immediate and urgent action to deal with the problem. Piracy was no longer conducted only by the Arabs and Turks, but also by the French, Spanish, Italians, Maltese and even Greeks. In 1626 we learn of the case of a Greek sea captain of Patmos who embraced the faith of Islam along with his son and became a notorious pirate, attacking merchant shipping in the seas to the north of Candia.

CHAPTER VI

EDUCATION-LITERATURE-THEATRE-ARTS

1. Education and intellectual life

There is no evidence for the existence of schools in Crete during the first century of Venetian rule. It is probably safe to asume, however, that the Byzantine school tradition would have been continued at the numerous monasteries on the island, but the greater part of the people of the island, especially in the rural districts, would have been uneducated and illiterate. Continual rebellion and civil strife were hardly conducive to the flourishing of schools.

There is some fragmentary evidence which dates to the early fourteenth century, although it is hardly sufficient as a basis for generalisation. In 1317 the priest Michael Pediotis undertook to teach reading and writing of Greek to children in Candia. In the relevant contract his wage and gifts are defined according to the old Byzantine custom. This type of popular education, based chiefly on the musical text of the *Oktoëchos* and the Psalter, continued throughout the entire Venetian period in Crete, as is manifest in published documents of both the sixteenth and seventeenth centuries. Alongside the Greeks, in the towns, there were also Italian schoolteachers who taught both Italian and Latin. These latter teachers are ridiculed in the Cretan comedies of the last years of the Venetian period. The notaries who were obliged to draw up their documents in both languages, had to learn their terminology and knowledge from special teachers. A document dated 6 November 1645 gives us an idea of the education that a prospective notary underwent: studying for four years he had to learn 'to read and write Roman (ie. Byzantine Greek) and Frankish in the vernacular and not in the ancient learned Greek idiom or the learned Latin idiom, but simply vernacular, and not in a florid style, but ordinary and plain'.

The existence of bilingual education, chiefly for the Venetian children, is also attested by the poet Leonardos Dellaportas in the following verses:

Since I was just a child I have sat at school
Learning my letters, both Frankish and Greek.

This bilingual education at its higher levels, especially during the last century of Venetian rule, gave the Cretans the opportunity to read foreign works and to follow the literary fashions of western Europe.

We know more about higher education since sources from the late fourteenth century onwards become more plentiful and reliable. A highly learned Cretan monk, Athanasios, who corresponded with many other scholars of his age, had a school in Candia with a considerable number of pupils (1389). It was during this same period that the Cretan scholars and monks Neilos Damilas and Joseph Philagris were at their most active. In about the year 1390 we know that Joseph Philagris wrote his commentary on the works of Aristotle at the monastery of the Three Hierarchs in Kophina.

A considerable number of the dated manuscripts today held in the library collections of Europe are known to have come from Crete, a fact which presupposes the existence of libraries and the function of organised scriptoria on the island at this time.

We have already mentioned the career of Joseph Bryennios in Crete (1382/3-1402/3). A number of Byzantine scholars who foresaw the historical fate of the Byzantine capital had already begun to seek refuge in Venetian Crete before the time of the fall of Constantinople to the Turks. Such scholars included the pro-western theologian Demetrios Kydones, who died on the island in 1397/8, Manuel Kalekas (1399-1401), Maximos Chrysoverges (1399-1400) and Demetrios Skaranos.

The wave of refugee scholars to Crete increased during the years around the capture of Constantinople by the Turks (1453). These learned Byzantine scholars strengthened Greek education on the island by setting up schools and by teaching. The most famous of these figures was Michael Apostolis who founded a school in Crete and was closely involved with the copying and transmission of manuscripts. Apostolis and his son Aristobolos (later to become a member of the church orders with the adopted name Arsenios and to take up residence in Monemvasia) made a very significant contribution to Greek education on the island in the fifteenth century. A pupil of Michael Apostolis was Laonikos the Cretan who was to produce a printed edition of the *War of Frogs and Mice* by Homer. This movement of intellectuals to Crete was to produce a generation of Cretan scholars and learned individuals contibuting broadly to education, letters and the intellectual life of the day. This generation included eminent men such as Markos Mousouros, Ioannes Gregoropoulos and Demetrios Doukas.

From the late fourteenth century onwards the Cretans also turned to Italy for a broader education, and especially to the University of Padua. Many went on afterwards to pursue successful political or religious careers in Europe, or became prominent merchants in various branches of commerce. Others achieved distinction for their learning and came to occupy university posts in Europe. Petros Philagris was the first Greek professor at the university of Paris (1378-1381), later to become cardinal (1405-1409) and finally Pope, with the name Alexander V (1409-1410). In Milan Demetrios Damilas, a profusive writer, published in 1476 the *Grammar of Constantine Laskaris,* the first Greek book to be published in Europe. The publishing activity of Cretans was impressive. At the end of the fifteenth century Zacharias Kalliergis founded a printing house in Venice with the collaboration of other Greeks, while in 1515 he founded the first Greek printing house in Rome. Markos Mousouros (1470-1517), one of the most famous Greeks of the diaspora, was in Venice during this same period: he was critic, philologist, poet, editor, professor of Greek at the university of Padua and Venice, and collaborator of the famous Venetian publisher Aldus Manutius. He was also the first editor of the collected works of Plato for which he wrote a famous *Ode to Plato,* characterised as the 'finest example of eloquence and poetry in the ancient Greek idiom to have been composed in the period of the Renaissance.' Besides many texts of both ecclesiastical and secular literature, Mousouros also published the so-called *Mega Etymologikon* (1499) at the printing house of Zacharias Kalliergis, and financed by the Cretan Nikolaos Vlastos. This edition is prefaced by a short epigram composed by Moussouros himself praising the publishing activities of the Cretans in Venice:

Cretan he who edited. Cretan he who printed.
Cretan he who paid the costs, and I myself Cretan am.
The mild aegis-bearing Cretan among Cretans...

Following the fall of Constantinople, therefore, Crete played the role of guardian of the intellectual heritage of the Greeks. One Greek historian, Therianos, has commented enthusiastically that 'Crete after the disaster that befell Byzantium proved itself to be the heart of Greece and the firm acropolis of Hellenism. Renowned scholars, fine artists, eloquent poets and noble heroes went there and served to sustain and succour the unfortunate Greek people. The printing house of Kalliergis in Venice was in fact a Cretan workshop. Cretans polished the metal, Cretans laid out the type-set, Cretans produced the type-face, Cretans supervised, and Cretans took care to select suitable editions for the enlightenment of the Greek people; and finally it was Cretans who so freely gave of their money to ensure the successful publicaton of the Greek poets and writers.'

Elsewhere in Europe Cretans achieved distinction. Demetrios Doukas was invited by Cardinal Jimenes in Spain to teach Greek at the university of Alcala, and the calligrapher Angelos Vergikios in Paris was appointed to the post of chief librarian to Francis I of Fontainebleu. The distinguished Hellenist Franciscus Portos taught Greek at the Calvin Academy in Geneva (1561-1580). As professor Yannakopoulos has remarked, 'for over two centuries, from 1400 to 1600 and later, Crete exported not only select wines and olive oil but also a large number of learned men and artists who wherever they went in western Europe obtained important positions and high office. We find Cretans from one end of the Mediterranean to the other, from the monasteries of Sinai and Mount Athos to the Iberian peninsula, northern Europe, England and Russia. They were commissioned to paint churches and produce pictures of the finest art, they worked as secretaries, teachers and advisors to the western humanist monarchs, and they founded printing houses for the publication of the ancient Greek authors.'

Within Crete itself there was a significant development in intellectual and artistic activity, especially during the last century of Venetian rule. The improvement in living conditions, the development of the economy, the steady hellenisation of the Venetian element on the island, and above all the change in Venetian policy which, under pressure from the manifest Turkish threat, had to become more considerate towards the Greeks of the island, all went to create the necessary preconditions for the flourishing of an urban life that demanded intellectual and artistic commodities besides much else. What is more, easy communication with the West favoured intellectual development, while more and more Cretans went to study in the universities of western Europe, and above all Italy. Many of these scholars later returned to Crete where they established schools and attracted pupils. Today we know the names of many Cretan scholars who were members of Italian universities and later became teachers in Crete. Members of the Greek College of Rome (from 1576 onwards), such as Markos Moussouros (a different individual to the famous humanist mentioned earlier), Michael Melinos, George Logothetis, George Querinis, Frangiskos Gozadinos, David Dioscouros (or Dioscourios), Malachias Kyriakos, Markos Donos and many others all later went to teach in Crete.

The Cretan monasteries also flourished in this period, and many of them developed into eminent centres of learning, with libraries and scriptoria. The monastery of St. Katherine's of the Sinaites at Candia was perhaps the most famous on the island. A lot has been written about the monastic school of St. Katherine's, much of it verging on myth and lacking documented evidence. It was only natural that a school of ecclesiastical learning functioned in the monastery, as was the case with all large monasteries, but claim for the existence and function of an official school of higher education is not confirmed by the sources. However, a number of famous men of learning have been linked to this monastery, such as Ioannes Moresinos and Joasaph Dorianos, the teacher of the highly learned Maximos Margounios who later became bishop of Cythera. In his will Margounios left his large collection of books to the monastery 'for the good', he writes, 'of the monastery and of the Greek people in general'. A whole series of learned ecclesiastics, such as Meletios Pegas, Maximos Margounios, Meletios Vlastos (perhaps the same person as Meletios Makris), Gerasimos Vlachos, Meletios Syrigos and others who were all well-versed in ancient Greek literature (some were acquainted with Latin literature as well), were either members or abbots or teachers at Cretan monasteries. They all corresponded or composed or wrote poetry in classical Greek. These men may be taken as an example of how the Renaissance spirit, with its rediscovery of classical antiquity, also had its representatives in Crete.

Another example of the flourishing intellectual life on the island during the last years of Venetian rule was the institution of the Academies which were organised in the three main centres of Crete on western (and chiefly Italian) lines. They functioned as a kind of literary society, with select scholarly members who held conversations on subjects concerning literature and art, aiming to cultivate themselves intellectually and to follow the trends of the European Renaissance. Our knowledge concerning the existence and function of these Academies is based on research that has been carried out by professor Panayiotakis. The first of the Academies, known as the Academy of the *Vivi* (of the Living), was founded in Rethymnon in 1561/2 by the scholar Francesco Barozzi (1537-1604). It is the earliest known literary 'club' to have existed in the Greek world and the first manifestation of organised intellectual life in Crete. Barozzi, in his official speech on the occasion of the foundation of the Academy, outlined its aims: 'The Academy aims to achieve virtue and wisdom, the best and most precious things that can be given a man.' About thirty years later the Academy of the *Stravaganti* (the Extravagants) was established at Candia by the Venetocretan Andreas Cornaros, poet and writer of a still unpublished history of Crete. A short time later the Academy of the *Sterili* (of the Fruitless) was established at Chania. These centres served as the gateways for the movements of the Italian Renaissance and were to help the penetration of European culture into the island.

2. Cretan literature. The early period

The history of the literature of Venetian ruled Crete is generally divided into two chronologically and qualitatively uneven periods: the formative and the high point. During the first formative period, which lasts until the end of the sixteenth century, Cretan literature generally follows the trends of late Byzantine literature, characterised chiefly by didactic and satirical literature. The language is that met with elsewhere in late Byzantine vernacular literature, mixed with elements of the learned classical Greek language (appearing more often in ecclesiastical texts) and the Cretan dialect. The verse metre which is employed by poets is known as the fifteen-syllable, or 'political', verse, which to begin with was unrhymed, but from the fifteenth century was usually in rhyming couplets. Occasionally eight-syllable verse is also encountered.

The oldest examples of literary expression in Venetian ruled Crete are demotic popular songs, and particularly those known as 'akritic' (of the frontier), that were inherited from the preceding period. The new times and events of the early Venetian period gave rise to new demotic songs expressing the new style of life.

The earliest known poet of this literature is Stephanos Sachlikis, member of an important bourgeois family of Candia. Recent studies place his literary career in the second half of the fourteenth century. He is a fascinating character who gives us a picture, based on the experiences of his dissipated lifestyle, of Cretan society and manners of the age. In his poems we 'taste something of the tumultous life of the world and the underworld of a large town of the period, as was Candia.' In his poetry, some of which was written in prison, didactic and satirical modes are combined, not infrequently becoming wholly bawdy in tone.

A contemporary of Sachlikis was Leonardos Dellaportas (1350?-1420), again born of a well-to-do family of Candia, and who served in Venice in various posts and on various missions. Fairly late in life he was the victim of calumny and was imprisoned in Candia. While in prison he wrote a lengthy autobiographical poem with the title *Dialogue with Truth,* as well as a version of the Passion of Christ in verse.

Marinos Falieros (early sixteenth century) was a writer of love poetry, born of a hellenised Venetian family of Candia. His poems *Erotikon Enypnion* (Love vision) and *History and Dream* belong to the genre of dream-vision poetry. He also wrote admonitory and consolatory works such as the *Rime of Consolation, Didactic discourses* and a religous poem *Lament on the Passion and Crucifixion of Christ,* an elementary Mystery play.

In the early sixteenth century Manolis Sklavos wrote a poem with the title *The Calamity of Crete* about the terrible earthquake that occurred on 29 May 1508 which flattened Candia and other parts of the island.

The most important poet of this early period, however, was Bergadis (from the Venetian name Bragadin) of Rethymnon who was active in the early sixteenth century. His poem *Apokopos* in 558 lines of rhyming fifteen-syllable verse has been described as a masterpiece of the sixteenth century. This also belongs to the genre of dream poetry and its subject is an imaginary descent into Hades, a favourite theme of didactic literature in the Byzantine period. The poet, with a rare touch of lyricism and a rich, dense, evocative language, turns his subject into a paean for the joys of life and the beauty of this world. His brilliant detailed desciptions remind us of Renaissance paintings.

Bergadis was imitated by his contemporary and fellow citizen of Candia, Ioannes Pikatoros, in a poem with the title *Rime of Consolation*. This was also a vision poem of a descent into Hades, but this time painted in macabre tones and with terrifying descriptions that are a far cry from the graces and light touches of Bergadis. The poems contain elements deriving from many sources, both Byzantine and Western, religious and popular.

At the end of the fifteenth century the priest and monk Nathanael Bertos wrote poetry (chiefly in the style of verse homilies) in which he reviles the clerics for their violation of ecclesiastical rules.

Purely religious poetry was composed by George Choumnos and Andreas Sklentzas. The former, a notary of Candia at the end of the fifteenth century, wrote a work with the title *Kosmogenesis*, a lengthy verse composition (2800 rhyming fifteen-syllable lines) which constituted a working of folk traditions centred on the Old Testament. Andreas Sklentzas, a Catholic monk, wrote various other religious works, prayers and chants, and also translated into Greek the well-known work by Thomas Aquinas *Prayer for the Holy Communion*.

Gabriel Akontianos, the last representative of the Byzantine rhymed romance, in around the year 1500 wrote his *Rime of Apollonius of Tyre,* a Cretan version of a western medieval romance, that was itself based on a lost Greek original of the Greco-Roman period, and which was then received back into the Greek tradition via a translation into Greek in about 1400.

Antonios Achelis of Rethymnon described in verse the siege of Malta by the Turks (1565).

Besides the poetry by these known poets there are also many poems by anonymous writers which are generally held to be Cretan. These include *On being away from home, The restoration of Constantinople, Tale of Venice, The speech of the dead king, The fair tale of the donkey, the wolf and the fox, The rimada of the daughter and son, Lament for Cyprus,* and others. Many of these poems have survived until recent years in popular vernacular versions both in Crete and elsewhere.

3. The high point of Cretan literature. Cretan theatre

The last decades of the Venetian period (ca. 1590-1669) were a golden age for Cretan literature. The necessary preconditions for such a flourishing had been created by the favourable political, economic and social circumstances of the time. A developed and precocious urban society, with a distinctly Greek character, yet open to the influences of the European Renaissance, became the vehicle for a brilliant culture whose finest expression was to be found in its rich, vigorous and bountiful literary production. It was one of the greatest periods in the history of modern Greek literature. The main distinguishing feature of this period was the inspiration derived from Italian Renaissance literature. This influence, however, should by no means be interpreted as a slavish dependence on Italian models, and nothing can detract from the originality and freshness of these Cretan works. The instrument for expression in this literature was the local idiom of Crete which now came to assert itself as a literary language and attained impressive heights of strength and musicality. For the first time in the history of modern Greek literature a regional dialect elevated itself to such a degree that it became a literary tool of seemingly unlimited potential. The Greek philologist Alexiou has said the following about this literature: 'the great virtue of the mature Cretan literature is its perfect language'. The linguist G. N. Chatzidakis also claimed that the dialect of Crete may have formed the basis of standard modern Greek, if Crete had not been so unfortunate as to fall into the hands of the Ottoman Turks in 1669.

The earliest of the works from the high period of Cretan literature is *Voskopoula* (Shepherdess), a delightful pastoral idyll written in finely crafted eleven-syllable verse. The poet, however, remains anonymous. It first appeared in a printed edition in Venice in 1627, published by Nikolaos Drimytinos of Apokoronas, and it subsequently ran into many further editions. It was a popular favourite and it even became a demotic song in Crete and the other Aegean islands.

The finest products of this period of Cretan literature, however, were theatrical. For the first time since Late Antiquity we discover true theatre once again in Greek lands, as both poetry and theatrical action. It seems that the man responsible for introducing this genre to Crete was George Chortatsis of Rethymnon (late sixteenth-early seventeenth century), one of the first learned Cretans to attempt to transfer to Crete poetic and theatrical forms of the Italian Renaissance. His masterpiece is the work *Erophili*, a tragedy dated to ca. 1600. The work, whose immediate prototype was the *Orbecche* of Giambattista Giraldi, impresses not only for the perfection of its theatrical structure and the nobility of its style, but also for the craftsmanship of its language and verse. It made a great impresion on the people of the period, as is evidenced by the many vernacular versions which subsequently sprang from Chortatsis' original and which have survived down to this day in the oral tradition of Crete and other parts of Greece.

Chortatsis was also the author of a pastoral drama with the title *Gyparis* and of a comedy *Katzourbos,* which is both the oldest and the finest of the surviving Cretan comedies.

Two other comedies, the anonymous *Stathis,* and *Fortunatus* by the Cretan noble Markos Antonios Foskolos, have survived. The latter was written during the last years of the siege of Candia (1655-1656). Both are works of fine craftsmanship, although they do not share the brilliance of *Katzourbos.*

Towards the end of the period two other tragedies were written: *Zenon* by an unknown poet, and *King Rodolinos* by Ioannes Andreas Troilos of Rethymnon. The latter was published in a printed edition in Venice in 1645.

ΒΑΣΙΛΕΥΣ, Ὁ

ΡΩΔΟΛΙΝΟΣ

ΤΡΑΓΩΔΙΑ ΣΥΝΘΕΜΕΝΗ.

ΠΑΡΑ

ΙΩΑΝΝΟΥ ΑΝΔΡΕΑ τοῦ ΤΡΩΙΛΟΥ.

Con licentia de' Superiori, & Privilegio.

ἘΝΕΤΙΗΣΙΝ, παρὰ Ἰωάννῃ Ἀντωνίῳ τῷ Ἰ χμζ.

Figure 11
The front cover of the first (and only) edition of the tragedy *King Rodolinos,* published in 1647 (reproduced by kind permision of the Gennadeion Library, Athens).

The most perfect product of the Cretan theatre, however, must surely be the *Sacrifice of Abraham,* generally thought to be a youthful work by Vitsentzos Cornaros and dated to the early seventeenth century, shortly before the composition of *Erotokritos.* It is a developed form of the medieval mystery play with a clearly theatrical standing. The characters are impressively real. The lyrical tone, along with the fine language and poetry go to make it a brilliant work of literature, that is the product of a highly talented individual. The work was printed for the first time in 1696 in Venice and ran into many editions. It even circulated in popular pamphlets and was an extremely popular work throughout the years of Ottoman rule.

However, the supreme achievement of Cretan literature, and modern Greek literature in general, is *Erotokritos,* a verse tale that runs to over 10,000 rhymed fifteen-syllable lines. The poet was Vitsentzos Cornaros of Siteia, a writer of genius who has risen to the rank of national poet of the modern Greeks. Vitsentzos Cornaros, as a later Greek poet, Palamas, wrote, 'is the great immortal poet of the Greek people'.

From the point of view of the tale and its plot the poem is not particularly original. It is based on the medieval French romance *Paris et Vienne* which was translated and reworked many times. An Italian prose translation of the work is believed to have been the source for Cornaros, who also borrowed many other techniques from Italian poets, and particularly Ariosto. All these elements, in a new, enchanting combination were given Greek form and adapted to the rich world of the poet and his sensitivity. Today *Erotokritos* is justly held to be one of the outstanding works of the European Renaissance. As Alexiou, the recent editor of Cornaros' work has remarked, it is an 'enchanting combination of ideas, emotions, pictures and a fastidiousness and vigour of style and composition'.

Literary problems associated with Erotokritos and above all the poet and date of composition still cause debate among scholars. The most likely case is that Vitsentzos Cornaros was a hellenised Venetocretan, the son of Jacob and brother of Andreas Cornaros, an eminent scholar of Candia. Vitsentzos Cornaros was born in Siteia in 1533 and died in Candia in 1613 or 1614. *Erotokritos* may therefore have been written in the early years of the seventeenth century.

The arts

The Renaissance style in Cretan culture is also to be seen in the field of art, and especially in architecture and sculpture. The Cretan towns were adorned with fine buildings and other public and private works, attested both in our sources and by the remains which can be seen today. Chania, the second largest town of the island, had impressive buildings which provoked the admiration of visitors. An Italian traveller of the seventeenth century compared the town with Capri in Italy and wrote that the buildings of Chania were similar to those in Venice. The Englishman William Lithgow counted ninety-seven palaces in Chania in 1632. The town also had thirty Orthodox and fifteen Latin churches. The church of St. Francis, one of the few Venetian buildings still standing, today houses the Archaeological Museum.

Rethymnon had a similar appearance. A superb fountain, built by the rector A. Rimondi in 1629, the famous Lodge (late 16th or early 17th century), the clock tower and the Porta Guora are the most impressive monuments of the town.

The Venetian monuments of Candia, capital of the kingdom of Crete, were of even greater importance. Again, the most imposing and elegant building was the Lodge, a fine example of the Palladian style, built in 1626 to 1628 by the Provveditor Francesco Morosini. The restoration of the monument confirms its reputation as the most beautiful building of Crete. Morosini also managed to have his name associated with the famous aquaduct that terminated at the Fountain of Morosini (built 1628), which is still standing. Besides solving the problem of water supply for the town of Candia, it also served as an attractive work of art and adornment of the town.

Figure 12
Drawing of the Lodge of Rethymnon (G. Gerola, *Monumenti Veneti* III, 64, fig. 29).

The general Renaissance style also influenced to some degree Orthodox monastic architecture. At two large monasteries in Crete, at Arkadi and at Holy Trinity of Tzagarolon, there is clear evidence of Renaissance influence, chiefly in the decorative features on the façade with their Greco-Roman columns and other features of the Gothic style.

Cretan painting

The painting of portable icons and of frescoes was a highly cultivated and much practised art in Crete and it developed specific aesthetic rules. Early examples of this sacred art, which continued the Byzantine tradition without interruption, have not survived in Crete. In the strife of the rebellions of the thirteenth and fourteenth centuries many priceless works of art were destroyed. For some of these we have historical and literary evidence that furnishes us with information. It is known, for example that, already from the beginning of the eleventh century, with the reorganisation of monastic life and institutions on the island by Saint John Xenos, portable icons were brought to Crete from Constantinople. Also it is probably safe to assume that painters came to Crete from the Byzantine capital at times when it provided a safe haven for inhabitants of the frequntly beleaguered imperial capital. One example of this earlier period of art in Crete is the portable icon of the Virgin at Mesopantitissa, a work that is undoubtedly Constantinopolitan and had been deposited in the church of St. Titus in Candia and was a highly revered object by the faithful throughout the period of Venetian rule. This is one of the few works of art that the Venetians managed to save after the conquest by the Turks and which is now to be found in the church of Santa Maria della Salute in Venice. It has been dated to the twelfth century.

The first examples of genuinely Cretan art are frescoes. The oldest known church with frescoes is the church of St. John in the village of Stylos, near Apokoronas, and which is dated to the years 1271-1280. From that date until the early sixteenth century over one thousand churches were built and decorated with wall-paintings. These wall-paintings therefore enable us to form an idea of the evolution of the art of icon painting on Crete. The essentially provincial character of the art of icon painting on the island as it appears in the oldest churches, is gradually injected with features from the large Byzantine centres, such as Constantinople, Nicaea and Mystra. From the second half of the fourteenth century Cretan painting shows obvious signs of influence from the Palaiologan style, as displayed in the works of Ioannes Pagomenos who worked in west Crete. These influences become more marked in the following century and especially around the time of the fall of Constantinople, and they clearly had an impact on the character of early Cretan painting. Constantinopolitan painters such as Nikolaos Philanthropenos, Emmanuel Ouranos, Alexios and Angelos Apokaukos, Andronikos Sinodenos, Manuel Phokas and others, who came to Crete for refuge during these hard times, were the bearers of artistic influences of the Palaiologan school of art. There are some examples of this art style still preserved today in monasteries, such as at Vrontisi and at Varsamonero, as well as at community churches at Potamies in Pediada (church of the Virgin Guverniotissa), at Sklaverochori (Eisodia of the Virgin) and at Embaro.

Crete under the rule of the Venetians, and especially its towns, was open to western (Renaissance) influences which began to make themselves felt in Cretan art of the early fifteenth century. Indeed there are painters who can paint with equal ease and skill in both the Byzantine and the Italian styles. the so-called 'Italo-cretan' icons, indicative of these new trends, are unique. The number of painters who were working in the main centres and towns of Crete during the last two centuries of Venetian rule was surprisingly large. Research into the archive sources for the period 1527-1630 has brought to light the names of over two hundred painters working in Candia alone. Today we know that these painters were organised into guilds for the better protection of their profession.

Gradually, therefore, a Cretan School began to develop (16th to 17th centuries) marked chiefly by an academic perfection, subtle technique and a chromatic richness. It was in the Cretan School that the long Byzantine tradition reached its greatest degree of perfection, as has been remarked by the art historian L. Brehier. Supreme masters of the art of icon painting were Theophanes 'the Cretan' Sterlitzas, otherwise known as Bathas, and Michael Damaskinos. Theophanes was commissioned to paint the monastery of Anapausa (1527) at Meteora in central Greece and the monasteries of Lavra (1537) and Stavronikita (1545-1546) on Mount Athos. He was largely responsible for transmitting the artistic techniques of the Cretan School outside Crete, and his extensive and imposing style became a model for monastic church painting throughout the Orthodox East.

While Theophanes spread the style of Cretan painting within the sphere of wall-painting, Michael Damaskinos painted mainly portable icons, of which a considerable number survive today in museums and collections. With Damaskinos the Cretan School reached its zenith. It is in the art of Damaskinos that we see the blending of the conservative Byzantine tradition with the influence of Italian painting. Damaskinos was undoubtedly influenced by the Italian style during his long stay in Venice, where he decorated the representation of the twelve great church festivals on the iconostasis of the church of S. Georgio. Another important Cretan painter of the period was George Klontzas whose works, however, have not survived on the island.

It was into this sophisticated artistic environment in Venetian ruled Candia that Domenikos Theotokopoulos, otherwise known as El Greco (1541-1614), was born. He is Crete's greatest artist, and one of the finest in the history of art. Today we know that El Greco was already a recognised painter before he left Candia at the age of twenty-eight in 1569. Crete was the departure point for his artistic career.

The fall of Candia in 1669 put a swift end to the glorious tradition of Cretan painting. Cretan painters of the diaspora, such as Philotheos Skouphos, Theodoros Poulakis, Iliou Moskos, Viktor and Emmanuel Tzane Bounialis, went to settle in other Aegean islands or in the Ionian islands where they also brought their art. They were the last representatives of a School which finally eclipsed with their generation. After 1700 one can no longer talk of the existence of a Cretan School of art.

Music

Music, both ecclesiastical and secular, was another of the arts to enjoy a high reputation in Crete. As the old cantor and composer Chrysanthos Prousis wrote: 'when the muse of psalmody finally faded from Constantinople, it was saved in the churches of the Peloponnese and Crete'. Psaltes -Orthodox church cantors- were also among those who fled to safety in Crete, judging by the names that are recorded, after the fall of Constantinople in 1453. In Crete a specific style of ecclesiastical chant was developed which, having been given the name 'Cretan Chant' later passed on to Zante along with the Cretan refugees who fled Candia in 1669. There in the Ionian islands this style of music survived until relatively recent years. Today we know the names of many *Protopsaltes* (leading cantors) in Candia and the other centres on Crete, who are mentioned in the sources as being great practioners of their art.

Recent research by Panayiotakis has expanded our knowledge of the history of secular music. Of these secular musicians the most famous seems to have been Frangiskos Leontaritis (ca. 1518-1572), perhaps the earliest representative of modern Greek music.

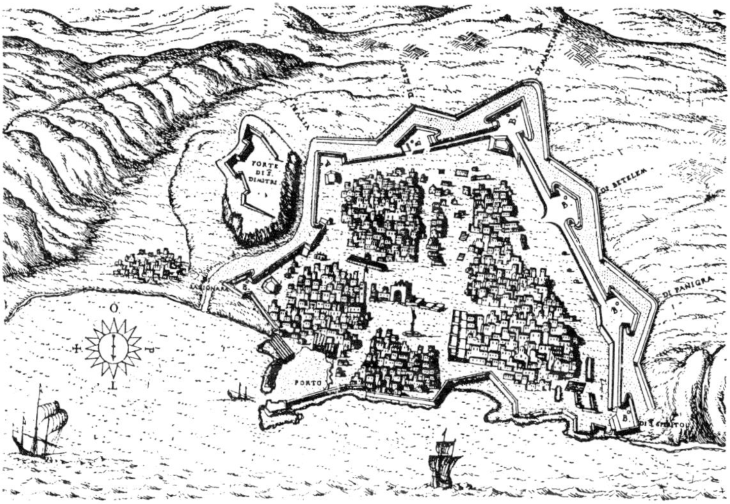

Figure 13
The town of Candia in 1651 (drawing by M. Boschini, *Il Regno tutto di Candia,* Venice 1651). It is possible to discern in the drawing the vast walls of the town with their frontal towers and the entrance way of the Pantokrator (Panigra), of Bethlehem (di Betelem), of Martinengo, of Jesus, of Vituri and of Sabionara.

CHAPTER VII

THE CRETAN WAR
(1645 -1669)

One of the major events of the seventeenth century was the Cretan War, a prolonged, bloody struggle waged by Venice against the Ottoman Empire to prevent the Kingdom of Crete from falling into the hands of the Turks. The contest soon took on European dimensions since many of the European princes of the period became involved in the conflict, especially during the last years of the siege of Candia.

By the mid-seventeenth century Crete had become the last bastion of the Christian East. Its salvation was not merely a question of prestige for the Christian world; it was a matter of extreme political and strategic importance, since it was to determine the boundary between two wholly different worlds and cultures. This explains why the war became the subject of detailed histories written by Europeans and Turks, both at the time of the war and later, and why it stirred passions to an extent seldom seen in world history. Alexander Komnenos Ipsilandis wrote in his work History of events after the fall of Constantinople that 'If this war had been followed by the poets of the past it would have exercised the quills of all of them, and Parnassos itself would have found material of greater import than the Trojan War; for whoever wishes to compare the two will find that the battles conducted below the walls of Troy were less bloody than those that took place in the war of Crete at Candia.'

Following the subjugation of Cyprus in 1570, Crete had remained the sole bastion of Christian Europe in the Levant. Its strategic position, its large ports and fortifications, and the quantity, wealth and variety of its products had constituted an age old attraction and challenge for the Turks. After the fall of Cyprus it was clearly only a matter of time before the Turks would turn their attention to Crete. With its submission they would achieve mastery of the entire eastern Mediterranean.

However, the course of political and military events after the sensational Battle of Lepanto in 1571 postponed Turkish designs on Crete for some time. The destruction of the huge Turkish armada and the political crisis that ensued in the Ottoman Empire, with economic and military collapse and with the reorganisation of the whole administrative machine, delayed Turkish expansion westwards for many decades. On the other hand, the Christian European princes, deeply divided among themselves by the Church reformation now under way and exhausted by prolonged foreign wars, were no longer willing to become involved in new ventures. This is why they failed to exploit to the full their victory at Lepanto. The result of this lull in activity was a long period of peace that lasted three quarters of a century (1571-1645), and which constituted one of the longest periods of peace that the eastern Mediterranean has known. It was under these favourable circumstances that the promising cultural flowering of Crete developed, a flowering, however, which was to be brought to a sudden and violent end in the mid-seventeenth century.

Venice and the Ottoman Empire in the first half of the seventeenth century

By the early seventeenth century the Ottoman Empire appeared to have recovered from its internal crisis and to have restored stability. The rise to the throne of the Sultan Murat IV (1623-1640), one of the most dynamic sultans in the history of the Ottoman Empire, was to inject new life into the empire and create new impetus immediately after the reorganisation of the army and the recovery of the economy. Within just one decade the Ottoman Empire felt ready for further expansionist military campaigns.

Venice, on the other hand, was plagued at this time by grave and incurable economic ills, which had begun to appear at the end of the sixteenth century and became more and more acute as time passed. Just prior to the Cretan War Venice was capable of maintaining a force of only four thousand mercenaries throughout the entire island. For the first time in the long history of Venetian rule on Crete, Venice no longer kept up regular payments for the officers and soldiers who served in its name: they were therefore compelled to take up various other occupations, such as that of tailor, barber and cobbler, in order to secure a living. The once invincible Venetian fleet had become considerably reduced in number, and the Venetians themselves seemed less and less willing to serve in the galleys.

Crete's defences were in no better shape. From the early seventeenth century the Dukes and Provveditors General were pointing out in their reports the weaknesses in defences and they made urgent requests that the city walls, aquaducts and cisterns be repaired, that new fortifications be constructed, and that the fleet and army be reorganised. But such projects were not executed. Another reason that partly explains Venice's nonchalence with regard to the Ottoman threat to Crete was that Venice was under the impression that any renewed Ottoman aggression would be aimed primarily at Apulia in southern Italy, and not at Crete. This was a victory for Ottoman diplomacy that had let out the rumour that they had designs on Italy itself.

Venice could have relied now on the Cretans themselves who constituted a civil guard of some 14,000 men at this time. In the face of the Ottoman threat Venetian policy towards Crete had become more relaxed and relations between the two peoples on the island were now close and harmonious. Venice, however, never managed to overcome its fears, and failed to appreciate the gravity of the situation: it was reluctant to give arms to the Cretans and let them take an active role in the defence of their island. The feudal spirit, however, which continued to inspire the attitude that Crete was simply a colonial domain to be exploited, died hard, even in the face of the final menace. Crete thus found itself both ill prepared for the conflict and faced at the same time by a historical dilemma, expressed eloquently by a contemporary Cretan poet, Marinos Tzane Bounialis:

Their clouded souls did fall from bad to worse
and little knew they who to fear the most,
the Franks or Turks!

The pretext for war

A pirate raid served as the pretext for the Ottomans to launch their attack on Crete. In 1644 the Knights of St. John of Malta, who during this period had devoted themselves to piratical ventures in the Mediterranean, captured a Turkish ship close to the coast of Crete which was carrying pilgrims to Mecca. The Turks claimed that the pirates took the captives to Chania and gave a part of their prize to the Venetian commander. Venetian historians deny categorically that there was any involvement on the part of the Venetians and assert that the whole episode was a premeditated Turkish ploy. Whatever the case, the whole episode acquired legendary dimensions since it was rumoured that one of the pilgrims on the boat that was seized by the pirates was none other than the Sultana, whose capture understandably stirred the Turks to swift revenge. The legend, however, was most probably created by ship's name 'Sultana', and the episode in fact had no connection with the Sultan's wife. Piracy was once again the cause, as it had been in the time of the Romans, for an invasion: this time of the Turks.

The Turkish landing and the fall of Chania

A huge Turkish force, consisting of 100 warships, and 350 transport ships carrying 50,000 men, of whom 7,000 were Janissaries -the Sultan's crack force- set out for Crete in the early summer of 1645. The commander of the fleet was Yusuf Pasha and the commanders of the army were Musha Pasha and Murat Aga. They landed on the island on 23 June 1645 close to the monastery of the

Virgin at Gonia, at the western end of the Bay of Chania, and met with no resistance. A few hours later they attacked the islet of Thodoros which was defended by a small garrison commanded by a Venetian, Julian. After a desperate four hour struggle the Venetian garrison commander decided to blow up the entire fortress at the moment that the enemy breached its walls.

Figure 14
Chania. The so-called Rethymnon Gate (Porta retimiota). The Turks called it Cale Capi (G. Gerola, *Monumenti Veneti*, I, 461, fig. 267).

On the afternoon of the same day, plundering and destroying everything in its path, the Turkish force reached the edge of Chania which was already being bombarded by the Ottoman fleet, and the siege promptly commenced. The commander Cornaro and the rector Fenarolo were responsible for the defence of the fortress. The garrison consisted of eight hundred mercenaries and an armed civil guard of one thousand who were mostly Greek. The Chania garrison put up a brave defence in the face of constant and repeated attack and fierce battles were staged outside the walls of the castle. In the meantime the bombardment from the Ottoman fleet continued day and night. The Venetians attempted to create a diversionary attack by mobilising Cretans from the districts of Selinos and Sphakia, but it came to nothing. The disorganised groups of Cretans, led by Michael Kallergis of Sphakia and Loukas Barotsis of Selinos, were crushed by the numerically superior and better equipped Turkish soldiers. Yet even in these early days of the Turkish presence on the island bands of irregular soldiers were gathering together: the Cretan resistance was already under way among the intractable country people. These rebel bands, who will be discussed in the next chapter, came to be called 'Haynis' by the Turks, and they are mentioned even in the very earliest of Turkish records for Crete.

The Venetians also attempted to mobilise a large force of Maniots from the Peloponnese, but this too was unsuccessful. The siege became daily more relentless and the stranglehold on the town tighter and tighter. The Venetian naval commander Marino Capello was powerless with his ships in Suda Bay and was in no position to offer support for the beleaguered inhabitants of Chania, apart from sending three ships with supplies. A note written by a scribe in a manuscript now in the Historical Museum of Herakleion accuses Capello of shirking his responsibilities: 'June 29th, 1646: the Turkish armada arrived at Chania, and general Capello offered nothing but a few supplies and anathema'. The Venetian naval squadron based in the Ionian Sea did not dare to attack the huge Turkish fleet. The people of Chania, now afflicted by hunger, disease and the ceaseless Turkish bombardment, were now in utter despair.

A considerable number of Greeks, and especially clerics such as the abbots Cyril Syrigos and Philotheos Skouphos, distinguished themselves for their bravery in this critical but fatal hour for the beleaguered island. The former with the help of one hundred monks put up a brave defence of Revellino, while the latter defended his monastery, along with thirty-four of his monks, before escaping to Suda. The Venetian reports of the time even mention the heroic contribution of the women who not only kept the soldiers fed and supplied but also even fought on the fortress battlements alongside the men.

By early August the situation looked grim. The besieged were still holding out against the Turkish onslaught, but the walls had suffered severe damage and the fortress was ready to collapse in parts. The suggestion that they surrender to the Turks was rejected as being out of the question. However, on 17 August the Turks stepped up the pressure with an all out onslaught that was once again held off by the defenders, but at great loss of life. Six hundred men were killed or wounded. Resistance seemed hopeless now and the leadership within the fortress considered surrendering on honourable terms. These terms were accepted by the Turkish pasha and the city was eventually surrendered to the Turks on 22 August 1645 after a two month siege. The few remaining soldiers of the garrison along with most of the inhabitants left the town for Suda Bay. Whoever remained in the town was sold into slavery, and the monasteries and churches were looted. Even the tombs were opened in the hope that they contained treasure.

The loss of Chania was the first major blow to the Venetians and a fearful omen for the rest of Crete. The Turks were now well entrenched in and within a short time they had subjugated most of west Crete, including the districts of Kisamos, Kydonia and Apokoronas along with their fortresses. The capture of the castle at Suda Bay no longer posed much strategic importance for the Turks, especially after 1646 when the Turks built their first fortress at Kalami. Chania was lost for good, and the various attempts by the Venetians to recapture it all resulted in failure.

The fall of Rethymnon

The next main objective for the Turks was the town of Rethymnon. Another large Turkish force of 40,000 men landed at Suda Bay on 2 July 1646 under the command of Deli Hussein, and immediately headed eastwards, plundering and burning the villages on the way. The Turkish leadership, however, had given strict orders forbidding acts of violence towards the Cretan population and requiring that respect be shown towards the property of the Cretans, in the hope that thus the Turks would gain the support of the native population. To this end the Turks were also keen to reestablish the Orthodox hierarchy on the island and appointed Neophytos Patellaros, a monk from the monastery of Arkadi, as the first new Orthodox metropolitan bishop of Crete. Political measures, however, could do little to control the zeal of the Janissaries. Marinos Tzane Bounialis has preserved for us vivid descriptions of the Turkish atrocities carried out at the time of the conquest of Crete.

The Turkish attempt to storm the castle at Suda failed, but the Venetian ships anchored in the bay were exposed to the savage bombardment of the Turkish cannons firing from the new castle at Kalami overlooking the bay. They were compelled to leave the port at Suda and seek shelter at Rethymnon.

The siege of Rethymnon began in late September 1646. Rethymnon had just a small garrison led by Don Camillo Gonzaga and Molino. The general command was in the hands of the Provveditor General of Crete, Andreas Cornaros. From the first days of the siege the Venetian authorities, perceiving the hard times ahead, decided to send a large number of the town's inhabitants to Candia (mostly women and children). These unfortunate refugees, however, were to find little relief since the authorities and people of Candia refused to give them shelter and drove them out of the town, mainly because of fear of the plague which had broken out that same summer. Their welcome was no better elsewhere during these difficult times. Itinerant, hungry and embittered they were frequently compelled to resort to seeking protection form the Turks. Marinos Tzane Bounialis wrote in restrained tones of frustration:

They found no charity in Candia,
but groaned again from like evil.
Words fail me when I think on what they suffered
but I accuse none, nor put the blame on anyone...

Many succeeded in obtaining favours from the Turks and later rose to positions of high rank in the Ottoman administration. One such case was that of Andreas Miliotis, who became Grammatikos of the Porte in Ottoman ruled Crete.

The descriptions of the siege of Rethymnon are distressingly vivid. Continual bombardment, lack of food supplies, and the numbers of dead and wounded made the town a living nightmare. Despite all this, however, the defence remained spirited and surrender was not as yet contemplated. The Turks fired leaflets into the fortress on arrows, inciting the besieged to surrender and promising their safe treatment after the entry of the Turks into the town.

Help and reinforcements never arrived. A small French naval squadron attempted to land troops but was compelled to retreat under heavy fire from the Turks. In a major assault launched on 11 October the enemy managed to take control of a part of the battlements and then open the gates of the castle. The Cretan garrison and a number of the civilians, however, managed to find haven in the castle of Fortetsa. The siege thus continued for another 23 days. A treaty was signed on 13 November 1646 whereby this castle was surrendered to the Turks. Some of the inhabitants fled to Candia and others to the Ionian islands. The fine town of Rethymnon with its enviable intellectual and cultural tradition had thus fallen victim in its turn to the darkness of slavery to the Turk.

The Turkish campaign continues
The march to Candia

The fall of Rethymnon concluded and consolidated Turkish control of west Crete, leaving only a few small pockets free by the end of 1646. The Turkish military plan was to steadily conquer the island thereby leaving Candia totally isolated. They were well aware that the final battle would be decided under the enormous walls of the great fortress that had the reputation of being the strongest in the entire east Mediterranean, and recognised as being one of the finest examples of medieval fortress architecture. The walls of Candia,

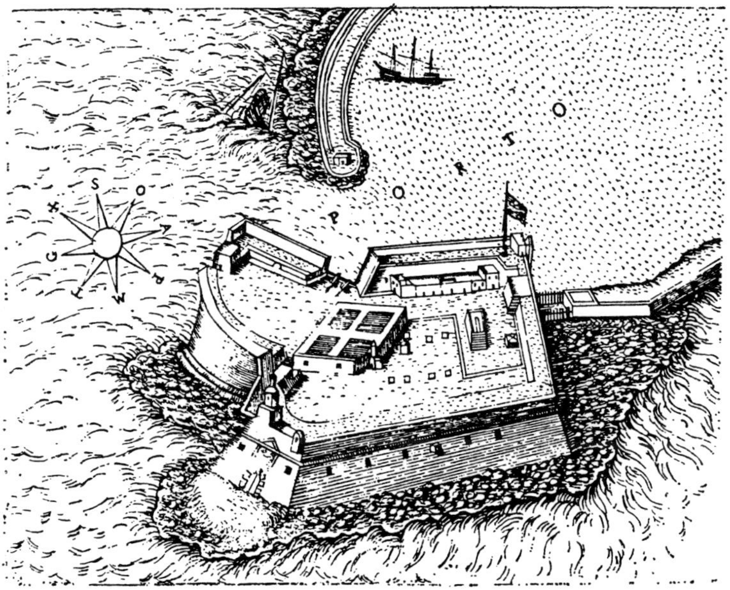

Figure 15
The headland castle of Candia (known in the Turkish period as the Great Kule) was built between 1523 and 1540, on the site of an older castle. It was one of the largest and most imposing fortificatons of the eastern Mediterranean. (Drawing by M. Boschini, *Il Regno tutto di Candia,* Venice 1651.)

whose construction had begun in 1462 at the point of the huge castle (subsequently named Kule by the Turks), on the headland of the harbour, were considered to be impregnable.

Just a month after the fall of Rethymnon the Ottoman forces had reached the district of Candia. In the spring of 1647 further Turkish reinforcements arrived on the island and occupied themselves with plundering raids in the villages of central and east Crete. The Venetians attempted to check the Turks with surprise attacks. Venetian forces landed at Mylopotamos and at Merabello, and achieved a certain amount of success under the leadership of the commander Gil d'Has. He was finally defeated, however, on campaign at Charax, in the Mesara district.

At the same time the Venetians tried to mobilise the Cretan population, and the clergy in particular who constituted a major force by exercising great influence on the peasantry. The abbot of the monastery of Agarathos, Athanasios Christophoros, was one such member of the Church who fought with outstanding bravery and, according to the account of Marinos Tzane Bounialis, set up the heads of Turks about the defences of Candia, to impress the Venetian general Dolphin:

And the abbot and the Greeks came out
carrying the heads of Turks who'd ventured in the town
and presenting them they showed their joy...
And they decked them out around the gate,
over the arch and all around so that the general,
Dolphis could pass by them...

After the destruction of Agarathos in 1648 the abbot Athanasios Christophoros fled to Italy, taking with him many relics and manuscripts from the monastery.

The famous learned ecclesiastical figure Gerasimos Vlachos undertook to encourage the villagers of Pediada and Merabello to fight the Turks. He also provided economic assistance for the struggle against the Turks and later fought on the walls of the castle of

Candia in defence of the town alongside his two nephews, Gregory Vlacos and Arsenios Kaloudis.

In the spring of 1648 virtually the entire Cretan countryside was in the hands of the Turks. Certain areas, such as Siteia, suffered unprecedented damage. The Venetians now had control of just three coastal sites: that of Grambousa, Suda and Spinalonga. The villagers were in a desperate plight, with their homes destroyed and their possessions seized, and now faced with the imposition of fearsome taxation by their new masters. It was indeed a grim time for the inhabitants of the island. There are accounts of villagers selling their wives and children and then disappearing or embracing Islam in the hope of improving their lot. Conversion to Islam, which will be discussed in greater detail below, was now already under way in Crete. If we believe the account left us by the traveller P. Richard, by 1657 some 60,000 Cretans had already embraced Islam. Bounialis refers to the phenomenon with obvious despair:

that many Christians to save themselves
did discard their crosses and lay aside their faith.

The siege

The siege of Candia began in May 1648. The Turks, under the leadership of Deli Hussein, set up camp in the district of Yiofyros about four miles west of Candia, and prepared for the last great assault. The first main attack took place on 2 July 1648, and was aimed at the castle of St. Demetrios, at the present day site of Analypsi near Herakleion. The assault was countered successfully by the Venetians and the Turks were forced to retreat. Having realised that their position was not entirely safe at Yiofyros the Turks organised in the summer of 1648 a new site for their base near Marathitis on the hill south of the present day site of Fortetsa, which they named Nova Candia. They destroyed the aquaduct which carried water to Candia from the springs at Agia Eirini, and they began to carry out attacks on the castle on a daily basis, accompanied by relentless cannon fire. The siege from the land was practically total. Candia was cut off from all directions apart from the sea, where for the time being they were able to hold off the Turks.

For no less than sixteen years (1650-1666) the siege of Candia seemed to be at a stalemate. The bombardments, the attacks and the counterattacks, all succeeded in producing weariness in both sides. The fortress, however, which the Turks began to believe was haunted, remained impregnable. The foreign wars of the Ottoman Empire in the northern Balkan region did not leave it enough leeway to assist the besiegers of Candia. The Venetian fleet, which had still managed to maintain superiority in the Aegean, followed closely the movements of the Turkish fleet and repeatedly harried its ships. The admiral of the Aegean fleet, Francesco Morosini, the later valiant defender of Candia, succeeded in inflicting very severe damage on the Turkish fleet at the mouth of the Hellespont in 1658.

In the meantime the war started to take on pan-European dimensions. Venice made repeated requests to the other European leaders for military support imploring them to put aside their various differences and conflicts in the case of Crete, and it succeeded in stirring up interest in the fate of Candia. European interest in the fate of Candia first manifested itself in 1650-1. Spain undertook to supply Candia with grain and also gave 154,000 realia and eight warships as part of its contribution to the Cretan struggle. In 1660 cardinal Mazarin of France sent prince Almerigo d'Este with 4,000 men. The prince's efforts to win back Chania ended in failure and the destruction of his force, as well as the destruction of the Cretan villagers who had risen up in support of the French. This disaster was further aggravated by a new outbreak of the plague in 1661. A few months later Almerigo d'Este died from fever in Paros.

The Cretan war was also conducted on the level of religious propaganda. The Turks promised the islanders that they would restore the Orthodox hierarchy to the Church in Crete and that they would remove the Latin prelates. As early as 1646 they appointed a Cretan, Neophytos Patellaros, as metropolitan bishop of the island.

The Venetians, in a somewhat meanly motivated about-turn of policy, also made similar promises to the Cretans in order to secure their support and loyalty. In the autumn of 1657 the ousted Ecumenical Patriarch Ioannikios II arrived in Candia and gave moral and spiritual support to the Orthodox Christians, declaring holy war on the infidel, and assuring the Orthodox that the killing of an infidel would secure them with remission for their sins! However, when he attempted to make the Orthodox church of Trimartyr the base of a new Cretan patriarchate, the Latin element put pressure on the Venetian authorities to remove Ioannikios from the island.

In August 1664 the Treaty of Vasvar was signed between the Ottoman sultan and Leopold I of the Holy Roman Empire. The Turkish forces were now relieved of their duties in Europe and free to support the assailants of Candia. Venice became alarmed at the turn of events and decided to prepare to send strong reinforcements to Crete. The recruitment and command of this new force was entrusted to the French general Chiron François, Marquis de Ville, who arrived in Crete on 26 February 1666. His presence failed to make any change whatsoever in the situation.

The Turks, too, had decided to bring the long and exhausting conflict to a conclusion. The Turkish commander-in-chief Hussein was recalled to Constantinople and beheaded (1666) and the Grand Vezir Ahmet Köprülü (meaning 'of Cyprus'), dubbed Fazil (The Just), was appointed in his place. A valiant soldier with immense experience in the field of war, and victor over the Austrians and Germans at Neuhäusel, Köprülü was to put both his reputation and his life at stake by undertaking to finish the Cretan campaign. He arrived in Crete on 3 November 1666 and took over the command of the Turkish forces and the Cretan campaign.

The Venetians, too, sent a highly experienced commander-in-chief and admiral to Crete in the figure of Francesco Morosini, the last defender of Candia and a worthy opponent for Körpülü. From this moment the Cretan War entered its last and most dramatic phase. These last three years (1666-1669) were to be filled with dramatic and momentous events. A true battle of the giants was to take place both on and below the walls of the Cretan capital. The latest and most powerful weapons of the age was employed and the flower of European and Ottoman soldiery was put to the test. The war now took on international dimensions and was considered a matter that concerned the whole of Christendom.

Köprülü began his action in earnest in the spring of 1667 when sixty-four Turkish galleys arrived in Crete carrying 40,000 Turkish soldiers from the Peloponnese. From this moment Candia entered its death throes, being daily bombarded by cannon fire that gradually destroyed everything and inspired panic in the people of the besieged fortress. Marinos Tzane Bounialis once again gives us a vivid picture of the terror that took hold during the final stages of the siege:

Stones rain down on me, and cannon-balls like hail,
Thunder and lightning leave nothing unscathed.
Destroyed my churches, and towers all felled,
as if a whirlwind would snatch me up.
No man went to sleep in his home,
No man could walk the streets without fear.
I am sorely grieved, for I, Candia, am adorned
with the bodies of dead Christians and am bloodstained;
Mute bodies lying in pieces,
heads, hands and legs scattered all over...

The Christian forces defended the town courageously and Francesco Morosini commanded the defence with the greatest earnestness and untiring vigilance. From November 1667 the position of the besieged inhabitants became much more difficult when colonel Andreas Barotsis deserted to the side of the Turks and revealed the weak points in the fortification's defences to the enemy. This betrayal was to be decisive for the course of the siege since the Turks now knew at which points they had to apply the most pressure. The Cretan oral poetic tradition has preserved the following song which refers to the treachery of Barotsis:

O Castle, where now are your towers and belfries,
where now your valiant and handsome young warriors?
-My warriors, my handsome young knights
are now the joy of the earth, down in dark Hades.
I have no quarrel with the Turk, with the decree of Hades,
my quarrel is with that treacherous dog
who betrayed all to them.

Barotsis was not the only one to desert. Despair and wretchedness led to increased desertion, especially among the crews of the Venetian galleys. The Turks made the most of the situation by offering large rewards to all those who deserted and went over to their side. It is recorded that Köprülü spent 700,000 gold pieces for this purpose.

The ranks of the European mercenaries fared no better. The difficulty that the northern warriors found in adapting to the climatic conditions, their disaffection because of the irregularity of their pay, the poor food and lurking disease, and above all the constant disputes among the leadership all served to weaken the defence of the fortress. The Marquis de Ville, who had conceived the plan to recapture Chania in order to bring some relief to Candia, had argued with the Dutch general Werdmüller (the cartographer of Candia); then his campaign met with failure and he was recalled. When he returned to Crete he was wounded and died shortly afterwards in December 1667.

Yet the castle walls remained unbreached. The defenders' hopes were raised when a new division of reinforcements, French mercenaries recruited by Venice, arrived. The French force of some 600 men arrived at Candia on 2 November 1668, only to be wiped out in an unsuccessful assault carried out against the Turks on 16 December 1668. Yet more reinforcements arrived in early February. The Holy Roman Emperor Leopold I sent 2,000 men, the Duke of Hannover sent 4,000 men, the grand master of the Teutonic Order sent 200 men, and Venice sent 900 Italians. Large quantities of food and other supplies also arrived as well as money to pay the mercenaries. A few months later on 16 May another force of 2,500 Germans arrived at Candia with Count De Valdek. Finally on 19 June the last noteworthy French force (6,000 men) arrived, led by the Duke of Navaille, generals Colbert and Bresse and admiral François de Vendôme, the Duke of Beaufort. Further reinforcements of 1,300 men and 60 artillerymen arrived on 30 June from Bavaria and Strasbourg.

The new high hopes were quickly dashed. The foreign commanders failed to agree among themselves on the best course of defence, while the losses were becoming increasingly alarming. In just one foray to the east of the fortress the French lost 500 soldiers along with the Duke of Beaufort. The total of dead or wounded French rose to over 2,000. Moreover, the Duke of Navaille decided to leave Crete (16-20 August 1669). The departure of the French left the besieged town with little hope of salvation. The commander-in-chief could see that the end was imminent. They maintained a valiant defence for a few days longer, but no one was under the illusion that they could hold out any longer. Morosini therefore decided to open negotiations with the Turks for the surrender of Candia.

The negotiations began in top secret at the end of August and lasted for about twenty days. Köprülü's representatives were Ahmet Agas and the Greek interpretor Panayiotis Nikousios whom the Turkish commander had brought with him for precisely this purpose. Morosini's representatives were a Scotsman, Annant, and the Cretan noble Stephanos Skordilis. The treaty, which was drawn up with the greatest of care, was concluded on 16 September and hostilities ceased immediately. The Venetian commander had twelve days to evacuate the town.

According to the terms of the treaty the Christian population was allowed to leave the town with whatever possessions it could carry. By 27 September the town was evacuated. The last Christian to leave the town of Candia was the German officer Christopher Degenfeld. It is related that just two old men and a woman were the only ones who did not leave. There were also a few Jewish families who remained behind. When Köprülü entered the town on 4 October 1669 he came across a ghost town, scarred by mounds of rubble. Morosini took the unfortunate inhabitants over to the islet of Dia some way off the coast of Herakleion, and from there they took the road of flight to the Heptanese (Ionian islands) and elsewhere. The poet of the Cretan War writes of the plight and troubles of the refugees:

If one took all the Cretans together, I believe
they amounted to little more than ten thousand,
for most had been killed or sold into slavery,
and scattered, O the unfortunate souls, to distant lands.
And if they meet, they know not each other, unless they ask,
'And where are you from, stranger?' Other opportunity
had they none to meet. 'Why, from Crete!' they would say,
and they would clasp each other's hands and weep...

It is interesting to note here that Morosini had the good mind to include in the terms of the treaty a special provision for the retention of the entire state archive of the kingdom of Crete. Five ships were loaded with state records and books, of which three reached Venice. The Venetians always held onto the hope of regaining their lost dominion of Crete and that they would need the information contained in the archives in order to restore the administration of the island. This was never to be, of course, but thanks to Morosini's foresight a large part of our sources for the history of Crete has been preserved for the long period of Venetian rule.

The cost of the siege of Candia in human terms was immense. According to a Turkish source, during the course of the twenty year siege 137,116 Turks were killed, including 25,000 Janissaries, 15 pashas, 80 çorbacis and 120 çavuss (high ranking officers).

With the fall of Candia the entire island of Crete was now in Ottoman hands. Venice maintained control of just three fortresses: those of Grambousa, Suda and Spinalonga. They were the last remnants of its once great colony, but in essence they were no longer of much value to the maritime republic now that so much had changed in the region. Their continued possession by Venice simply allowed the Venetians to hold on for some years longer to the vain hope that they might recover their lost kingdom in the Levant.

PART SIX

THE PERIOD OF OTTOMAN RULE IN CRETE
(1669-1898)

I
THE EARLY OTTOMAN PERIOD
(1669-1821)

CHAPTER I

ORGANISATION AND ADMINISTRATION OF THE EYALET OF CRETE

1. The consequences of the Ottoman conquest of Crete

The Ottoman conquest put a sudden end to the promising flourish of the Cretan renaissance of the seventeenth century. The island had been the only source of light and hope for the rest of Ottoman ruled Hellenism, but now it too was to suffer the same fate. The population was drastically reduced by the trials of the long Cretan War and by the mass evictions from the urban centres. Many of those who remained converted to Islam, a phenomenon that continued throughout the whole period of Ottoman rule. Town life, the existence of which constitutes a precondition for any cultural creativity, was devastated, with the destruction of the large urban centres of Crete that were subsequently settled by Turks. The French traveller Tournefort described Candia just thirty years after its conquest as the 'remnant of a city'! The Cretan economy shrank to an elementary form of agricultural and pastoral life, while trade, for at least the first fifty years of Ottoman rule, was practically moribund. To this grim picture the Ottoman conquest of 1669 was to add the imposition of extremely burdensome taxation and a host of other hardships that were now the lot of the Cretan people.

One of the more positive consequences, however, of the Ottoman conquest was the restoration of Orthodoxy on the island and the reconstitution of the Church and its hierarchy. The reorganisation of the Cretan Church was of course one of the permanent features of Ottoman policy by which the state could exercise influence over its Orthodox subjects. Crete was now cut off from the West, but rejoined to the centre of Orthodoxy -the Ecumenical Patriarchate- and hence with the rest of Orthodox Hellenism. As happened in the rest of the Greek lands the Church immediately undertook the spiritual and national guidance of the subjugated Cretan people.

2. The Ottoman administration

Immediately after the fall of Candia and the final, decisive conquest of the whole of Crete, the Turks applied themselves to the administrative and military organisation of their new, prized possession. To begin with they simply maintained the administrative system of the Venetians, with the division of Crete into four areas (formerly *territoria,* now *pashalikis* or *sançak*): those of Siteia, Candia, Rethymnon and Chania. Very shortly afterwards, however, they reduced the divisions to three, joining Siteia with Candia. And so the *Eyalet* (a large administrative region) of Crete was formed. It remained in this form for roughly two hundred years until 1867 when the separate region of Lasithi was set up with the secession of the four eastern districts of Crete.

Historians studying the period of Ottoman rule in Crete used to believe that Sphakia was the only part of the island which enjoyed administrative independence -with low taxation- as it had been placed under the special protection of the *valide sultan* (the Sultan's mother). Recent research, however, and above all the publication of Ottoman historical records, have overturned these older views.

Sphakia was granted as a *timar* (the Ottoman equivalent of a fief) to the commander-in-chief Gazi Hussein as a reward for their subjugation in 1652. Hussein then gave them to the holy cities of Mecca and Medina as Islamic monastic properties in 1658. The people of Sphakia were henceforth obliged to pay a sum of 5,000 piastre per year as Holy Tribute and they were not exempted from the payment of the poll tax which was applied to the bondsmen throughout the rest of Crete from 1690 onwards. The Sphakians, as appears in the relevant records of the period, initially protested at this unfair tax burden. But it was not until 1760 that, after repeated pleas and requests from the *hanum sultan* Fatma Hatun, grandson of sultan Ahmet III, who had been entrusted with the protection of the region, that special *firmans* (Ottoman imperial decrees) were issued relieving the Sphakians from some of the heavy taxation.

The main administrative centre of the *eyalet* of Crete was based at Candia. The Turks kept the historical name of the city in the form Kandiye. Each district of Crete was run by a Pasha (with the title sançak bey) appointed by the sultan. The Pasha of Candia was officially recognised as being superior to the other two Pashas of Rethymnon and Chania, and had the additional title of *serasker* (commander-in-chief) of Crete, as chief of the armed forces of the eyalet. He appointed the garrison commanders of the lesser fortresses of the island in the main towns of the smaller administrative districts. The districts (known as *kandiliks*) were under the control of the local Pashas. The Pasha of Candia had control of the eleven eastern districts (seven in the modern day *nomos* of Iraklion, and four in Lasithi). The district of Mylopotamos was sometimes under the control of the Pasha of Candia and sometimes under the control of the Pasha of Rethymnon.

In theory the Pashas were the official representatives of the sultan's power in Crete, the enforcers of his commands and the word of the holy law of Islam. Their most important task was the collection of revenue and its transport to the Ottoman imperial capital in Constantinople, as well as the equipping and training of an

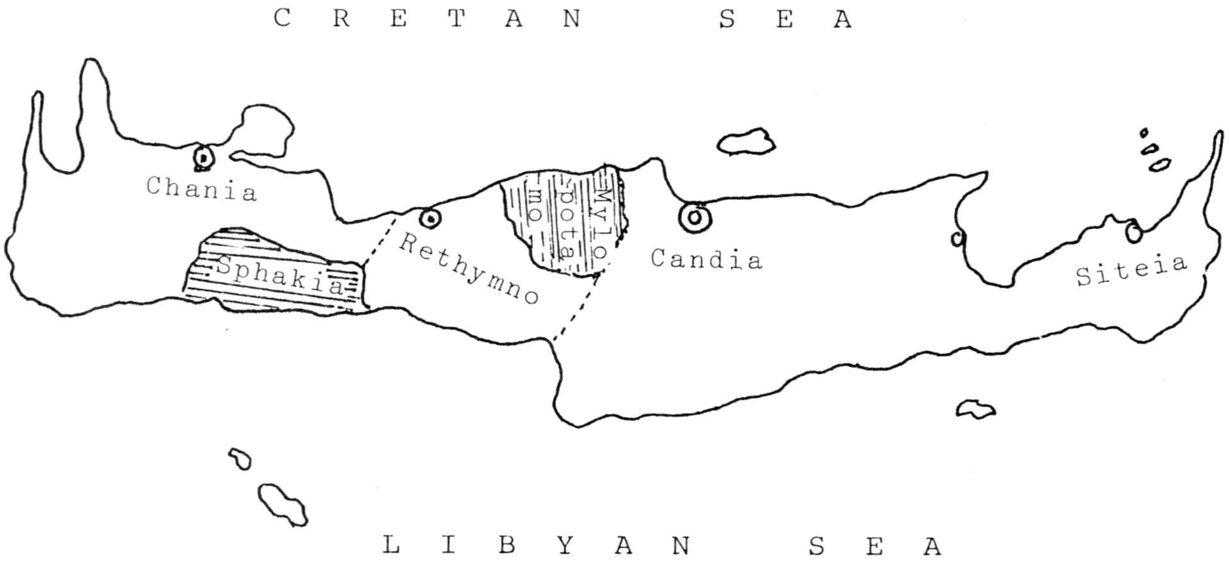

Figure 16
Map of the adminstrative division of Crete during the period of Ottoman rule (1669-1867). The district of Mylopotamos was subject sometimes to the pasha (sançak bey) of Candia, and sometimes to the pasha of Rethymnon. The Spahkia region was a *vakufi,* or holy dependency (of Mecca and Medina) from 1658 onwards.

armed and ready military force capable of maintaining internal and external security. In practice, however, their powers were somewhat ill-defined since they were constrained by the immunity and un-accountability of the Janissaries, who, with the passing of time, ended up by becoming a scourge to the island, and even to Ottoman authority itself.

Each Pasha had his own council, known as a *divan,* a small-scale equivalent of the Grand Divan of the sultan. The divan met regularly once a week, and could be called for emergency sessions if circumstances required. The following individuals were members of this council: the Pasha as chairman, the *Kadi* (Muslim magistrate), the *mufti* (expounder of Muslim law), the Janissary leader (*Janissar aga*) and the head of the military divisions. The sultan's decrees (*firmans* and *berats*) were read out and explained at the sessions of the divan and various decisions were taken on matters of local importance, such as administrative, economic, military or police affairs. Ultimate responsibility for the enforcement of the sultan's decrees lay in the hands of the chief-commissioner, the *sirturnas.*

The long distance that separated Crete from the administrative centre of the Ottoman empire, the fear of internal rebellion on the part of the island's population and, above all, the need for vigilance against the possibility of any Venetian attempt to regain control of her old kingdom kept the Turks constantly on the alert. This state of military alert was maintained for over fifty years until 1715 when the Turks seized control of Spinalonga, the last stronghold of the Venetians on Crete, and succeeded in wiping out altogether any trace of Venetian military presence from the area.

3. Military organization

The Ottoman military force on Crete consisted of two main divisions of Janissaries: the imperial Janissaries (Kapu-Kulu) and the local Janissaries (the Yerli Yeniceri). The latter were composed of Islamicised Cretans, the much feared Turko-cretans. The leader of the imperial Janissaries held the title of Janissar-agasi, while the leader of the Yerli Yeniceri held the title of Yerli-agasi. The administrative hierarchy of the Janissaries' ranks was particularly elaborate. At Candia there were five battalions of imperial Janissaries each composed of 5,000 men, and 28 ocaks (barracks) of local Janissaries. The same forces were also based at Chania for the control of west Crete. This system was maintained right up until 1826 when the sultan Mahmut disbanded the Janissary forces throughout the entire empire.

At the major strongholds of Crete and especially at Candia and Chania there were large weapons and supplies stores. The authorities were always careful to ensure that food supplies, and particularly grain and rusk supplies, were sufficient for the needs of the army. At both Candia and at Chania there were vast underground grain stores. In a Turkish document dated to 1753 it is recorded that in that year 9,131 *muzurs* (roughly 225,000 kilos) of grain were stored in the state grain stores of Candia.

4. The judicial system

As in other parts of the Ottoman empire, Islamic law constituted the core of Cretan law, based as it was on the holy precepts of the Koran. The most important courts on Crete were the so-called *mehkeme* in each of the regional capitals of the island. The *kadi,* or Muslim magistrate, had broad judicial powers. All cases of criminal, civil, succession and property law were handled by the *mehkeme.* The court decisions were recorded in special legal codices and this was sufficient to give the decisions authority and status as precedents for further decisions of a legally binding nature. It is worth adding that any order of whatever authority, including the sultan's *firmans* and *berats,* could only achieve validity and legal status by being recorded in these legal codices. This is the reason why surviving codices in Turkish archives constitute such a rich source of historical information: they not only contain records of legal proceedings but also official copies of orders issued by the Ottoman authorities. The cadi was appointed by the *chief jurisconsult* of the Ottoman state -the *seyhulislam* and was the highest ranking state functionary. His salary was largely borne by the convicted.

Besides the *mehkneme* there were also lesser courts at the main towns of the districts (kadiliks). These were equivalent to a magistrate's court, and settled cases of local and minor importance. The head officials of these courts were called Na'ip.

The procedure for the dispensation of justice was simple and was based on the sworn evidence of the litigants and their witnesses. The oath was legally binding for both judges and litigants. Christians swore on the Gospels and in the name of Jesus Christ, Muslims swore on the Koran and Jews on the Torah (Pentateuch).

5. The tax system. Land distribution.

One of the first concerns of the Ottoman administration on Crete was the distribution of land and the organisation of the system of taxation. Immediately after the fall of Candia in 1669 and the final subjugation of Crete a land census was carried out whereby the taxable population was assessed, after which the first regulatory tax decree was issued in 1671. A complex and grievously burdensome tax system -the most burdensome of all the Greek lands under Ottoman rule- was implemented in Crete within just a few years of the Ottoman presence on the island. Although our sources are scant for this early period it is possible to draw a rough outline of the principles of the Ottoman tax system.

Villages and property were divided into five categories. The first category consisted of the public property of the Venetians, which was now delivered into the hands of the sultan (*havassi hümayun*, 'imperial or state property'). The second category consisted of the temliks, ie. property that was granted to high ranking officials and functionaries, pashas and beys in recognition of the services they had offered the empire during the course of the Cretan War. This granting of land was conducted on the basis a special imperial decree (the *melikname*) issued by the sultan. The third category consisted of the smaller *timars* (or *ziyamets*) that were granted to military officers who had been charged with the task of maintaining internal security and order on the island. These were the military fiefs: eight in the region of Candia, four in Rethymnon and five in Chania. A fourth category included even smaller timars, known as *mukats,* that were granted to ordinary Turkish citizens who were under the obligation to provide particular services to the state. Candia contained 1400 such mukats, Rethymnon 300 and Chania 800. Finally there was a fifth category consisting of land known as *vakuf* (ie. a religious dependency). The revenues from the vakufs were designated for the maintenance of mosques and other public works or charitable institutions.

The cultivators of the land in all five cases listed above were the Christian serfs, former owners of the land but now obliged to pay a tribute. Any Christians who had managed to hold on to their property after the Ottoman redistribution of the land had to pay a special land tax called the *toprak vergisi*. The land taxes were a fixed lump sum paid on a yearly basis and were related to the total produce of the land and any form of goods produced on the land. These taxes were termed the *mukataa,* a word derived from Arabic of the Ottoman period. The land tax was fixed at a rate of 20%, or one fifth, of the land's revenue, double the tithe which had been imposed on other Greek regions. In reality, however, the avarice and whims of the administrative officials meant that this tax amounted to far more than the official 20% determined by the state. In a dramatic report sent by the Christian district representatives, dated to 9 January 1692, they accuse the tax officials of estimating the grain produce not at the moment it is collected on the threshing floor, but long before it is even harvested, thus making an arbitrary calculation that was as much as three times the true harvest, simply in order to reap in more taxes. Besides the official taxes there was a host of other taxes devised by the local Ottoman authorities for their unfortunate subjects. The peasants were thus obliged to provide the Ottoman officials with all kinds of products such as olive oil, honey, cheese, raisins, mutton, lamb, sheepskins, straw, firewood, poultry and pigeons. In the summer months they were obliged to transport 6,300 loads of snow from Psiloritis and Madares down to the towns for the production of cool refreshments for the pashas and agas. In desperation the peasants frequently attempted to avoid cultivating their land, but this led to worse consequences: by a decree of 19 March 1685 uncultivated farms had to pay a special tax based on the produce of previous years.

The Sublime Porte had in fact issued stern orders forbidding tax abuse on the part of state officials and it had few qualms about beheading offending pashas who had been proved to have oppressed the Christians of Crete. In 1694 Fidik Hadji Mehmet Pasha was beheaded and in 1728 the chief accountant of the island, Osman, was beheaded for oppressive tax collection and irregularities in the conduct of his office. However, it was only very rarely that the sultan's orders were actually implemented by his Janissaries in far away Crete.

The situation became worse after 1720 when a new system was introduced for the *mukataa.* While in the past the *mukataa* were put up for auction each year and awarded to the highest bidder, from 1720 onwards the life tenure of the right to collect land tax, known as *malikyane,* became the established method of tax collection. In other words, the highest bidder rented the taxes of an entire area for the rest of his life. This system was to prove disastrous both for the tax-paying subjects and, ultimately, for the Ottoman empire. These *malikyane agas,* or Ottoman tax farmers, grew into ruthless exploiters and masters of the people, concerned simply with acquiring wealth quickly and easily. They managed to amass vast economic power and developed into a strong force that came to conflict with the interests of the central power whose demands it grew to respect less and less.

It was not only Turkish officials who brought this oppression on the Christian serfs. The Christian district chairmen, and the Christian *grammatikoi* (officials) to the Porte often competed hard with the Turks for the distinction of most oppressive exploiter of the tax-payers. It is hardly surprising, therefore, that the Christian serfs were frequently compelled to submit petitions of protest to the authorities, and sometimes even to the sultan himself. In N. Stavrinidis' work *Translations of Turkish Historical Documents* there are many documents of the years 1701-1703 concerning the matter of irregular tax collection. Even Meletios, the bishop of Pediada, is sued, since as chairman of his district he over-oppressed economically his Christian subjects.

The Church of Crete had various specific economic obligations to fulfil towards the Ottoman authorities, whose burden, however, was borne by the Christian subjects. The Metropolitan diocese of Crete existed in return for a lease payment of 66,000 aspra, which were collected by the chief accountant of Crete and were delivered to the state treasury of the island as regular state income. Another 10,000 aspra had to be payed by the Metropolitan of Crete as a gift to the imperial treasury of Constantinople. In order to raise the above sums of money the Church had to impose a tax that amounted to 12 aspra for every married tax-paying Christian on the island.

Other forms of taxation included the so-called peskeks, which the archdiocese of Crete had to pay regularly to the pasha and other high functionaries on the occasion of religious feasts.

The most important and long-lasting tax which the Christian Cretans had to pay in money was a tax of tribute, a form of poll-tax known as the cizye. Immediately after the conquest of the island draft census charts were drawn up whereby the Cretans were divided into three categories: the wealthy, the moderately well-off and the poor. The poll-tax was fixed at the corresponding rates of 48, 24 and 12 drams of silver for each class, equivalent to 672, 336 and 168 Turkish aspra respectively. The first tax lists were drawn up by the chief accountant of Crete, Mehmet Pasha, and the beylerbey of Chania and published on 6 February 1686. These contained 26,720 tax-paying families: 12,700 wealthy, 9,850 of moderate means and 4,170 poor. The total revenue from the poll-tax was calculated at 19,019,712 Turkish aspra. However, since the collection of taxes by family was inefficient and created many problems for the tax collectors, it was later determined by an imperial decree issued on 19 June 1691 that tax would be paid by means of tax forms on which were written the name, surname and physical features of the tax-payer. The total number of tax-payers was estimated from the tax forms to be 18,046 in 1691, and rose to 21,900 tax forms in 1728 (1900 wealthy, 16,816 of moderate means, and 3,184 poor). This tax system was to undergo various modifications as time passed. In 1696, for example, after complaints that the method of dividing the subjects into categories was not working properly, all the tax-payers were lumped together into a single middle category. The poll-tax was then reckoned to be two gold pieces. In 1705, by a new decree, the sultan reintroduced the sytem of three classes. With just a few small changes this system survived until 1821. The continual rebellions of the Cretans after 1821 (the year the Greek War of Independence broke out) led to further changes in the tax system, until the poll-tax was finally ditched by the Treaty of Haleppa in 1878.

6. Ottoman-Venetian relations

Venice never forgot its former dominion of the Regno di Candia and it never ceased to entertain the hope of one day repossessing it. By the treaty of the surrender of Candia in 1669 Venice sought to hold on to, and maintain control of, the three coastal strongholds of Grambousa, Suda and Spinalonga. These fortresses would protect Venetian commercial shipping and could also serve as a base for any likely Venetian attempt to recapture Crete.

After 1685 the relations between the two sides became tense once again, with the result that war was declared between Venice and the Ottoman Empire. It was during the course of this conflict that Venice attempted to recapture Chania, whence it hoped to extend its campaign to regain the rest of Crete. In the summer of 1692 Venice sent the naval commander Domenico Mozzenigo to Crete with the order to try and stir up rebellion in the west of Crete and to capture Chania. He landed on the island on 17 July 1692 but his campaign was to last no longer than forty days. Mozzenigo began the siege of Chania. The villages of Apokoronas and Sphakia were incited to rebel and hundreds of Cretans, under the leadership of Ioannis Machairiotis, rushed to help Mozzenigo 'save Crete from barbaric slavery', as the historian Pietro Garzoni remarked. The expedition, however, ended in failure. The Turks had received intelligence in advance of the Venetians' intentions and prepared their defence at Chania with strong forces before the siege even began, while further reinforcements were mobilised from Candia in the direction of west Crete. On 7 September 1692 Mozzenigo retreated after a futile struggle and many losses. The villages of Apokoronas and Sphakia were destroyed by the Turks and 2,000 Cretans were forced to leave Crete and follow the Venetians to the Peloponnese and the Heptanese (Ionian islands).

Venice, however, lost its fortress of Grambousa. On 6 December 1691 the Napolitan Capetan della Cioga betrayed the Venetians and surrendered the fortress to the Turks in return for a large reward. He spent the rest of his life in Constantinople where he was known as Capetan Grambousa.

Venice managed to hold on to its two large coastal fortresses of Suda and Spinalonga for a while longer. Many Cretan families and individuals had sought refuge in these strongholds in order to avoid the Turkish yoke. According to a census of 1713 a total 582 individuals are recorded as living in the Suda stronghold in the most wretched conditions. Spinalonga seems to have had a similar number of inhabitants.

During the course of the new war waged by the Ottoman Empire against Venice for the repossession of the Peloponnese (1714-1715), the Turkish naval commander sailed to Crete and succeeded in capturing the Suda fortress after a siege that lasted just a few days (late September 1715); ten days later (4 October 1715) he took Spinalonga. The captives were sold off as slaves in the slave markets of Candia and Chania while the younger and sturdier of the captives were enlisted into service as oarsmen on the Turkish frigates. With the loss of these fortresses Venice lost all hope of ever regaining the kingdom of Crete.

CHAPTER II

CRETAN SOCIETY IN THE EARLY PERIOD OF OTTOMAN RULE

1. Ethnographic and demographic features of the island

As was mentioned in the previous chapters, one of the most serious consequences of the Ottoman conquest of the island was the fall in population. The mass conversions to Islam in the years immediately after the conquest reduced greatly the Christian population in the countryside. Unfortunately we do not have any detailed statistics, but it is possible to get a rough idea of the composition and size of the population of Crete from the various censuses carried out by the Ottoman authorities and from descriptions and estimations (although these need to be viewed with considerable caution) of foreign travellers to the island.

For 1671 we have the Ottoman source for the tax-paying members of the population in the twelve eastern districts (covering the present-day *nomoi* of Lasithi and Iraklion, and the district of Mylopotamos). The total number of people listed for the payment of the poll-tax was 16,516. If we make a rough reckoning of the proportion of tax-payers to the total population as being 1 : 4, the Christian population in the above areas may be estimated to have been around 65,000. It is worth noting here that the English merchant Bernard Randolph who visited Crete in 1687 wrote that he believed the population of the island to be about 80,000: 50,000 Christians and 30,000 Muslims. These figures may be inaccurate but they do at least tell us how sparsely populated the island must have become in this period.

The far more reliable account of L. Pitton de Tournefort, a French traveller to Crete towards the end of the seventeenth century,

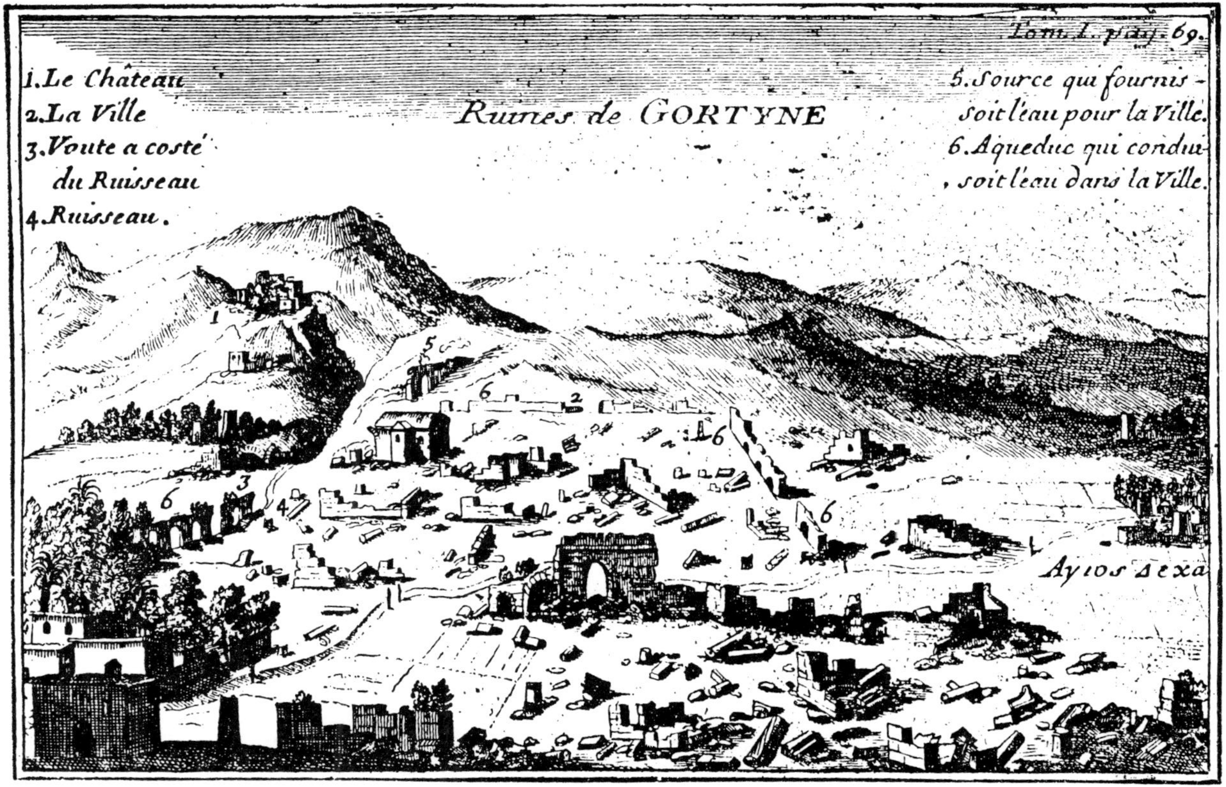

Figure 17, The ruins of Gortyn as viewed by the French traveller Tournefort in 1699.

gives us some details about the population in the towns. Chania had 2,000 Greek and 1,500 Turkish inhabitants as well as twelve French merchants and two Catholic monks of the order of the Capucini. Candia, however, shows a much changed figure: 2,000 Turks, 800 Greeks and a thousand Jews.

In the first decades of the eighteenth century, however, the population appears to rise significantly. An Ottoman source quotes the number of tax-payers as being 53,753 which corresponds to a likely total population of about 200,000. Again we should be cautious here because it is known that the Ottoman authorities had made efforts to increase the number of tax-payers very much beyond the instructions given by the sultan.

In about 1730 the population must still have been fairly sparse from what we can gather from travellers' accounts. After the first half century of Ottoman rule, however, renewed strength seems to be injected into the island accompanied by a steady increase in the population of the rural areas. By the late eighteenth century the Cretan population is reckoned to have reached about 350,000, according to travellers' accounts. The most interesting feature of these figures is the proportion of Greeks to Turks, estimated respectively as 200,000 and 150,000. Such a massive influx of Turks was a unique phenomenon for the Greek lands, even during the period of Ottoman rule, and it was a decisive factor in determining the lifestyle of the inhabitants on the island, and also of the exceptionally oppressive conditions under which the Christian population was forced to eke out its existence.

Greek sources for the period immmediately prior to the Greek War of Independence of 1821 give much lower figures: 113,320 Christians and 99,764 Turks.

2. Islamisation. Turko-cretans. Crypto-Christians

The problem of Islamisation in Crete is a vast issue. The general hardship and the burden of taxation and social pressures, as well as the indescribable ruthlessness of the occupiers frequently drove the

Cretans to denial of their faith and conversion to Islam. Mass conversions took place even during the course of the Cretan War, but after the final subjugation of the whole island and the consolidation of Ottoman power on the island the phenomenon took on unprecedented dimensions. Two main kinds of Islamisation took place: individual and group. In the first instance isolated individuals with a loose sense of national and religious allegiance converted to the Muhammedan faith in order to maintain their property, wealth and privileges. This was generally a very simple procedure. They had to recite their confession of Muslim faith before the Kadi and change their name. This act was then recorded in the Muslim religious codex. This kind of Islamisation continued throughout practically the entire period of Ottoman rule, right up until the mid-nineteenth century.

Mixed marriage also usually involved conversion to Islam. We know, for example, that the Turks who came to Crete did not bring women with them. Consequently they married local Christian women and made families, despite the fact that officially mixed marriages were not allowed. On marriage the partner was supposed to embrace the Muslim faith; if they did not, the marriage was automatically dissolved. However, it is known that many Turks, and, above all, Turko-cretans allowed their wives to remain Christian and practise their faith according to the dictates of the Christian religion.

The Islamisation of one member of a family did not automatically mean that the rest of the family had to change faith. It was quite possible for the father to be Christian and the son to be Muslim, or vice versa. Later repentance and conversion back to Christianity was also not unheard of. If one partner of a married couple converted to Islam it generally meant that the marriage was dissolved.

More serious social and ethnic problems were caused by the phenomenon of mass conversions to Islam. Entire villages changed their faith, sometimes along with their priest. This was the case at Selinos and Monofatsi where, according to the historian B. Psilakis, the inhabitants became the 'most religious and fervent Muslims of the whole island'. In some cases there is evidence that Islamisation was compulsory. The strongest motive for denying one's traditional faith and consequently one's national consciousness was calculation and personal interest. This is evident in the case of the villagers of Maroula, near Candia, who refused to pay their taxes in 1659 because they claimed that they had converted to Islam and consequently were exempted from payment. The French traveller Tournefort describes how over 60,000 Cretans had converted to Islam by 1699. The population therefore was Cretan by origin, language and customs, but Muslim by faith. These were the so-called Turkocretans who very often proved themselves to be more savage and cruel than the Turkish Muslims. The curious fact is that these Turkocretans had a distinct Cretan national consciousness, they were passonately patriotic and were strict in observing the local customs. In this respect it is interesting to note the declaration sent by the caretaker Greek government at the start of the Greek War of Independence in 1821 to the Cretans. The declaration attempted to secure, if not the full blown support, at least the understanding and neutrality of the Cretans in the national struggle against the Turks, by appealing, however, to the fact that the Cretans were a special case of Muslims: 'For your houses are besides ours, and you wear the same clothes as us, and you have the same boldness, and the same gait, and the same language. For all these reasons you must join us, so that we can all live together like good fellow citizens... For we ask you again to join our cause, for deep down you are not Orientals, or Arabs, you are rather true Cretans and you have Greek blood and you must abide by this...'

Some accepted Islam for appearances' sake, while secretly maintaining their Christian faith. They came to be known as the crypto-Christians. This same phenomenon was observed right from the earliest Ottoman period in other parts of the Greek world, both on the Black Sea coast and in Cyprus. Of course the official Church was unequivocally against the denial of the Christian faith. Yet there were some prelates of the Church, such as the Cretan Nektarios

Jerusolymon (1664-1682), who showed sympathy for the crypto-Christians and were known to forgive certain cases of Christians who made an outward show of observing the Muslim faith. A famous family of crypto-Christians in Crete was the Kourmoulis family of Mesara who converted to Islam in 1680. Immediately following the declaration of the War of Independence in 1821 they offered great services to the national struggle. However, the number of crypto-Christians in Crete was probably never very high. In the popular dialect the crypto-Christians were known as 'linen-cottons' or 'secrets'.

3. Community organization of the Christians of Crete

The system of local administration that was in force in the Ottoman ruled Greek lands and which was to prove particularly beneficial later to the reorganisation of Greek nationalist forces was never applied in Crete, at least during the earlier Ottoamn period. Our sources, even following the publication of Ottoman historical records by N. Stavrinidis, are very few indeed and cannot allow us to conclude that such a system of local administration existed and was in operation in Crete. A remark made by B. Psilakis that in Crete there were 'none of the local Greek representatives or community elders and *koçabashis*' such as existed in the rest of Greece, is probably close to the historical truth. A recently published Ottoman document, dated 10 September 1762, states clearly that town representatives (*koçabashis*) were appointed in Candia for the purpose of tax collection. However, such representatives do not seem to have been more widely present. One exception was Sphakia where, according to all the sources, there was some kind of rudimentary community organisation. In a document dated 24 October 1695 the names of various community leaders, or Kapetani of the villages in the district of Sphakia and community elders are mentioned.

One institution which became established in Crete and existed until the end of the eighteenth century was that of the *proedros* 'chairman' of the district, known in Turkish as the *kethüdas.* Each district elected its own proedros whose responsibility it was to deal with the affairs concerning the Christians of that district, to represent them before the Ottoman authorities, and to ensure the proper collection of taxes. It was a post similar to that of the koçabashis in other Greek regions of the Ottoman empire, though at district level rather than community level. The election of the proedros of course presupposes that each local community also had its distinguished citizens who represented it and who were responsible for electing the proedros.

4. The dragomans to the Sublime Porte

The institution of the provincial dragomans (interpreters), which existed throughout the Ottoman ruled countries (Egypt, Syria, Cyprus, the Peloponnese and so on) was also applied to Crete. These Interpreters to the Sublime Porte, as they were known, were local inhabitants who knew Turkish and who were appointed as official interpreters of the pashas and were naturally entrusted with the pashas' absolute confidence. Besides their role as interpreters they also had to work closely with the *defterdar* (director of finances) of the island on matters related to taxation, and they were responsible for finding workers for public labour and personal services for the Ottoman officials. They each had three Christian secretaries who helped them in their task and above all in the work of collecting the tithe tax.

In the beginning the dragomans to the Sublime Porte were elected by the district chairmen, but later their appointment was proposed by the Kadi or by the Pasha of Crete for consideration by the government. The residence of the Interpreter was at Candia although he had representatives at both Chania and Rethymnon. We have still not been able to reconstruct a full list of the Interpreters to the Sublime Porte in Crete. It is known that the first dragoman appointed in Crete was Andreas Miliotis from the village of Magarites near Mylopotamos, who had worked for the Turks from as early as 1646. Later, however, he was hanged in his own village by the Turks. The last Interpreter to have been appointed in Crete in the later Ottoman period was Lazarakis Jordanou who just managed to save his skin in the Herakleion massacre of 1821, disguised as a woman. With the outbreak of the Greek independence movement in 1821 the institution of Interpreter was abolished.

Most of the men who became Interpreters to the Sublime Porte, as can only be expected, were people of little national or religious loyalty to the Greek cause. They tended to be avaricious, mean and unhesitating oppressors of their fellow nationals and Christians. Many of the published Ottoman documents mention the irregularities and injustices committed by the dragomans.

5. Economy and trade

As has already been mentioned, with the Ottoman conquest the Cretan economy slid into a primitive mode. For the first fifty years of Ottoman rule it is difficult to talk of anything more than very rudimentary economic life on the island. The decline in the population due to excessive hardship, waves of emigration, and executions, the poor living conditions that excluded any possibility of creativity and above all the burdensome taxation left no room for the development of the Cretan economy.

The Turks were naturally concerned to reorganise the economy and commerce. Just two years after the fall of Candia they allowed the establishment of a Venetian Consul, Ricardo Contostavlo, on the island, who was responsible for overseeing Venetian trade relations with Crete. A French consulate was set up at Chania in 1674 with a vice-consul at Candia and an office at Rethymnon. Nonetheless, trade activity remained at a depressingly low level. Even in 1725 the French consul reported that the Cretans live in a most wretched state and that the whole island had not bought more than fifteen rolls of French cloth.

The product which was produced in the greatest quantities during this period was grain. Published records held in the Ottoman Archive of Herakleion and the French consulate reports show that Crete exported both grain and legumes to large commercial centres such as Bengazi, Tripoli, Rhodes, Chios and Euboia. During the time of the major crop failure in northern Europe in 1678 France bought grain from Crete. Salt was also produced in large quantities at the salt flats on Spinalonga (30,000 muzurs in 1672). Sheep and goat breeding do not seem to have been so active during this period. In the census of 1699 the eleven eastern districts are listed as having a total of 109,845 sheep and goats, and Sphakia as having 11,000.

From the early eighteenth century onwards there was a steady increase in trade activity, conducted chiefly by French shipping. The development of soap production turned the inhabitants interests to olive production, which suddenly boomed. Gradually grain cultivation gave way to other farming. The island was to find itself in the position of no longer being self-sufficient in wheat and it had to import large quanities from the capital, Constantinople, in 1715, Asia Minor and Euboia. Crete, however, was now exporting large quantities of olive oil to Constantinople and especially to Marseilles where soap production, for which olive oil was the raw material, was carried out. The soap industry also developed in Crete itself. The establishment of soap manufacturing workshops is mentioned in sources for the year 1696, but the number of such workshops seems to have grown dramatically after 1715. In 1717, for example, there were only two soap factories in Crete, in 1723 there were more than twenty, and in 1732 they had risen to over twenty-five; by 1749 in Candia alone there were twenty soap factories. Being profitable enterprises the soap factories belonged almost exclusively to the Turks. With the passing of time and the steady improvement in the standard of living there was also the appearance of soap factories run by Christians. In 1742 Candia had twelve soap factories of which just two were owned by Christians, while in 1749 there were twenty, of which seven were owned by Christians, and in 1765 there were eighteen, of which eleven were Turkish and seven Greek, capable of producing two thousand hundred-weight of soap a year. The quality of the Cretan soap was not particularly high since it contained a large proportion of olive oil. The French merchants preferred to buy the Cretan soap and then process it a second time in Marseilles.

Crete produced other select goods such as almonds, chestnuts, honey, wax, wool, raisins, silk, wine, and even rice, cotton and flax. The author of the work *Chorographia of Crete* (1818) discusses at length the plain of Mesara whose 'fruits not only go to feed practically the whole island, but are sometimes even exported to Malta and other islands.' The same writer goes on to say that 'the following products are exported from the harbour of Candia: soap, raisins, wine, carob, cheese products, almonds, flax, snails, silk and others which are all transported by Cretan shipping.' Other products not mentioned in the list above include medicinal and aromatic herbs and plants such as laudanum and saffron, praised highly by the foreign travellers of the time, as well as Cretan fabrics and embroideries, especially those produced at the island's convents (such as the convent of Paliani).

Products imported by Crete were sugar, coffee, rice, leather, fabrics, salted fish, and timber and metal goods. Most of these came from Constantinople, Alexandria, Marseilles and Venice. Crete also imported books -chiefly ecclesiastical- from Venice.

The general form of the Cretan economy during the earlier Ottoman period was agricultural and pastoral. The flourishing shipping activity of past times was all but forgotten. Only at Sphakia was there a small merchant shipping fleet which appears to have developed significantly in the mid-eighteenth century. This commercial and maritime activity of the Sphakians was to give a rare opportunity to the people of this part of the island to better the quality of their lives. These promising developments were to suffer a major setback with the rebellion of Daskaloyannis. Generally Crete during the period of Ottoman rule was not in a position to follow the naval and commercial developments of the other Greek regions of the Ottoman empire. The harsh living conditions were not conducive to the vitality and optimism necessary to engage in such activities.

6. Professional life - the guilds

The vast majority of occupations with which we are familiar for the Venetian period appear to have continued to exist in the Ottoman period. Chiefly in the towns and in the larger villages of the rural areas, besides the farmers, livestock breeders and merchants and traders, we also come across builders, blacksmiths, tile makers and potters, tailors, shoemakers, carpenters, painters, bakers and many others. Most of these occupations, being the most profitable, were almost exclusively carried out by Turks. In 1685, for example, thirty-eight bakeries were functioning in Candia, of which thirty-one were Turkish, two were owned by Cretans, four by Armenians and one by a Jew. In 1763, however, just eighteen bakeries were functioning in Candia, all of which were owned by Turks. The same was the case with the butchers. Seven are recorded as functioning in Candia in 1735 and they were all Turkish. The various ethnic groups tended to have a tradition in a particular occupation. The Armenians, for example, were builders, while Ethiopians were porters and donkey-drivers.

The tradesfolk in the larger towns were organised into associations that had their own rules and a president recognised by the Ottoman authorities. Some of these associations, or guilds, had a Christian president. However, they never managed to acquire the status and power which they had enjoyed in Venetian times, and they could not be compared with the much stronger guilds that existed in other parts of the Ottoman empire, such as in Thrace. Only in the later Ottoman period (1850 and after) did stronger guild organisations start to develop in the Cretan towns, with their patron saint and a special emblem.

7. Lifestyle

Under such grim living conditions it is hardly surprising that there was a general dissoluteness of morals. Theft, and above all rustling, was the scourge of the countryside (this had been the case in other periods of Cretan history). The towns saw an increase in prostitution. The authorities sometimes took steps to try and remove the prostitutes from Candia after complaints from the citizens of the town. Besides the prostitutes there were also the so-called *kapatma,* Christian girls who Muslims, despite the strictures of the Koran, took into their homes and with whom they had illegitimate children who were abandoned at the doors of the hamams and mosques. The following is an interesting and illuminating extract from an order issued by Kyamil Ahmet Pasha of Candia, dated 1 January 1763: '...the Muslims take into their homes and maintain *kapatma* -or *pesleme*- women without the sanction of a lawful marriage who are selected from among the young girls of the Christians and, being exposed to adultery, leave their illegitimate infants in the doorways of the mosques and hamams or they abandon them in remote places, where they are either devoured by the dogs or taken up by the reviled infidel and, having been transported to their churches, are then exposed to the eternal darkness of their faithless Christian religion...' This order was addressed particularly to the imams of the Turks and it accused them of being responsible for the spread of these cases of unlawful cohabitation. It continues: 'Search and discover the houses of those who are unlawfully living with an adopted non-Muslim partner within the town, and all those who show a willingness to enter into marriage let them proceed to wed with proper sanctity, whether the partner is a second, third or fourth wife; for those women whom the man refuses to marry and who are in an interesting situation (ie. pregnant), you must designate a sum for maintenance, and return them to their guardians or relatives. Whichever women do not wish to marry, yet do not wish to stop their relations with the man, or have nowhere else to go and are wholly helpless, you must hand over to their priests...'

This policy, however, of Kyamil Ahmet Pasha was not implemented by the other pashas of Crete. The evil continued and infants were still exposed, so much so that at some periods the phenomenon constituted a grave social problem, especially in Candia. The Ottoman authorities arranged some elementary form of social welfare and designated a small sum of money for the maintenance of the women and their children when it was established that they were the illegitimate children of Muslims. In 1754 the kadi of Candia fixed a sum of four paras daily for every underage child who had been parented by the Christian girl Margia and the Turk Karemfili Mehmet *beshi* (Islamised Cretan).

CHAPTER III

JANISSARIES AND HAYINS

1. The Janissaries of Crete

The savagery of the Janissaries of Crete was notorious. No other region of the Ottoman ruled Greek lands, with the exception perhaps of Macedonia, suffered their depradations to such an extent. Both the imperial Janissaries and the local Janissaries (known as yerlis) showed scant respect for the law and would be constrained by no one. They even ignored and contravened the sultan's own orders. The regional power of the pashas who represented the sultan's administration was ill-defined and frequently simply a matter of formality. The pasha could hardly intervene in cases of Janissaries' irresponsible actions, since the Janissaries were subject only to their own whims and desires. In fact the 'hoodless' *(xekoukoulotoi),* as the Janissaries came to be known in Crete, were so lawless that they sometimes even threatened the lives of the pashas themselves. In 1690 they showed few qualms about doing away with the Pasha of Chania, Sulfikar, and throwing his body to the dogs because he foolishly attempted to implement the law and restrain their arbitrary acts. The Sublime Porte became concerned about the situation in Crete and, by various means, tried to put these unbridled forces under some kind of control. After 1750 the situation became chronic. The years that were to follow, right up to the eve of the Greek war of independence, were to be the amongst the hardest that the Cretan people had ever known, as they were subject to the lawless whims of the Janissaries. Foreign travellers to the island describe the most horrifying incidents and the historians of Crete never tire of re-counting the atrocities committed by the Janissaries and their bestial behaviour towards the Christian population. Here is a characteristic extract taken from an imperial decree dealing with the excesses of the Janissaries of Candia, dated 6 July 1762:

'The brigands and malefactors in the employment of the guard of this fortress, cheating and deceiving their superiors and neglecting their duties, have found the opportunity to openly devote themselves to robbery and crime and, in drunkenness, they tour the neighbourhoods bearing their weapons, and insult the honour of the inhabitants and attack families and their children. And besides these attacks on the honour and good repute of the citizens, they have proceeded to commit further outrages by attacking with unprecedented audacity the Porte and the Aga of this great fortress... This god-protected and grand frontier stronghold must be purged and cleansed of the blight of these ruffians and their base deeds so that the people may find some respite...'

Ottoman imperial decrees did not suffice to restrain the misdeeds of the Janissaries. In the late eighteenth and early nineteenth century some of these Janissaries in fact became famous for their atrocities and they had the dubious honour of being preserved in folk song and memory. Alidaki of Chania, Arif Aga of Rethymnon, Bedri efendi and Haniali of Candia, and Memet Aga or Memetakas of Siteia were among this category of Janissaries.

In 1812 the Sublime Porte took the decision to intervene forcibly and to crush the insubordinacy of the Janissaries of Crete. The Porte sent Hadji Osman Pasha to Crete and he managed to destroy many of the Janissaries by hanging (for which he was given the nickname 'the throttler'). It is also recorded that 'In 1813 Hadji Osman Pasha organised on the same day and at the same hour a true night of St. Bartholomew at the three Cretan strongholds, slaughtering about 500 agas and beys.' This incident made a deep impression on the Chirstians as well, and the legend grew up around the figure of this strange Pasha that he was a crypto-Christian archimandrite of the patriarchate of Constantinople, named Vasileios, and that before the slaughter he attended a Christian service in the basement of his palace at Chania and that he was given holy communion from the hands of a terrified Cretan priest. His outrageous behaviour earned him the derogatory name 'Papayannis' amongst the Turkish community of Rethymnon. The Cretan people's secret wish that the Janissaries be destroyed is expressed lucidly in the following demotic folk song:

'Lord, may a Pasha come who they call Antonis,
to liberate the Romioi [Greeks] and enslave the Turks...'

Figure 18
The tower of Alidakis at Brosnero in the province of Apokoronas (drawing by R. Pashley, *Travels in Crete,* II, 159).

The policies of Hadji Osman Pasha were continued by his successor Reshid Mustafa Pasha, otherwise known as Kyutahis who later went on to overpower Ali Pasha of Jannina. As *serasker* of Crete (1815-1816), Kyutahis executed many of the insubordinate Janissaries, a fact attested by the records in the Ottoman archives.

2. The Hayins

Already from early Ottoman times in Crete many young adventurers fled to the mountains from where they were able to operate and launch attacks against the Turks in night raids. The Turks called these mountain outlaws *Hayins* (from the Arabic word *hayin*, meaning perfidious, treacherous, thankless). The number of hayins increased after the fall of Candia and the final subjugation of Crete. Without ever becoming quite as endemic as in the rest of Greece it is possible to compare the hayins with the *klephts* (organised bandit communities) of mainland Greece. Most of the hayins of Crete had taken to this lifestyle for entirely personal reasons. They carried out acts of revenge for grave family injustices perpetrated by the Turks against members of their families. After the fall of Candia the hayins sought refuge in the three remaining Venetian fortresses of Grambousa, Suda and Spinalonga. Once these fortresses succumbed to the Turks in 1715, the hayinis then fled to the mountains and the monasteries. Their existence was a continual struggle for survival. Even priests are mentioned as being among their number. In a document dated 1 September 1672 it is recorded that papa-Janis, formerly *kethüda* of Kastelli, in Merabello, became a hayin and fled to Spinalonga. Popular Cretan songs have preserved the memory of some of these hayinis.

The Turkish tried their best to clamp down on the activities of these dangerous misfits. It is interesting to note here that they attempted to implement the institution of the *armatoloi* here in Crete as they had done elsewhere in the Greek areas of the Ottoman empire. As early as 1686 the inhabitants of many of the Cretan regions had petitioned the Pasha of Candia to appoint Christian armed guards ('armatoloi') in the villages. And in fact this institution does seem to have worked for a number of years, for we have an Ottoman document (probably dated to the year 1689) which contains a full list of the armatoloi of Siteia.

The Turks, however, were distrustful of the existence of armed

Figure 19
The hideous 'çinkeli', devised for the execution of the hayins. (Drawn by Tournefort, 1699.)

Christian forces within their domains and they seem to have preferred to organise special bands (çete) of fanatical Muslims whose task it was to hunt down the hayins. At the same time they implemented a general policy of intimidation by declaring the inhabitants of the villages as being in league with the Christian hayins. In 1689 the Ottoman authorities compelled the Christian inhabitants of the eastern regions of Crete (Pediada, Lasithi, Merabello, Ierapetra and Siteia) to sign declarations whereby they accepted responsibility for the activities and harbouring of the hayinis.

Arrested hayins were subjected to the most hideous tortures and were executed on a *'çinkeli'*, a frightful contraption which is known to us from the sketch made by the French visitor to Crete, Tournefort. Under circumstances such as these the hayins' activities were severely restricted. Especially after the fall of the Venetian fortresses of Suda and Spinalonga in 1715 little hope was left for these first representatives of Cretan resistance to Ottoman rule. For many decades to come Ottoman rule on the island was to remain unshaken. Cretan resistance was only to reemerge after the rebellion of Daskaloyannis during the period of the domination of the Janissaries. It was then that these Cretan avengers were to act as a fearful countermovement against the injustices perpetrated by the agas. Bold and free-booting young men, fired by the spirit of revenge for some injustice carried out against their families, took up arms and made their base in the mountains. We know the names of some of these brave mountain fighters from the harsh period of 1790-1820: the Chalis and Yannaris families of Chania, the Deliyannakis and Koutsouris families of Sphakia, Siphakas of Apokoronas, the Tsouderos family of Rethymnon, Yannis Palmeris of Mylopotamos, and Stavros Xetrypis, Stavroulis Niotis and Vasilis Sbokos of Anogeia. Famous in east Crete was Dimitris Logios or Varouchas from the village of Agios Thomas, in Monofatsi. In an attempt to kill the much feared Janissary Agriolidis at Mesara, Logios was fatally wounded and died in 1811. Others such as Xopateras Markakis, the Leratoi brothers, Malikoutis, Romanos, Petroyannis, Tsakiris,

Michael Korakas were active in the region of the plain of Mesara. The hayins of Mesara were supplied with weapons by the Sphakians who exchanged weapons and muskets for grain. Michael Vlachos became famous in Malevizi, George Vergas was famous in east Pediada and Manolis Kazanis in the Lasithi plain. Popular Cretan songs and tales have preserved the memory of many of these figures and their daring acts of revenge.

CHAPTER IV

THE REBELLION OF DASKALOYANNIS (1770)

A major event of the early Ottoman period in Crete was the rebellion of 1770. This rebellion needs to be seen within the more general perspective of the policy of the day of Catherine the Great of Russia and the Orlof strategy. We have already mentioned the special status of Sphakia under the Ottoman administration. The nature of the terrain did not enable the Turks to make their presence much felt in this area and as a result the Sphakians, having paid their burdensome taxes, were not subject to other forms of oppression. Furthermore the Sphakians' access to the sea enabled the area to escape from its isolation. Using locally produced timber the Sphakians built small ships at Brosyalo and at Loutro, and were thus able to travel throughout the Mediterranean and even north, through the Black Sea, to Russia. Shipping became a source of wealth for the Sphakians and this mountainous and infertile area now enjoyed a period of economic development:

'They had their ships which carried them about;
like beys and princes they headed for Sphakia...'

The figure of Yannis Vlachos, otherwise known as Daskaloyannis, stands out in the mid-eighteenth century. He was a wealthy shipowner, with four three-masted ships, and had travelled widely throughout the Mediterranean. Besides his personal fortune he had also acquired a broader knowledge of the world and of the problems of his age. He was undoubtedly the leading figure of the area of Sphakia. He is already mentioned as holding the office of Interpreter in 1750 and in 1765 is recorded as being the chairman (*Kethüda*) of his region. Daskaloyannis, along with his brother Nikolo Sgouromallis, represented his region for taxation and other public affairs. His reputation and plans were, however, chiefly bolstered by his acquaintanceship with other distinguished Greeks and foreigners of the day. He met Emmanuel Benakis in the Mani and, perhaps through Benakis, Theodore Orlof whom Catherine the Great of Russia had sent to the Peloponnese in 1769 in order to incite rebellion among the *prokritoi* of the region. Daskaloyannis' plans for a revolutionary liberation movement in Crete backed by Russian support was in harmony with the general political climate and ideals of the time. Daskaloyannis himself was convinced of the sincerity of the Russian pledges, as can be seen in the following lines from his ballad:

'Every Christmas he doffed his cap
and said to the priest, "I'll bring the Muscovites".'

Events suddenly took off after the rebellion in the Mani in 1769, in which many Sphakians took part. Throughout 1769 and up to the spring of 1770 Daskaloyannis made preparations for the revolt at Sphakia, amassing weapons and provisions and fortifying various strategic positions. He was aware that it would be both impractical and unfeasible to expect an uprising to take hold throughout the whole of Crete. It was for this reason that he limited his action to the region of Sphakia, though even here he was to meet with resistance. His uncle, a priest, appears to have had grave reservations about the wisdom of such an undertaking. In the ballad of Daskaloyannis, composed by Barba-Pandzelios, a semi-literate cheese maker of the village of Mouri, near Sphakia, the objections of the priest are expressed sincerely and simply:

'And then the priest shook his head,
deep in thought, his soul was full of consternation,
'Teacher Yannis,' he said, 'Come to your senses,
you'll drag the whole of Crete into dire distress,
And you'll bring ruin on Sphakia,

And all the Pashas and the Turk will descend on us.
By the time the ships of Muscovy reach us
The Sphakians won't have a home in Sphakia to rest...' '

The Turks in Crete were in continual fear of foreign armed invasion. The movements and plans of the Russian fleet became known to the Ottomans by their spies and merchants. On 7 February 1770 the agas of Chania sent an urgent message to the sultan notifying him of the 'alarming' news that the envoy Miri Mahmut, on returning from the Netherlands, 'had seen with his own eyes at the port of Gibraltar... 28 ships each with sixty cannon, 22 frigates and four ships of the *bomba* class. These ships were fully manned with soldiers from Denmark and Great Britain, and were flying the Russian flag, and their commanders and admirals had been appointed in the name of Russia. On asking them of their intentions, the envoy was informed that they were bound for the Mediterranean, and the Morea and Suda in particular.'

It is not known precisely under what circumstances or on what date the revolt broke out at Sphakia. It seems most likely that the first unrest occurred at Easter (4 April 1770). Previous to this the Sphakians had refused to pay the poll tax and had driven out the Ottoman tax collector.

The total Sphakian force numbered no more than about 2000 men, but they were well armed and had plenty of supplies in case of prolonged conflict. They first aimed their attacks against the neighbouring areas of Kydonia, Apokoronas and Agios Vasileios and they forced the terrified Turks living in these parts to seek refuge in Chania. The Turkish response, however, was as swift as it was ruthless. By May of the same year a force of some 15,000 Turks had gathered in the district of Apokoronas ready to enter Sphakia. In the face of the obvious danger the Sphakians had the foresight to send their women and children to the southern Peloponnese and the island of Kythera. An attempt by the Turks to reach a compromise with the surrender of the rebels and assurances of safe conduct proved fruitless. They then began a simultaneous attack from three separate positions. After the first major battle at Krapi the Sphakians were compelled to retreat to their highest mountain fastnesses. Throughout the summer and autumn of 1770 they defended themselves with astonishing bravery in the mountains and gorges of Sphakia and managed to stave off effectively the onslaughts of the enemy. However, their villages were totally destroyed, their flocks were scattered, the entire region was subjected to unprecedented plundering and many of the people were led into captivity and taken to the slave markets of Candia. Among those who were taken to Candia was the priest, and uncle of Daskaloyannis, who it seems gave information to the Turks about the relations between his nephew and the Russians. The worst consequence for Daskaloyannis, however, was the fact that his wife and two daughters were arrested.

The following winter was hard. Daskaloyannis' hopes of support from the Russians proved ill-founded, and disaffection set in. The only solution to the drama was to submit to the dictates of circumstance. Having received assurances from the Turks that they would be granted amnesty the rebels accepted the following terms recorded in a legal document dated 18 March 1771:

1) that they pay the poll tax which thay had refused to pay the previous year,

2) that they surrender their weapons and provisions to the Ottoman authorities,

3) that the ringleaders of the revolt -'the knavish violators, flaunters and perpetrators of deeds against the rules of service and obedience to the state be sent to his highness the governor of Candia for the imposition of a fitting punishment,'

4) that the Sphakians no longer come into contact with, or supply with food, any Christian ships which approach their harbours,

5) that they attempt to arrest the crews of any Christian ships and send them to Candia,

6) that all judicial powers in Sphakia be conducted by an official and kadi to be appointed by the divan of Candia,

7) that no repairs or restoration be carried out on churches, and no new ones built,

8) that the Sphakians pay the tithe according to the orders of the sultan,

9) that no tall buildings such as towers be erected, and no Christian symbols be placed in the buildings,

10) that religious ceremonies be forbidden and ringing of church bells,

11) that all Muslim captives be released,

12) that the Sphakians be obliged to wear the dress worn by the peasantry of the rest of the island. It is worth noting that it was forbidden for Christians in Crete to wear the same style of clothes as those worn by Muslims. Various documents have survived which concern this issue.

Before this disastrous turn of events and clearly under the pressure of the general outcry over the failure of his rebellion, Daskaloyannis decided to give himself up in the hope that he would thereby reduce the severity of the Turks' treatment of his fellow Sphakians. It is recounted that the Pasha of Candia compelled Daskaloyannis' brother Nikolo Sgouromallis, who was already captured by the Turkish authorities, to write a letter to Daskaloyannis assuring him of the good faith of the Turks. Daskaloyannis gave himself up, along with his trusted companions, but the Pasha of Candia reserved for him the most frightful of punishments. On 17 June 1771 the Pasha ordered that Daskaloyannis be flayed alive. Nikolo Sgouromallis was tied up and forced to watch the hideous spectacle of his brother's execution. According to tradition, Sgouromallis was unable to endure the sight and lost his senses, dying a madman. The other Sphakians after three years of captivity managed to escape and return to Sphakia, devastated by their experiences, only to be greeted by the desolation of their land and villages. Barba-Pandzelios gives a dramatic description of the Sphakians' despair on seeing the ruin of their homes:

'Sphakia was no longer recognisable to them,
they could no longer find their neighbourhoods,
And all seemed like a bad dream as they looked on.
Here and there stood the ruined remains of their homes,
and hunger, poverty, desolation, tears and lamenting
were heard on the shore as they looked toward the hills.'

The rebellion of Daskaloyannis was the first bid for freedom to be made in Crete during the period of Ottoman rule; it was also the first bitter taste of the tragic consequences of failure.

CHAPTER V

EDUCATION AND CULTURAL LIFE

1. Education

With the fall of Candia in 1669 Crete was plunged into a cultural dark age. The Cretan Renaissance was suddenly cut short. All those scholars and men of learning who managed to save themselves from the Turks, fled their home island of Crete, taking their books and manuscripts with them. Large and important Cretan libraries, both private and monastic, were destroyed and the island was left in a state of culutral barbarism. Nevertheless, during the first fifty years following the fall of Candia there were a few scholars who remained scattered throughout various parts of the island. Sources for this period, though meagre and limited, have preserved for us the names of some of these scholars. The owner's note in a manuscript dated 1700 gives us the name of a teacher, Ioannis Daphnomilis, as well as that of a calligrapher, Georgis, of Candia (1701).

Up to the year 1700 the Cretans of the diaspora continued the renowned intellectual tradition of the island. In 1681 Marinos Gianne Bounialis (originally from Rethymnon) published in Venice a lengthy verse work on the Cretan War. In the same year Francisco Skoufos published his work *Art of Rhetoric,* which was to exert especial influence on ecclesiastical rhetoric during the period of Ottoman rule, and above all on the figure of Ilias Miniatis. Gerasimos Vlachos, metropolitan bishop of Philadelphia (1679) and the monk Athanasios Varouchas were active in the Heptanese (Ionian islands), and corresponded in the ancient Greek language while preaching in the modern-day vernacular, after the example of Maximos Margounios and Meletios Pigas. The profusive writer and monk Agapios Landos became a popular teacher by virtue of his works. His highly popular work *Salvation of Sinners* went through numerous editions in the eighteenth and nineteenth centuries.The last representative of this tradition was the patriarch of Alexandria, Gerasimos Palladas (1677-1699). His homiletic works written in a popular idiom still remain unpublished.

The eighteenth century was a period of utter darkness for the cultural and intellectual life of Crete. For while in other parts of the Ottoman dominated Greek lands promising signs of a revival of intellectual life can be seen to emerge from the beginning of the century, Crete seems to have fallen into total obscurity. Learning appears to have become restricted to the simple teaching of reading and writing by the unsophisticated monks at the schools in the monasteries. And even the higher ranking clergy was composed for the most part of poorly educated men, if their surviving works are anything to judge by. In his book *Short History of Crete,* published in 1824, the historian P. Nikolaidis made the following observation: 'It is indeed distressing to think that even the smallest island in Greece can boast at least two native born men of learning and education, while in Crete, the largest of the Greek islands, there appears to have been none worth speaking of... For there were a few Cretans (those who dwelt in the three large coastal strongholds) who were men of commerce and possessed some knowledge of the world, while the rest of their fellow men sank into total uncouthness...'

It is surely characteristic that in all the many Turkish records which have been published to date there is not a single mention of a Cretan teacher, although there are references to Turkish schools and teachers. One might expect to find at least a rudimentary form of school life being offered at the numerous monasteries of the island (if not in the towns) during the eighteenth century. It is known that at some monasteries, such as at Arkadi, Apanosephe and Gonia (near Kisamos), the copying of manuscripts was still carried out. We also know the names of many Cretan scribes from the period of Ottoman rule in Crete, such as Arsenios, bishop of Kydonia and outstanding musician, Gerontios Kalamaras, Meletios Kallergis, Pavlos Klados (or Kladopoulos),

George Gounales, Konstantinos Kypraios, a monk of Ilarion and Gerasimos of Kalognomon. Some of the manuscripts are of exceptional interest on account of their artistic merit, such as the codex in the British Museum Library (Additional 41483), copied by George Gounales at the monastery of St. George at Apanosephe in 1784.

In some areas, such as at Sphakia, thanks to more favourable conditions, elementary schools started to function from the middle of the eighteenth century onwards. Various educated Sphakians undertook the role of teacher: Ioannis Vlachos (Daskaloyannis) was one such case.

By the end of the eighteenth century an educational movement had begun to appear in Crete. Schools began to be founded and well-known teachers were sought from other parts of the island. In 1791 two schools were functioning at Chania, maintained by wealthy merchants of the town. An Austrian, F. W. Sieber, who visited the island in 1817 relates that the oldest school in Crete had been founded about fifty years earlier and that 'it was originally founded at the instigation of French merchants. Later another was founded in the capital of the island, Herakleion, and in Rethymnon.' In the early nineteenth century renowned teachers were working in Crete. Kallinikos Verroiaios, well-known for his modern teaching method, was summoned to teach in Chania. Soon after 1800 Gregory Perdikaris of Rethymnon, Jacob Manolesis of Santorini, Jacob Kalogeros and a certain Stephanos are recorded as teaching in Chania. The school at Chania, which at some point was in danger of closing on account of lack of funds, was eventually saved by the generous donation of 25,000 rubles from the Cretan Ioannis Vamvakis after pleas for support from the bishop of Kydonia, Kallinikos and the *prokritoi* of the town. This money, however, took several years to arrive and in the end it was used almost entirely to help fund the needs of the struggle for independence in 1821.

The Cretan-born scholar Gregory Megalovrysanos ('worthless head of the school of Candia', as he himself writes with humble modesty) taught in Herakleion. He also taught in Chania (1800-1805) before being summoned to Herakleion by the educationally-minded bishop and martyr of the town, Gerasimos Pardalis, and by Hadji Ioannis Psarakis, father of the Psaroudakis brothers who also became well-known teachers. There also seems to have been a seminary functioning in Herakleion before 1800, with a certain Synesios, a learned monk of the monastery of Apanosephe, as its head, and which also appears to have had an ordinary school for a period. The anonymous author of the *Chorographia of Crete*, published in 1818 (and wrongly attributed to Zacharias Praktikidis), informs us that in 1818 Candia had 'one hospital and one school in which the pupils learn grammar, logic, poetics, and rhetoric, and sometimes mathematics, two schools of art and one of music'.

Another school functioned at Rethymnon under the supervision of George Vaos of Siphnos, and a Greek school under the supervision of Ioannis Metaxas Lazaridis, bishop of Rethymnon and later of Avlopotamos. The Austrian visitor to the island F. W. Sieber (1817) described the Rethymnon school as being excellently organised and having fourteen pupils. The subjects taught were morals, Aesop's fables, Plutarch, Plato, Homer, arithmetic, geometry, algebra, history and philosophy.

One of the most outstanding scholars and teachers of the period immediately preceding the outbreak of the war of independence of 1821 was Zacharias Praktikidis (or Tsirigotis) of Herakleion, who also acquired fame for his activity during the struggle for independence. Praktikidis taught at Rethymnon (1802-1808) and later at Herakleion (1808-1818). He was ordained a deacon by bishop Gerasimos Pardalis and then departed for Mount Athos. In about 1820 he returned to settle in Sphakia where he set up a Greek school in the small monastery of the Virgin at Thymiani. Here he taught until the eve of the Greek revolution.

Closely related to the issue of education is the existence of libraries in Crete. The larger monastic centres of the island were generally availed of well-stocked libraries with both printed and manuscript books. Savary, a French traveller to the region, informs us that in 1779 at the monastery of Arkadi there were 'two hundred volumes of ecclesiastical and theological works and one Homer manuscript'. Similar libraries existed at the monasteries of Gonia, Apanosephe, Apezonon, Agarathou, Toplou and elsewhere. There were also private libraries: not only the well-known teachers of the day such as Ioannis (Ioannikios) Lazopoulos, Gregory Megalovrysanos, Synesios, and Zacharias Praktikidis possessed large libraries, but also other well-to-do people of a more modest education such as the doctor George Nikoletakis of Candia, of whose personal library a large part is preserved in the Archaeological Museum of Herakleion.

Another educated Cretan of the years prior to the Greek revolution and war of independence who possessed a large collection of books and manuscripts was the Herakleian doctor Ioannis Leftheraios, slaughtered in the massacre of 24 June 1821. The Austrian traveller Sieber tells us something about this personality: 'There [at Megalo Kastro] I met the renowned doctor of the island, Mr. I. Leftheraios, a highly cultured man, who not only spoke the Italian and French languages with uncommon ease, but what is even more unusual he spoke Latin quite eloquently. He also knew ancient Greek and spoke Arabic and Persian. He was unsurpassed in his knowledge of Turkish, its literature and the cultivation of its style. Because of his knowledge he was often asked to interpret the firmans [Ottoman imperial decrees] that arrived from Constantinople and to explain many of the more obscure phrases of the administrative language of the Dirvan. This scientifically trained doctor was educated by his father who had also studied in Padua.' Leftheraios was an exceptional and impressive case of a Cretan man of learning and culture of the years prior to the Greek revolution.

2. Art

With the fall of Candia (1669) the large artistic workshops of Crete ceased to exist and the fine tradition of the Cretan School of painting was brought to an abrupt end. Many painters (Philotheos Skouphos, Theodoros Poulakis, Emmanuel Tzane Bounialis, Ilias Moskos, Victor and others), treading the general path of flight and the diaspora, went to the Heptanese and other parts of the Greek world still free of Ottoman rule where they were able to continue their work and keep the tradition alive. Today we know more than fifty names of Cretan artists of the period 1669-1750. However, after 1700 it is no longer possible to talk of a Cretan school of painting. Both the factors and circumstances which had led to its rise were now extinguished for good.

There are several painters of note who lived and worked in Crete during the dark years of the early period of Ottoman rule (1669-1821). The first that we know of after the fall of Candia were Makarios Skordilis (*ca.* 1674) and George Stais (1705). In about 1700 the monk Jakovos painted a superb icon of the Virgin at the monastery of Myriokephalon.

The most important Cretan painter of the first half of the eighteenth century was George Kastrophylakas (1723-1752). Many of his beautifully painted icons can be seen today in the museum of St. Katherine's in Herakleion. Another noteworthy painter who worked in Cyprus, Sinai and Crete was Ioannis Kornaros (1745-1806). One of his icons (dated 1770), depicting the theme 'Thou art great, O Lord' can be seen today in the monastery of Toplou. A contemporary of Kornaros was the painter Polychronis (1775-1810) who also worked in Cyprus, Sinai and Crete.

Evidence suggests that a number of schools of art functioned in the large towns of Crete and at the monasteries. There were two art schools in Candia in the early nineteenth century according to the author of the *Chorographia of Crete.*

II

THE PERIOD OF CRETAN UPRISINGS
(1821-1898)

CHAPTER I

THE UPRISING OF 1821 - 1830

1. The activity of the Philiki Etaireia in Crete

The activity of the Greek independence organisation the *Philiki Etaireia* (Friendly Society) in Crete has still not been fully studied. It is safe to assume that the leaders of the Society neither planned nor were able to systematically organise revolutionary activity in this corner of the Greek world, where both its distance from the rest of Greece and unfavourable local conditions did not foster much hope of swift success. Nevertheless the pronouncements of the Society had reached Crete and many of the leading Cretan ecclesiastics, merchants and intellectuals who lived in Constantinople or in the Danubian principalities of the Ottoman empire had been intitiated into the Greek revolutionary struggle from early on. The family of Daimonakis which had fled Crete for Moldavia after the abortive uprising of Daskaloyannis, the Herakleian merchant Magdalenos (or Ladas) who lived in Smyrna, the bishop Ieras Artemios, the metropolitan bishop Gerasimos Pardalis, Kallinikos Kritovoulidis, the Sphakian ship owners Panayiotis Psaroudakis and Andreas Fasoulis, as well as many others besides all supported the activities of the Society. On 1 September 1816 the Cretan scholar Emmanuel Vernardos joined the Society in Moldavia to become the first official representative of the Friendly Society in Crete. He went to Sphakia in September 1819 under the pretext of taking money and books to the school at the monastery of the Virgin at Thymiani; in fact he was on a mission to sound out the situation on the island and to spread the word for revolution among the local Greek community. Among the many whom he converted to the cause for independence was Anagnostis Manousoyannakis from Nimbros. The Cretan historian Psilakis records the 'unspeakably terrible' oath sworn by Manousoyannakis: 'I accept to undergo and suffer the cruellest death if I fail in any way to stand by the aforementioned pledges or if I become a traitor or informer against my people and partners in the national struggle.'

In December 1819 another spokesman for the Society, the Chiot teacher Varnavos Pangalos (descended, however, from a Cretan family that had fled Crete many years earlier), arrived in Chania. He was highly effective in winning people over to the Greek cause. He managed to secure the support of the doctor Renieris, Kouvaritis and the renowned crypto-Christian of Mesara Hussein (Michael) Kourmoulis. He also won the support of the bishop of Kisamos, Melhisedek Despotakis, the abbot of the monastery of Preveli, Melhisedek Tsouderos, the abbot of the monastery of Gonia, Parthenios Raptanis, Ioannis Damvergis of Rethymnon, and Andreas Pachynakis (or Pachynandroulis), one of the most distinguished figures of the Greek revolution, and many others. The deacon Kallinikos Verroiaios, who founded a school at Chania had also been sent by the Friendly Society. As Zacharias Praktikidis wrote, Kallinikos 'established some of the most distinguished citizens of the town as members of the Friendly Society, along with bishop Kallinikos of Kydonia.'

A rare document written in the code of the Friendly Society also confirms the initiation of the Sphakian Ioannis Birakis into the Society. It says, 'In the name of the Salvation to come, I confirm Ioannis Birakis son of George, of Sphakia, and aged fifty-five, to be a member and supporter of the Friendly Society and ardently to desire the well-being of his nation, initiated and sworn in by myself [the signature is illegible] at Sphakia on 20 April.'

It appears then that the Friendly Society was considerably active in Crete. The revolution that was shortly to break out against Ottoman rule had already found the support of some of the most distinguished citizens of the island. A list of the Cretan members of the Friendly Society was recently published by the historian Stergios Manouras.

2. The outbreak of the 1821 revolution

Spiridon Trikoupis, the historian of the Greek revolution and war of independence accused the Cretans of being slow to respond to the national cause: 'Despite the fact that the revolution spread throughout the entire Peloponnese and thence to the Aegean, and despite the fact that ships bearing the Greek flag could be seen off the coast of Crete, the inhabitants of Crete, both in the plains and on the mountains, were not moved to join in; the clergy made every effort to maintain peace and order on the island by issuing pastoral decrees for the purpose.' This view today is considered both inaccurate and exaggerated. Another historian, D. Kokkinos, has given a more fair account of Crete during this period: 'The phenomenon of the revolution in Crete is unique in the history of the Greek struggle for independence. It was an uprising of an incarcerated and bound titan armed with nothing more than its Greek consciousness, its vigour, sense of honour and anger. This source of strength was enough not only to start the revolution itself but also to enable it to continue unabated, a shining epic in the history of the Greek revolution, almost savage in its untold sufferings, continually submerging and reemerging from waves of blood, deriving further strength from the harshness of the struggle'.

The outbreak of the revolution against Turkish Ottoman rule in Crete immediately after the raising of the national banner in the Peloponnese was initially weak. Crete was confronted by two main obstacles: firstly, the lack of weapons and other supplies, and secondly, the large Turkish population of the island whose probable savage reprisals were a just cause of fear. Indeed, the decision of the Cretans to support the revolution seems irrational if one takes into account the unfavourable balance of numbers. Kallinikos Kritovoulidis, a reliable witness and writer about the Cretan uprising, wrote the following: 'Unprepared and cut off from the rest of the Greek world they looked to their own resources and entered the national struggle... In the beginning their weaponry amounted to no more than four hundred barrels of gunpowder... And what about lead and paper? Ecclesiastical books and weights of the steelyards and whatever else could be found were used to begin with for making cartridges and rounds. For many months the Cretans bought at their own expense a barrel of gunpowder for three, four and sometimes five Spanish gold peices. The number of weapons that were available was extremely limited during the early period of the revolution and those bearing arms probably amounted to no more than about 1200, of whom 800 were Sphakians.'

Moreover, Turkish vigilance was constant. On learning of the outbreak of unrest in the Peloponnese the Turkish authorities in Crete ordered the metropolitan bishop Gerasimos Pardalis to summon all the bishops of the island to Herakleion, clearly with a view to holding them there as hostages. Pardalis sent out the summons asking them to come to Herakleion but he also secretly notified the bishops that they should not come. He was clearly concerned about what might be in store for them. Five hundred bishops eventually came to Herakleion and none of them was spared in the massacre that followed.

The revolution first broke out in Crete in the region of Sphakia in early April 1821. On 7 April the Sphakians held a meeting at Glyka Nera to discuss the general situation on the island and the possibilities for the participation of more regions of Crete in the revolution. The bitter experience of the Daskaloyannis rebellion of 1770 gave the Sphakians every cause to be cautious about any such uprising. They met again eight days later at the monastery of the Virgin at Thymiani. It was here that they decided to take up arms against the

Turks, although it was not until June that the conflict finally began. The official start of Cretan participation in the war of independence was 14 June 1821, the day on which the Cretan revolutionaries won their first battle at Loulo, near Chania. The first official proclamation of the General Assembly of the Cretan provides us also with the same date: 'The inhabitants of the island of Crete, full of the noble and lofty spirit of freedom, took up arms against the Ottoman tyranny on 14 June 1821...' Within a few days the conflict spread to the rest of the island and Crete now entered the Greek national struggle for freedom.

3. Turkish atrocities

Turkish reprisals were ruthless. On 19 June bishop Melhisedek Despotakis of Kisamos was hanged and the bishop of Kydonia, Kallinikos Sarpakis, was imprisoned along with his deacon Artemios. The abbots of the monasteries were also killed. A group of incensed Muslims entered the convent of St. John the Baptist (a monastic dependency of the monastery of Gdernettos) at Korakies, near Akrotiri, and raped and slaughtered the nuns. The chronicle of these events gives the following description: '*A second band, equally enraged, descended on the convent and violated all those nuns who had not been quick enough to flee; they then put the monastery to the torch and left... Later the monastery was abandoned and uninhabited.*' The massacres were savage and in the town of Chania 400 Christians lost their lives in a few days.

Similar events occurred in Rethymnon where the bishop Gerasimos Perdikaris (or Kondoyannakis) was imprisoned 'in a base and miserable hovel..' In the following year he was hanged. We are also informed that the Turks smeared their banners with the blood from his heart in the belief that they would be victorious by doing so.

It was at Herakleion that atrocities reached their height. The Turks of the town asked Serif Pasha for permission to bear arms. On 23 June a Turkish ship arrived at the harbour, bearing news of atrocities in Constantinople and Smyrna against the Greeks and the hanging of the Greek patriarch. This served to trigger off the most violent massacre that Crete had known and was to remain indelibly engraved in the people's memory. On the morning of 24 June the Turks killed the metropolitan bishop Gerasimos Pardalis and the bishops Neophytos of Knossos, Ioakeim of Cherronesos, Ierotheos of Lambi and Sphakia, Zacharias of Siteia and Kallinikos of Diopolis. The cathedral was plundered and put to the torch. The abbots of the monasteries and other clerics were all killed. It is estimated that the number of dead on that day in Herakleion and its outlying districts was no less than 800. The highest ranking Greeks of the island were among these, such as Ioannis Leftheraios, the learned doctor already mentioned. Only strong protests from the British and French vice-consuls of the island restrained the Turks from perhaps carrying out the total annihilation of the Christian Cretans.

Similar events took place in east Crete. The bishop of Petra, Ioakeim, was killed by the Turks at the monastery of Aretiou. The monastery of Toplou was looted and many of the monks killed. A document from Sphakia gives us an idea of the Turkish savagery: 'so, so many evils and woes befell us and all the Greek people at the hands of our enemies, the godless and faithless Agarenes [Turks], in the pitiful island of Crete, however, terrible evil befell the Christians; they began with the prelates and priests, the monks and the laity and went on to slaughter everyone... Some they strung up and killed with the sword or by lead shot. Abbots of the holy monasteries, priests and monks and whoever else they found in their path were cut up, others were thrown from cliffs, the fair women were held to satisfy their evil desires, babies sucking at the breast were slaughtered, children of six or seven years old were taken off to be made Muslims, the churches were burned... and every kind of wickedness was committed by the unholy barbarians...' Under circumstances such as these it is indeed remarkable that the revolution in Crete grew in intensity and lasted for a total of ten years.

4. The first year of the revolution

The Cretan revolutionary struggle had as its base the region of Sphakia. From Sphakia it quickly spread to the whole of west Crete. The Turks repeatedly tried to root out the rebel bases in the mountain villages of Kydonia and Apokoronas, in order to descend on the villages in the region of Sphakia. Fierce battles took place in the summer of 1821 at Kerameia, Malaxa and Apokoronas. The revolutionaries were led by the chieftains A. Panayiotou and George Daskalakis (or Tselepis, grandson of Daskaloyannis), Sephakas of Apokoronas and the Halis brothers (Ioannis and Vasileios) of Theriso. Turkish efforts at suppressing the revolt failed. The *agas* of the villages were obliged to seek refuge in the walls of Chania where the situation was becoming ever more difficult on acount of shortages of food and supplies. The Greeks won an important victory on 15 June at Lakkos near Kydonia. Latif Pasha of Chania and his five thousand men were defeated and then routed when they attempted to attack Theriso, one of the main rebel bases in the mountains of Kydonia. In their retreat the Turks left their weapons and supplies. This victory gave the revolution a firm foothold in the area of Chania.

Events took a similar turn in the region of Rethymnon. A Turkish expeditionary force that attempted to break through to Sphakia was attacked by the chieftains of Rethymnon, Anagnostis and Petros Manouselis, Deliyannis, Helidonis, George Tsouderos and others, at Rustika and Agios Konstantinos and was wiped out. The Turkish leaders Koundouris and Glymidis were killed in these battles. On the same day the chieftains Rousos Vourdoumbas, Vasilis Kourmoulis, George Tsouderos, Pologiorgis and Melidonis countered an attack from the Ambadiot Turks of Amari at the site of Agios Ioannes 'the Wretched'. Again the revolutionaries won an important victory and they succeeded in seizing a large supply of weapons.

Revolution broke out a few days later in the eastern districts of the island. The flatter terrain, especially around Herakleion, the long distance from Sphakia -the natural base for the revolutionaries- as well as the massacres carried out by the Turks as a deterrent naturally made the local inhabitants more wary about embracing rebellion. In the region of Herakleion rebel fighting broke out at Mesara which borders on Mylopotamos and Agios Vasileios. The main inspiration behind the revolutionaries' actions in this part of the island was Michael Kourmoulis a member of a notable family of crypto-Christians of Mesara. From the first moments of the revolution the Turks considered it prudent to retreat into their larger strongholds and the more easily defended positions in the rural plains.

The Turks were fully aware that the Cretan uprising could only be suppressed if Sphakia, the heart of the rebels' operations, was destroyed. In late July 1821 Serif Pasha of Herakleion, in the capacity of *serasker* of Crete, organised a large force in which the other Pashas of the island participated. It consisted of 3,500 men with an artillery and cavalry force and set out from Herakleion under the command of Kaounis. Omer agas of Siteia sent a force of 1,500 men and Osman Pasha managed to amass a force of over 2,500. The whole Turkish force gathered from the east of the island and Rethymnon therefore amounted to around eight thousand men. The Greek attempts to check the Turkish force near Rethymnon failed and many of the chieftains such as papa-Yannis Skordilis were killed. The revolutionaries were compelled to withdraw to safer positions while the Turkish force laid waste the villages in the region of Apokoronas and reached Suda Bay, where it joined up with the army from Chania. It inflicted terrible destruction on the region, and the victims -chiefly the elderly and women and children- of the Turkish assault amounted to over 3,000. Only at Theriso did the revolutionaries manage to check the Turkish advance. On 19 August at Theriso the Turks lost two hundred men and the commander, Kaounis, was killed. Many Cretans, however, also lost their lives, including Stephanos Halis.

The Sphakians were quick to perceive the gravity of the situation and they made urgent requests for help. In a document dated 14

August 1821 addressed to the naval forces of the island of Spetsai, they wrote the following: 'We are in great distress, and no longer have the strength to carry on since the enemy is warring against us both by land and sea certain that the absence of Greek ships will mean the destruction of the Christians...' They desperately asked for supplies of gunpowder, lead shot and guns, but above all some ships that would make their presence felt along the coast of the island in order to terrify the Turks. In another document of the same date they wrote again to the *prokritoi* of Spetsai: 'We have neither the time nor the ability to describe to you the sorry situation in which our island now finds itself. Kapetan Pavlos Belivanakis whom we have sent to you will tell you in his own words of the final destruction of our homeland. The enemy has now ventured out of the three main strongholds of the island with as many as 25,000 men along with the three Vezirs of Crete and they have surrounded us from the landward side and hour by hour they assault our position... So, for the love of God, please do something, send some of your precious ships, as many as you can spare, so that we may counter the enemy attack...'

The hoped-for help never arrived and the Turks led by Osman Pasha of Rethymnon managed to break through to Sphakia on 29 August. The whole district was subjected to total destruction much like that of 1770. The chieftains, in their desperate struggle to save their families and the unarmed civilians (who had fled in fear to the gorges and the coasts in the hope that ships would come to save them) no longer put up any resistance. The various chroniclers of the Cretan revolution (Kritovoulidis and Praktikidis, for example) openly accused the Sphakians of bringing disaster on the revolution because of their arrogant indifference, their inertness at the crucial moment and their meanness of spirit and petty quarrelling. And so a golden opportunity to smash the Turkish force, by means of ambush and guerrila tactics in a region highly suitable for this kind of warfare, was lost. After the destruction of Sphakia the Turks returned to their fortresses. The Cretan revolution seemed to have been suppressed and the Turks hastened to inform the Sublime Porte of the news.

However, the revolution did not die out and it was not long before it revived. In September and October of 1821 the revolutionaries managed to regroup their ranks and to expel the Turks from Apokoronas and Kydonia. But it was obvious that the struggle could not result in success if there was not to be a united military and political administration behind it. Lack of central leadership, personal ambition and constant disputes among the chieftains, and especially the Sphakians and Katomerites, all constituted an obstacle to a common, coordinated plan of war. The election of a single leader would have created closer links with other Greek areas and would have fostered support for the Cretan struggle. The Cretans eventually addressed themselves to Dimitrios Ypsilandis, a leading figure of the newly independent Greece, and asked him to appoint a chief commander for Crete.

5. The political organization of Crete Michael Komninos Afendoulis

The Sphakians, who are often accused of being power hungry and undisciplined, organised from the time of the inception of the revolution a supreme political office known as the Chancellory of Sphakia, a collective body responsible for the planning of the revolution. Kritovoulidis wrote the following: ‘At the time of the assembly of the various districts of Sphakia it was decided that a political committee be set up which adopt the title that was popularly current of Chancellory of Sphakia, that had its own seal with a depiction of the Virgin and an inscription reading ‘Virgin of Loutro’ derived from the church at the harbour of Loutro’.

The Chancellory was ratified by the General Assembly at the church of the Virgin at Thymiani (29 May 1821). The Chancellory’s task was an important one despite inherent difficulties. It not only served as the ruling body of the revolutionary movement but also undertook to direct the supplies of arms and provisions to the chieftains, to protect the civilian population, and to manage fund raising and the foundation of a hospital at Loutro near Sphakia. However, the Chancellory was not in the position to control the many local disputes and ambitions of the leaders and chieftains. For this reason it requested the Greek Government -and Dimitrios Ypsilandis as the leading representative of the supreme revolutionary power- to appoint a chief commander of the Cretan revolutionaries, 'to whom all the Cretan leaders would be subordinate and no chieftain would be superior to.' The post of chief commander was not proposed for a Cretan, apart from the famous chieftain of Mesara, the crypto-Christian Hussein-Michael Kourmoulis, but this suggestion was not taken up. Ypsilandis proposed Alexander Kantakouzinos but Kantakouzinos declined the offer. He then turned to Michael Komninos Afendoulis (or Afendouliev) who was honoured to accept the post. Afendoulis went to Crete in November 1821 and remained on the island for exactly one year with the somewhat pompous title of General Eparch and Commander-in-Chief of Crete.

The appointment of Afendoulis to the post of Chief Commander of Crete did little to solve the problems, and it probably served to aggravate them. The Cretans were ill inclined to be commanded by a non-Cretan who was ignorant of the nature and problems of the island. His personal appearance and weak physique did little to inspire confidence and respect, while his whims and unbridled ambition and superciliousness made him unpopular. In any case his position was undermined by the overt and hidden disputes among the Cretan leaders and especially the Sphakians with whom Afendoulis was constantly at odds. In order to strengthen his position he attempted to cultivate the friendship of some of the chieftains by awarding them various titles and honours. This, however, was a grave error, for he simply succeeded in aggravating the disputes still further and eventually led the Cretan campaign into crisis. Some of the chieftains actually carried out murders against their rivals. The Sphakian Vourdoumbas killed Antony Melidonis who had been awarded the title of *quincenturion* by Afendoulis.

A number of military failures, that were generally blamed on the

Figure 20
Seal of the General Staff of Crete on a document of 22 April 1822 with the signature of the commander-in-chief and governor of Crete Michael Komninos Afendouliev (Historical and Ethnological Society of Greece, *Sfrayides Eleftherias,* Athens 1983, no. 195).

incompetence of Afendoulis, made his position even more shaky. In March 1822 he organised a siege of Rethymnon believing that it would easily fall into his hands. The siege, however, failed and Cretan losses were heavy. Among the dead was the French philhellene colonel Valestre. Two months later the revolutionaries were defeated at a battle near Malaxa (10-11 May 1822).

Both contemporary and later historical writers are severely critical of Afendoulis and give a damning verdict of his conduct. However, it should be recognised that he had undoubted organisational skills and his work in Crete was not totally unsuccessful. On the contrary during his term of office in Crete the revolution was put on a firmer basis and spread to the whole island, achievements which cannot be ignored. Moreover the period in which he was in Crete (November 1821 to October 1822) was surely the most successful period of the revolution in Crete. Although there were mistakes and military failures, there were also important successes and the revolution was kept alive across the island. The Turks of Crete did not manage to suppress the revolt as they had originally hoped. It is also significant that Afendoulis attempted to give political shape to the freedom struggle and to plan a form of political organisation. This was one of his main aims right from the start: 'to put affairs in order and to establish a system of political assembly,' as he said in a communication to Koundouriotis (26 November 1821). It was for this reason that he requested the assistance of his friend Petros Omiridis Skylitsis, who had already served as representative of the island at the first National Assembly that was held in Epidaurus.

6. The caretaker government of the island of Crete

From 11-21 May 1822 a General Assembly of the Cretans was summoned at Armeni near Apokoronas with the purpose of voting a caretaker form of government for the island and of appointing the chief leaders of the freedom struggle. Skylitsis, after persistent pleas from Afendoulis, chaired the Assembly in which about forty representatives participated from all the Cretan regions. Skylitsis maintained a position of flexibility and worked for the restoration of reconciliation between the parties concerned and for the successful procedure of the Assembly.

In accordance with the system adopted in other parts of Greece the General Assembly of the Cretans issued a 'Declaration of Freedom', and voted for the planning of a constitutional system with the title 'Caretaker Polity of the island of Crete'. The plan contained seven sections: 1) Religious faith, 2) the general right of the inhabitants of the island, 3) regional concerns of the island, 4) administration, 5) election of the administration, 6) the duties and rights of those in the administration, and 7) general procedure and correspondence. The first two sections (articles 1-11) are identical, even in wording, with the constitution of Epidaurus.

The General Assembly at Armeni also approved a Plan for a caretaker administration of the island of Crete which provided for the division of the island into four regions (departments, or *nomoi* in Greek), themselves subdivided into provinces and communities.

Central power was to be exercised by the General Eparch and the General Chancellory which was composed of the General Secretary and secretaries for the economy, police, war, sea and justice. At the capital of each of the nomoi there were to be an eparch, secretaries and harbour authorities. The constitution also provided for the design of the Cretan flag and the Cretan seal bearing the title 'Administration of the island of Crete'. The representation of Crete in the Greek national parliament would be by members called *Parastates* whose number was determined by the ratio of 1 : 30,000 inhabitants.

One day after the ratification of the caretaker government, the General Assembly elected Afendoulis to the post of General Eparch and then went on to appoint the general secretaries.

In practice the above decisions were never fully implemented. Skylitsis fled from the island on hearing the first reports that the Egyptian force had landed on the island (late May 1822) while Afendoulis remained for just a few months longer though without any real power. Anarchy ensued and was to afflict and weaken the island for a long time to come.

7. The Egyptian force in Crete

The fact that the Turkish army was fully occupied with the campaign in the Peloponnese and further north in mainland Greece against the Greek revolutionaries and the inability of the Turks of Crete to bring the rebellion under control meant that the Sultan Mahmut IV sought the aid of Mehmet Ali of Egypt. Mehmet Ali, hoping that in the long run he would acquire Crete for himself, willingly accepted the invitation for intervention and sent a large force to the island under the command of his brother-in-law Hassan Pasha. On 28 May 1822 the Egyptian fleet of thirty warships and 84 transporters sailed into Suda Bay while the General Assembly of the Cretans was still in session at Armeni.

Hassan immediately set out on campaign. In early June he attacked the fortified position of Malaxa where the revolutionaries had managed to hold out till then. Disagreement amongst the Cretan leaders and failure to organize any coordinated action meant that there was little hope that Hassan Pasha could be held off for long. Kritovoulidis wrote: ‘One can expect nothing with any certainty from an army in which there is no clear hierarchy or strict discipline, even if its men can fight like lions.’ The Cretans attempted an assault on Tsikalaria on 12 June, but they were defeated and many lost their lives; Malaxa which till then had been held at great cost was abandoned now to the Turkish Egyptians on 13 or 14 June 1822.

On these same days Serif Pasha of Candia ravaged the area of Anogeia from where the inhabitants fled to the mountains. The chieftains of the district of Anogeia then organised a counterattack and struck at Serif Pasha’s force at Agios Myronas. Near here at Krousonas the Cretans managed to draw off a select band of 350 Turkish Albanian soldiers and surrounded them at the church of Agios Charalambos where they were all killed.

In the summer of 1822 the revolution in Crete was faced by grave difficulties. Afendoulis received no response to his urgent requests for outside support. In July 1822 Stephanos Vasilopoulos brought to Crete 900 weapons which had been bought in Marseilles with money donated by Varvakis; they were distributed in east Crete in order to revive the revolution.

After his first few operations Hassan realised that the suppression of the revolt in Crete would not be such an easy undertaking. He therefore tried a different and more subtle approach. He released the bishop of Kydonia Kallinikos from prison and compelled him to send a pastoral encyclical to the revolutionaries commanding them to put down their arms and submit to the authorities (4 July). At the same time Hassan issued declarations summoning the people to submit to the ‘beneficent’ ruler of Egypt, Mehmet Ali, and promising that there would be a just and honest administration. The Halis chieftains of Chania requested permission from the revolutionary administration to reply to the bishop of Kydonia and proudly declare their unswerving dedication to the cause of the revolution.

Hassan therefore resumed his military operations on 1 August. A large force set out from Platania with the goal of rooting out the revolutionary bases in the mountains of Kydonia. By 6 August Hassan's force had driven its way through the villages of Lakkoi and Theriso despite relentless harrying from the chieftains' guerilla bands. Hassan, however, lost six hundred men in this campaign and this made him more wary. Leaving the mountain villages of Kydonia he passed through Apokoronas laying waste all the villages in his path and proceded on to Rethymnon and Mylopotamos. In a report to Ioannis Kolettis, the minister of war, dated 15 August 1822 Afendoulis gives a vivid picture of the situation in Crete and the critical state of the war.

Hassan set up camp at the monastery of Christ at Halepa in Mylopotamos where he was then subject to fierce attack from the chieftains of the districts of Anogeia and Mylopotamos (30 August) and suffered heavy losses. On the next day he was attacked another time and the ensuing engagement developed into a long and bloody battle near Sklavokambos. Because the area was vulnerable to attack and did not offer good ground for the cavalry Hassan moved eastwards to the district near Herakleion. He then descended on the district of Pediada with the intention of working his way through to Lasithi which was the granary and base of the revolutionaries' operations in the east of the island. The revolutionaries, however, held the main passes through to the area and it was impossible for Hassan to break through. He therefore decided to head towards Viannos where he then set up camp again. In late October he moved on to Ierapetra and from there, in a circular movement, he went to the villages of Males, Kroustas and Kritsa near Merabello. Leaving these villages he managed to reach the mountain plain of Katharos from where he finally launched his attack on Lasithi plain (November 1822) laying waste the villages in his path.

While these events were taking place and the revolution was in danger of being suppressed, internal anarchy amongst the revolutionaries reached its height. Michael Afendoulis had a bitter disagreement with the Cretan chieftains and secretaries and his position was now seriously undermined. He himself made repeated reports to Kolettis and Koundouriotis requesting that he be replaced, declaring that he was incapable of carrying out his duties. The General Secretary of the Chancellory Neophytos Oikonomos and the other secretaries, without waiting for the reply to arrive from the central administration arrested Afendoulis and locked him up (15 November 1822) accusing him of negligence, inertia, excessive ambition and even having treasonable inclinations. Revolutionary Crete was now without a leader and the other representatives and attorneys of the free Greek state, Anagnostis Panayiotou, George Papadakis, Nikolaos Andreou, Anagnostis Ieronymakis and Emmanuel Antoniadis who had been sent by the caretaker administration of Crete to the Peloponnese requested the appointment of Emmanuel Tombazis of the island of Hydra to the post of Governor General (28 November 1822). Six months went by, however, before Tombazis arrived in Crete and the island was both leaderless and the revolutionary struggle for independence had flagged to a worrying extent.

Having laid waste the Lasithi plain Hassan wintered at Merabello where, in February 1823, a dramatic episode took place. Some two thousand civilians and a few armed revolutionaries had sought refuge in a cave near Milatos. The Egyptian force laid siege to the cave and bombarded it with cannon fire for a fortnight. The Sphakian Rousos Vourdoumbas and his men, who had been trailing Hassan's force, tried in vain to save the besieged civilians in the cave. In mid February the besieged, 'miserable from thirst and despairing of any aid', surrendered to the vengeful Turkish-Egyptians. Most were slaughtered on the spot and the rest were sold into slavery.

A few days later, however, Hassan was killed at Kastelli in Pediada when he fell from his bolting horse.

8. Emmanuel Tombazis, Governor of Crete

Emmanuel Tombazis, the new Commissioner of Crete, arrived on the island on 21 May 1823 accompanied by a naval squadron of five warships and three transport ships and a force of 600 volunteers, chiefly from Epirus in northern Greece. He was accompanied also by distinguished political figures of the day, including the British philhellene Hastings who was commander of the artillery, doctor Stephanos Kanelos, Skourtsis of Hydra and many others. The arrival of Tombazis on the island at a moment when the revolution had reached its nadir on Crete was to revive the Cretans' hopes and give new life to the struggle for independence. An important military victory for the Cretans was soon to follow: on Tombazis' arrival at Kastelli in Kisamos the alarmed Turks in the fortress surrendered control to the Greeks (25 May) after being assured that they would be allowed safe passage to Chania.

However, Tombazis' strategy did not prove to be the best. Instead of attempting to take control of the stronghold of Grambousa and thereby creating a large and impregnable naval base which would ensure control of the coast and the supply route to the island (till now only the small harbour of Loutro near Sphakia had served this purpose), he directed the military campaign against the region of Selino where the most notorious Janissaries were based. A large number of Turkish civilians were besieged at Kandano, and were in danger of dying from hunger and the plague (brought to the island by the Egyptian forces). Negotiations for their surrender broke down and the Turks attempted to play for time in the hope that help would arrive from Chania. In the end the Turks were forced to come to terms and to abandon the fortress and go to Chania; on the way, however, they were ambushed and killed by a force of Sphakians in the district of Sebronas (6-7 June).

In the meantime the Turks were busy reorganising their defences. Hassan's successor was a young general called Hussein bey, also brother-in-law of Mehmet Ali of Egypt. The Egyptian fleet under the command of Ismael Gibraltar arrived in Crete in early June bringing a force of some 3,000 men and abundant supplies.

In the face of this new turn of events Tombazis summoned the

Figure 21
Cretan seals
1. Seal of the isle of Grambousa, 1828 (Historical and Ethnological Society of Greece, *Sfrayides Eleftherias,* no. 827).
2. Kretikon Symboulion (Cretan Council), 1829 (*op. cit.,* no. 507).
3. Directorate of Crete, 1829 (*op. cit.,* no. 504).

chieftains to an assembly at the village of Arkoudaina on 22 June. Representatives from all the regions of the island, including Sphakia, attended the meeting despite their original objections. At this meeting they approved a proposal for the 'Organisational body of the annual local administration of the island of Crete', which was founded on the main directives of the constitution of Epidaurus. According to this organizational body the Commissioner was the representative of the Greek National Administration in Crete, and was responsible for the organization of military and political affairs. The ministries were limited to three -internal affairs, war and the economy- and five secretaries of equal status were appointed to each one. A sixteen member commission was also set up and established in Vryses in the Amari district, and for the first time a judicial body was set up with the task of establishing courts for the dispensation of justice. However, there were no fundamental changes from the situation that existed under Afendoulis. All power was again concentrated in the hands of the Commissioner, who was not obliged to seek approval for his actions from the central administration. The internal situation on the island, instead of improving, in fact became worse, anarchy reigned and a new period of tension between the revolutionaries arose. Tombazis could neither satisfy the Sphakians nor the Katomerites.

Tombazis was also accused of carrying out reckless actions. N. Nikolaidis in his small but fascinating work *Historical and critical essay on Cretan affairs* criticises Tombazis for losing valuable time by occupying himself with administrative affairs rather than the pressing needs of the day.

9. Hussein in Crete

The new commander-in-chief of the Turkish-Egyptian forces devised a brilliant strategy that was based on speed of action and daring. His plan aimed at suppressing the revolt first in the east of the island so that he would be free to set about subduing the west part of the island without fear of attack from the east. Heading a highly disciplined and well-equipped force of 12,000 men, backed by artillery and cavalry, he arrived in Herakleion and set up camp at Agia Varvara. Commissioner Tombazis just managed to muster 3,000 men and position them opposite at Gergeri. At the battle which took place on 20 August near the village of Amourgelles the Cretans, despite a brave defence, were unable to hold off the overwhelming superiority of the enemy forces, and they retreated after losing 300 men. Tombazis was unable to gather further forces in the region of Mesara and departed for the western part of the island. Having taken control of Mesara, Hussein headed in the direction of Rethymnon. In early October 1823 he camped at the village of Melidoni in Mylopotamos and laid siege to 370 women and children and about thirty armed men who had taken shelter in a nearby cave. The siege lasted three whole months in which Hussein mercilessly bombarded and attacked the cave. The drama of the siege reached its climax when, in

January 1824, the Turks threw burning materials through a hole in the top of the cave. Everyone inside died of asphyxiation.

Hussein now moved west unhindered. Tombazis attempted to capture the stronghold of Grambousa but failed, the Greek side suffering severe losses, and his plan to bombard the Egyptian ships anchored in Suda Bay was never realised. Urgent requests for help from other parts of Greece met with no response since the rest of Greece where the revolution was still raging was now passing through a period of political and economic crisis and civil war. Tombazis wrote the following to George Koundouriotis, president of the Executive Council (dated 2 March 1824): 'Sir, hard-pressed Crete is now breathing its last. A little military help and the arrival of ships could relieve the island of the threat of annihilation. It is a rich land and could repay the cost many times over; it needs only to be saved from the enemy and the plunderers who squander the national wealth. Sir, if the Greek nation loses Crete, it will lose its right eye and independence will not amount to much. May the honourable Commission therefore hasten to secure the salvation of the island while the enemy still leaves us time to do so; otherwise all will have been in vain'.

Unfortunately Crete was abandoned to its fate. Having plundered the villages of the district of Apokoronas and having taken many captives during February 1824, Hussein descended on Sphakia in the next month, from the approaches of the Kattre gorge and Krapi. Many of the Sphakian chieftains lost heart and capitulated. This was to have a dire impact on the morale of the rest of the revolutionary movement. The enemy reached the harbour of Loutro almost unhindered. Tombazis had ordered that the food and weapons stores be burnt in order that they not fall into enemy hands. The terrified civilians sought salvation with the ships anchored off the coast, and in the gorge of Agia Roumeli. The Greek fleet removed 10,000 people from the harbour of Loutro and 2,000 more from other harbours. The number of Cretans who fled the island during the first months of 1824 is estimated to have been around 60,000.

Hussein swiftly proceeded to Selino and Kisamos in order to wipe out the last remnants of resistance. Over 1,500 are known to have died in the region.

Tombazis no longer had any reason to remain in Crete. In his last announcement to the Cretan people dated 12 April 1824 he simply urged that they try to continue the struggle for independence. He left Crete in the company of the brave chieftain of Mesara, the crypto-Christian Michael Kourmoulis, who died of grief a short while later on the island of Hydra, having given his all on behalf of his homeland.

With the withdrawal of Tombazis the revolution in Crete essentially came to an end. On the same day Hussein made a declaration from the harbour at Suda Bay granting a general amnesty which was largely greeted with relief. There were only a very few whose will remained unbent and who were determined to continue the struggle which now took on the character of bandit warfare. Various partisan bands now formed and they operated by carrying out flash nightime raids and sabotage. They became known as the Kalisperides (literally, the *Good evenings*). The Turks, using the same tactics, set up terrorist groups composed of fanatical Janissaries. They were known as the Zurides (from the Cretan dialect word for fox) because they carried out devious night raids.

By late May 1824 Hussein had totally stamped out the Cretan revolution. The Turkish-Egyptian force was now free to assist Ibrahim in the Peloponnese. Crete was now to become a supply base for the Turks in the attempts to contain the revolution in the rest of Greece.

10. The Grambousa period (9 August 1825 - 1828)

In mid-1825 the Cretans who had fled to the Peloponnese and were now fighting alongside their fellow Greeks decided to revive the revolution in Crete. A small force of 300-400 men led by Dimitrios Kallergis and Emmanuel Antoniadis arrived in ships from

Spetsai in the area of Grambousa. Thanks to a brilliant plan they managed to become masters of the stronghold of Grambousa (9 August 1825) and on the same day other revolutionaries captured the fortress at Kisamos. The Cretan revolution was suddenly revived in the west of the island and entered on a second phase, known as the Grambousa period (1825-1828). The rekindling of the revolution in the other parts of the island proved to be a slow process. Most of the chieftains had sworn obedience to the Turko-Egyptians, and Mustafa Pasha, who had succeeded Hussein as governor of Crete, appeared to be in a strong position on the island. In endeavouring to appear to be a man of peace and fairmindedness he issued strict orders to the Janissaries threatening to stop by any means, including hanging, excesses carried out by them against the Christians. He gave a similar order to the Christian Cretans, aimed particularly at the Sphakians, with regard to the Muslims.

The capture of Grambousa and Kisamos by the revolutionaries was a grave cause for concern for Mustafa, and he immediately sent out a force of 2,000 men to recapture the fortresses. He failed to win back Grambousa but he did manage to halt the spread of the revolt further in the west of the island. The revolutionaries were contained within the fortress of Grambousa where, in order to maintain their presence, they had to resort to piracy. For about two years the fortress was a base for pirate raids carried out against Cretan coastal areas and approaching shipping, both Turkish and European. A community was organised in Grambousa and a church of the Virgin 'Kleftrina' ('of the Pirates') was built within its walls at the instigation of the abbot of Gonia, Parthenios, and Dimitrios Chrysaphopoulos. The church was opened by the bishop of Ardameri, Ignatius, who also taught at the Greek school in Grambousa.

The stronghold was organised and strengthened. The ship 'Perikles' was bought from Tombazis with contributions from Greeks and Cretans and it carried food and supplies to Grambousa. A caretaker administration was set up with the title Cretan Council and constituted the official revolutionary authority on the island. The president was B. Halis and the other members were Martimianos Perakis, D. Vlastos, N. Papadakis, P. Ioannou, N. Georgiou, B. Ioannidis, I. Xanthis and N. Limbritis. The secretary was A. Pothitos.

Figure 22
Cretan seals
1. SF[RAYI]S T[IS] N[ESOU] GRAMBO[USIS] 1828 (Historical and Ethnological Society of Greece, *Sfrayides Eleftherias,* no. 827).
2. KRITIKON SYMVOULION, 1829 (ibid., no. 507)
3. DIEFTHYNSIS KRITIS, 1829 (ibid., no. 504)

The Treaty of London (6 July 1827) was to have an impact on affairs in Crete. Tombazis sent a communication to the Cretans urging them to revive and extend the revolutionary movement at all costs because, according to his information and estimations, only those areas of the Greek speaking world that were in rebellion against the Ottoman empire would in fact be incorporated within the borders of the newly established Greek state. Crete would therefore have to be in a state of uprising in order that it might have a chance of being included in the Greek borders. In the early autumn of 1827 Cretans and other volunteers in the Peloponnese and other islands were shipped back to Crete. A force of 1,000 Cretans and 100 others was transported by Miaoulis and other naval commanders of Hydra to the fortress of Grambousa in October 1827 with the aim of mobilising a general uprising throughout Crete. As the Sphakians did not appear keen to lead the rebellion the revolutionary forces decided to organise the campaign from the area of Merabello and to begin the uprising in the east of the island. On 20 November a large force led by Halis landed at Agios Nikolaos. Turkish resistance was quickly crushed and the revolutionaries headed for the village of Kritsa and from there made their way towards the area of Neapoli. 400 Turkish Cretans were besieged and killed at the mosque of the village and the Turkish force which had been sent from Herakleion under the command of Ladaoglu was defeated and Ladaoglu killed. In the meantime more and more Cretans from elsewhere in Greece were arriving on the island and their numbers had now reached about 3,000 men. However, the absence of any high command and the lack of discipline led the whole campaign to a bad end. A few days later (9 December 1827) the revolutionaries who had taken control of the eastern villages of the district of Pediada (Malia Stalida, Mocho and Krasi) were not able to withstand the counterattack of the Turkish Albanians and were forced to make a disorderly retreat. The retreat would have been a total disaster if the chieftain of Lasithi Manolis Kazanis had not intervened in time. Some returned to Grambousa and others left Crete for the islands, while still others fled to the inaccessible fastnesses of the mountains.

11. Hadji-Michaelis Dalianis in Crete (1828)

In the early months of 1828 prime minister Ioannis Capodistrias decided to put a halt to banditry and piracy around Greece. He sent Alexander Mavrokordatos to Grambousa in Crete, one of the most notorious bases for piracy, along with the British and French fleets. The pirate ships were destroyed and the fortress was handed over to the British colonel Urquehart who was killed a few months later. In order to secure order and prevent any reemergence of the piracy commander Stains of the British naval squadron took a number of measures.

Shortly before these events took place the bold Epirote fighter Hadji-Michaelis Dalianis had landed at Grambousa on 5 January

1828 at the head of a small force of 600 men and 100 cavalry. After prolonged recriminations and disagreements among the chieftains for the drawing up of a coordinated plan of action it was decided that military operations should commence from Sphakia. In early March Dalianis seized Frangokastello and secured his defences there and was shortly joined by Halis. However, circumstances were running against them. There was a serious shortage of food supplies and other provisions and attempts to stir up revolt in other districts had proved fruitless because Mustafa had already sent threatening communications to the villages describing the reprisals the inhabitants would suffer if they rose up in rebellion. Therefore Hadji-Michaelis, left to his own defences and the help of a few Sphakian chieftains, had to face the whole Turkish army that had been mustered by Mustafa. Dalianis' insistence that they stay to fight out the decisive battle at Frangokastello, despite the advice of the more experienced Sphakians that they should retreat to the mountains, proved to be disastrous. Mustafa, with a force of 8,000 men and 300 cavalry reached the mountain plain of Askypho on 13 May 1828. Five days later the Turkish army had reached Frangokastello where one of the fiercest and bloodiest battles of this entire period of Cretan uprisings was fought. Hadji-Michaelis was killed along with 385 of his finest fighting men. 800 Turks were killed. Just a small number of rebel fighters held on inside the fortress for a few days longer, only to end up by coming to terms with the Turks and being allowed to withdraw. This decisive defeat of the Greeks at Frangokastello (18 May 1828) has become linked in popular Cretan tradition with the so-called Drosoulites -a curious and inexpicable optical phenomenon which can be observed in the area in late May and early June under certain atmospheric conditions.

On his way back to Chania Mustafa suffered serious losses when the Sphakians made surprise attacks and prevented his force from proceeding by burning the forests they were marching through. At Chalara near Agios Antonios Mustafa lost 1,000 men and could have suffered worse if the Turks had not simply dropped their weapons and supplies and fled. Mustafa eventually arrived back in Chania on 30 May with his force shattered.

In June of the same year Capodistrias sent Baron Rheineck to Crete as his representative, who stayed on the island until late March of 1829. Because the stance of the Great Powers was not favourable, Rheineck recommended that the Cretans call a halt to hostilities in accordance with Capodistrias' order. This recommendation was ignored by both the Spjhakians and the chieftains of the other parts of the island. On the contrary the hostilities continued and actually spread further into the region of Siteia. The Cretan Council was reestablished and was composed of representatives from all the regions of Crete. Councils were appointed for all the areas and were assigned the task of supplying weapons and provisions and for protecting the Christian population.

The Cretan revolution revived yet again in almost all parts of the island and the Turkish response was marked by incredible violence against the Christians. In Turkish manuscripts it is mentioned that the Pasha of Herakleion Suleiman had announced that gifts would be given to all those Turks who brought him the heads or limbs of Christians. Fierce fighting took place throughout the summer of 1828 in the region of Mesara where the chieftains Michael Korakas, N. Malikoutis, Ioasaph Xopateras and others managed to confine the Turkish to the larger villages. Here it is worth mentioning a dramatic episode which took place. Ioasaph Xopateras was under siege from a large Turkish force at the tower of the monastery of the Virgin 'Hodegetria' and finally came to a tragic end in March 1828. His death was soon avenged by his friends the chieftains of Mesara when they killed the notorious Janissary Agriolidis in August of the same year. Agriolidis' death and the transfer of his headless body to Herakleion so incensed the Turkish crowd that this served as a pretext for the second major massacre to occur in the town and its surrounding area. About 800 people are thought to have died in this new atrocity which remained in popular memory as the 'Vengeance of Agriolidis'. Similar atrocities took place in Rethymnon, Arkoudaina and Armenokamboi. In Chania Mustafa did not dare to stir the Turkish mob to committing massacre because he was afraid of the likely response of the Great Powers.

The massacres of the civilian populations in Herakleion and Rethymnon had provoked an outcry among the Europeans and a certain amount of pro-Cretan sentiment now made itself felt. In October 1828 both the British and French fleets arrived in Suda Bay and Admiral Malcolm acted as an intermediary in negotiations for a ceasefire and a halt to Egyptian forces arriving on the island. Capodistrias sought to make the most of the pro-Cretan sentiment of the European powers. In November 1828 he sent Emmanuel Tombazis to Crete as his representative in negotiations with the local leaders and chieftains with the purpose of taking control of Siteia, the only Cretan district that still remained under the absolute control of the Turks. In spite of the objections expressed by Rheineck a military campaign was organised in early December 1828. A large force of some 2,500 men led by G. Protopapadakis, G. Tsouderos, P. Zervoudakis and others set out from the village of Kavousi near Ierapetra and attacked the district of Siteia from the direction of Roukakas. The terrified Turks shut themselves in their fortified towers while others fled to the fortresses at Ierapetra and Spinalonga. All 400 Turks who were under siege in the tower of the village of Lithines were killed when the tower exploded, and another 3,000 who had fled to the village of Ethia surrendered when they were given assurances that they would receive safe passage to Asia Minor. Around 1,200 other Turks who had sought refuge in the monastery of the Virgin 'Akrotiriani' (at Toplou) also surrendered when they learnt the news from Lithines and Ethia, and they were transferred to the island of Chalki.

However, Siteia was not to remain in revolutionary hands for long. While the revolutionaries, drunk with unexpected success, had devoted themselves to plundering, a large Turkish force of 4,000 men was on its way to Siteia and managed to recapture it without significant resistance, laying waste the villages in the district and taking thousands of Christians prisoner. Only a handful of Sphakians remained to lay siege to Ierapetra.

In early February 1829 Rheineck was replaced by the Englishman Hain who stayed in Grambousa as the representative of Capodistrias until October of the same year. Fighting was still going on in the region of Chania (Malaxa and Tsikalaria) without, however, reaching any decisive outcome. In October Hain was replaced by the Greek Renieris, 'a man quite advanced in years, with a mild temperament and a fine patriot.' The revolution was kept alive for only a few months longer. Practically all the rural areas were under the control of the revolutionaries while the Turks had been confined to the three main strongholds of the island at Chania, Rethymnon and Herakleion.

12. The end of the Cretan revolution

After ten years of hard fought struggle and bloodshed the revolution in Crete came to an arbitrary end. The Protocol of 22 January 1830 officially left Crete outside the borders of the newly established Greek state, to remain under the absolute jurisdiction of the Ottoman sultan. This solution was imposed by British diplomacy which had always been opposed to Cretan independence. The news of the decision was a cause of great disappointment to the Cretans. They protested in frustration and anger against both the Great Powers and the prime minister of Greece Capodistrias. The Cretan Council which was composed of K. Kritovoulidis, A. Stephanakis, Georgis Saounatsos, N. Limbritis, G, Kalomenopoulos, M. Chionakis, A. Ioannidis, I. Michael, G. Venetikos, G. Sakkorafos, A. Aretinis, A. Papadakis, I. Kondylis and M. Lidas, with N. Damvergis as secretary, called an emergency meeting at the village of Magarites near Mylopotamos on 22 April 1830 and issued a dramatic statement 'To the Greeks': 'Crete has always been and will remain to be an inalienable part of Greece, having fought and still fighting with the rest of the revolutionary parts of the country since the beginning of the struggle for freedom, and no one can understand how, with the various manoeuvres of the representatives of respected monarchies, these same powers can simply neglect to take Crete into account while a violent war is still raging on its land and the Turks have been pushed back by the Greeks into their strongholds... We can find no other salvation than in our arms and in honourable death; and if Christendom wishes to abandon us to the ferocity of the Turks, having seen our women, children and parents slaughtered, let us then too become victims -but noble victims of constancy of spirit and belief in our inalienable rights...'

The final request of the Cretan Council that Grambousa be allowed to remain in the hands of the Cretans was never answered and attempts to take it by force failed. In June 1830 the ships of the Great Powers arrived in the bay of Palaikastro west of Herakleion in order to impose order on the island. The Cretans were compelled to submit to their wretched fate and accept the ceasefire with the proviso that clear guidelines and policy be introduced on the island protecting both the Christian and Muslim elements. This directive was immediately violated by the Turks who carried out further massacres and took more prisoners. 'In the streets of the towns of Crete the daughters, sisters, women and beloved children of the Greek Cretans are sold like pieces of meat': so wrote a group of citizens to N. Renieris in a document signed at Kalyves in the Apokoronas distrirt on 17 August 1830.

CHAPTER II

EGYPTIAN RULE
(1830-1840)

1. The general situation

The Protocol of London granted Crete to the Regent of Egypt Mehmet Ali in exchange for services he had provided the sultan during the course of the Greek revolution in Crete and the Peloponnese. Thus Crete now entered a new phase of 'grim enslavement', as the historian Psilakis phrased it. The ambitious monarch of Egypt was well aware of the significance of possessing Crete and was concerned to secure permanent control of the island. For this purpose, and to avoid possible intervention on the part of foreign powers, he took a number of measures whereby he hoped to achieve internal peace and order. He appointed Mustafa Naili Pasha as governor of the island, who came to be dubbed Giritlis (Cretan) because of his long service in Crete. He assigned military control of the island to his trusted commander Osman Nur-El-Din bey.

The Egyptian administration in Crete wished to appear to be just and impartial, and dealt with Christians and Muslims on an equal basis. With the granting of a general amnesty it summoned all the inhabitants of Crete to lay down their weapons and live peaceably together under a regime of peace and equality. It was during this period that many Muslims, unable to live according to the orders of Mustafa or to come to terms with the prospect of a quiet civilian life, sold their belongings and moved to Asia Minor. There were also many Cretans who refused to lay down their arms, and chose instead to leave Crete and settle in Greece. By a synodical letter (January 1831) the Patriarchate implored the Cretans not to leave their homeland and assured them that they would be fairly treated by Mohammed Ali of Egypt.

Two administrative bodies, called *surades,* were set up for the administration of the island, one at Herakleion and the other at Chania, while two smaller councils were set up in Rethymnon and Sphakia. Besides the Turkish functionaries, one Christian and one Muslim representative from each district of the island participated in these bodies. This, however, was a mockery of fairness since the representation of the Christians always left them in the minority and incapable of imposing their views or suggestions.

It is true, however, that the Egyptian administration was in many respects beneficial and helped to reconstruct the island after the damage caused, socially and economically, by so many years of revolution. A broad programme of works for the common good was implemented: roads, bridges, aquaducts and harbour construction were all undertaken for the first time since the Venetian period on the island. The Egyptian administration gave especial attention to organising education by founding schools for Muslims and Christians. Similar measures were taken for the spheres of justice, social welfare and public health. In 1832-33 a census was carried out on the population and for the first time a newspaper titled *Kritiki Ephimeris* (The Cretan Daily) was published in two languages (1831).

2. The movement of Mournies (1833)

In order to execute such an ambitious programme of public works it was necessary of course to gather vast amounts of money that could only be obtained by increases in taxation and better exploitation of the local resources. The tax measures were extremely oppressive and they provoked general discontent and strong protests from the Cretans; the situation reached it climax with the movement of Mournion. In September 1833 a crowd of about seven thousand Christians gathered at the village of Mournies near Kydonia in order to protest their opposition to the economic oppression of the Egyptian administration. In order that the demonstration not appear to be

Αρ. 12.

ΚΡΗΤΙΚΗ ΕΦΗΜΕΡΙΣ

Τῇ 19. Μαρτίου. 1831, ἐν Χανίοις.

Βαρόμετρον τοῦ ἀέρος Χανίων.

Ε. 1831. 18 Μαρτίου.

	Αὐγή	Μεσημ.	Δείλη Βαθεῖα	Δύσις	δ' Δύσις
Τρίτη	11	13	16	15	14

وقايع كريديه

يوم الاربعا في ١٦ شهر شوال سنة ١٢٤٦

ميزان هواى خانه

ل	ايام	صباح درجه	ظهر درجه	عصر درجه	مغرب درجه	عشا درجه
١٥	ح	١١	١٣	١٦	١٥	١٤

Ο ΜΟΥΣΤΑΦΑ ΠΑΣΣΑΣ ΚΑΙ ΟΣΜΑΝ ΝΟΥΡΕΤΗΝ ΜΠΕΗΣ

Εγκύκλιος. Πρὸς τοὺς Χριστιανοὺς τῶν Επαρχιῶν Κρήτης.

Στοχαζόμενοι, ὅτι ζητεῖτε καὶ θέλετε τὴν ἀνακαίνησιν τῶν Εκκλησιῶν σας ἀπὸ Ημᾶς, διὰ νὰ κάμνετε τὸ Προσκύνημά σας ἐλευθέρως κατὰ τὴν θρησκείαν σας, Ημεῖς κατὰ τὸ πνεῦμα τοῦ Μεχμὲτ Αλῆ Ερένδη μας, τοῦ ὁποίου ἡ μόνη ἐλπίδα εἶναι εἰς τὸ νὰ εὕρωσιν οἱ ἄνθρωποι τῆς Κρήτης ἡσυχίαν, ἀνάπαυσιν, καὶ ἐλευθερίαν, (τὰς ὁμιλήσαμεν πολλὰς φορὰς) θέλομεν ἀπὸ καρδίας νὰ ζῆτε ἐλευθέρως καὶ μὲ εὐχαρίστησιν. Τὸ ἴδιον σᾶς λέγομεν καὶ τώρα διὰ περισσοτέραν σας βεβαιότητα. Νὰ ζῆτε μὲ καθε ἄνεσιν, καὶ ἐλευθερίαν, καὶ νὰ ἔχετε τὴν ἄδειαν νὰ ἀνακαινίσετε καὶ νὰ ἀνακτίσετε τὰς Εκκλησίας σας ὡς ἔχετε τὸν τρόπον καὶ θέλετε, μένοντες ἀπαραίτητοι [illegible] χωρὶς καμμίαν ὑποψίαν καὶ φόβον, διὰ ὅτι Μοναστήρια καινούργια [illegible] Εἴθε πληροφορηθέντες [illegible] εἰς τὸ νὰ κάμνετε ἐλευθέρως τὸ ἔργον [illegible], κατὰ τὸ ζήτημά σας καὶ κατὰ τὴν ὄρεξίν σας. Καὶ κατὰ τοῦτο μένομεν καὶ Ημεῖς εὐχαριστημένοι μὲ τὴν ἰδικήν σας εὐχαρίστησιν.

Figure 23, Page 12 of the first official Cretan newspaper *Vakay Girit* (Cretan Daily), dated 19 March 1831 and published by the Egyptian administration in Chania.

an armed uprising it was forbidden for those present to bear arms. The Sphakian general Deliyannakis who wanted to participate with his men who were all armed was obliged to leave the gathering. On 20 September 1833 those present at the meeting composed and signed a petition to the Great Powers in which they described in detail the new distress they were now suffering and sought their protection.

The Mournies meeting, however, did not just concern itself with economic matters. It took on the character of a general protest against the arbitrary exercise of political and military power on the island: '...The soldiery has been scattered throughout the island and they dishonour us, they divide husbands from wives, they commit whatever their barbaric nature and Asian ferocity leads them to...'

Mehmet Ali's response was immediate and harsh. Osman Nur-El-Din bey attacked the gathering with his cavalry chargers and forcibly dispersed the people. The ringleaders were arrested and 41 of them hanged. In order to terrorise the people into obedience and to pre-empt any attempts at further protest, the authorities arrested and hanged many other preeminent Christians and Muslims who viewed the movement sympathetically or secretly supported it. The new regime was in a sufficiently strong position to prevent the Great Powers from becoming involved in the Cretan issue.

The Cretans were now aware that without the support of the Great Powers they could not entertain any hopes of freedom. In late 1838 exiled Cretans submitted a proposal to the British to invade Crete and declare it a British protectorate. This proposal, however, which was submitted a second time in 1839 met with no response.

3. The end of Egyptian rule. The uprising of 1841

The crisis in the Eastern Question during the years 1839-1841 was to have an impact on the course of events in Crete. The involvement of Mehmet Ali in a war against the Ottoman empire and his defeat in Syria was to shake the basis of Egyptian power in Crete.

The Great Powers, who for reasons of their own national interest had maintained a policy in favour of keeping the Ottoman Empire intact, decided at the Treaty of London (3 July 1840) to secede Crete from Egyptian control and bring it back under Ottoman rule.

Before the Treaty was signed the exiled Cretan chieftains (B. Halis, I. Koumis, Emmanuel Patellaros, Anagnostis Tsouderos, Vasilogeorgis, Hairetis and others) decided to return to Crete in order to organise a new uprising in the hope that this would bring the Cretan issue to the forefront of the discussions. They arrived in Crete in late 1840 accompanied by the young politician Alexander Koumoundouros. The uprising broke out on 22 February 1841 simultaneously across the whole island. In the western regions the leaders were the Hairetis brothers (here the uprising came to be known as the Hairetis Uprising) and in the eastern parts of the island the uprising was led by Vasilogeorgis (hence the Vasilogeorgis Uprising). In their declaration announcing the uprising, the leaders of this new revolution endeavoured to remind the people of the blood that had been shed before in their national struggle and that the time had come for further self-sacrifice in order to win freedom at last, since now European diplomacy was in favour of a liberated Crete.

It is necessary to see the movement of 1841 as a continuation of the similar freedom movements in Thessaly and Macedonia in the years 1839-1841, and it was part of the same historical context. Unfortunately the situation on the island was not conducive to a general uprising such as that of 1821. The Sphakians appeared to be unenthusiastic to risk such an uncertain confrontation and other chieftains from elsewhere also seemed reluctant to embark on a new revolutionary enterprise. Mustafa Pasha, after an abortive attempt to negotiate with the rebel party resorted to force of arms and began a harsh and bloody campaign to stamp out the revolt. Fierce battles took place in the district of Apokoronas (Provarma, Vafe, Vryses) and in the east of Pediada (near the village of Xida). Remarkable as it may seem, during the course of these fierce conflicts, the resourceful Cretan Emmanuel Vyvilakis managed to transfer his printing house to the village of Vafe near Apokoronas and for two months published a paper entitled *Rhadamanthys*.

The Greek government of the day was in no position to come to the aid of the insurgents and the Great Powers put pressure on the rebels to call a halt to their fighting. On 5 April when it seemed clear that it was futile to continue the struggle the rebels composed and submitted a communication to the kings of France and Great Britain and the czar of Russia in which they bemoaned the plight of Crete and implored them once again to intervene. Of course, they received no response and the uprising ended with the mass flight of the rebels and many civilians to Greece.

CHAPTER III

THE PERIOD OF PEACE
(1841-1866)

The internal situation on Crete did not change in any fundamental respect as regards the administration. Mustafa Naili Pasha returned to Crete as General Commissioner on 31 October 1842 and remained in power until 1850 when the sultan promoted him to the office of Grand Vezir (prime minister) and replaced him with Salih Vamik Pasha. The powerful beys of Crete tried to overturn the appointment of Salih 'because they hoped to seize the opportunity to pursue again their own interests', as the newspaper *Rhadamanthys* wrote (p. 46, 14-11-1842).

A few small administrative reforms should be mentioned here. In 1851 the capital of the Ottoman domain *(eyalet)* of Crete was transferred to Chania. The island was divided into 23 provinces *(kazades).* Provincial councillors were apointed in the main centre of each province and they were served by one Muslim *(bulukbasi)* and one Christian sergeant-at-arms *(kastelkiagasi).* The provincial councils were charged with administrative, judicial, policing and economic (tax collection) duties.

The European liberal movements of 1848 also found their counterpart in Crete where once again a revolutionary mood was in the air, although no actual revolutionary act manifested itself. The successor to Mustafa, Salih Vamik Pasha governed the island fairly and generally left a good impression on the people. Salih's successor, however, Veli Pasha, the son of Mustafa the Giritli, brought a return to the old harsh ways.

The Crimaean War (1853-1856) was to have important consequences for the course of Cretan affairs. With the Treaty of Paris

(1856) the sultan was obliged to declare the famous Hatti Humayun by which he granted important privileges to his Christian subjects, such as religious toleration, personal freedoms and assurance of prices and private ownership. Although the Ottoman authorities in Crete refused to put the Hatti Humayun into practice and continually violated its directives it should nonetheless be seen as an important step in the struggle towards achieving recognition of basic rights. The next forty years of the history of Crete (up to the time of autonomy in 1898) is a movement along the path opened up by the Hatti Humayun. The Turkish violations of its clauses were the pretext for the uprisings that occurred in the following years.

The uprising of Mavrogenis (1858)

The administration under Veli Pasha remained authoritarian and harsh, despite the directives of the Hatti Humayun. The imposition of new tax measures and a general curfew sparked off more protests from the Cretans. In April 1858 5,000 Cretans gathered at a protest meeting at Boutsounaria near Chania, and here they elected a Committee that would compose a communiqué to be sent to the consulates of the Great Powers on the island and to the sultan. This political movement, which was named the Mavrogenis Movement on account of the name of its leading figure, led to a number of positive results. Veli Pasha's attempt to use force was blocked by the refusal of the military commander to comply and envoys from the sultan, who arrived in Crete in June 1858, showed considerable understanding and agreed to satisfy, to a large degree, the just demands of the Cretans. Veli Pasha was removed from office and succeeded by Sami Pasha who at once commenced negotiations with the chieftain Manousoyannakis. By a special Ottoman imperial decree issued on 7 July 1858 the Cretans were granted and guaranteed religious, tax, administrative and judicial privileges. The Christians were also granted the right to bear arms, and were charged with setting up councils of elders.

The institution of the Councils of Elders, which was established with the sultan's decree of 1858, was of immense significance for the life of the Christians and its role, especially as regards questions of social welfare, hereditary and family law and education, was particularly important in the decades to come. The elders who were appointed to the boards of the three main departments of the island (Chania, Rethymnon and Herakleion) where directly dependent on the Church. At Chania and Herakleion the council of elders had seven members and at Rethymnon six. One of the members was a clergyman appointed by the Church, while the other members were selected by elective bodies composed of members of guilds, merchants and other well-to-do bourgeois citizens. Similar councils were also set up for the Muslims.

It was also during this period (1858-1866) that an 'anti-revolutionary' movement began to emerge in Crete which wished to promote the idea of an autonomous island Greek state, independent of mainland Greece, under the protection of the British. This movement enjoyed considerable support from notable Cretans, clerics and laity, as well as from the metropolitan bishop Dionysios Charitonidis. The main inspiration behind the 'anti-revolutionaries' was a highly resourceful woman, the teacher Elizabeth Kontaxaki (or Vasilakopoula). The Historical Archive of Crete (at Chania) contains interesting records concerning the activity of the 'anti-revolutionaries'.

CHAPTER IV

THE GREAT CRETAN REBELLION (1866-1869)

The rebellion of 1866-1869 constituted the climax of the Cretans' desire for freedom and union with Greece. It also made plain the clear nationalist character of the Cretan Question and as events developed it began to occupy European diplomacy as an important part of the Eastern Question in general.

There were two main causes behind the Cretans' new and decisive reckoning with the Ottoman empire: the imposition of new taxation, despite the directives against this in the Hatti Humayun, and the so-called monastery question. After a short period of just and mild rule (which led the Cretans to request that he stay on in his post) Ismael Pasha, governor of Crete from 1861, changed tactics and proceeded to enforce a harsh tax policy, aimed chiefly at agricultural produce. The people, however, became particularly angered when Ismael attempted to intervene in the monastery question which had arisen during this period in the eastern provinces. Various enlightened clerics and members of the laity such as Argyrakis and Georgiadis had requested since 1862 that the property of the monasteries be placed under the control of the councils of elders, for the purpose of founding schools. The metropolitan bishop Dionysios, the other bishops and the abbots of the monasteries were opposed to this proposal. The scandalous involvement of Ismael in the selection of representatives who were to debate the issue, the nullification of the election of 'undesirable' figures and the arrest and imprisonment of the members of the committee who had intended to go to Constantinople to discuss the matter with the Patriarch all sparked off violent reaction amongst the Christian population of the island.

From the spring of 1866 meetings had been taking place in several villages: at Atsipopoulo, Anogeia, Agios Myronas and Krasi. On 14 May the first pan-Cretan assembly was held at Boutsounaria near Chania in the monastery of Agia Kyriaki. They drew up a petition to the sultan and conveyed a copy of the petition to the consulates of the Great Powers in Chania: '35 years have passed and during this period the lives of our fathers as well as our own has been just a series of oppressive measures, injustices and misfortunes... we have to pay the most burdensome taxation that gets worse and worse each year... and justice is something quite unheard of for us... for we are but slaves of another people'. The meeting broke up on the same day but on the next many of the representatives signed another petition addressed to the kings of Great Britain and France and to the czar of Russia expressing the wish for union with Greece.

The reply of the Sublime Porte arrived in Crete in mid-July and it rejected in threatening tones the Cretans' demands. Immediately the representatives of the Cretan provinces called a meeting at Brosnero near Apokoronas and signed a declaration of revolution which they then conveyed to the consulates of the Great Powers (20 July). On 21 August the revolutionary assembly summoned the Cretan people to rise up against the Ottoman yoke, issuing a declaration from the village of Askyfou near Sphakia: 'Standing by the oath we swore in 1821 and inspired by national pride in the greatness of Hellenism and national unity, and the justice of our cause, we reject all offers of compromise and boldly declare before God and men that our only unanimous and constant desire is for Crete to be united with the motherland Greece, and we implore almighty God to bless our arms and grant us full success'.

The decision to raise the banner of revolt had been taken, but the prospects did not look promising. British and French diplomacy was opposed to any change in the status quo of the Ottoman empire. Only Russia, which had been humiliated at the Treaty of Paris (1856), favoured the uprising in Crete and supported it through its representatives on the island, Spyridon Dendrinos at the Russian consulate in Chania, and Ioannis Mitsotakis at the vice-consulate in Herakleion. Mitsotakis, in fact, had set up a group entitled the *Secret Society* whose purpose was to prepare the ground for the rebellion and to mobilise forces both within and outside Crete.

Within free Greece popular enthusiasm was a positive factor, but the official state was unable to help either economically or militarily, especially at this time when the Turkish threat appeared to be looming on the borders of Thessaly where Ottoman forces were gathering. Also the politicians were divided in opinion. Dimitrios Voulgaris who supported British policy was decidedly reluctant to express support, while Alexander Koumoundouros, who favoured Russian policy, was more determined. The government of Benizelos Roufos was clearly opposed to the rebellion as is evident in a communiqué sent by the minister of foreign affairs Spyridon Valaoritis to the Greek consul in Chania Nikolaos Sakopoulos (16 April 1866): 'Under the present state of affairs in Europe and the East any imprudent move in Crete would certainly be disastrous. The Cretans... must be extremely cautious and not be drawn into any kind of insurgency, whether from a poor estimation of the political situation in Europe or from the irresponsible exhortations and incitements of hasty and reckless persons.'

With the outbreak of the uprising, Cretans and other Greeks in free Greece immediately mobilised to help collect money, food and supplies. In Athens a Central Committee for the Support of the Cretans was set up, largely run by the distinguished lawyer Markos Renieris (1815-1897), himself of Cretan descent, then governor of the National Bank of Crete. In Syros another special supply committee was set up to support the Cretan struggle with weapons and volunteers who would be transported to the island by Greek coastal shipping. Throughout the course of the rebellion the ships *Hydra, Panhellenion, Arkadion, Krete* and *Henosis,* sailed by brave and courageous captains, carried out numerous missions to supply the Cretan rebels, breaking through the Ottoman exclusion zone and picking up refugees and the wounded to take them back to Greece.

Admiral Nikolaos Sourmelis with his ships *Krete* and *Henosis* carried out no less than twenty-five missions to Crete, transporting a total of 2,310 tonnes of supplies.

All this, however, was quite insufficient for a conflict with the Ottoman empire. Patriotic enthusiasm could not make up for the serious weaknesses that were evident in the Cretan campaign. Already in the early summer of 1866 Turkey had sent a strong military force of some 4,600 men which was joined to the permanent force of Egyptians stationed on the island. Before open confrontation had even begun the enemy army amounted to almost 25,000 men. Immediately after the outbreak of hostilities new reinforcements arrived from Turkey. By September 1866 no less than 45,000 Ottoman Turkish and Egyptian troops were in Crete, not including the 10,000 or so Turkish Cretan inhabitants of the island who had also been mobilised. The Turks were not just immensely superior in numbers, they were also equipped with modern weaponry, abundant supplies and virtually unlimited economic support. Their forces were highly disciplined, the commanders all experienced men of war and the Ottoman fleet was formidable. The Cretan rebels numbered no more than 25,000 and many were experienced fighters and undoubtedly courageous and accustomed to hardship, and also knew the land well and could easily seek refuge in the mountains and turn the conflict into guerilla warfare. But the Turkish force easily swept across the plains, plundering and burning the villages as it did so. The unarmed civilians, the main victims of the rebellion, had to seek refuge in the mountains or outside Crete, while the rebels were frequently obliged to abandon the struggle in order to take care of their families. The rebellion thus developed into a tragedy which was faced by the people with remarkable fortitude.

One of the major weaknesses of the Cretan rebellion was the lack of a commander-in-chief. There was no leading figure for Crete as a whole. The highest revolutionary power was exercised by the General Assembly and later (from early 1867 onwards) by the Caretaker Government, though this had neither a fixed location nor a fixed number of members. It moved around the mountains according to the needs of the rebellion. In place of a commander-in-chief there were a number of important figures who served the Cretan cause. Cretans who had served in previous rebellions, young men who were entering the battlefield for the first time, volunteer officers, clergymen and ordinary individuals all played their part in this great Cretan uprising. It is impossible here to recount the names of all the leaders and chieftains who took part. Ioannis Zymvrakakis, brother of the minister of the armed forces of Greece, was leader of military operations in the region of Chania. The Greek colonel Panos Koronaios, who arrived in Crete in September 1866 with a small force of volunteers, was stationed in the area of Rethymnon. Michael Korakas was in charge of the eastern provinces. These three leaders all had the title of commander-in-chief. There were other leaders in the various provinces: Hadji-Michaelis Yannaris in Kydonia, Konstantinos Kriaris in Selino, Kostaros Voloudakis in Apokoronas, Stamatis Hionoudakis in Sphakia, Michael Tsouderos in Agios Vasileios, Michael Skoulas in Mylopotamos, Paul Dedidakis in Malevizi, Nikolaos Theiakakis in Monofatsi, A. Katechakis in Temenos and Kainourio, Antony Zographos (Xanthoudidis) in Pediada and K. Sphakianakis in Merabello. Learned clerics such as Parthenios Kelaidis of Sphakia and Parthenios Peridis of Kisamos undertook the delicate and difficult task of corresponding with the foreign consuls on the island and handling the diplomatic side of the rebellion.

The first year (1866)

The first preparations and stirrings of rebellion took place long before official outbreak of the uprising. Revolutionary bands of Cretans, known as 'columns', were formed as early as the summer, while the Turks started to flee their villages and seek shelter in the strongholds of the larger towns and the Christian population did the opposite, fleeing the large towns for fear of massacre and heading for the mountains.

The first fighting broke out in mid-August at Selino, before the rebellion had officially started. Kriaris seized the well-fortified position of Stavros and forced the Turks to retreat within the walls of Kandano. The Egyptian Sahin with a force of 5,000 men attempted to take control of the area around Vryses near Kydonia in order to cut off the rebels' communications with Sphakia. The rebels of Apokoronas, however, laid siege to Sahin's position and forced him to seek terms with them and then withdraw to Chania, leaving behind all his provisions. These early successes of the Cretans caused alarm amongst the Turko-Egyptians. Sahin was recalled to Egypt and replaced by the minister of the armed forces Ismael Pasha.

The sultan charged Mustafa Pasha Giritli with the difficult task of suppressing the rebellion. He arrived in Crete on 30 August and immediately issued a statement summoning the rebels to lay down their arms within five days and calling the people to order, with the promise that their just demands would be satisfied. The General Assembly which convened at Kamboi near Kydonia, unanimously rejected the Mustafa's proposals (7 September): 'The rallying call "Union or Death" which rang throughout Crete was the proud response.' The conflict was under way. Mustafa, with a strong force, expelled the rebels from Malaxa (8-11 September) and promptly headed towards Selino in order to relieve the besieged troops of Kandano. He achieved his aims, but on his return to Chania his forces were subject to surprise attacks and he lost many men (21 September). On a third campaign Mustafa attacked the mountain villages in the area of Kydonia where many of the rebels were based, and burnt down the village of Lakkoi, the home of Hadji-Michalis Yannaris, the village of Theriso and Meskla. The rebels, however, managed to fight off Mustafa's forces at Aliakes and totally defeated a force of 1,500 Turks at Kerameia. Mustafa retreated from the mountains of Kydonia and descended on the area of Apokoronas where one of the Cretan high commanders, Ioannis Zymvrakakis, was defeated at the village of Vafe and suffered heavy losses (12 October).

The defeat at Vafe had a serious impact on the morale of the rebels. Many now had the impression that the rebellion did not have any hope of lasting for much longer. The Greek consul, Nikolaos Sakopoulos wrote in his report to the foreign ministry: 'I am very much afraid that we are about to witness a most distressing drama.' Mustafa was quick to exploit the low morale of the enemy and, in a new delaration, called the rebels to lay down their arms and promised a general amnesty, allowing the Greek volunteers safe passage back to Greece. In particular he sought the submission of the Sphakians. Many villages in the region of Sphakia did in fact declare submission, as did also the inhabitants of other villages in other regions of the island, such as in Merabello, Pediada, Rizo and Lasithi. And so the rebellion seemed to have come to a premature end.

The Arkadi carnage

After his victory at Apokoronas, Mustafa left Mehmet Pasha in Vryses while he, at the head of a force of 15,000 men and a powerful artillery unit, descended on the region of Rethymnon. The revolutionary committee of Rethymnon had its centre at the monastery of Arkadi where Panos Koronaios had appointed Ioannis Dimakopoulos as garrison commander accompanied by the valiant abbot of the monastery Gabriel Marinakis. On 8 November 1866 Mustafa's forces surrounded the monastery, while Resit Pasha of Herakleion invaded the region of Mylopotamos in order to prevent the rebel fighters there from being able to cross to Arkadi. 300 armed rebels and 600 women and children had taken refuge in Arkadi. The attack began after Gabriel and Dimakopoulos rejected Mustafa's proposals for their surrender. Despite the enormous strength of their forces the Turks did not manage to storm the monastery on the first day. Only with the deployment of a huge cannon did the Turks manage to smash down the west gate of the monastery, by which entrance the troops burst in at daybreak on 9 November. The abbot had already been killed fighting on the walls of the monastery; but at the critical moment when the Turkish soldiers rushed in Kostis Yamboudakis (or, according to a folk song, the teacher Emmanuel Skoulas of Anogeia) blew up the powder magazine and the entire monastery was reduced to burning rubble. Most of the Greeks were killed along with hundreds of Turks. Just three or four managed to get away free while about 100 were taken prisoner including Dimakopoulos. Dramatic details of the horror of this incident were recorded by the American consul at Chania, Stillman, and the writer Timotheos Veneris in his monumental work *Arkadi Through the Centuries* (Athens 1938) gathered details from a number of soures.

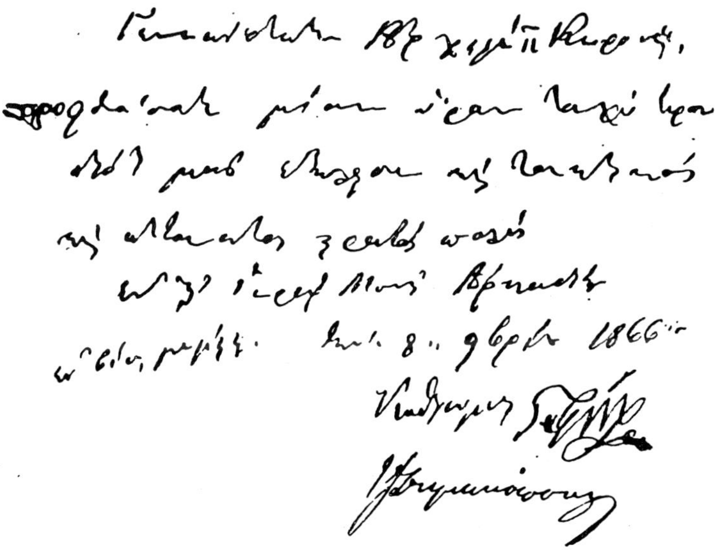

Figure 24
The dramatic letter written by the defenders of Arkadi to the leader P. Koronaios: 'Most valiant leader P. Koronaios, Please hurry to be here even just one hour earlier, for we have been surrounded by a large regular and irregular force. The monastery of Arkadi, 8th September 1866. The abbot Gabriel I. Dimakopoulos. In most urgent haste'. (Timotheos Veneris, *To Arkadi dia ton aionon* [Arkadi through the centuries], p. 250.)

The heroic sacrifice of the monastery made a great impression throughout the world, becoming an event reminiscent of Mesolonghi and Kungi from the days of the Greek war of independence. People of liberal sentiment and philhellenes rose in support of the Cretans, setting up committees and charities and writing in favour of the Cretan cause. The Anglo-Greek Committee in Athens, run by the old British general R. Church, was particularly active in its charity work. The committee provided care and shelter for 4,600 Cretan refugees in Athens. The American philhellene Samuel Gridley Howe was also highly active in supporting the Cretan cause. Volunteer Serbians, Hungarians and Italians also came to Crete, as well as journalists such as H. Skinner, Edmond Desmaze, J. Ballot and others. Letters written by Victor Hugo, published in the newspaper *Kleio* in Trieste, were to help alert public attention in the outside world to the events in Crete. In part of the letter Hugo wrote: 'The heroic monastery, struggling like garrison post, died like a volcano. The tragedy of Psara was no more epic, the Mesolonghi siege does not stand higher.' Hugo was comparing the Arkadi explosion to two of the heroic though tragic exploits of the Greek revolution and war of independence of 1821.

The rebellion in the east of the island

Military operations began in the area of Herakleion on the first days of September 1866. The Turkish army entered the village of Agios Myron and slaughtered the women and children who had taken refuge in the cave of Sarchou nearby. They then proceeded to attack the rebels at Almyro, but were repulsed and suffered heavy losses (8 September). However, at the battle that took place on 13 October near the villages of Kastamonitsa and Amariano in eastern Pediada the rebels were unable to withstand the 8,000 strong enemy force and retreated leaving seventy dead, including the local leader Emmanuel Tyllianakis.

In late December the steamer *Panhellenion* arrived in Crete with the Maniot colonel Dimitrios Petropoulakis and a force of 350 volunteers. They landed at Fodele where they were immediately attacked by Turkish troops and forced to take to the mountains of Malevizi. A short while later, however, on 15 January the Turkish army suffered a major defeat in the battle of Tylissos, where 600 of its men were killed. On the Cretan side, though, the valiant leader of Malevizi, Paul Dedidakis, was killed.

Mustafa's final campaigns

After the catastrophe at Arkadi Mustafa decided to direct his operations for a second time against the mountain villages of Kydonia (27 November) and against the area of Selino. At this time disagreement had broken out between the commanders Zymvrakakis, Koronaios and Korakas over the organisation of the supreme command of the Cretan forces. The bickering between the Cretan leaders and the lack of weapons and supplies were all to play into Mustafa's hands, who now found little resistance to his movements. His main objective now was Sphakia. In late December part of Mustafa's troops were transported by ship to Agia Roumeli and Frangokastello where Mustafa himself arrived in early January. The Sphakians were in a dire position. Their main concern was to save the civilian population which had fled to the shores hoping to find salvation in the Greek and European ships anchored off the coast.

The rough terrain and the harsh winter conditions that now set in forced Mustafa to leave Sphakia after he had received declarations of obedience from various villages and their leaders. On his return from the region, however, he was to suffer extensive losses in the Katre gorge where 500 of his men were killed. The Turkish army left its arms and supplies to the rebels. The American H. Stillman considered this to be Mustafa's most disastrous expedition of the whole campaign against the Cretan rebellion.

Despite heavy loss of life and equipment Mustafa believed that he had achieved his goals. But the rebellion had not been suppressed and the Sublime Porte (which now had to face an outcry from the international community and a temporary change in European, and especially French, diplomacy in favour of the Cretans) was well aware of this. In January 1867, in order to appear to be conciliatory and to try and improve the image of the Ottoman empire, the sultan sent Server efendi to Crete with an imperial decree arranging for the election and sending of representatives -one Muslim and one Christian from each province of the island- to Constantinople in order to submit proposals for the solution to the Cretan question. Server's mission, however, did not lead to any fruitful results. The sultan recalled Mustafa and replaced him with the Croatian convert to Islam, Omer Pasha, one of the most able generals of the Ottoman Empire.

Omer in Crete

Omer arrived in Crete in March 1867 and immediately took charge of the 25,000-strong Turkish-Egyptian forces. His military plan, quite different to that of Mustafa, was to be directed against two main targets: Sphakia and Lasithi. In April 1867 Omer attempted to invade the region of Sphakia by striking it on a number of fronts, but despite ferocious attacks he failed to achieve anything. He then decided to direct his efforts against the eastern part of the island, leaving Mehmet Pasha at Apokoronas and Ali Sarchos at Kydonia in order to prevent the rebels in those parts from being able to move east. Continually harrassed by the Cretan forces of Mylopotamos and Malevizi, Omer eventually reached Herakleion on 10 May where he drew up his plans for the campaign against Lasithi. Lasithi was to eastern Crete what Sphakia was to western Crete: the base and supply point of the rebels. Korakas and the local leaders sealed off the main paths of access through to Lasithi, but Omer concentrated his forces at Kastelli in the region of Pediada where the Egyptian Ismael and Ali Sarchos had arrived from western Crete. Having deceived the rebels about his real intentions Omer managed to go from Yerakiani in Lagada to the summit of Mount Afendis, from where he descended on the rebels at Kara and crushed all attempts at resistance by Petropoulakis. On 21 May the Turkish forces descended on the plain where the rebels had now gathered. Korakas managed to hold off the Turkish attacks for a while with his small cavalry regiment but eventually superiority of numbers and better equipment defeated them. Lasithi was destroyed a second time.

Omer's success, however, about which he boasted so confidently, was not to be long-lived. Immediately after the departure of the Turks the rebels and inhabitants of the plain returned. Omer went back to Herakleion and from there made towards Chania, while the forces of Resit Pasha and Ali Sarchos (Ismael had died at Kastelli in Pediada) headed towards Mesara. At the battle of Gergeri on 13 June the Turks once again suffered heavy losses. A few days later Omer arrived by ship at Tymbaki in the district of Mesara in order to organise his campaign against Sphakia. On 23 June a part of the army was transported to Sphakia by ship while other divisions marched into the area of Sphakia overland. Invading on two fronts Resit and Mehmet moved towards the plain of Askypho where they joined forces with Omer. Thanks to careful coordination, and despite the brave resistance of the Sphakians and other Cretans who had come from other parts of the island, Omer managed to subdue the whole region and, for yet another time, to inflict immense destruction on Sphakia. However, there was a heat-wave during this time and water shortage and the Turks were forced to abandon the unfortunate area. Resit, seriously wounded, returned to Herakleion, Mehmet returned to Apokoronas and Omer, by ship, to Chania. Another Turkish campaign, this time against Omalo and the Samaria gorge, which began on 31 July was not successful.

The campaigns led by Omer served to show that the Turkish army was able to prevail in the battles with the rebels, but it could not impose permanent and stable hegemony in the more remote regions of the island. The moment the Turkish forces withdrew from the area the rebels reappeared from their remote fastnesses. The result was a vicious circle, and the rebellion had developed into a long, drawn out tragedy for both sides. It was clear, as far as the Ottoman empire was concerned, that the achievements of the Turkish military campaigns were not proportionate to the cost in money and human life.

This situation and the increasing indignation of the international community at the crude tactics of the Turks in Crete, compelled the sultan to change direction for yet another time and adopt a policy of concession and conciliation.

Aali Pasha in Crete. The Organic Act

The sultan recalled Omer and announced a ceasefire for five weeks in Crete, from 5 September 1867, and granted a general amnesty. The Grand Vezir Aali Pasha was sent to Crete bearing a number of administrative concessions which constituted the foundation of the so-called Organic Act of 1868. In essence it promised an elementary form of autonomy for Crete, with various privileges being granted to the Christians of the island. Aali Pasha arrived in Crete on 22 September 1867 and straight away issued a proclamation summoning the rebels to lay down their arms within a period of 45 days and inviting the people to elect representatives within a period of just two weeks. He informed the Revolutionary General Assembly of the Cretans that he was prepared to sanction practically any form of government provided that the basic demand of union with Greece was withdrawn. The Cretan response was negative and hostilities continued, though this did not prevent Aali Pasha from proceeding with his plans. He announced elections in the Turkish occupied parts of the island and in the three main towns and convoked a puppet assembly at Chania, composed of 30 Muslims and 20 Christians none of whom were recognised or esteemed members of the community and all of whom had been chosen under pressure or bribed. Moreover, the courts were manned with individuals drawn from the manual trades: craftsmen, wine merchants and grocers.

British policy favoured the plans of Aali Pasha in Crete and its representatives supported him and tried to encourage the people to submit to the Pasha's designs. We mentioned earlier the activity of the so-called 'anti-revolutionaries' of the period, such as Elizabeth Kondaxaki at Chania, friend and sympathiser of the British consul.

On 11 November Aali outlined to the Chania Assembly 14 basic directives of an administrative regulation for Crete, which later came to be termed the Organic Act. In accordance with these new reforms Crete was to constitute a *vilayet* (administrative province) of the Ottoman empire, supervised by a Governor General (*vali*) appointed by the sultan. The island was divided into five councils and twenty provinces, as follows: the Chania Council with the provinces of Kydonia, Selino and Kisamos, and the capital at Chania; the Sphakia Council, with the provinces of Sphakia, Apokoronas and Agios Vasileios, and the capital at Vamos; the Rethymnon Council, with the provinces of Rethymnon, Mylopotamos and Agios Vasileios, and the capital at Rethymnon; the Herakleion Council, with the seven moden day provinces of the *nomos,* Temenos, Malevizi, Kanourio, Pyrgiotissa, Monofatsi, Viannos and Pediada, and the capital at Herakleion; and the Lasithi Council with the provinces of Lasithi, Merabello, Ierapetra and Siteia, and the capital at Neapoli. In both the central and provincial councils Christian employees were appointed according to a fixed ratio with the Muslims. Law courts were to be composed of both Muslims and Christians, while elected councillors were to participate on the board of the General Council and at the administrative councils of the five main regions and the provinces. Both Turkish and Greek were recognised as official languages.

These directives along with other articles concerning tax concessions and the setting up of a Commercial Bank were all included in an Imperial Decree which was issued on 8 January 1868 and circulated among the Cretans on 3 February. This was the Organic Act by which Crete was to be governed throughout the next decade (1868-1877).

The end of the rebellion

Aali Pasha returned to Constantinople satisfied with the policies he had implemented in Crete, but the rebellion had not been finally put down. In November 1867 the governorship of Crete was put in the hands of Hussein Avni Pasha who followed a totally different political line to that of his predecessors. Having realised that organised military campaigns were merely damaging the army and failing to produce stable results he decided to consolidate control of the provinces by constructing towers at strategic points where permanently based squadrons would be installed. It was to these towers, which formed a chain of communication between themselves, that he entrusted the permanent military control of the provinces and the vigilant surveillence of the insurgents. This system proved to be efficient, though the rebels changed their struggle into a kind of guerilla warfare that lasted throughout 1868 without producing any clear results.

The rebellion came up against other difficulties, both internal and external, and started to peter out. The people had become weary and the means for continuing the armed struggle had been reduced to a minimum. The sending of supplies from Greece had now become a problem since the landing places and harbours of Crete were now inaccessible to unapproved foreign shipping and the patrols of the Turkish fleet had been stepped up, particularly when the naval command was taken over by the ex-British officer Hobart Pasha. The steamer *Arkadion* had been sunk off the south coast of Crete, while in December 1868 Hobart pursued the Greek ship *Henosis* as far as the port of the island of Syros, where he then prevented it from being able to leave. Turkey then proceeded to accuse Greece of actively supporting the Cretan civil unrest and a Greek-Turkish conflict was threatened though finally averted thanks to the intervention of the Great Powers.

Greece, however, was forced to accept the terms of the Turkish ultimatum and to cease sending volunteers and supplies to Crete. By

October 1868 the rebellion in west Crete had expired and was definitively laid to rest with the destruction of Sphakia. Attempts by Korakas and his rebel companions in the eastern provinces of Crete to keep the insurgency alive at all cost were in vain.

The rebel 'caretaker government' was to come to a tragic end on 11 December in Gonia, Kisamos province. It was suddenly besieged by the Turks and most of its members were killed. The decision taken on 30 December by the rebel leaders of six eastern provinces to continue the armed struggle could only now be described as wishful thinking dictated merely by the general disaffection and disappointment of the people.

In January 1869 events suddenly took a new turn. European diplomacy had now turned in favour of the Ottoman Empire. At Paris (9-20 January) the Great Powers agreed to forbid Greece from setting up volunteer bands aimed at stirring up rebellion within Ottoman territory or sending provisions with ships 'destined to assist in any manner attempts at rebellion on the domains of His Majesty the Sultan.' Following this Turkey took determined measures to stamp out all remnants of insurgency within the eastern provinces of the island. The final blow came when a price was set on the heads of the leading rebels. On 18 January the Pasha of Herakleion stuck up an announcement commanding the ringleaders to give themselves up within a period of ten days with the promise of a general amnesty for all. After the deadline had passed a price of 500 Ottoman sovereigns was placed on the head of each rebel leader. This new development caused alarm amongst the rebel leaders of the eastern provinces who then called a meeting at Tzermiado in Lasithi (26 January) in order to decide on the matter. As was to be expected, at the dramatic meeting that was held, opinions were divided. The leader of the six eastern provinces, Konstantinos Sphakianakis, decided to give himself up to Adosidi Pasha in Neapoli, and many others followed suit. A tiny number, out of stubbornness and frustration refused to lay down their weapons and chose to become outlaws (Zographos, Tyllianakis, Tryphitsos, Angelidakis, Tongos and Spyridakis).

The rebellion had finally ended without the basic desire of the Cretans for freedom and union with Greece being fulfilled. Human and material losses and destruction had been incalculable both for the Cretans and for the Ottoman Empire which irreparably damaged its prestige and reputation by its handling of the whole episode. The carnage and bloodshed had only served to prove that the solution to the Cretan Question would not be possible without a general conflict throughout the Balkans that would finally cut the Ottoman Empire down to size. The only positive gain for Crete was the Organic Act and the privileges which it conceded, and which served to place the Cretan Question on a new footing as well as constituting a constant point of reference for all the liberation movements that were to emerge during the years up to autonomy in 1898.

CHAPTER V

THE DECADE OF THE ORGANIC ACT
(1868-1878)

The Sublime Porte viewed the Organic Act as a gesture of good will and an important concession to the Christian population of Crete. By ignoring the distinctly nationalist character of the Cretans' demands it appeared to believe that it could displace the problem by granting 'equal' privileges to both the Christians and Muslims of the island. The Organic Act, however, amounted to little more than a sleight of hand. It contained wholly unacceptable clauses as well as deceiving the Christian element into thinking that it was represented at the General Assembly. The 250,000 or so Christians were represented by 38 members, while the 70,000 Muslims had 36. Even the Jews, who amounted to no more than 50 families, had a representative. This highly disproportionate representation meant that the Christians, once again, had very little hope of having their proposals adopted. Despite the deliberate weaknesses and obscurities built into the Organic Act, the Muslims themselves were able to obstruct its implementation in many ways and continually sought its abolition. In reality the Organic Act was never fully implemented. Its continual violation led to repeated protests from the Cretan representatives and to petitions for modifications in the Act which, however, were never adopted by the Sublime Porte. On the contrary the authorities harassed and imprisoned or exiled those who protested against the flouting and violation of the Act. Christopher Argyrakis of Herakleion and K. Mitsotakis of Chania who 'protested repeatedly against the gross flouting of the Christians' rights and the scandalous mockery of the Act, and demanded that the Act be simplified and that many of its clauses be abolished', were expelled from the island, the former being sent to Asia Minor and the latter to Constantinople. The ironic expression 'Organic Act for Crete, and glitter for the *dovleti*' reveals the Cretans' feelings for the new situation on the island.

Following the uprising of 1866-69 the internal situation on the island did not leave much lea way for strong protests, while at the same time it favoured political experimentation for Turkey. For five years at least (1869-74) the situation on Crete was grim. The population had been reduced in the carnage of the rebellion and the mass expulsions, villages had been deserted, houses were in ruins and abandoned, and the land had been left uncultivated. Crete had to be reconstructed from the ruins, and it had to do this equipped solely with its own resources. During the course of the decade from 1869-1878 Turkey sent Muslim military leaders as Governors General of the island, who were hostile to any kind of reform and progress. With the exception of the brief term of office of Reuf Pasha (1871), a man educated in France and possessed of a more progressive, dynamic and, above all, just spirit, and who succeeded in winning the affection of the Christians, the Ottoman administration of these years was characterised by rigidity and an anti-Christian fanaticism. It is worth bearing in mind that from 1871 onwards the Ottoman Empire entered a phase of great political instability. It was at this time that the Panislamic movement took root and that attempts to introduce liberal principles into the Empire came up against strong reaction. In Crete the main group representing this reaction was composed of the Beys, a strong force that opposed in every way possible the moves for equal rights for Christians and Muslims that had been given shape by the privileges contained in the Organic Act. It was for this reason that important public works in Crete were not undertaken, and those that had been planned, such as a road link between the three main towns on the north coast, were not realised. Social welfare was virtually non-existent and the Orphan Fund that had been set up in 1858 for the purpose of protecting the property of orphans eventually ended up by serving the purpose of lining the pockets of the Turkish organisers.

The major European events of the period were not without their impact on Crete. The Franco-Prussian War of 1870 forced the Turks to step up their vigilance and supervision of the situation on the island. However, it was the revolution in Bosnia-Hercegovina which broke out in the spring of 1875 that was to have the strongest influence on the internal situation in Crete. Revolutionary fervour was suddenly rekindled and various signs of insurgency reemerged, both on the island and elsewhere. The Sphakian abbot Parthenios Kelaidis, dubbed Kapetan-Papas by Hadji-Michalis Yannaris, sounded out the Cretan exiled leaders from his base in Trieste as to the possibilities of reviving rebellion in Crete along the lines with that in Bosnia-Hercegovina. The All-party Government in Greece was in no position, however, to voice open support for such ideas, but already in Crete revolutionary committees had been set up. The more prudent and moderate of the Cretans rejected the proposal for another rebellion that might simply lead to the total destruction of the island; others favoured the idea of making Crete a British protectorate, thereby abandoning the tactic of seeking union with the rest of Greece, which had in any case been systematically and persistently rejected by European diplomacy. The idea of Crete as a British protectorate, which had been promoted earlier, was supported by the Anglophile element on the island, the leaders of Sphakia and Konstantinos Sphakianakis and the General Commander of the six eastern provinces from the time of the rebellion of 1866. Sandwith, the British consul at Chania, after a tour of the island wrote in a report to the British government in late 1875 that 'I was not aware of this earlier, but have since learnt that there is a pro-British party on the island, opposed to both Greece and Russia, and that it seeks British protection for the island'. This idea, however, was not particularly popular, and could not very well be promoted considering that Britain itself had not declared, at least openly, any desire to play the role of protecting power. In mid 1876 another group of Cretans, whose number included Parthenios Kelaidis, put forward the idea of declaring Crete an autonomous principality. They even suggested that Gregory Ypsilandis, Greek ambassador to Vienna, should be the ruler, but Ypsilandis rejected the proposal.

In the same year (1876) the General Assembly of the Cretans had petitioned for the safeguarding of the Organic Act by means of an imperial decree from the sultan and with some fundamental modifications of its clauses, and in particular of those which concerned the representation of the religious components of the population in the provinces and towns. The petition was not even discussed by the Sublime Porte. In early 1877 the internal situation on the island was again in turmoil with the referendum for the first Turkish constitution of Midat. The Christians of Crete submitted a petition to the Gorvernor General Samih Pasha requesting that Crete be excepted from the rulings of the Turkish constitution and that it be considered a self-administrative province as provided by the Organic Act. Samih Pasha dissolved the General Assembly and the Christian representatives sought refuge in Apokoronas. Tension had once again risen and it seemed likely that a new rebellion was about to break out.

CHAPTER VI

THE REBELLION OF 1878

This was the situation in Crete at the time when the Russo-Turkish War broke out in the spring of 1877. This new period of crisis in the Eastern Question was seized upon as a golden opportunity for a new revolutionary movement in Crete and the Cretans and supporters of the Cretan movement started to mobilise themselves once again. In July 1877 a 44-member committee was elected in the western provinces in order to deal with the Cretan Question. A 'Cretan Centre' was set up in Athens at the instigation of Markos Renieris for the purpose of gathering weapons and supplies for Crete where three revolutionary committees had been set up at Vamos, Chania and Rethymnon. In August of the same year the committee of Chania elected a post-revolutionary committee to be based at Krapi, and shortly afterwards representatives from all the committees decided to call an all-Cretan revolutionary assembly in the village of Fres in the province of Apokoronas for the purpose of electing a Presidium.

The likely defeat of Turkey in its conflict with Russia finally determined the Greek government's position. Harilaos Trikoupis, minister of foreign affairs in the all-party government led by Koumoundouros announced on 27 December that Greece would actively support an uprising in Crete, while exiled Cretan leaders and fighters were already on their way to the island. The first to arrive back in Crete was Hadji-Michalis Yannaris, who had been in exile in Russia, and he was soon followed by the clan leaders of west Crete, Korkidis, Boyatzoglou, Kriaris, Skalidis, the monk Parthenios Peridis and others. Similar activity took place in the eastern provinces under the general command of Michalis Korakas. In January

1878 the Pan-Cretan Revolutionary Assembly, the largest meeting of its kind to have taken place in Crete, met in the village of Fres, with a multitude of representatives.

In the meantime Turkey was preoccupied with its war against Russia and was unable to send forces to Crete. Instead it attempted, at the suggestion of Britain, to resort to a policy of compromise and pledges. Two envoys of the Sublime Porte, Kostis Adosidis Pasha, former governor of Lasithi, and the Turko-Cretan Selim Efendi were charged with the task of negotiating with the Cretan revolutionaries, and offering further concessions and privileges within the framework of the Organic Act. The revolutionary assembly charged Ioannis Tsouderos of Rethymnon with the task of composing the reply which included the following terms: 1) that Crete be declared an autonomous principality, paying tribute to the sultan, and 2) that the governor be a Christian and that he be elected with the Great Powers as guarantors. Adosidis asked to be given ten days to convey the content of the Cretans' proposals to Constantinople. The ten days passed but no Turkish reply was forthcoming.

And so rebellion broke out, firstly in west Crete in mid-January, soon to spread across to the eastern provinces. Once again the Turks left the countryside to seek refuge in the large fortified towns. By the

Figure 25. Seal of the revolutionary caretaker government of Crete, 1878. Stamped on a document dated 10 July 1878 (Historical Archive of Crete, Chania).

end of March the whole of Crete was under rebel control apart from the strongholds of Ierapetra, Spinalonga, Herakleion, Rethymnon, Itzedin, Chania, Kisamos and Grambousa, none of which could be breached without the aid of heavy artillery.

The collapse of the Turkish front in its war with Russia was to have fateful consequences for the development of Cretan affairs. Article 15 of the Treaty of San Stefano (February 1878) merely obliged Turkey to comply to the stipulations of the Organic Act of 1868. In July 1878 the consuls of the Great Powers in Crete insisted on a ceasefire, promising that the Cretan Question would be considered at the Berlin Conference which was to revise the Treaty of San Stefano. The General Assembly of the Cretans decided to send two representatives, Kostaros Voloudakis and Ioannis Sphakianakis, to the Berlin Conference. The Greek government, however, objected to this and refused to transport them to the conference because it suspected that the Cretan representatives would suggest the solution of a principality, thereby abandoning, for diplomatic reasons, the demand for union with Greece.

The Great Powers' decision at the Berlin Conference did not differ greatly from that of the original Treaty of San Stefano. It simply obliged Turkey to implement the Organic Act along with any alterations deemed necessary. It was for this reason that the Cretans decided to continue the armed uprising, despite the internal difficulties that had started to appear. Irregularities in the management of the war supplies and above all the food supplies, divided the clan leaders and led to distressing incidents, particularly in the area of Mesara, in August 1878.

The Haleppa Agreement (October 1878)

Turkey, now satisfied that the solution of union with Greece had been ruled out for the Cretans, gladly accepted British proposals for new concessions to the Christian population of the island. Two new negotiators, Gazi Ahmet Muhtar Pasha and Selim Efendi, arrived in

Crete, while the Governor General Kostis Adosidis Pasha and Sandwith, the British consul at Chania, persuaded the General Assembly of the Cretans to appoint representatives to conduct talks with the Turks. Among the representatives was the young doctor Ioannis Sphakianakis, son of K. Sphakianakis the leader of the six eastern provinces of Crete during the rebellion of 1866. Ioannis was described in the following words: 'his imposing presence, and his twenty-eight years, gave a certain tone to the talks and exercised a positive influence of discretion and higher patriotism in all there'.

In October 1878 the so-called Haleppa Agreement was signed (the name of a district in Chania) which was immediately ratified by imperial decree from the sultan and comprised the new political constitution of Crete. Its main clauses were the follwing:

1) The Governor General of Crete could be a Christian. His term of office was to be five years, and could be renewed.

2) The Governor General was to have a councillor of the other faith (ie. Muslim, if he was a Christian, and *vice versa*).

3) The General Assembly was to have eighty deputies (49 Christians and 31 Muslims).

4) A Cretan gendarmerie was to be set up.

5) Greek was recognised as the official language of the courts and of the General Assembly. Only the Proceedings, court rulings and official correspondence would be composed in both Greek and Turkish.

6) A general amnesty was to be granted.

7) There would be temporary tax exemptions.

8) The establishment of literary societies and associations was to be allowed as well as the publication of newspapers.

The Haleppa Charter was without doubt an important step towards resolving the Cretan Question since it turned Crete into a semi-autonomous province with specific privileges. The first governor to be appointed under this new constitution was Alexander Karatheodoris. He was in office for just a few months until succeeded by Ioannis Fotiadis, a highly educated and energetic figure with both administrative and diplomatic experience and one time ambassador of Turkey to Greece. He was governor until 1885, and his term of office was characterised by moderation and justice. He supported the establishment of new schools, he promoted attempts at solving serious economic problems, such as customs and monastic property, and he laid the foundations for the better internal organisation of the island. Educational associations were set up in the larger towns and measures were taken to protect Cretan antiquities. However, the next three governors (Savvas Pasha, Anthopoulos and Sartinsky) were not able to govern so efficiently and were drawn into the local disputes and domestic political wrangling that now started to appear on the island.

CHAPTER VII

THE SITUATION IN CRETE UP TO THE TIME OF THE REBELLION OF 1889

During the decade between the Haleppa Agreement and the next rebellion of 1889 Crete was marked by intense political disputes and party intrigue which were to have a debilitating effect on the internal order and development of the island, turning the whole people -in the words of the future prime minister of Greece, Eleftherios Venizelos- into 'fanatical politicians'. Two major parties were created: the Karavanades party and the Xypoliti party. The former which represented the conservative element of the island was largely formed of the more serious, educated and powerful members of Cretan society, such as Hadji-Michalis Yannaris, his brother Professor Antonios Yannaris, N. Stavrakis and I. Sphakianakis. They also occupied the highest posts in the administrative hierarchy of Crete; it was for this reason that they were dubbed derogatorily by their political opponents 'Karavanades', implying that they drained the public treasury of its funds. The Xypoliti on the other hand represented the liberal and progressive tendencies of the age. Leading members of this poitical group were the lawyer Konstantinos Mitsotakis, the Fumis brothers, the Sphakian A. Michelidakis and others. A similar division of political alignment was also to be observed amongst the Muslims of Crete. The curious aspect of the Muslim allegiances was that it was the lower social group of the agas who supported the Karavanades, while the powerful beys tended to support the Xypoliti. Political fanaticism now split the people and frequently led to acts of violence, vandalism and murder. At the same time this period also saw a great increase in livestock theft, an endemic phenomenon of Cretan rural life.

The Cretan Question seemed to have been forgotten in the turmoil and disturbances of political passions. In 1888 there was a revival of the idea of seeking British protection, also supported by foreign figures such as the old American friend of Crete Stilmann. This idea was not to find much support among the people; rather it was fiercely rejected: 'We prefer Turkish rule a thousand times more than British', wrote the newspaper *Lefka Ori*.

The rebellion of 1889

In the elections of 1888, which were marked by gross irregularities, the Xypoliti party won. The Karavanades, however, reacted in a wholly unprecedented and unforeseen manner which was to have grave consequences for the political life of the island. At the General Assembly of 6 May 1889 they tabled a motion supporting the union of Crete with Greece. This move was illegal and tantamount to revolution. The Governor General N. Sartinsky hastened to dissolve the General Assembly and to issue a warrant for the arrest of the leading members of the Karavanades who had already taken flight to the mountains where they declared the commencement of a new rebellion. And so while the General Assembly was now bereft of the official opposition and left in the hands of the Xypoliti, the Karavanades-inspired revolution rapidly gained ground amongst the popular consciousness. The people now abandoned political passions and once again embraced the dream of union with Greece.

However, conditions for the spread and consolidation of a new uprising in Crete were far from favourable. The government of Harilaos Trikoupis was quick to dissociate itself from the rebellion, and Turkey, exploiting the situation, hastened to recall the Governor General Satinsky and replaced him with the uncompromising military figure of Sakir Pasha. The new Governor General immediately imposed a state of martial law. The Turkish army tool control of key points of the island, while the Muslim population once again took to violence and looting. Courts-martial were installed and the death penalty became a daily occurrence in Crete.

This luckless rebellion had further consequences. Turkey, using the excuse that the parliamentary institution had failed to work in Crete, revoked the Haleppà Charter by a decree dated 17 December 1889 which was issued in wholly unorthodox fashion and not revealed beforehand to the Great Powers, and which brought a return to the Turkish style of government of the past. All political and religious privileges were revoked and heavy taxation was imposed. The only course of action available to the Cretans was passive resistance which was manifested by mass resignations from public posts.

CHAPTER VIII

THE POLITICAL ACTION COMMITTEE AND THE REBELLION OF 1895

The five years from 1890-1895 were among the most bleak of the entire period of Turkish rule in Crete. Old passions and hatred reemerged and acts of violence became a daily phenomenon. The new developments had convinced Cretan leaders that union with Greece could not be achieved by means of locally centred uprisings, but would only be possible within the context of a wider crisis throughout the Balkans. This is how the idea first took root of setting up an autonomous or semi-autonomous state in Crete under the protection of the Great Powers and postponing until later and under more favourable circumstances union with Greece. This idea was warmly promoted by the dynamic abbot Parthenios Kelaidis up to June 1892 when he was expelled from the island.

In the same month a small rebel movement emerged in Sphakia but it soon died out, having failed to spread to the other provinces (September 1892). It was clear that it would take a long time before the people and the leaders of Crete would be ready psychologically for a new uprising. With this in mind a secret fraternity of Cretan clan leaders was set up in February 1893 at Sphakia and it set about winning other Cretan clan leaders and political figures over to its cause and preparing for a new rebellion and the retrieval of their lost privileges. This fraternity, however, which was fired with enthusiasm and numbered some 150 members -all sworn to secrecy- was not able to undertake wider action, having neither a specific plan nor a generally recognised leader.

In 1895 circumstances seemed to favour Cretan affairs. The massacre of the Armenians (January 1895) shocked world opinion and created a poor image for Turkey which now received formal protests from all quarters. Fear of further massacres that might occur in Crete made the Cretan people wary of action, but affairs were to evolve differently. The Sublime Porte attempted to alter its image by contriving a spectacular act. In March 1895 it suddenly replaced the severe Mahmut, Governor General of Crete, with the Christian Alexander Karatheodoris. The Cretans took courage and responded positively to his plea for them not to leave public office and to send representatives to the General Assembly. However, the Cretan Turks were wholly opposed to the appointment of Karatheodoris and organised a pan-Cretan terrorist group which then committed murders and other acts of violence with the intention of provoking a state of emergency on the island and forcing Karatheodoris to step down. The people could not react but there appeared fearless guerilla fighters who organised bands who carried out revenge killings. Two figures, Joseph Liapis and P. Yiparis, became notorious for their organised acts of revenge. In this climate of general anarchy the Governor General was unable to carry out his duties. When the Cretan representatives demanded the reinstatement of the Haleppa Charter, Karatheodoris became alarmed and dissolved the Assembly on 18 June 1895.

At this critical stage in Cretan affairs there appeared on the scene the Sphakian politician Manoussos Koundouros, one of the most important figures in Crete in the last decade of the nineteenth century and magistrate at Vamos from 1890. He was one of the few people to seek public office at a time of passive resistance because he believed that in such a post he would be able to help more effectively his homeland. He believed that autonomy would serve as a first step towards union with Greece and secretly made moves to set up a political action committee that would prepare the ground for a new rebellion. His views which were supported by Billioti, the British consul at Chania, were clearly and fully set out in a note that he was to submit to the General Assembly as well as to the consuls of the Great Powers. Most of the members of the secret fraternity joined forces with Koundouros and Joseph Lekanidis, despite his initial reservations, took up the post of secretary of the action committee.

Figure 26
Seal of the Central Political Committee of Crete (1895). (*Sfrayides Eleftherias,* no. 1566.)

Koundouros' note was approved at a meeting held in the village of Klima in the province of Apokoronas on 3 September 1895, and on 10 September at a General Meeting held in Krapi; it was then sent to the consulates of the Great Powers. The basic principles of this new policy were as follows: Crete should be declared an autonomous political entity paying a tribute of 15,000 Ottoman sovereigns annually to the sultan; it should be ruled by a Christian governor serving a five year term of office without the sultan having any right to replace him; and the privileges granted to the Cretans in the Haleppa Charter should be restored with certain fundamental improvements.

This proposal put forward by the political committee was immediately held to be seditious. The Governor General Alexander Karatheodoris ordered that its members be arrested but the gendarmerie and the Turkish forces failed in their attempts to find them. Karatheodoris' efforts proved futile and he was replaced by Turkhan Pasha in March 1896. Turkhan brought with him a firman decreeing a general amnesty, but the political committee rejected the gesture. A strong new patriotic movement revived in Crete as the old political squabbles and disputes were put aside. The Cretan struggle seemed now to acquire new signs of unity and it was strengthened by its leaders who were bound to one another by the ancient custom of 'brotherhood'.

A decisive event for the consolidation of the political committee and the development of the rebellion was the siege of the Turkish garrison at Vamos (4-18 May 1896). The Cretan victory was a great boost for the morale of the rebels and also influenced the attitude of the Great Powers. Once again a General Revolutionary Assembly of the Cretans was organised in Crete and in Athens the Central Committee for the Support of the Cretans was reformed. Volunteers started to head towards Crete from June 1896 led by Konstantinos Manos and Ioannis Dafotis, the founder of the Order of Select Cretans.

Acts of violence perpetrated by the Turkish element of the island had led to a rise in tension. On 11 May killings and looting were carried out against the Greeks of Chania and quickly spread to the countryside around, and especially to the villages of the provinces of Kydonia and Kisamos. Similar incidents also took place in Herakleion and in the villages of Pediada. On 26 June 1896 the Turks slaughtered the monks of the monastery of St. John in Anopoli in the province of Pediada and laid waste the villages of the district.

These acts of violence eventually compelled the Great Powers to intervene and put pressure on the Sublime Porte to make new concessions. After protracted talks and negotiations the consuls of the Great Powers at Chania delivered a new consitution to the Christian representatives, containing the following features: a Christian governor was to be appointed by the sultan for a five year term of office and would have to be approved by the Great Powers; the number of posts for Christian public employees were to be double those for Muslims; the Cretan gendarmerie was to be reorganised with European officers in the higher posts; and the island was to be granted full economic and judicial independence with the Great Powers as guarantors.

The revolutionary committee under the chairmanship of Manoussos Koundouros agreed to the terms of the new constitutional organisation of the island. The rebellion thus ended successfully in August 1896.

CHAPTER IX

THE REBELLION OF 1897 -1898 AND THE AUTONOMY OF CRETE

In September 1896 George Verovich Pasha, formerly governor of the island of Samos, was appointed Governor General of Crete. But within a month of his appointment the situation again deteriorated. The public prosecutor Kriaris was murdered in Chania and a threatening declaration was circulated aimed against the Christians. The Great Powers became concerned by these developments and put pressure on the Ottoman state to implement the new rulings of the constitution as quickly as possible. The Cretan gendarmerie was set up in January 1897 under the supervision of the British major Boor. The Turkish element, however, was quick to set about undermining the rulings of the constitutional arrangement, and murders and acts of violence again broke out. In mid-January the bishop's residence was burnt down along with the Christian neighbourhoods of Chania, leading to fears that the violence would spread to other areas.

While the Great Powers were making efforts to prevent disturbances from spreading further throughout the island, the Greek government of Deliyannis, under pressure from the opposition and public opinion, decided to intervene in Crete. To begin with Greece sent warships under the command of Prince George to obstruct Turkish attempts at transporting military supplies and personnel, and it ordered seventeen Cretan officers to hand in their resignation in order to set up insurgent squadrons for Crete. However, when the Great Powers decided to proceed to international occupation of the island (3 February 1897) the Greek government tried to anticipate the Powers and sent colonel Timothy Vassos, representative of the king of Greece with 1,500 men to take control of Crete and declare union with Greece. Timoleon Vassos landed at Kolymbari on 1 February and immediately issued a declaration whereby he took over control of Crete in the name of the king of the Hellenes, and announced the union of Crete with Greece in an atmosphere of widespread jubilation.

The new rebellion quickly spread and tough fighting broke out throughout the island. Vassos seized the tower of the Turks at Voukolies (7 February) and their military bases at Agia and Livadia. However, he was prevented by the Great Powers from approaching Chania by their implementation of a six-kilometre exclusion zone. An engineered violation of the exclusion zone by the Turk Ibrahim resulted in a formidable bombardment (9 February) of the Revolutionary Miliary Camp of Akrotiri, that had been set up by A. Sephakis, Eleftherios Venizelos, N. Pistolakis, K. Fumis and G. Makriyannis. This incident provoked widespread outrage in Europe and demonstrations and articles in support of the Cretans and against the European admirals who had bombarded the Christians on the side of the Turks.

In the face of these new developments the Great Powers suggested (17 February) the solution of autonomy, but the Cretans and the Greek government categorically rejected the proposal, as they also rejected the idea of a principality. The Great Powers sealed off the coasts of Crete and prevented the Turks and Greeks from transporting men and supplies to the island. Despite this, however, the struggle continued unabated in Crete. Fierce battles were fought in all parts of the island and especially in the district of Herakleion. The centre of Turkish military operations from January to June 1897 was the small town of Archanes around which fierce fighting took place, described in moving words by Ilias Voutieridis in the '*Journal of the Order of the Select Cretans*' (1898). It was in one of these battles, at Episkopi in the province of Pediada, that Antonios Tryphitsos, the valiant clan leader of the province of Pediada, was fatally wounded (25 June 1897).

The luckless Greek-Turkish war (8 April - 8 May 1897) forced

Greece to recall its forces from Crete on 21 April. The Cretan dream of union with Greece had proved to be illusory for yet another time. The leaders of the Cretan uprising were obliged to accept the solution of autonomy. At the third General Assembly, chaired by Ioannis Sphakianakis, the unionists voted with the pro-autonomy faction and the decision was unanimous. There remained only the question of the precise nature of the new political entity of Crete, and, above all, the personage who was to become governor. The Cretans requested a European, 'for only a European governor would possess the prestige on an international scale that would be necessary to defend effectively the autonomy of the island in the instance of any likely intervention from the Sublime Porte'. But as the Great Powers could not agree on a generally accepted figure for the post of governor they proposed Prince George of Greece as High Commissioner of the island.

The General Assembly announced this decision to the Cretan people in the following statement (dated 18 July 1898): 'The Assembly of the Cretans, working with exemplary order and unanimity of purpose, has decided to accept the plan for a caretaker administration of the island proposed by the commanders of the fleets in accordance with the decision of the Protecting Powers. For this reason the General Assembly has elected a five member Executive Council which, in cooperation with the high council of the commanders, will undertake the organisation and administration of the island in accordance with the rulings and regulations that will be drawn up for the purpose'. The Executive Council took over the internal administration of Crete for the period until the arrival of the High Commissioner Prince George. It was composed of Eleftherios Venizelos, I. Zacharakis, I. Sphakianakis, G. Mylonoyannakis, N. Yamalakis and G. Hatzidakis.

The last act of the Cretan drama was the massacre of Herakleion which took place on 25 August 1898. As a detachment of British soldiers was leading the officials of the Executive Council to their temporary headquarters at the tax office of the town in accordance with the decision of the fleet commanders, the infuriated Turkish mob saw fit to commit a fearsome massacre that was reminiscent of the worst days of Ottoman rule. Besides hundreds of Christian civilians they also killed 17 British soldiers and the British Consul on the island L. Kalokairinos, and they burnt and looted shops and offices. The British were swift to react: they hanged seventeen leading Turkish Cretans who were considered the ringleaders and *agents provocateurs* of the riots, while others were condemned to prison sentences or expelled from the island. A large squadron of British ships under the command of Admiral Noel sailed into the port of Herakleion and the Turkish force was ordered to leave the town as well the other strongholds of the island. On 2 November 1898 the last Turkish soldier left Crete. Just one month later on 9 December 1898 the High Commissioner Prince George landed at Suda. The centuries' long servitude of the island had ended for good. The bishop Petras Titos wrote exultantly in a letter dated January 1899, 'now we Cretans are able to call ourselves by that sweet word *free*.'

CHAPTER X

CRETAN SOCIETY DURING THE PERIOD OF UPRISINGS (1821 - 1898)

1. Population

The Cretan population underwent great fluctuations during the period of uprisings. It was reduced by the bloody fighting and emigration and increased again during the intervening periods of peace. During the great rebellion of 1821-1830 the population was halved. While it is estimated that the population amounted to about 213,000 shortly before the rebellion, it had fallen to little more than 129,000 by the time of the census carried out in 1832-33 by Mustafa Pasha at the request of Mehmet Ali of Egypt. The figures are preserved in the journal of R. Pashley, an Englishman who visited the island in 1834. The census was carried out by family which means that the figures can only be a rough approximation. In the countryside 21,535 families are recorded (16,133 Christian and 5,402 Muslim). If one reckons on each family as having four members on average, then the total is around 108,000 inhabitants (81,000 Christians and 27,000 Muslims). To this figure can be added the inhabitants of the three main towns of the island (Herakleion 12,000, Rethymnon 3,200 and Chania 5,800) which gives us a total of 129,000 according to Pashley's calculations. The table below, compiled by Stylianos Spanakis, gives a detailed picture of the population of Crete by province:

Province	main town	families		
		Christians	Muslims	Total
1. Kisamos	Kastelli	1458	337	1795
2. Selino	Rodovani	500	451	951

3. Chaniotika	Chania	1655	252	1907
4. Sphakia	Askyphou			
	Anopoli	848		848
	Sphakia (Chora)			
5. Apokoronas	Fres			
	Kephalas	1562	197	1759
6. Agios Vasileios	Melambes	818	218	1026
7. Rethemniotika	Rethymnon	652	552	1204
8. Amari	Ano Meros	497	246	743
9. Mylopotamos	Margarites	920	310	1230
10. Priotissa		268	91	359
11. Kainourio	Ambelouzos	406	278	684
12. Monofatsi		238	585	823
13. Malevizi	Agios Myron	901	94	995
14. Temenos	Archanes	289	118	407
15. Pediada	Mochos, Malia	1330	396	1726
16. Rizokastro	Viannos	663	443	1106
17. Merabello	Kainourio Chorio	1390	235	1625
18. Siteia	Mouliana	898	324	1222
19. Ierapetra	Kastelli	840	285	1125
	Total	16133	5402	21535

The relatively long period of tranquility which followed and the improvement in the quality of life naturally favoured an increase in population, especially in the countryside. According to the census of 1858, ordered by Veli Pasha, the population of Crete was 278,908: in other words it had doubled within the space of thirty years. The figures from this census are recorded by N. Stavrakis (according to a note by a certain N. Moutsonikolakis) and are as follows:

Christians from new-born to the height of old age were:	
names:	215,863
Ottomans	62,138
Israelites	907
	278,908

During the period of the long rebellion of 1866-69 the population again fell because of widespread warfare and emigration. The dead and the emigrants are reckoned to have amounted to around 30,000. It took about fifteen years for the population to reach once again the level of 1858. According to figures of 1881, reproduced in detail in the valuable work of N. Stavrakis *Statistics of the population of Crete* (Athens 1890), the total Cretan population was 276,208 (202,934 Christian Orthodox, 72,353 Muslims, 253 Catholics, 13 Protestants, 8 Armenians and 647 Jews).

An interesting feature of the make up of the Cretan population at the end of the nineteenth century is the drastic change in the proportion of Christians to Muslims. While on the eve of the revolution of 1821 the Muslims were almost equal in number to the Christians in Crete, by the time of the census of 1881 the ratio is 3 : 1 in favour of the Christians. This meant that the Christians were now able to influence decisively the course of historical events.

2. Work

In the field of work and the economy the proportions were almost always in favour of the Turks who generally owned the largest properties (*çifliks*), and held the most important and profitable posts and crafts, an exclusively Muslim privilege until 1868. The table below is taken from the work of N. Stavrakis (Vol. I, p. 197) and is headed ‘Population according to profession’:

Male

Profession	Christians	Ottomans	Total
Crafts	6090	3818	9908
Merchants	1956	1858	3814
Seamen	230	953	1183
Landowners	1612	1210	2822
Farmers	32715	8080	40795
Herdsmen	6869	600	7469
Labourers	4043	2432	6475
Pupils	10799	3140	13939
Teachers	271	157	428
Doctors	83	15	98
Surgeons	7	14	21
Pharmacists	14	8	22
Solicitors	49	19	68
Journalists	3	1	4
Artists	54	6	60
Engineers	6	4	10
Churchmen	733	113	846
Employees	798	694	1492
Servants	1621	856	2477
Total	67,953	23,978	91,931
In monastic orders	753		753
In mosques		147	147
In hospital service	22	27	49
In prison service	284	146	430
In the gendarmerie	854	543	1397
Without work	33565	12863	46428
Total	103,431	37,704	141,135

Female			
Teachers	41	73	113
Pupils	5172	2451	5623
Midwives	281	81	362
Servants	1501	1144	2645
Total	4,955	3,749	8,844
In monastic orders	141		141
In hospital service	74	12	86
In prison service	8	6	14
Without work	96,421	31,763	128,184
Total	101,579	35,530	137,109

From the above tables it is clear that the vast majority of the Cretan population was composed of farmers and herdsmen. It should be pointed out that by the term 'crafts' is meant chiefly soap manufacturers and tanners who constituted the highest class economically. The middle and lower classes of the Christian and Muslim populations were involved in various trades and jobs. Organized professional life with guilds and a specific hierarchy, patron saints and a special emblem only appear in Ottoman Crete after the Haleppa Agreement of 1878. Stephanos Nikolaidis wrote the following: 'November 21 [1879]: Today was the festival of the wine merchants' guild with the procession of their flag which was led in before the icon to the home of the guild president. Since then the Turks have started grumbling about this new celebration'.

3. Economic life

Throughout the second period of Ottoman rule the character of the Cretan economy continued to be agricultural. The economy was almost exclusively based on a highly varied agricultural order which nonetheless was unable to cultivate more than about a third of the

Cretan land. Extensive regions remained uncultivated or were used for grazing goats and sheep. The Ottoman administration viewed the peasant farmer merely as a source of revenue without taking the slightest measures for the development or protection of agricultural production. A picture of the Cretan economy is given us by the 'Note on the Cretan Question by the Central Association of the Eastern Federation in Athens' (1889): 'In a land where trade is still in its swaddling clothes one shoud not even begin to talk of industry, but agriculture, the only source of production and the only taxable occupation is in a very sorry state. The Cretan farmer, working under the most harsh conditions and without protection or development of any means of transport becomes the prey of the first trader he chances upon, and he thinks himself lucky if he can get a loan (with the strictest of terms) of 25-30%. Under such circumstances it is impossible for the agricultural class to avoid utter desolation unless the imperial [ie. Ottoman] administration hasten to establish an agricultural bank with moderate interest rates'.

The basic agricultural product was olive oil whose annual production was between 9,000 and 13,000 tonnes -an amount that fell far short of the actual potential of the island. Viniculture had developed in some areas, such as in Kisamos and Malevizi. Other important products were grain, carob-beans, citrus fruits, honey, silk, cotton and linen. Livestock breeding was also important: in 1837 Crete had 600,000 sheep and goats, rising to 908,000 in 1844.

Industry was virtually non-existant. A certain degree of cottage industry had developed, producing woollen bedspreads, rugs, materials and clothing made from cotton and silk. Many of these goods were exported to markets abroad. Increased silk production led to the setting up of spinning-mills in Chania and Herakleion which produced silk of the finest quality and exported to Trieste and Marseilles.

However, the most important industrial product of the time was soap. We have seen how the soap industry developed in the early 18th century. Despite the competition of the French soap industry

Cretan soap found export markets and was the main export product of the island alongside olive oil. In 1881 there were fifteen soap factories in Herakleion and ten in Chania. After 1850 the tanning industry also started to develop.

Despite these activities the Cretan economy was never self-sufficient. Imports were always greater than exports and the gap continually widened. In 1873 the French consul at Chania spoke of the irreversible decline of the Cretan economy. The rebellions and internal anomalies only served to aggravate the economic situation on the island.

4. Education

With the outbreak of revolution in 1821 in Crete the few schools that were actually functioning closed since they were considered hives of 'sedition and war', and the teachers were subject to harrassment from the regime. One of the first victims of Turkish atrocities was the well-known teacher at Chania Kallinikos Verroiaios who was hanged with the bishop of Kisamos Melhisedek Despotakis on 15 June 1821. Another teacher, Nikolaos Fourakis, pupil of Konstantinos Koumas, managed to escape from prison but later died from his hardships. The people of Rethymnon managed to save two teachers -Ioannis Metaxas and George Vaos- by paying a huge ransom for their release. Most of those who were able to, fled to the Peloponnese and the islands of the Aegean where they continued their work and frequently made a name for themseslves. Among these Cretan exiled teachers were Kyriakos Hadji-Petrou Venizelos, father of the future prime minister of Greece Eleftherios Venizelos, the brothers Konstantinos and George Psaroudakis of Herakleion, Ioannis Daskalakis of Siteia, George Logios and many others. Many of these had graduated at the Central School of Aegina where they had acquired their training in mutual teaching techniques. Some of them returned to Crete after 1830 and taught at various schools.

The harsh conditions of the period of the revolution between 1821 and 1830 was not conducive to the functioning of schools. However, the rebels at Grambousa managed to set up a school within their small stronghold to which Dimitrios Vlastos was invited to come and teach. The school was founded on 16 November 1826. A document of the period refers to the school: '...The patriots, realising the necessity of educating their children decided to set up a school, but since there was not a suitable building available for conducting lessons within the stronghold they laid the foundations for a new building for this most worthy purpose. They have appointed Mr. D. Vlastos as teacher, who should be quite adequate for the time being, and have set up a committee in the community composed of Messrs. Parthenios Oikonomos, Pavlakis Iatros and K. Kritovoulidis who will undertake to supervise the improvement of the educational establishment...' The philo-Cretan bishop Ardamerion Ignatios, having been invited by the rebels to conduct the inauguration ceremony and sanctification of the new church of the Virgin, was later to teach at this same school.

Chrysanthos Vandouri, another Cretan teacher, had also spent a period in exile in the Peloponnese and in a petition to the Ministry of Ecclesiastical Affairs and Public Education (dated 23 October 1829) he asked for financial support from the government of Capodistrias in order to set up a school in Kisamos.

During the period of Egyptian rule (1830-1840) the administration of Crete allowed and supported the establishment, wherever necessary, of schools where the Greek language would be taught. On his first visit to Crete in 1833 Mohamet Ali encouraged the local councils to establish schools, stating that 'it is only right that the government should save the people of the island from ignorance and perdition and that they should be enlightened by knowledge and education'. The Englishman R. Pashley, who visited the island, wrote that in 1834 there was a school at the monastery of Arsani and another in Rethymnon. In 1836 the energetic bishop Lambis Nikodimos founded the school of Agio Pnevma (Holy Spirit) in the province of Agios Vasileios which was to grow into an important training centre and later became a seminary. In 1950 Professor N. Drandakis brought to light some interesting information concerning education in Rethymnon during this period. We also have some scattered evidence for other areas. A note written by K. Kozyris in his diary informs us, for example, that in Kritsa a school functioned from 1832 onwards.

Two important teachers from this period were the brothers Konstantinos and George Psaroudakis. They were the sons of Hadji-Ioannis Psaroudakis, a wealthy merchant of Herakleion, and had fled to the island of Spetsai in 1824 where they founded a school and tried out new teaching methods which they had learnt from George Kleovoulos in Syros. They enjoyed a considerable reputation as teachers and the Cretans repeatedly pleaded with them to come back to their home island. In the spring of 1837 an American, George Benton, who was sent to Crete by the American Education Association, set up an American School in Chania and invited George Psaroudakis to take up the post of headmaster, having been recommended him by another American, John-Henry Hill, who had already set up a similar school in Athens, and the Cretan university professor Misael Apostolidis. George Psaroudakis arrived at Chania in April 1837. The school quickly grew in size and acquired a considerable reputation. It had 400 boys and 150 girls, with four men and two women teachers. Despite the negative response of the Ecumenical Patriarchate in Constantinople that suspected the school of being a den of pernicious Lutheran and Calvinistic ideas, the school continued to have a large number of pupils and continued to function until 1843 when the Turkish authorities shut down all American schools within the Ottoman Empire.

In this same year (1843), at the instigation of the metropolitan bishop Kallinikos Houyas and local community personages, a school was set up in Herakleion and George Psaroudakis was invited to teach there, but the citizens of Chania set up new schools at their own expense and asked him not to leave Chania, but to carry on teaching there, which he did until his departure for Athens in 1851.

The career of Konstantinos Psaroudakis was similar to that of his brother. From 1842 he taught at the progressive school of Rethymnon and was highly successful there. In his book *Report of the Schools Committee of Crete for 1844,* Emmanuel Vyvilakis wrote that 'The most important contribution of K. Psaroudakis was that, after persistent requests and pleading on our part, he undertook, in cooperation with the supervisors of the school, to teach in particular the *Teaching Guide* [of Saraginos] as well as more general teaching techniques to his best 24 pupils of whom 15, as he informed us, received diplomas from him, qualifying them through public examinations to hold the post of teacher in whatever village or province of the island they might be asked to go. We considered this to be the most effective way of spreading literacy and learning throughout the island, since each of these qualified pupils is able to open a school, with the aid of the reading charts and other teaching books provided, in his village content with a modest salary. On account of his dedication and enthusiasm for the school Mr Psaroudakis has earned the gratitude of all his compatriots in Greece'. Konstantinos Psaroudakis also wrote history and geography books for schools.

Dorotheos Scholarios, a respected man of learning of the nineteenth century, taught at the school in Rethymnon between the years 1844 and 1847, before becoming metropolitan bishop of Larisa.

In 1836 a committee was set up in Athens to supervise education in Crete. It was composed of K. Asopios, George Gennadios, Misael Apostolidis, Philip Ioannou and L. Fotilas, all professors of the University of Athens. Reports and information were published by the committee in the Cretan newspaper *Rhadamanthys.* At the instigation of the committee 15 junior schools were founded, and within a few years they had risen to the number of 27 with the help of funding from wealthy Cretans abroad. The committee also collected books and various other equipment for the Cretan schools.

Education in Crete, however, was mostly catered for by the Church. There were not only the schools in the monasteries which pupils from the surrounding villages attended. The metropolitan bishop and the bishops from the local dioceses took pains to find teachers and means to establish elementary schools. Nikodimos bishop of Lambi, Dorotheos bishop of Petra, Ioannikios bishop of Rethymnon and himself teacher in the Greek school of the town, the metropolitan bishops Kallinikios Houyas and Dionysios Haritonidis, Evmenios also bishop of Lambi and later metropolitan bishop, as well as many others were all especially active in encouraging schooling on the island.

With the concessions granted by the Hatti Hümayun of 1856 conditions became more favourable for the foundation of schools and their number immediately increased dramatically. There was a crisis in 1859 when Husni Pasha began harrassment of teachers who had Greek citizenship. His successor, Ismael Pasha (1861-1865) initially supported improvement of education and encouraged the Christians of the island to open schools; however, he later changed policy and began to expel teachers with Greek citizenship from Crete. Fortunately many Cretans were now studying at the University of Athens and they often returned to support education on the island and were instrumental in improving the quality of education offered. From 1855 onwards the Cretan historian Vasileios Psilakis taught Greek history and philology at the grammar school in Chania, and later became headmaster. The politician Antony Michelidakis, while still an undergraduate at the University of Athens, spent time teaching at the grammar school in Herakleion (1865-1866) at which he too was later to become headmaster in 1871. Nikiphoros Zachariadis the bishop of Arkadia and, subsequently, Kydonia taught at the grammar school of Neapoli as a teacher of scripture.

In the years immediately preceding the rebellion of 1866 boys and girls schools were to be found in all the main towns of the island. It is known that in 1862 there was a grammar school in Herakleion called the Epimenideios School, and that in this same period there was also a public library in the town. The schools were financed chiefly by the Church and wealthy individuals, while receiving further funding from charities and lotteries. Funding from the state treasury of Crete was meagre: 7,000 piastres annually for all the schools of Crete, Christian and Muslim.

We have already referred to the so-called monastery question which constituted one of the causes of the rebellion of 1866. This issue, created by various men of learning of the day (and chiefly by Christopher Argyrakis and Leonidas Georgiadis) and affecting east Crete, concerned the management of monastic property by committees with the intention of making monastic income available for the education of the people. In 1865 the committee concerned ended up by reaching a unanimous decision to implement these proposals, but the controversial involvement of Ismael Pasha prevented the matter from proceeding any further. The rebellion which followed (1866-1869) prevented any schools from functioning and Cretan education was to be totally disrupted.

With the Organic Act of 1868 the Greek language was established as the official language of Crete and it was ruled that it should be taught even in the Turkish schools on the island. Education was soon to be reorganised, however, and the old schools were reopened and new ones also founded. In 1870 regulations were drawn up for the organisation of the monasteries in Crete. One of the chapters dealt with the schools that were funded by the monasteries and run by the clergy and the Central Council of Elders, and it also provided for the foundation of secondary level schools in the larger centres.

After 1870 education embarked on a new phase. As Antony Michelidakis remarked in a speech which he gave at the Cretan Parliament in 1901, '...from 1870 to 1878 the Muses began to establish themselves in Crete'. A report by the Greek Philology Association of Constantinople on the state of education in the Greek provinces of the Ottoman Empire in 1872 gives some interesting facts about Crete. In the provinces of the administrative region of Herakleion there were 18 elementary schools: four in the province of Malevizi, three in Temeni, six in Pediada, four in Kainourio and one in Monofatsi. In the region of Lasithi there were 1,456 boys and 68 girls attending school and the local council recommended that 'at least two new schools be set up in the provinces of Ierapetra and Arkadi (Viannos) where the inhabitants live in extreme poverty and suffer the bitter spectacle of their children roaming the streets without hope for the present or the future'. The same report does not discuss the schools of Rethymnon and Chania for which our evidence comes from a letter of the bishop of Kisamos Misael mentioning the foundation of 19 elementary schools in the province of Kisamos and 10 in Selino.

By the Agreement of Haleppa (1878) a number of Educational Associations were founded in Crete and new cultural activity started to develop, with the publication of newspapers and the creation of libraries. At the same time a large number of schools were opened, especially during the period of the governorship of Ioannis Fotiadis Pasha. In 1881 the General Assembly of the Cretans passed the Education Bill which came into force as from 24 June 1881 and applied until 1898. This Act, drawn up by Michelidakis and Antony Voreadis, made elementary education compulsory for both sexes and provided for the foundation of an elementary school which was to have 30 pupils, and a Greek school that was to have 80. Secondary level schools were established at Chania, Herakleion and Neapoli. A lower-grades high school functioned also at Rethymnon.

Despite these efforts, illiteracy remained worryingly high in Crete. According to the census of 1881 82% of male Christians were illiterate and 97% of women. The corresponding figures for the Muslim population were 81% for males and 88% for females. The difference between the two groups is accounted for by the fact that the majority of the Christian population belonged to the agricultural class while the majority of the Muslim population lived in the towns where their numbers in the schools were always higher. The sudden increase in the number of schools in the 1880s made a significant contribution to reducing illiteracy, especially among the Christians. It should be stressed that many of these schools were founded at the expense of wealthy or successful benefactors. The old Cretan rebel fighter and, later, politician George Xenoudakis bequeathed his estate to his province of the island, Sphakia, in order that schools be opened up in all the villages of the area.

CHAPTER XI

THE CRETAN CHURCH DURING THE PERIOD OF OTTOMAN RULE (1645-1898)

1. The reestablishment of the Orthodox hierarchy

One of the first political moves of the new Ottoman rulers in Crete was the reestablishment of the Orthodox metropolitan see and its subject dioceses and the restoration of the Orthodox hierarchy in the Cretan Church. This concession was part and parcel of the constant religious policy of the Ottoman sultans and was aimed at exerting psychological influence over the Orthodox Cretans who would now have, for the first time since 1204 and the arrival of Venetian rule in Crete, Orthodox prelates. It was probably at the suggestion of Panayiotis Nikousios, who accompanied the Ottoman campaign in Crete as an interpretor, that Neophytos Patellaros (a monk and man of learning from the monastery of Arkadi, and relative of the Ecumenical Patriarch Athanasios III Patellaros) was ordained as early as 1647 as the first Orthodox metropolitan bishop of Crete. The new metropolitan proposed to the Turkish commander Hussein that the dioceses be restored (1653/54), to be run initially by tutelary bishops until the right personages had been selected and ordained. The earliest evidence we possess for the existence of Orthodox dioceses in Ottoman ruled Crete is in a manuscript dated 1659. At that time there were twelve dioceses in Crete, retaining their ancient names as was the custom in the Church: Gortyn, Knossos, Arkadia, Cherronesos, Avlopotamos, Agrio (ie., Rethymnon), Lampe, Kydonia, Iera, Petra, Siteia and Kisamos. For the same year mention is made of another bishop, besides the metropolitan, Theophanes of Arkadia.

The number of dioceses did not always remain the same throughout the period of Ottoman rule. It fluctuated between ten and twelve, while in the years immediately preceding the rebellion of 1821 there was also a titulary bishop (assistant to the metropolitan), of Dioupolis.

Around the year 1820 therefore, the Cretan Church had a total of 13 dioceses including the metropolitan. Episcopal lists for the period of Ottoman rule have been compiled by N. B. Tomadakis (1940) and Theoharis Detorakis (1977).

The metropolitan bishop of Crete (who, after 1700, bore the title 'Metropolitan of Crete and all Europe') was to supervise a see that was composed of the ancient diocese of Gortyn, and the province of Sphakia which was to remain practically unministered on account of its remoteness and rough terrain. In October 1779 the Cretan, Zacharia, assigned the pastoral administration of the province of Sphakia to the bishop of Avlopotamos Parthenios with the privilege that 'he be named and corresponded with as Parthenios of Avlopotamos and exarch of Sphakia'.

2. Privileges and obligations of the Cretan Church

The restoration of the Orthodox hierarchy in Crete was accompanied by privileges that were granted, in accordance with Ottoman practice, to the Orthodox prelates. The Church was the natural head of the subject clergy and laity to which all were obliged to show obedience. The various spiritual, administrative, judicial and economic privileges of the Church were assured by official written ruling from the Sublime Porte (in documents entitled *berats*) and they were to be respected by the Muslims. The Ottoman authorities did not have the right to interfere in the work of the Orthodox ecclesiastics and lower clergy. The family law of the Christian population in Crete (covering issues such as marriage, divorce, inheritance and endowments) was applied according to the rules of the Orthodox Church and not according to those of Islam. Church personages and the exercise of their duties were protected by imperial order of the sultan: 'Except in the case of contravention of the law, they shall not be subject to any kind of pressure or intimidation whether from governors, vice-governors, *subashis* (police), voyvodas, bursars, tax collectors, or officers of the villages and other military personnel'. None of this, however, prevented the Janissaries from committing acts of violence, and even murdering members of the clergy. A well known incident was the murder of bishop Methodios Siligardos of Lambi in 1793 by the Janissaries of the region. Usually the prelates and lower clerical orders had to buy their personal safety by giving money and bribes which the unbridled Ottoman greed both silently and overtly encouraged.

The tax imposed on the metropolitan of Crete was 66,000 Turkish silver pieces annually to be paid to the state treasury of the island, as well as another 10,000 as tribute to the imperial treasury in Constantinople. This annual levy of 76,000 silver pieces, for which the metropolitan bishop was personally responsible, was handed over to the director of finances (*defterdar*) of Crete. In order to collect this vast sum of money an annual tax of 12 silver pieces had been imposed on every Christian family from the earliest years of Ottoman rule.

The patriarchal tax was of a similar amount and had been sanctioned by imperial decree immediately following the reestablishment of the Orthodox hierarchy in Crete. Again, this tax amounted to twelve silver pieces per family and one gold sovereign per church figure, while there were other emergency taxes and a variety of levies, such as an olive oil levy for the patriarchal oil lamps! There is no doubt that the policy of the Ecumenical Patriarchate towards the newly reinstated Cretan Church was authoritarian and oppressive. Even in the earliest years of Ottoman rule the Patriarch Dionysios IV (1676-1679) was responsible for provoking a flood of imperial decrees demanding prompter payment of taxes by the Cretan Church. The patriarch's representative on the island was granted the right to proceed, through the Turkish authorities, to the termination of office of the metropolitan and other bishops in the instance that tax contributions were not forthcoming. In 1679 Neophytos Patellaros was forced to resign on account of these pressures.

3. Relations between the Cretan Church and the Ecumenical Patriarchate

The demanding policies of the Patriarchate naturally caused a negative response in Crete which was also encouraged by local Muslims. During the period when Konstantios Siphnios was metropolitan bishop (1711-1716 and 1719-1722) a crisis broke out which had been fomenting for some time. The clergy and the laity became divided into two opposing factions, the 'metropolitans' (on the side of the patriarchate) and the anti-metropolitans (opposed to the patriarchate). The anti-metropolitans were backed by various powerful groups of the day such as the Sinaite monks of Candia, the Interpretor for the Porte Yannias Moskakis of Rethymnon, and Bonnakis, *prokritos* of Archanai. This faction, which had its supporters both in Crete and in Constantinople, succeeded in influencing many Ottoman officials and especially the director of finances who then filed the proposal to the Sublime Porte to declare the Cretan Church autocephalous, breaking away completely from the Ecumenical Patriarchate. The relevant imperial decree dated 23 April 1715 is one of the major sources of information on the Cretan Church for these years of tribulation.

The sultan therefore accepted the proposal of the antimetropolitans of Crete, he removed Konstantios, against whom a whole range of slander had been concocted, and forbade the Ecumenical Patriarchate from involving itself in the ecclesiastical affairs of Crete, especially those touching on finance.

The crisis was quickly diffused. The Patriarchate eventually managed to have the imperial policy changed and thus prevent the Cretan Church from becoming autocephalous. The metropolitan Daniel (1723-1725), previously bishop of Rethymnon, who appears to have secretly collaborated in the 'rebellion' of the Cretan Church, was expelled from the island. The Patriarchate ordained Gerasimos Letitzis (1725-1756), Cretan born and formerly bishop of Monemvasia, as metropolitan bishop. An energetic and charismatic figure, he managed to have his name linked with many large ecclesiastical works, such as the construction of the cathedral of Agios Minas. During his days relations between the Cretan Church and the Patriarchate were fully restored. The Great Church (as the Orthodox Church was dubbed) now harvested its taxes in Crete, while in return Crete was assured religious freedoms that could only be guaranteed by the prestige of the Great Church and would help preserve the national consciousness of the subject Cretans.

Questions of dogma and the such were not to disturb the Cretan Church during the earlier period of Ottoman rule. The subject population was therefore undivided from a religious and ethnic point of view. The Latins and their sympathisers abandoned Crete at the time of the fall of Candia and there were never to be again conditions under which Roman Catholicism was able to exert any influence on the island. In any case the only Catholics to remain on Crete were the handful of merchants and consuls from the European states, all concentrated in the three main towns of the island.

4. Christian worship and the main religious centres

Officially there was freedom of worship for the Christians of Crete. Various rulings had even been passed for the protection of freedom in conducting established Christian festivals and ceremonies. By request of the first metropolitan Neophytos Patellaros (16 December 1670) the pasha of Candia ordered the *voyvodas* of the imperial villages of Crete not to prevent the Christians from carrying out their ceremonies. In reality, however, things were quite different and far from rosy. The poet Marinos Tzane Bounialis as early as the seventeenth century describes in verse the vandalism carried out by the Muslims against the Orthodox Churches.

The churches in Candia (113 Orthodox and 16 Catholic), just as in other towns and larger villages, were either destroyed or turned into mosques, baths, storehouses, barracks and even public urinals! It was only with great difficulty that the Sinaite monks of the monastery at Candia managed to save the small church of Agios Matthaios which had been given to them by Panayiotis Nikousios, by securing a decree from Ahmet Köprülü the conqueror of Crete. It is easier to determine more precisely just how free Christian worship was from the case of the cathedral. Candia, the place of residence of the metropolitan bishop of Crete, did not in fact have a cathedral, which the Sinaite monks themselves had not got round to building chiefly for economic reasons. A religious dispute, partly incited by the Turks, kept the Christian population of Candia divided for no less than 66 years. Throughout this whole time the metropolitan of Crete was obliged to tour the villages and monasteries or to humble himself before the Sinaite monks asking them to allow him to conduct the liturgy in their church. The controversy between the metropolitan and the Sinaite monks became so acute that when, in 1688, the metropolitan Anthimos Kallipolitis managed after great efforts and expense to restore the old cathedral of the Taxiarchs (Archangels), the Sinaite monks provoked its demolition on the eve of its inauguration! The priest Paul Kladopoulos, bursar of the Church of Crete, gives a vivid account of these events in his verse work on Agios Minas (1736):

He is a bishop, and has charge of Crete,
but no church has he to sing and pray,
and roams the villages to hold his services
and night and day bemoans his fate...

According to one source the metropolitan during this period resided in the small monastery of Agios Minas at Skalani in the province of Pediada. In 1735 the metropolitan Gerasimos Letitzis succeeded after great effort and expense in securing permission from the Turkish authorities to restore the old church of Agios Minas and to make it the metropolitan cathedral of the island. The inauguration ceremony was held on 10 November 1735, although its actual restitution to the metropolitan see of Crete was made official by legal ruling on 19 June 1742. This church came to be linked with the history of Turkish ruled Herakleion. In 1800 the metropolitan Gerasimos Pardalis transferred six large icons by the famous Cretan painter Michael Damaskinos from the monastery of Vrontisi to adorn the new cathedral.

5. The monasteries

During the course of the Cretan War (1645-1669) the Cretan monasteries suffered from the ravages of looting and destruction, especially those that showed resistance to the Turks such as the monastery of the Virgin of Gonia in the province of Kisamos and the monastery of Angarathou in the province of Pediada. Icons, holy vessels, sacerdotal vestments, books and manuscripts all fell victim to wanton destruction. Only a very small number of the artifacts in the monasteries were saved and transferred to the West (chiefly Italy) by the fleeing inhabitants of the island.

After the fall of Candia (1669) and the consolidation of Turkish rule on Crete the monasteries in the towns were either destroyed or turned into mosques and barracks. Those monasteries that were located on the *çiftliks* (farm property) belonging to the Janissaries were also destroyed for good. Of the many hundreds of monasteries known to have existed on Crete during the last years of Venetian rule only a very few survived and were left to function. A few place names, such as Kellia (Cells), Kalogeroi (Monks), Kalogres (Nuns), Pano Kyres (Ladies), Kato Kyres, Monastiri and Monastiraki preserve the memory of the monastic history of the island.

Islamic law (the Seriat) forbade the foundation of new monasteries and churches. Even to repair and maintain old church buildings required a special permit which usually cost many times the estimated cost of repair. Documents of the period give us a clear picture of this situation. In 1745 the pasha of Candia received an application from the metropolitan Gerasimos Letitzis for permission to repair and restore various parish and monastic churches in the provinces of Malevizi and Temeni. Here is an extract from the permit that was issued:

'For the repair of the two doors and sixteen windows of the great church in Kera Eleousa (Malevizi province), 32 feet in length and 20 feet in height. For the restoration of the window panes and door boards. For the repair of its one iconostasis and the twenty-four pews. For the repair of the three pulpits where the gospels are read out, and the cupolas. For the repaving of the floor with slate. For the mortaring of the external walls with lime and plaster. Materials required: 2,000 tiles, 200 loads of lime, 100 loads of sand, 1000 okas (800 kilos) of clay mix, 60 Venetian boards, 200 rafters, 40 chestnut pillars, 2500 nails, 150 working days for builders, 150 working days for labourers, 60 working days for carpenters.' There were some monasteries, however, which the Turks refused to grant permission to be restored or maintained. The author of the *Chorographia of Crete* (1818) wrote of the monastery of Agarathou, that 'Ottoman law does not simply forbid the monastery to be restored, it even forbids one stone to be placed on another, because at the time of the fall of Candia a monk of the monastery caused considerable damage to the Ottomans'. This 'monk' was the abbot Athanasios Christophoros who had set up a fence spiked with the heads of decapitated Turks in 1648. Other large and important monasteries were left to fall into disrepair. Again the writer of the *Chorographia* writes about Vrontisi: 'On the foothills of Mt. Ida there stands the once famous monastery of St. Antony, known as Vrontisi, now bereft of both monks and abbot. One can see many old artifacts in this monastery, such as icons by the famous painter Michael Damaskinos, twelve large chestnut crates full of old books and parchment manuscripts'.

Therefore only a few monasteries managed to survive these hard times of subjugation, and these were chiefly the largest and richest - those that were able to pay the heavy taxes and emergency levies and the lavish bribes demanded by the Turkish officials. The custom of having a powerful Turkish aga (known as a *muteveli* or *monastiragasi*) on the committee of the monastery became established from very early on. With the help of lavish bribes and gifts he undertook to protect the monastery from the raids and plundering of the Janissaries. The payments made by the monasteries are mentioned in the Chronicle of Agia Triada (the Holy Trinity) of Tzagarolon: 'the monks and other brethren of the monasteries were not obliged to carry out other labours or services, but they were subject to other distress and unbearable tribulations. For, besides the fact that they had to give one seventh of all their produce (including olive oil) to the mukata-aga, they also gave him four times a year gifts of rams, honey candle lamps. And they not only had to furnish gifts for them, but also for all the other officers and notorious Turks, whose number might reach twenty-five or more for each monastery. These gifts were offered on the feast of the birth of our Saviour and again on the feast of His resurrection, and the profane feast of *vayrami'*.

The Ecumenical Patriarchate hastened to put many monasteries under its protection, making use of its authority and declaring them *stavropegiac* (subject to the Patriarchate). It was for precisely this reason (ie. the salvation of the monasteries) that Neophytos Patellaros conceded a number of the wealthier monasteries (such as those of Arkadi, Arsani, Agia Triada of Tzagarolon, the Virgin at Gdernettou, Chrysopigi at Chania and Ierousalim in the province of Malevizi) to the control of the Patriarchate.

In general the Cretan monasteries of this period are comprised of the stavropegiac, ie. dependent on the Patriarchate, and the parishional, ie. dependent on the local bishops. This situation, however, was not very constant. According to the circumstances and the current line of policy of the patriarchal throne, patriarchal decrees could be issued changing the status of the monastery from stavropegiac to parishional and vice versa.

The long period of internal stability in Crete during the first period of Turkish rule (interrupted only by the rebellion of Daskaloyannis in 1770), was conducive to the economic development of the monasteries and the increase in the number of monks. Using the pretext that there was a need to train the higher grades of the clergy schools were opened at many of the monasteries, especially after 1750. Once again the monasteries were gradually becoming centres of at least a basic level of education and artistic training. We know

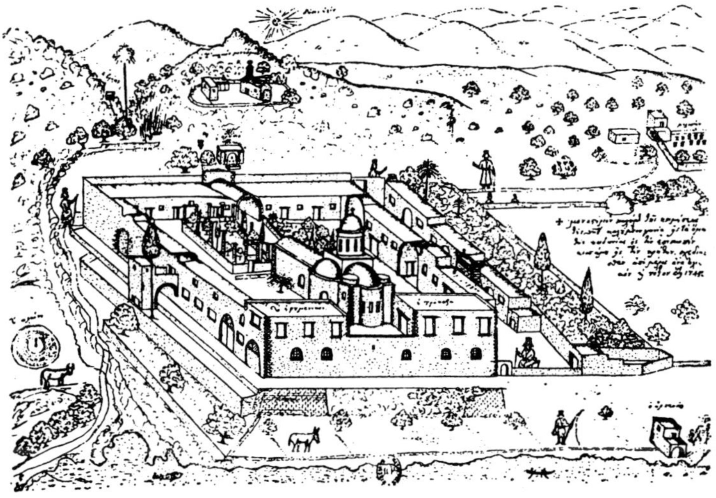

Figure 27
The monastery of Kyria Hodegetria (Gonias) in the province of Kisamos, drawn from the south-east in 1745 by the Russian monk Vasileios Plakas. (G. Gerola, *Monumenti Veneti* III, 160, fig. 69.)

today, for example, that the larger Cretan monasteries of Arkadi, Apezonon, Agia Triada of Tzagarolon, Apanosephe, the Virgin at Akrotiriani (Toplou) and others provided schooling and libraries with both printed and manuscript books. Savary, a Frenchman who visited the island, wrote that in 1779 at the monastery of Arkadi there were 200 volumes of ecclesiastical books and one manuscript of Homer. In some of the monasteries there were scriptoria, such as the monastery of St. George at Apanosephe where the illustrator George Gounales worked (1794) and where the teacher Synesios taught.

The Cretan monasteries today contain very few manuscripts since many of those that had survived into the nineteenth century were destroyed during the long period of rebellions (1821-1898). They were used for filling weapons and thus served to help win freedom for Crete.

6. The cultural and moral level of the clergy

The high cultural tradition of the Cretan clergy during the last years of Venetian rule came to a sudden end with the Ottoman conquest. Those learned men of the Church who survived the wars and hardship fled to the Ionian islands and Italy, taking their books and manuscripts with them. The monastic schools were shut down or confined themselves to the teaching of the rudiments of education. The French consul on Crete gives us a picture of the cultural level of the island in the early 18th century from his visit to Arkadi in 1730. He was disappointed by the gross ignorance of the monks at a monastery he visited, which just fifty years earlier had enjoyed a high reputation as a thriving centre of scholarly activity: 'When I asked whether I might see, feigning simple curiosity, their collections of books, I saw nothing but a few volumes, mostly of more recent times, and others in shabby cupboards or stacked on mere boards, exposed to the air and the ravages of insects which turn them eventually to dust. Nevertheless, in my determination to stir up this pile of rubbish I discovered a large parchment manuscript of very great age that contained works by St. Chrysostomos. None of the monks there was able to translate to me a single line of the text, and they told me that it was in "old" Latin that none of them could understand'.

It was not until the late 18th and the early 19th centuries that we find again men of learning in the ecclesiastical circles of Crete, with figures such as the bishop of Chersonnesos Gerasimos Kalognomon (died 1812), the teacher Gregorios Megalovrysanos, Synesios Cretan, Zacharias Praktikidis, Neophytos Oikonomos and Kallinikos Kritovoulidis.

Lack of education and learning was compensated for by the moral uprightness of the clergy who so staunchly stood by the faith of their fathers and their national consciousness. Professor Tomadakis wrote the following: ‘The works of the Church were greatly facilitated during the period of Ottoman rule by the high moral standards of the clergy. The Venetians, by cutting the clergy off from the leadership of the Orthodox Church, had provoked ignorance, exploitation and unprecedented corruption. The presence of the prelates and the unhindered movement of the Patriarchate during the course of Ottoman rule meant that central Church control was far tighter and more direct, and as a result the Cretan Church was freed of various offences (vagabonds, bigamous clerics, illiterate priests, monks living licentiously). Both clergy and laity felt the need to distinguish themselves from the sacrilege and lechery of the Turk by living more purely and piously. The populous and economically strong monasteries were to exert a great influence, and many people sought refuge in them -the poor and unjustly treated and those who were in search of education. The figure who was to be the main consolation for the peasantry, however, was the simple village priest, dressed like the villagers in the Cretan breeches, carrying out all the peasant’s tasks, living in exemplary manner with his family and fulfilling the function of adviser and guide to his fellow villagers: like a bird the Church sheltered under its wings its nestling peasantry. The priest felt the same as his fellow villagers, he suffered with them, and since he was a leading member of his community he was frequently to be found at the vanguard of his parish during the course of the numerous Cretan rebellions, following the example of the Orthodox priests in the time of Venetian rule’.

7. The Cretan Church during the period of the great Cretan rebellions (1821-1898)

Many of the leading Church figures of Crete had been initiated into the secrets of the Friendly Society (see *Part Six II, chapter 1*) and they had been prepared psychologically for the struggle for liberation that lay ahead. It is certain that bishop Artemios Pardalis of Iera and Melhisedek Despotakis of Kisamos had become members of the Society while staying in Constantinople. The metropolitan Gerasimos Pardalis was converted to the cause by his nephew Artemios bishop of Iera. Members of the lower orders of the clergy such as Zacharias Praktikidis and Neophytos, *oikonomos* of the Sinai monastery dependency of Agia Triada, had also been introduced to the Society.

When rebellion broke out in Crete the clerics were the first victims of Turkish reprisals. We have already discussed at length the killing of the bishops in June 1821. The bishop of Kisamos Melhisedek Despotakis was hanged on 15 June. The bishop of Kydonia Kallinikos was imprisoned along with his deacon Artemios about whom a popular verse has survived:

The dear departed Artemios, who they so sorely tortured,
was three years in the dungeon, suffering at their hands,
and when he asked for water, they poured urine over him...

Five prelates were killed in the Herakleion massacre of 24 June 1821, having been invited to the town by the metropolitan bishop, who himself had been ordered to do so by the pasha. These prelates were the metropolitan Gerasimos Pardalis, bishop of Knossos Neophytos Fyndikakis, bishop of Cherronesos Ioakeim, bishop of Lampi Ierotheos, bishop of Siteia Zacharias, and perhaps also the titulary bishop of Dioupolis Kallinikos. The bishop of Petra Ioakeim was killed by the Turks of Humeriako on the following day. The bishop of Iera Artemios happened to be out of Crete when these events occurred and when he learnt what had taken place he took refuge in

Alexandria where he later became patriarch. By order of Herif Pasha of Herakleion Neophytos of Arkadia, the only prelate to survive the massacre, was appointed as the new metropolitan bishop, only to die a month later from the plague. The Church of Crete was without a head.

The lower grade clerics -the village priests, the abbots, monks and nuns were to suffer a similar fatc, as surviving chronicles attest and the Turkish *Codex of Victims* in the Turkish Archive of Herakleion.

During the long rebellion of 1821-1830, as well as the later rebellions, the clerics helped serve the Cretan cause and struggle for freedom, as fighters, military leaders, politicians and diplomats. Many, such as the well known memoirists of the rebellion Zacharias Praktikidis and Kallinikos Kritovoulidis, and the valiant fighter at the monastery of the Virgin Hodegetria Ioasaph Xopateras (died 1828), left their religious vocation in order not to contravene ecclesiastical rules by fighting in the cloth. Others fought as normal men of the Church and succeeded in making a name for themselves on account of their gallantry: Melhisedek Tsouderos, abbot of the monastery of Prevelis, who fell at Polemarchi in the province of Kisamos, the protopapas of Sphakia George Morakis, abbot Anthimos of the monastery of Chrysopigi, the deacon of Galaktia Psaromilingos, the members of the Skordilis family and many others. Other clerics played a political role. Neophytos Oikonomos made an admirable political contribution by running the General Secretariat of Crete from 1821 to 1824, and was described as a 'learned man with a perfect command of the Greek language, sound administrative abilities and moral strength'.

The Cretan Church served the struggle for liberation in other ways as well. The riches of the churches, both parish and monastic, were made available for the needs of rebellion. Here is an extract from a revealing document that mentions the contribution of the large monastery of Prevelis and which is signed by the commander-in-chief and governor general of Crete Michael Komninos Afendouliev, October 1821: 'I, the undersigned, hereby declare that I have received from his most gracious and holy abbot Melhisedek of the monastery of Prevelis in the district of Rethymnon eight thousand and forty-five silver pieces from the aforementioned monastery... and this document of confirmation has been signed by myself and stamped with the stamp of my regiments so that it may be used on any occasion and for any matter concerning the nation of Greeks, that they repay and recognise the great service which the aforesaid abbot did at a particularly critical and difficult moment in our struggle...' A vast number of ecclesiastical objects from Crete, which had been scattered for safety among the Cyclades islands, were sold off by the Greek government in 1826 in order to finance the new campaign in Crete.

The Church and the clerics made similar contributions in the later rebellions. The dramatic events at the monstery of Arkadi are a typical example of this. Many clerics also played a leading role in the handling of the Cretan Question: men such as Parthenios Peridis who acted as Chairman of the Assembly of the Cretans (1866) and his one time pupil Parthenios Kelaidis -dubbed 'Kapetan Papas' by Hadji-Michalis Yannaris- who proved to be one of the key figures of the 1866-69 rebellion. Finally, the bishop of Kisamos, Dorotheos Klonaris, was chairman of the revolutionary Assembly of the Cretans during the last rebellion of 1897.

8. Organization of the Cretan Church (1821-1898)

After the gruesome slaughter of the bishops in 1821 the Church of Crete was left without a head for about two years. In 1823 Kallinikos of Anchialos, who joined the diocese of Knossos to the metropolitan see, was ordained metropolitan bishop (1823-1830) with the permission of the sultan Mahmut IV. It should be noted that the Constitution of the Caretaker Government of the Island of Crete which was approved by the General Assembly of Armeni (May 1822) did not mention the Church of Crete, but only the official religion: 'The dominant religion of the island will be Eastern Orthodoxy, but the government will be tolerant towards all other religious faiths' (Article 1). During the period of the revolution (and war of independence in Greece) pastoral care and supervision was hardly viable on account of warfare and other tensions. In 1826 Ignatios, the bishop of Arkadia, was invited by the revolutionaries to come to Grambousa and inaugurate the church of the Virgin Kleftrina (protectress of pirates) in the capacity of 'high-priest and vicar of the free provinces of Crete.' There he also taught in the school.

During the time when Meletios I Nikoletakis was metropolitan bishop (1830-1834) the dioceses of Crete were merged into just five by decree of the Patriarchate dated 24 November 1831, because of the drastic decline in population. The dioceses of Knossos, Lambi and Cherronesos were merged with the metropolitan see. The diocese of Petra was merged with that of Arkadia, Iera with Siteia, Rethymnon with Avlopotamos, and Kydonia with Kisamos. Later (1842-1843) the metropolitan bishop Kallinikos Huyas (who was himself of Cretan descent) proceeded to the restoration of the dioceses of Knossos and Cherronesos, but this did not meet with approval from the Patriarchate and Houyas was removed from the metropolitan see. In 1845, however, the diocese of Cherronesos was given official recognition by the Ecumenical Patriarch, and in 1859 the diocese of Kisamos was once again separated from that of Kydonia. Finally in 1862 all the dioceses of the island were restored apart from that of Knossos which was abolished for good as a separate diocese and joined with that of the metropolitan. This was the situation until 1900 when, by the Statute Act 276 of the Cretan State, the diocese of Cherronesos was finally abolished and added to that of the metropolitan, while the diocese of Petra was enlarged with the addition of the province of Viannos.

An important issue related to the hierarchy of the Church within Crete was the question of the salaries of the prelates of the island. In all the metropolitan sees and the dioceses answerable to the Ecumenical Patriarchate a special tax had been imposed on the Christian subjects, besides the ‘gifts’ and usual *peskesis* given by the monasteries to the bishops of their diocese. The metropolitan and episcopal tax had given rise to many objections, since it was believed by many ‘not to work well in Crete, being both oppressive for the people and damaging to the prelates, and altogether incompatible with the exalted position and independence of the prelacy.’ Satirical verses and polemical writings on the avarice of the metropolitans and bishops abounded in the 19th century, such as those by Kallinikos Gargalados (1839-1842) and Sophronios of Didymoteichon (1874-1877). For this reason the General Assembly voted in 1877 to abandon the old system and to pay the prelates of the Cretan Church from the state treasury of the island. In the budget for this year a sum of 264,000 piastres is recorded as being reserved for the payment of the metropolitan and the bishops.

9. Religious freedom

The Cretan rebellions led to the ovcerthrow of old religious barriers and gradually led to the abandonment of many restrictions and bans concerning questions of religious freedom. As early as 1827 permission was granted for the repair of the church of Agia Triada of Tzagarolon, and in the decade of the Egyptian administration (1830-1840) Mustafa Pasha granted general permission for the repair and restoration of all the Christian churches on the island, and he also sought the cooperation and advice of the metropolitan and the other bishops on building a new moral consensus and a renewal of Cretan society.

Religious freedom, however, was secured properly with the Hatti Hümayun of 1856 and was later extended with the Organic Act (1868) and the Haleppa Agreement (1878). The ban prescribed by Islamic law (the *Seriat*) on the building of new Christian churches was also lifted. In 1858 Velis himself granted an old church, which had been turned into a soap factory, to the Christian community of

Chania so that it could be restored and made into a new church of the Virgin (Trimartyri), to serve as a metropolitan church (of the Eisodia), which was eventually opened in 1861. On 25 March 1862, during the term of the metropolitan bishop Dionysios Charitonidis (later to become Ecumenical Patriarch Dionysios V) the construction of the large church of Agios Minas, one of the largest and finest in the eastern Mediterranean, was begun in Herakleion. The inauguration ceremony took place on 16 April 1895, during the term of the metropolitan bishop Timotheos Kastrinoyannakis, with all the bishops of Crete in attendance.

The Hatti Hümayun also allowed the erection of belfries on the Christian churches of Crete so that church bells were to be heard on the island for the fiirst time since 1669. The Turks had forbidden bell-ringing in Christian churches with the sole exception of the monastery of Arkadi, which for that reason came to be known as *Çanli monastir* (monastery with the bell).

The new developments in religious and political affairs in Crete were to make many of the crypto-Christians openly declare their faith and to return to the religion of their forbears. Turkish frustration now directed itself against these few crypto-Christians by mockingly calling them Turko-Manolis or Turko-Marias. They devised special laws by which these crypto-Christians were expelled from the island and their property seized by the state, while at the same time they protected by every means possible those Muslims who had converted from Christianity. During this period concerted efforts were made to win Christians, chiefly the young of the lower social classes, over to the Muslim faith with the promise of generous economic and social benefits. These neo-Muslims were scathingly dubbed *Kentrists* by the Cretans (from the Cretan verb *kentrizo,* meaning 'graft' or 'inoculate').

10. Ecclesiastical problems

As has already been mentioned, the Cretan Church did not have to face any disputes over dogma during the first period of Ottoman rule. In the mid-19th century, however, it was shaken twice by the activities of Lutherans and Calvinists, and slightly later by the Roman Catholic propaganda.

As noted earlier, the Patriarchate was highly suspicious of the American School founded by the Hills in Chania (1837), and it viewed it as a veritable lair of ungodly Lutheran and Calvinist propaganda. Patriarch Gregory VI sent a letter (dated May 1837) ordering the metropolitan Meletios Nikoletakis to act immediately and by every means to 'shut down the ungodly and soul-destroying school'. The headmaster of the school George Psaroudakis was obliged to reassure them of the Orthodox orientation of the teaching and wrote to the Patriarchate that 'if it seemed that even one of his pupils seemed to err in any way with respect to his religion then his (George's) life was in the hands of the Ecumenical Council to do with as it pleased'. The matter was not pursued further, and in any case in 1843 the Turks closed down all American schools within Ottoman territory.

More serious was the problem, which arose in 1859, of conversions to the Roman Catholic Church. The Catholic Church was able to exploit the sorry economic situation of the Cretans, especially after the harsh administration of Husni Pasha, and it began to spread the word that France would assume the role of protecting power of Crete if the Cretans converted to Catholicism and recognised the pope as head of the Church. This whole matter first took root in the villages of Apokoronas under the influence of the devout Capuchin priest Serapheim, and rapidly spread as many Orthodox (including clerics) hastened to join the neo-Catholic band-wagon in the hope that they could improve their pitiable situation. By the end of 1859 over 30,000 Cretans had converted to Catholicism and they were requesting the aid of the Vatican in organizing the local Church.

The Cretan Church was swift to react. The metropolitan Dionysios went to Chania and in an inspired declaration (31 December 1859) summoned the people to remain true to the faith of their forebears, and the Patriarchate sent an Exarch to Crete and a number of preachers. At the same time the Church of Greece and the Greek government mobilised to come to the aid of the Orthodox cause. But the whole matter quickly took on political and diplomatic dimensions. The Great Powers were alarmed by the French initiative in Crete and requested that it put a halt to the conversion campaign. The Ottoman state also expressed its concern since it was afraid that the phenomenon might spread to other areas of the Ottoman Empire. And so the wave of conversions to Catholicism died out as quickly as it had begun.

A half-hearted attempt at reviving the Catholic issue was made in April 1874 when the Vatican, for the first time since 1669, sent a Catholic bishop to Herakleion. The Stephanos Nikolaidis wrote that 'For the first time since the fall of Crete to the Turks a Western bishop, called Aloisius, set foot here [ie. Herakleion], with the title Bishop of Candia of Crete. He conducted just one mass, and preached many times in the Greek language, promising that his small flock would soon become large, but after a short time he left for Chania in order to set up his residence there for the benefit of the Westerners who lived there'. The matter, once again, ended without further consequences.

Of a more serious nature was the so-called Monastic issue which we discussed earlier, since it constituted one of the main causes of the rebellion of 1866-69 with the controversial involvement of Ismael Pasha. The attempt by the educated figures of Herakleion such as Ch. Argyrakis and Leonidas Georgiadis to fund elementary education with the revenue of the monasteries provoked a fierce dispute in east Crete. A solution was finally found in November 1865. As Stephanos Nikolaidis writes, in early November 'an assembly of bishops, abbots and representatives from Herakleion met to discuss the matter of the management of monastic property, and ten days later came to a settlement acceptable to all sides.' The involvement of Ismael Pasha, however, was to disrupt the agreement and lead to increased tension.

After the three year rebellion of 1866-69 and the restoration of order on the island the Church of Crete proceeded with the publication of the *Constitution of the Patriarchal and Parish Monasteries of Crete* (1870). This amounted to a charter for the Cretan monasteries which was to remain in effect until 1900 when ecclesiastical affairs were reorganised by Act 276 of the Cretan State. By this charter the Cretan Church undertook the responsibility of establishing schools using monastic revenues.

At the end of the nineteenth century relations became tense between the Cretan Church and the Ecumenical Patriarchate. The Patriarch Anthimos VII sent a synodical letter (4 September 1895) to the metropolitan, bishops, elders and Christian laity of Crete to oppose the Political Committee (see chapter 8 above). The committee banned the reading of the patriarchal letter in the churches, while a spate of polemical writings appeared in the press condemning the reactionary policy of the Patriarchate.

The last metropolitan bishop of the period of Ottoman rule in Crete was Timotheos Kastrinoyannakis (1870-1898). After his death there followed a fierce ecclesiastical dispute which came to be called the 'metropolitan controversy'. The Ecumenical Patriarchate appointed the bishop of Lambi and Sphakia Evmenios Xiroudakis as the new metropolitan, but the revolutionary government refused to recognise him, stating that it could not allow in future the Turkish-controlled Patriarchate to choose the prelates of the Cretan Church. Many local figures had considerable sympathy for this position, while others believed that it was not in the island's interest to throw aside the age-old bonds that linked Crete with the Great Church. The issue was settled by the Act 276/1900 of the Cretan State, in accordance with which the metropolitan of Crete was to be elected by the Patriarchate but his enthronement had to be approved by Act of the Cretan State. The key figures in the resolution of this dispute were the distinguished lawyer Ioannis Skaltsounis from the Ionian Islands and Eleftherios Venizelos, who at this time was minister of justice. Evmenios was enthroned as metropolitan on 14 May 1900 and here the dispute ended.

The same act also settled other issues, chiefly episcopal. The diocese of Cherronesos was abolished for good and added to that of the metropolitan see. Its last bishop Agathangelos Papadakis was transferred to the diocese of Lambi and Sphakia. The boundaries of the diocese of Arkadia were redrawn to bring it within the district of Mesara, and the episcopal residence was transferred to Agioi Deka, while the province of Viannos was added to the diocese of Petra (in Lasithi province). This situation was maintained until after the union of Crete with Greece in 1913.

A new ecclesiastical crisis broke out with the Greek Government Act 5621/1932 which reduced the dioceses of Crete to four, one in each administrative county of the island: the Metropolis of Herakleion, the diocese of Rethymnon, the diocese of Chania and the diocese of Neapolis. This act, which led to fierce argument between the prelates of Crete, was never in fact implemented. It was repealed by the Emergency Act of 21/25 October 1935 and Act 276 of the Cretan State was reintroduced.

By the Act 4149/1961 the diocese of Arkadia whose centre had been transferred in 1946 to Moires in the province of Kainourio was renamed the diocese of Gortyn.

In 1962, by act 812 of the Ecumenical Patriarchate all the bishops of Crete were given the title 'metropolitan' and, later, by act 283/28 February 1967 of the Patriarchate, the metropolitan see of Crete was declared an archbishopric and the metropolitan was now archbishop of Crete.

11. Ecclesiastical education

From the mid-nineteenth century Cretan clerics were able to train at schools of higher theological education, such as at the newly founded University of Athens where the leading divinity professor Misael Apostolidis taught, at the School of the Cross in Jerusalem and at the Theology School on the island of Chalki near Constantinople. From 1870 onwards all the Cretan prelates were Cretan by birth and all had passed through the highest levels of theology school. N. Stavrakis remarked that 'the bishops of Crete are all, without exception, highly educated Cretans, inspired with a sense of patriotism and full of the Christian virtues fitting to their high office'.

For the training of the lower grade clergy seminaries were opened on Crete itself. During the time when Evmenios was bishop of Lambi (1886-1898) the Greek school of Agios Pnevma which had opened in 1836 in the province of Agios Vasileios operated as a seminary for the training of the clergy. And during the last decade of the nineteenth century another seminary was opened at the monastery of Agia Triada of Tzagarolon which still functions today as the Seminary of Crete.

12. Cretan saints of the period of Ottoman rule

The Cretan catalogue of saints for the period of Ottoman rule on the island includes eleven individuals. The earliest of these figures was Markos Kyriakopoulos who was martyred in Smyrna on 14 May 1643. Manuel, born in Sphakia, was martyred in Chios on 15 March 1792. Myron of Herakleion was hanged in his home town on 20 March 1793. Without having been officially canonized, Methodios Siligardos, bishop of Lambi, is also generally ranked among the Cretan saints; he was killed by the Janissaries of his province on 9 July 1793. The monk Ilarion (known as Ioannis before entering holy orders), from Herakleion, was beheaded in Constantinople on 20 September 1804. Ioannis of Sphakia was martyred in Ephesos on 15 September 1811. Other saints who are still revered today are Angelis, Manuel, George and Nikolaos -the four crypto-Christians of Melambes, Agios Vasileios province- who were martyred in Rethymnon on 28 October 1824. The last Cretan saint was George Divolis of the village of Alikiano, Kydonia province, who was martyred on 7 February 1867.

PART SEVEN

AUTONOMY

CHAPTER I

THE GOVERNORSHIP OF PRINCE GEORGE

On 9 December 1898 Prince George of Greece disembarked at Chania in the capacity of High Commissioner of Crete, and was given a rapturous welcome by crowds of enthusiastic Cretans. Manousos Koundouros recorded in his diary: 'The national dream was at last fulfilled. Prince George of Greece landed here today bearing the title of High Commissioner of the Great Powers, but in essence he was prince regent. The naval commanders of the four Great Powers -Pottiers, Noel, Betollo and Skridlov- received him at Suda. An international force was on parade and a crowd of Cretans greeted him enthusiastically as he proceeded from Suda into Chania where he attended a thanksgiving mass in the cathedral of the Eisodia for his safe arrival and the liberation of the island. Pottiers, the French admiral and Chairman of the commanding council, presented George to the government house of Chania and formally handed over to him supreme control of the island. The Cretan flag was raised at this moment and it was greeted by a salute of cannon fire from the European ships anchored out in the port. The flag looks like this: a white cross, as with the Greek flag, divides the flag in four parts, of which the three are blue and the top square nearest the flagpole is red, in which is a white star; one of the rays of the white star (that which points downwards) is longer than the others'.

Having taken up the office of High Commissioner Prince George formally addressed the Cretan people, calling them to respect the laws and to live peaceably together: '... I shall work to the utmost of my abilities for your prosperity, I shall make every effort to govern well, justly and impartially, so that you may obtain true security, which will be guaranteed solely by the rule of law and benevolent institutions. I know that you will be prudent and that you will obey the authorities... You must now forget your old differences and, regardless of race or religion, you must now live in harmony together, under a common and benign state...'

The Cretan flag was raised on the fortress of Firka. The Turkish flag was left only on the castle of Suda as a last symbol of Turkish suzerainty on Crete. The four Great Powers placed the island under their protection by undertaking to oversee four separate regions of the island: the Italians in Chania, the Russians in Rethymnon, the British in Herakleion and the French in Lasithi. Chania, the capital of the Cretan state, was under joint control.

The foreign commanders departed on the next day (10 December) and the difficult task of organising the Cretan state was begun. A sixteen member committee (12 Christians and 4 Muslims), under the chairmanship of Ioannis Sphakianakis, was appointed and charged with the task of drawing up a constitution for Crete. Political matters proceeded without delay. On 9 January 1899 the official paper *On the Constitution of the Cretan Assembly* was published and general elections for the selection of state deputies were announced. In these elections, which took place on 24 January 1899 with exemplary calm and order, 138 Christian and 50 Muslim deputies were elected. The first sitting of the Cretan Assembly took place on 8 February amidst much celebration, and the Cretan constitution, having been approved by the Great Powers' council of ambassadors in Rome, was published in the official *Journal* of the Cretan State (16 April 1899) and immediately put into effect. A few days later (29 April) the first government of the Cretan State was formed composed of the following ministers: Eleftherios Venizelos as minister of justice, K. Foumis as minister of economic affairs, M. Koundouros as minister of foreign affairs and transport, N. Yamalakis as minister of education and religion, and Hussein Yenitsarakis as minister of public order.

This first government of the Cretan State worked with tremendous enthusiasm and carried out many important tasks. It lost little time in passing laws and acts, it issued a Cretan currency (the drachma), founded a Bank of Crete and organised a gendarmerie with Italian officers (carabinieri). It gave special emphasis to education and public health. Among the first public health measures taken by the government was the effective protection of the people from leprosy, a disease which had become endemic in Crete. For the isolation and health care of the victims of leprosy a special hospital was founded in 1903 on the island of Spinalonga. In general the first years of the governorship of Prince George 'proved to be happy years for Crete from the point of view of public order, and civil and organisational projects', as Koundouros noted in his diary.

The Cretan constitution, however, had a number of weak points. It was excessively conservative and conceded far too much power to the High Commissioner which could easily lead to despotism, if circumstances permitted. It was explicitly stated in the constitution that 'the High Commissioner actively participate in and supervise all the authorities, and in general govern and represent the State'. The lack of clarity over the precise nature of the services and organs of the administration was soon to create personal and administrative problems. The initial enthusiasm was soon succeeded by disappointment, which was further aggravated by the fact that the Athenian advisers of Prince George tended to grab all the best posts and offices, while the Cretans were pushed to one side. The old rebel fighter Hadji-Michalis Yannaris and other leaders signed a strong petition of protest and submitted it to Prince George on 30 July 1905.

Apart from these constitutional and administrative weaknesses, conflicting views soon arose over the burning issue of union with Greece. Prince George himself stood firmly by the principle of autonomy as specified and guaranteed by the Great Powers, and appeared to believe that the final solution to this major national issue would evolve and mature of itself through repeated international representations and petitions. It was not long before it became clear how unrealistic this idea was. The visit which the Prince made to the European courts in the summer of 1900 served to show that the Great Powers were not keen on rekindling the Cretan Question and they insisted on maintaining the status quo.

Eleftherios Venizelos (1864-1936), minister of justice, had different views however. He had already shown himself to possess remarkable qualities of leadership and charisma. On the question of union with Greece he believed that the solution would consist of gradual gains, the first of which must be the removal of foreign forces from the Cretan towns and their steady replacement by a local civil guard that would be headed by Greek officers. He expressed these views to Prince George and then outlined them in greater detail to the Commissioner's Advisory Council on 22 February 1901, without, however, finding any support for his ideas. Venizelos had already made it known that he did not recognise that the Prince had exclusive right to handle the question of union and expressed himself with impressive frankness: 'Speaking as one of the three hundred thousand Cretans, I do not surrender you the right to negotiate, without reference to others, the national interests of my homeland'. And so the dispute between Venizelos and the High Commissioner was now plain for all to see, and it was accompanied by a mass of mud-slinging writings and articles which Prince George's men in Athens were careful to leak to the Athens press in order to slur Venizelos. Venizelos' removal from the office of minister of justice was inevitable (18 March 1901). In reply to this slander and in order to explain his position Venizelos published five sensational articles in the Chania newspaper *Keryx* (Herald), which was edited by himself, under the title 'Let there be light'. He stated in these articles that he was not aiming to undermine the Commissioner's policy and he also declared with considerable self-denial that he was leaving his political office so as not to weaken the national cause of Crete. Prince George, however, yielding to the advice of his adamantly

Figure 28
German cartoon on the situation concerning the Cretan Question (1898). The title is 'The Cretan Labyrinth'. Europe isd shown cutting the thread which the king of Greece needs in order to find his way back out of the Cretan Labyrinth, above whose entrance are written the words: 'Crete. Entry to the Labyrinth is forbidden'. At the top the Peloponnese looks like the hand of Greece stretching down to seize Crete, which is shown as being full of nails. (From the rare book by John Grand-Carteret, *La Crète devant l'image,* Paris 1989, p. 70.)

anti-Venizelist advisers, pursued a policy of intransigence and cut off all the routes to a restoration of relations and dialogue with his former minister. Clearly piqued by the critical articles in both the Athenian and the Cretan press, he lost his self-control and proceeded to implement authoritarian measures such as the ban on freedom of the press and with political harrassment and detention of leading members of the opposition. It was under these circumstances that Cretan affairs appeared once again to be running into an impasse and the threat of a new crisis seemed to be looming, especially after the failure of a last attempt at bringing the two key political opponents, Venizelos and Antonios Michelidakis, back to the negotiating table.

CHAPTER II

THE THERISOS REBELLION (1905)

All those who had become disaffected by the authoritarian policies of the Prince gathered around Venizelos and formed a strong opposition force. The situation reached crisis point and the internal unity of the Cretan State was shaken when the opposition members signed a declaration on 26 February 1905 in which they demanded a change in the Cretan constitution. The declaration ran as follows: 'The undersigned, comprising the united Cretan opposition, have gathered in Chania on this day, 26th February 1905, with the aim of fulfilling the National Plan, and have decided: a) that our first priority must be the attainment of the long desired union of Crete with free Greece; b) if this is not possible, we will pursue the political orientation of our homeland towards free Greece, thus changing the present situation from an international point of view; c) and if this cannot be achieved we will seek to revise the Cretan constitution along the lines of the Greek constitution in order that the land may be freed of authoritarianism. We will pursue the realisation of this Plan even by means of popular armed insurrection. In pursuing these aims we are not interested in changing any particular personage, but if this does occur we shall take up arms and ever fight with all our might against any non-Greek ruler of Crete'.

This was the portent of rebellion which broke out just a few days later on 10 March 1905 and came to be known as the Therisos Rebellion. At the beginning of the year elections had been announced to take place on 20 March in order to select 64 deputies, to which number were to be added a further ten chosen by the Prince himself in accordance with the constitution. The opposition, having decided not to take part in the elections and accusing the Prince of implementing undemocratic measures and pre-electoral intimidation, called the people to abstain from the elections. Instead, therefore, of entering the electoral battle the opposition members gathered in the village of Therisos in the mountains of Kydonia province and declared the commencement of the armed struggle against the governorship. At the rebel meeting held on 11 March they declared union with Greece and the Greek flag was raised. Venizelos, self-appointed leader of this new movement, analysed the current political situation in Crete with great clarity and perception in a speech he gave at Kerameia on 25 March 1905, on the occasion of the anniversary of the outbreak of the Greek War of Independence. In his speech he said the following:

'From the outset they named the Prince representative of the national ideal in Crete. I, however, have had, and continue to have, cause for complaint with respect to this title. Crete has no need of a representative of the national ideal. The titles for this ideal are the repeated battles waged by us in its name. We accepted the High Commissioner only in the capacity of intermediary in the process of the union of Crete with Greece. He has played the role of intermediary for so long that patience has finally run out, since no progress has been made as had been hoped in the matter of winning our final freedom. Under this disgraceful regime various misconstructions have arisen which only serve to make the regime appear yet more disgraceful. With every journey abroad the Prince has made it was believed that union would be achieved. Already, however, six years have gone by. It was only natural that the Cretan people should resort to arms in order to make its desires more readily appreciated by all. There are those who believe that this movement is doomed. Has it not been realised, then, that the only solution to the Cretan Question is the union of Crete with the Kingdom of Greece? They say that union will be attained only when the son of the king of Greece sees fit! Well I protest against this view. We cannot entrust our national future into the hands of just one family [ie. the royal family]...'

The rebellion quickly spread, gaining the support of powerful local individuals and soldiers. Ioannis Sphakianakis, A. Stergiadis and Emmanuel Polychronidis of Herakleion immediately threw in their lot with the rebel movement, along with bishop Dionysios Kastrinoyannakis and Ioannis Tsouderos in Rethymnon, and bishop Titos of Petra and M. Sphakianakis in the province of Lasithi. Sympathy votes were passed throughout the island. Only the island gendarmerie remained under the control of the prince, and even this was not entirely loyal. The Great Powers were restrained in their response, with the sole exception of Russia which clearly supported the prince. The Russian warship 'Habri' under the command of vice-admiral Urbanovich repeatedly bombarded the rebel positions. Venizelos had correctly predicted international policy and was sure that the Great Powers would fail to reach agreement on strategy, thereby giving him room to manoeuvre.

Within a very short time Venizelos set up a caretaker government at Therisos and proceeded to issue bonds for 'patriotic' domestic loans amounting to a total of 100,000 drachmas, organised various government departments (economics, transport and internal affairs), issued postage stamps and published a newspaper named *To Theriso*.

The outbreak of the rebellion and its rapid spread naturally caused the prince and his supporters great alarm. His advisers led him astray by recommending ill-planned and inconsistent measures. He issued a 36-hour deadline to the rebels to lay down their arms. When the deadline passed he declared, after receiving the permission of the Great Powers, the implementation of martial law, while the Cretan Assembly, which was controlled by the prince, passed a bill approving the establishment of town guards. Events were leading to civil war, since two governments -that of the High Commissioner and that of the rebels in Therisos- were now functioning. Fortunately the conflict was confined to just a few minor encounters in the district of Chania and there were only a handful of victims.

The conflict quickly moved to the diplomatic sphere and requests were made for a political settlement of the crisis. The representatives

ΤΟ ΘΕΡΙΣΟ

ΕΚΔΙΔΕΤΑΙ ΔΙΣ ΤΗΣ ΕΒΔΟΜΑΔΟΣ

Διευθυντὴς καὶ Συντάκτης ΙΩ. Γ. ΠΑΠΑΔΑΚΗΣ § Τιμὴ ἑκάστου φύλλου Λεπτὰ [illegible]

ΠΑΡΑΛΛΗΛΙΣΜΟΣ

Τριακόσιοι περίπου ἦσαν οἱ ροπαλοφόροι τοὺς ὁποίους συνεκρότησεν ἡ Ἁρμοστεία ἐν Χανίοις κατὰ τὴν ἔναρξιν τῶν ἐργασιῶν τῆς τελευταίας Βουλῆς, οἵτινες ἀπὸ τοῦ ἐπιθετικοῦ ὅπλου τὸ ὁποῖον αὐτοὶ ἔφερον, καὶ τοῦ ὁποίου οὐχὶ ἅπαξ ἔκαμον χρῆσιν, ὠνομάσθησαν χουρχουδάδες. Καὶ λέγομεν ὅτι τοὺς συνεκρότησεν ἡ Ἁρμοστεία διότι εἰς τὴν πρωτοβουλίαν αὐτῆς ὀφείλετο ἡ συγκρότησις, ἥτις διενηργήθη διὰ ὀργάνων ποικίλους τίτλους ἀπὸ τῆς ἐν Χαλέπα αὐλῆς ἀντλησάντων. Μετὰ τῶν χουρχουδάδων τούτων ἠνώθησαν οἱ μπράβοι τῆς ἀστυνομικῆς ἐξουσίας, τῆς δημοτικῆς ἀρχῆς καὶ τῶν ἄλλων τροφίμων εὐνοουμένων τῆς αὐλῆς, οἵτινες ἀπετέλεσαν τὴν δύναμιν τῆς φρουρήσεως τῆς τάξεως (sic) καὶ τὴν προσωπικὴν ἀσφάλειαν τῶν πατέρων τοῦ λαοῦ ἀπὸ πάσης ἐξωτερικῆς πιέσεως, ὅπως ἀπερισπάστως καὶ ἐλευθέρως ἐξυφαίνωσι τὰς φιλελευθέρους αὐτῶν ἀρχὰς καὶ προβῶσιν εἰς τὰ ἀξιοθρήνητα αὐτῶν νομοθετικὰ ἔργα. Τὰ ἀργυρώνητα δημοσιογραφικὰ ὄργανα τῆς Ἁρμοστείας ἀπὸ τὰς βουλὰς τοῦ νέου Μίμου ἐξαρτώμενα ἐξῇραν τὴν δρᾶσιν καὶ τὴν ἐπίδρασιν τοῦ χουρχουδικοῦ σώματος, διὸ πάνυ εὐλόγως καὶ δεξιῶς ἐψηφίσθησαν ὑπὸ τῶν πατέρων τοῦ ἔθνους καὶ ἐκυρώθησαν προθύμως ὑπὸ τοῦ Ἁρμοστοῦ 800 περίπου λίραι ὡς ἀμοιβή.

Καὶ εἴδομεν τὰ γκαρσόνια καφενείων καὶ μαγειρείων νὰ τυλίξωσι τὰς ποδιάς καὶ νὰ παρουσιασθῶσι καὶ παραδίδοντες εἰς τὰς χεῖρας τῶν τυράννων καὶ καταπιεστῶν τοῦ Κρητικοῦ λαοῦ τὰ κατάλληλα φονικὰ ὄργανα. Καὶ ἤρξατο ἤδη ἡ περισυλλογὴ τῶν ὀργάνων καὶ ἀκονίζονται τὰ ὄργανα ταῦτα, ὅπως βυθισθῶσιν εἰς αἷμα ἀδελφικὸν πρὸς χαρὰν ἐκείνων, οἵτινες προοιωνίσαντο τὸν αἱματοκυλισμὸν τῆς Κρήτης ἀντὶ τῆς ἀπ' αὐτῆς ἀναχωρήσεώς των! Καὶ τὰ ὄργανα τῆς ἀπαισίας καταστροφῆς εὐχερῶς περισυνελέγησαν εἰς ἕνα νομὸν τῆς Κρήτης ὅπου ὑπὸ τὸ κράτος βαρβάρων λογχῶν ἐπετέλεσαν ἀληθῶς θαύματα, ἐξακολουθοῦσι δὲ κατὰ διαλείμματα παρόμοια ἐπιτελοῦντες. Καὶ μένει ἤδη νὰ περιμένωμεν ποία θὰ εἶναι ἡ προσήκουσα εἰς τὸ μέλλον διὰ τὰ ὄργανα ταῦτα ἐπωνυμία, τῆς ἀμοιβῆς πρὸς τὴν τῶν ῥαβδούχων ἐξισωθείσης περίπου, ἀφοῦ καὶ ἡ δρᾶσίς των εἶνε [illegible] καὶ ἡρωικωτέρα. Ἀλλ' ἄραγε δὲν θὰ μείνουν καὶ οὗτοι μόνον μὲ τὸν τιμητικὸν τίτλον, λήγοντος τοῦ ζητήματος ὡς λέγεται; Εἶναι εὐτύχημα ὅτι ἅπαντες ἐκ τῶν τεσσάρων ἄλλων νομῶν τῆς Κρήτης δὲν θὰ ἀποκτήσωσι τὸν ἀξιομνημόνευτον τίτλον τῶν ἐν Ρεθύμνῃ φρουρῶν, διότι ἡ Ἁρμοστεία ἀποτυγχάνει εἰς τὴν συγκρότησιν τῶν ἀντεπαναστατικῶν σωμάτων τῶν κατοίκων ἀρνουμένων νὰ δεχθῶσι τὰς προσφοράς της.

ΠΩΣ ΤΟΝ ΗΘΕΛΑΜΕΝ

Ἐὰν ἀπέβλεψαν οἱ ἐπαναστατήσαντες πρὸς στιγμήν, ὅτι τὸ σατανικὸν περὶ δημοφρουρῶν νομοσχέδιον ὅπερ ἐψήφισεν ἐσχάτως ἡ κατ' εὐφημισμὸν Κρητικὴ Βουλή, τὸ ἐψήφισε

Figure 29
The front page of the newspaper *To Theriso* which was published by the rebels. The article concerns the town guards who were organised by the High Commissioner in Chania.

of the Great Powers, realising that the prince had completely lost all popular support and that the rebel position enjoyed wide popular sympathy, attempted to bring the two sides back to the negotiating table. This was precisely what Venizelos wanted. After some preliminary fact-finding and discussions at Fournés, Therisos and Kalamitsi, Venizelos met the consuls of the Great Powers at Agia Moni of Mournies on 2 November 1905, where he signed an agreement on ending the rebel movement, after the acceptance of the main terms of the rebels.

The Cretan Question now entered a new phase. An international commission arrived in Crete in February 1906 and undertook to examine *in situ* the matter and to submit a report. After long and protracted negotiations with the Greek government and with Venizelos the Great Powers came to a new settlement proposal for the Cretan Question, the text of which was submitted to the prince on 23 July 1906. The settlement provided for the setting up of a Cretan gendarmerie on a totally different pattern, the establishment of a Cretan civil guard headed by Cretan officers taken from the Greek army, and the withdrawal of foreign forces once order had been restored on the island.

The Therisos rebellion produced positive results and Venizelos could well feel satisfied. On 26 July 1906 the Second Constituent Assembly of the Cretans, which undertook to draw up a new constitution, passed, amidst a general atmosphere of reconciliation, the unionist resolution. The task of reconstruction was begun once again and the Great Powers put up a loan of 9.3m French Francs for the Cretan government, at the same time rescheduling the interest payments on previous loans.

New ground had been gained on the political side. By a resolution passed on 14 August 1906 the Great Powers conceded to king George I of Greece himself the right to appoint the High Commissioner of Crete. This was a significant step forward in the Cretan issue.

After these developments Prince George was unable to remain any longer on Crete as High Commissioner and, despite the pleas of his anti-Venizelist advisers, he submitted his resignation on 12 September 1906 and, full of bitterness, departed from Crete.

CHAPTER III

THE GOVERNORSHIP OF ALEXANDER ZAIMIS
(18 September 1906 - 12 December 1908)

Immediately following Prince George's resignation, King George I appointed Alexander Zaimis as the new High Commissioner of Crete. Zaimis had already served as prime minister of Greece (and was later to assume the office of President of the Greek Republic), and had had a long and distinguished career in politics. He took up his duties on 18 September 1906 for a term of five years. The prime minister of Greece, George Theotokis, wrote the following to the president of the Cretan Assembly: 'by His Majesty the King's appointment of Mr. Zaimis a great step his been made towards the desired goal of the Cretans and the whole nation of Greeks for a solution to the Cretan Question'.

By joint agreement of the rebels of Therisos and the deputies of the Cretan Assembly, in June 1906 a second Constituent Assembly was set up under the chairmanship of Antonios Michelidakis. The Assembly worked intensively and on 2 December 1906 it submitted the draft for the new Cretan constitution to Alexander Zaimis. In the covering letter Michelidakis wrote the following: 'Herewith is enclosed for your inspection the new constitution which has been approved by the Second Constituent Assembly. The new period in domestic politics which Crete is now entering under the new parliamentary system, provides all the members of the Cretan electorate with the hope that, from the experience of the past and in the conviction that we have entered the last stage of our national goal, the period of internal unrest is now over and that we can devote ourselves to the completion of this task of common good and bring new advancement, both moral and social, to the island'.

Zaimis swore allegiance to the new constitution and formed a new government. A full state mechanism started to operate once more in Crete. The economy was soon put under full supervision, the state administration was organised, new laws were passed and efforts were made to deal with questions of public health and education for which Antonios Yannaris, professor at the University of Athens, was appointed minister. A special Bill was passed on 13 October 1907 for the setting up of a civil guard on the island, the first form of Cretan state militia that was soon to develop into a considerable military force, as was to become apparent in the Balkan Wars of 1912-1913 in which it played an important role.

In July 1907 a large part of the Great Powers' forces was withdrawn from the island. The rest were to evacuate the island within the next year, having received guarantees for the safety of the Muslim population. In fact all foreign forces were off the island in less than a year and the Cretan Assembly passed a vote of thanks to the protecting powers on 21 May 1908 for their contribution to the outcome of the Cretan Question. The existence now of a well-organised Cretan militia rendered the presence of foreign forces unnecessary.

The events of 1908. The end of the governorship

In 1908 the Cretan State entered a phase of rapid development, with a full state mechanism that worked smoothly. However, two major events took place that were to disturb the situation and influence decisively the course of Cretan affairs. The first of these was the annexation of Bosnia and Hercegovina by the Austro-Hungarian Empire and the second was the declaration of full independence by Bulgaria with the simultaneous annexation of eastern Macedonia in September 1908. The news caused outrage in Greece and Crete. The prime minister of Greece George Theotokis informed the speaker of the Cretan Assembly, George Papamastorakis, of the need for popular demands for the union of Crete with Greece and a referendum. Events moved fast. At midnight of 22 September 1908, while the High Commissioner was on holiday on the island of Aegina, the Chania politicians Venizelos, Emmanuel Xiras, Ch. Ploumidakis and Emmanuel Papayannakis issued a statement calling the people to a Pan-Cretan demonstration in Chania for the declaration of union with Greece. The statement was simple and direct: 'Beloved compatriots, now that Bulgaria has declared itself an independent kingdom, it is vital that we too declare our union with Greece'. At midday on 23 September, at a large meeting held in Chania, the first popular vote was passed approving union with Greece. In the days that followed further popular votes were held in other parts of Crete all supporting the union, and the government of the Cretan State also passed the following unionist resolution, which was published the next day (24 September) in the *Appendix to the Proceedings of the Government of the Kingdom of Greece in Crete* (as the *Proceedings* were named from that day forth):

'The government of the State of Crete, having accepted the unalterable will of the Cretan people, hereby declares the independence of Crete and its union with Greece, that it may now comprise an inalienable part of the Greek State. It beseeches His Majesty the King to assume control of the island. Until that moment it will continue to govern Crete, in the name of His Majesty the King of the Hellenes, according to the laws of the Greek Kingdom. It is therefore required that the Cretan authorities, in accord with this resolution, continue to conduct their duties'. The resolution was signed by the chairman G. Papamastorakis and the members Ch. Pologeorgis and E. Modatsos.

On the next day (25 September) the members of the government of Crete were sworn in by the bishop of Kydonia and Apokoronas declaring allegiance to the King of the Hellenes. The Cretan Assembly ratified the resolution for union and then issued its own celebratory resolution. It then formally dismantled the governorship. The Cretan constitution was annulled and the Greek constitution introduced. The Greek government informed Alexander Zaimis not to return to Crete, where a new (all-party) caretaker government was formed by Venizelos, Pitychakis, Logiadis and Pologeorgis, under the chairmanship of Antonios Michelidakis. The Greek government, in order to preempt the Turkish response and any international complications, did not yet proceed to a formal recognition of the union and merely confined itself to behind-the-scene guidance.

CHAPTER IV

EVENTS UNTIL THE FORMAL UNION WITH GREECE

The Great Powers appeared to quietly accept the new developments in Crete and did not react, despite the repeated and insistent protests of Turkey. However, when the Greek flag was raised at the castle of Firka, the representatives of the Great Powers demanded that it be lowered immediately. The government of Crete found itself in a difficult position and resigned. A foreign force landed at Firka and, unable to find a Cretan volunteer for the task, cut down the flag-pole with the Greek flag.

After the resignation of the caretaker government of Crete in August 1909 the Cretan Assembly appointed a new three-member committee (composed of N. Zouridis, Ioannis Saounatsos and M. Kapsalis) to carry out the task of governing the island. This committee was then succeeded on 29 December by a new government led by K. M. Foumis, G. Skouloudis and A. Papahatzis which immediately announced a general election for a new Cretan Assembly. In these elections which were held in the spring of 1910 Venizelos' party won a majority, and he formed a new government along with B. Skoulas and S. Mylonoyannakis on 17 May 1910. A few months later there was a government reshuffle when the Military League, which had taken control of political affairs in Athens following the Goudi *putsch* (1909), invited Eleftherios Venizelos to become prime minister of Greece in September 1910.

During the next two years Crete was governed by these three-member committees. The Greek government, even under the leadership of Venizelos, continued to reject the request of the Cretan deputies to be accepted in the Greek Parliament. This refusal was largely dictated by diplomatic concerns, in order to avoid any complications with Turkey, or of the Great Powers who had declared that they would not tolerate any change in the status quo of the Cretan political system.

At the end of 1911 new unrest was to trouble Crete. Venizelos' refusal to allow the Cretan deputies to enter the Greek parliament provoked a revival of the movement for rebellion in Crete. On 3 January 1912 a revolutionary assembly was once again set up, composed of armed forces and led by a three-member committee headed by Antonios Michelidakis who undertook to exert pressure to have Cretan deputies accepted in the Greek national parliament.

War, however, was to open up the paths that had been closed to access by diplomacy. With the outbreak of the Balkan Wars in October 1912 the doors of the Greek parliament were opened to the Cretans who were now welcomed with obvious joy. The Speaker of the Greek Parliament read out a resolution, according to which 'Greece recognises that there is just one parliament common to both the free kingdom [of Greece] and the island of Crete'. Of course the entry of Cretan deputies into the Greek parliament was not the same as formal recognition of the union. Even at this late stage, Venizelos preferred not to upset the state of autonomy that had been set up by the Great Powers. He confined himself to sending Stephanos Dragoumis as Governor General of Crete. Dragoumis arrived to take up his duties on 12 October 1912, and hoped to resolve the Cretan Question after the successful outcome of the Balkan Wars that had been waged between the various Balkan nations and Turkey.

In effect union had been achieved. On 14 February 1913 the flags of the Great Powers and Turkey were lowered from the walls of the castle at Suda. The symbols of suzerainty and of protection had at long last disappeared from Crete.

As had been expected, the successful conclusion of the Balkan Wars for Greece brought with it the long-desired solution to the Cretan Question. Article Four of the Treaty of London (30 May 1913) affirmed that the sultan resign all his rights over Crete to the Great Powers. By the terms of the separate treaty between Greece and Turkey (signed on 1 November 1913) the sultan renounced all claims to suzerainty over the island. The annexation of Crete by Greece had now been ratified. Dragoumis, in a statement addressed to the Cretan people on 28 November 1913, announced the expected arrival of King Constantine and his prime minister Venizelos at Chania where the formal declaration of union with Greece would be read out on the Sunday of the same week. Popular reaction was enthusiastic and spontaneous, with rejoicing everywhere. Centuries of struggle, bloodshed and tears had at last found their moment of historical justification. During the ceremony the Greek flag was raised high on the castle of Firka. And on the same spot, where until then the Turkish flag had flown, a marble plaque was set up with the following inscription written on it:

ΤΟΥΡΚΟΚΡΑΤΙΑ ΕΝ ΚΡΗΤΗ
1669-1913
ΗΤΟΙ 267 ΕΤΗ, 7 ΜΗΝΕΣ, 7 ΗΜΕΡΑΙ
ΕΤΗ ΑΓΩΝΙΑΣ

TURKISH RULE IN CRETE
1669-1913
267 YEARS, 7 MONTHS AND SEVEN DAYS
OF TRIBULATION

CHAPTER V

LIFE IN AUTONOMOUS CRETE

1. Participation of the Cretans in the Macedonian campaign

The declaration of Autonomy marked the end of Turkish rule in Crete. The Cretans' freedom had been secured and was guaranteed by the Great Powers. The age-long Cretan Question had reached its final stage. After centuries of darkness and bloodshed the Cretan people was once again allowed to taste freedom, domestic peace and security. 'Exemplary and unprecedented order for Crete prevails throughout the island', wrote Stylianos Xanthoudidis enthusiastically in 1909.

One of the most remarkable aspects of Cretan history during the first years of Autonomy was the voluntary participation of Cretans in the war effort on the Macedonian front from 1903 to 1908. Many Cretan leaders and rebel fighters, still fired by the enthusiasm of new-found freedom and national ideals, formed their own voluntary bands and joined up with the front ranks of the Greek forces in the struggle for the liberation of Macedonian Hellenism. Several Cretans, such as George Katechakis (Kapetan Rouvas) and George Tsondos (Kapetan Vardas), also served a distinguished career in the higher military ranks of the Greek forces during the time of the Macedonian campaign. According to the Greek historian Laourdas, 'it was the Cretans who, along with the native Macedonians, bore the brunt of the struggle and who paid the price of defending the just cause of the Macedonians most heavily with their blood'. In the official archive (set up in 1936) of the Macedonian campaigns the names of no less than 494 Cretans are recorded, 136 of whom died in action. This number is not accurate, however, because when the archive was initially set up many of the Cretan fighters of the

Macedonian campaign had since died or had not been notified to supply the necessary supporting documents showing their participation. We shall only learn the precise number when the archive of Tsondos, who succeeded Paul Melas as chief-of-staff, is published. P. Giparis, who also fought on the Macedonian front, wrote that of the 6,000 volunteers in Macedonia half were Cretans, and of those Cretans around 700 lost their lives. Melas wrote the following about a small force of Cretan volunteers in a letter addressed to the metropolitan bishop of Kastoria, Germanos Karavangelis: '...they are the perfect soldiers. Courageous, intelligent, daring, determined, ambitious and full of national pride: I am sure that that they will add enormous strength to your ranks'.

2. Population

The respite that the Christian element of the island could now enjoy from oppressive and unjust treatment at the hands of the Muslims had a favourable influence on movement of population on the island. For the first time the Turko-Cretans found themselves to be at a disadvantage, deprived of the administrative connivance which had allowed them to impose their will arbitrarily. The Muslim element had been particularly angered by the arrival of the Greek High Commissioner. The more fanatical of the Turko-Cretans, now unable to act as they pleased, decided to leave the island and make their homes elsewhere. Despite the repeated assurances of the High Commissioner and the guarantees of the Great Powers for their safety and equality with the Christians of Crete, there were mass migrations of Turko-Cretans to Istanbul and Asia Minor during the first two years of Autonomy. The Turko-Cretan population thus fell to about half its previous number: from 72,353 in 1881 it had fallen to 33,496 by the time of the census of 1900. During this same period there was a rapid increase in the Christian population, reaching 270,047 in 1900, having been just 206,812 in 1881.

The drastic decline of the Muslim element on the island was to have important social, psychological and economic consequences. Most of the Turko-Cretans who decided to leave Crete were those who dwelt in the rural areas. The Cretan villages were thus relieved of a Turkish presence and the villagers found that their land property had been increased. The Turko-Cretans who remained were chiefly those who resided in the towns or their environs. In the towns, however, where the Christians had been a minority during the period of Turkish rule, there was a sudden surge in the Christian population and it quickly reached levels almost equal to those of the Muslims. In the census of 1900 the urban Christian population was 25,561, while the Muslim population was 26,509. A natural concomitant of this development was that the urban economy (such as craft industry and trade) also passed into the hands of the Christians. As the historian Svolopoulos remarked 'the Greek element, strengthened numerically and politically, found in the urban centres those elements that allowed further economic and social development'.

3. The Economy

The newly formed Cretan State had to start life under difficult economic circumstances. The Protecting Powers granted a loan of 4m French Francs, but the problems facing the Cretan economy were both numerous and great. Moreover, the general economic crisis which hit Europe and particularly Greece in the early years of the 20th century inhibited any economic development on the island where the situation became even worse after two years of disastrous harvests (1900-1901).

Under these circumstances the High Commissioner's economic programme was under excessive strain from the very start. In a land, like Crete, that was overwhelmingly agricultural, government policy should have been directed primarily towards the development and modernisation of agriculture, and particularly the exploitation of the large and fertile plain of Mesara. In order to achieve a goal such as this, however, it was necessary to plan and execute other large infrastructural projects, and above all to construct a satisfactory road network on the island and to carry out port extension and improvements. Roads on Crete were very rudimentary and primitive; and the ports were too small for the requirements of modern shipping. Ships could only anchor in the large natural harbour of Suda Bay. At the other coastal towns ships were obliged to anchor out in the open sea and passengers and goods were brought ashore using small boats.

The Cretan government invited foreign experts to conduct studies and surveys in order to make proposals for the best ways in which to execute these large projects. The vast sums of money required for their execution, however, meant that they were a dead letter from the start. The estimated cost for the port of Herakleion alone was 10m drachmas, and the cost of the planned railway line between Herakleion and Mesara plain 9m drachmas: sums that were out of the question for an economy whose budget could only scrape together 450,000 drachmas for public works for the whole island.

After 1905 the economic situation began to improve. Domestic production, especially olive oil, increased and exports started to significantly outweigh imports. Yet the Cretan economy was still in no position to carry out the major works it so badly needed, and was obliged to depend on its traditional methods and resources.

4. Education and cultural life

The educational policy of the Cretan State was both dynamic and efficient. The stress that was laid on widely available elementary education is reflected in a whole series of legislative measures that took similar legislation in other countries as their model. The first Cretan constitution of 16 April 1899 stipulated that free education for boys and girls be compulsory. The increase in the number of schools, pupils and related spending was impressive. In the school year 1899-1900 523 elementary schools were functioning throughout Crete with a total of 35,844 pupils. In 1909-1910 there were 656 schools teaching a total of 40,559 pupils. Likewise, state spending on education rose from 406,193 drachmas in 1900 to 805,749 drachmas in 1910.

During this period there were two kinds of elementary school in Crete: the four-grade (lower school), and the six-grade (upper school). For middle-education there were six-grade grammar schools in the main towns of the island and semi-grammars (of three grades) in smaller centres. Three-grade high schools for girls were also set up in Chania, Rethymnon and Neapolis, and a five-grade girls' school opened in Herakleion. In 1903 a Public Education Act was passed setting up a three-year training school in Herakleion for state-school teachers, and also setting up a four-year seminary at the monastery of Agia Triada in Chania. This school legislation applied in Crete until 1914 when the general educational legislation of the Greek State was introduced on the island.

The most important cultural event of the years of Autonomy in Crete was the archaeological activity that was carried out at the various Minoan sites and the discovery of Minoan civilisation. Thanks to these large-scale archaeological projects, which began in the spring of 1900, Crete suddenly found itself at the centre of world intellectual attention as it yielded evidence of having been the cradle of European civilisation. The excavations were conducted by foreign archaeological schools and directed by highly distinguished archaeologists who had been granted permission by the Cretan State to excavate. It was fortunate for Crete that at this time two exceptional Cretan scholars and archaeologists had undertaken to supervise the archaeological activities of the foreign schools and were responsible for the protection of Cretan antiquities. The doctor Joseph Hatzidakis (1848-1936) and the archaeologist Stephanos Xanthoudidis (1864-1928) should be ranked as the twin heralds of Cretan archaeology. It was thanks to their zeal and patriotism that the Archaeological Museum of Herakleion was founded and many artifacts were kept in Crete that may otherwise have ended up in foreign museum collections.

Considerable cultural activity was taking place in many of the

Cretan towns during these years. Philological societies were particularly active and a number of important libraries were opened, such as the 'Athena' library of the Chrysostomos Philological Society at Chania and the Vikelaia Public Library in Herakleion. The latter owed its name to the distinguished scholar Dimitrios Vikelas who donated his valuable private collection of books to the municipality of Herakleion in 1908 in his enthusiasm over the archaeological discoveries at Knossos.

In the academic sphere Stephanos Xanthoudidis stands out for his work on archaeology, philology, history and folklore. He published numerous studies, thereby establishing himself as the father of Cretan studies. One of the major academic events of these years was the first full critical edition of the poem *Erotokritos*, published by Xanthoudidis in Herakleion in 1915 in collaboration with the scholarly publisher Stylianos Alexiou. In fact the Cretan Assembly had entrusted the task of producing a critical edition of this important Cretan poem to professor Antonios Yannaris as far back as 1886, granting him a generous sum of money for the purpose. When Yannaris died in 1909 Xanthoudidis undertook to complete the edition, and, following its publication, went on to produce editions of other Cretan works such as *Fortunatus* and *Erofili.*

The learned abbot Agathangelos Xirouchakis (later to become bishop of Kydonia) published his work *The Cretan War* in Trieste in 1908, along with the poetry of Anthimos Diakrousis and Marinos Tzane Bounialis.

A considerable number of journals were also published in Crete during this period. In 1912 the dynamic and learned metropolitan bishop Eumenios Xiroudakis began publication of the journal *Creta Christiana,* under the editorial supervision of Xanthoudidis. Its publication marked a serious academic step forward for Cretan studies. Its first two volumes, published in 1912 and 1913-15, contain a number of important studies and articles on the Venetian and Ottoman periods in Crete. In 1909 the short-lived folklore periodical *Kritikos Laos* was published in Herakleion, and in 1909-

1911 the learned journalist and historian Ioannis Mourellos published a notable periodical with the title *Kritiki Stoa*. Finally, another periodical *Kritikos Astir* was published in Chania between the years 1906 and 1911.

There was no literature that was particularly specific to Crete during these years. Writers tended to follow the literary trends of Athens. The most important man of letters was Ioannis Kondylakis (1861-1920), a fine writer on character and the father perhaps of the modern Greek 'genre' story, as Linos Politis termed the story describing Greek village life. In his works *Patouchas* and *When I was a Teacher,* Kondylakis gives a vivid picture of the life and manners of the Cretan countryside during the last years of Turkish rule.

It was in this social and intellectual climate that Nikos Kazantzakis (1878-1957), the major literary figure of modern Crete, was born and grew up. Kazantzakis later went on to describe brilliantly the Crete of the last years of Turkish rule in his story *Kapetan Michalis*. His character was formed and indelibly stamped by the Cretan ethos of this period.

EPILOGUE

LIBERATED CRETE
(1913-1941)

The separate history of Crete essentially ended when it became politically united with mainland Greece. Following the date of its union with Greece on 1 December 1913 it could not but share the same general history of the rest of Greece, of which it now comprised an organic part. By way of conclusion we shall just consider a few events which are specific to Crete.

1. Administration

After the union Crete comprised an administrative province with its capital in Chania where the leading state officials were now based. The governor general of Crete was appointed by the Greek government and bore the title of minister or secretary-of-state. This administrative set up, however, did not prove to be particularly stable and underwent a number of changes. As was to be expected the various national disturbances and tribulations that shortly followed the union were to have an impact on the Cretan administration as well. In 1915 the Cretan secretary-of-state was abolished, to be restored a year later by the revolutionary government of Venizelos based in Thessaloniki. At this time Crete was the bastion of Venizelism and firmly supported Venizelos during the period of national division when a rival government enjoying massive popular support was established by Venizelos in Thessaloniki in direct opposition to King Constantine and his policy of neutrality in the Balkan conflict of the First World War. Before embarking on his political plans and his open conflict with the king, Venizelos considered that it would be in his interest to visit Crete for a few days. The army division of Crete decided to back the pro-Entente rebel army group *Ethniki Amyna* (National Defence) in Thessaloniki. Once again, in 1925, the secretary-of-state was abolished, only to be reformed in July 1926.

2. The economy

The local economy continued to be based on its traditional lines. The main activity was olive cultivation. The olive groves of Crete now covered an area of some 80,000 hectares with an average annual yield of about 25,000 tonnes of olive oil. Whole olives were also produced and exported in large quantities. The second main resource of the Cretan economy was viniculture. Raisin production had developed and expanded in the region around Herakleion, while elsewhere, and especially in the province of Chania, good quality wine was produced. Grapes for fresh consumption were also produced, but in smaller quantities. Other agricultural products included cereals, citrus fruits and especially the citron, almonds, chestnuts, and carobs. Tobacco and silk were also produced in large quantities.

Livestock breeding also developed rapidly. According to the census of 1928, Crete had 700,000 goats and sheep, 50,000 cattle, 6,000 horses, 10,000 mules, 40,000 donkeys, 45,000 pigs, and 400,000 poultry. High quality cheese production yielded about 650 tonnes for export. A public cheese-dairy was set up in the village of Tzitzifes in the province of Apokoronas for the purpose of improving the quality and standardisation of the product, and elsewhere, in Sphakia and Anogeia (Mylopotamos), there were other cheese-dairies.

Large factories were not set up in Crete. Apart from the old soap factories, there were also raisin processing plants in Herakleion. In 1930 another factory was set up for citron processing.

The most important public work to be carried out during this period in Crete was the construction of the large harbour of Herakleion with a 600-metre jetty for the mooring of large ships.

Two aerodromes were also constructed, at Maleme in the province of Chania, and at Herakleion. Shortly before the war a military aerodrome was begun at Kastelli in Pediada.

In general the Cretan economy was in a relatively good state of health when compared with other parts of Greece. Exports were consistently in excess of imports. According to the survey conducted by the Herakleion Chamber of Commerce in 1928 exports were valued at 225,411,778 drachmas, while imports were valued at 196,488,492 drachmas.

3. Population. Refugees

An inportant aspect of Cretan social and demographic history during this period was the large number of refugees from Asia Minor (following the Asia Minor Disaster of 1922), mainly from the area around Smyrna, that fled to, or were resettled on, Crete chiefly in the area around Herakleion. As early as September 1922, according to the news reports and descriptions in the newspapers of the day, more than 20,000 refugees were in the harbour and roads of Herakleion and another 7,000 elsewhere on the island. Shelter and medical care for these unfortunate people had become a major problem for the secretary-of-state of Crete. A committee for the rehabilitation of refugees was set up and immediately began its task in the autumn of 1922.

In January 1923 the Treaty of Lausanne was signed by Turkey and Greece, whereby an exchange of populations was agreed upon. The entire Turkish population of Crete, which amounted to around 30,000 individuals, was obliged to abandon the island forthwith. The homes and property of the Muslims were handed over to the Greek refugees from Asia Minor. The final total of refugees to settle on Crete was 8,270 families, or 33,900 individuals. Most of them settled in the towns or their outlying districts where the Muslims had largely confined themselves since the beginning of the century. A few refugees settled in the rural areas, mainly in Monofatsi.

With the exchange of populations the Greek ethnic character of

Crete had been restored. After centuries of foreign domination the island now found itself to be of a homogenous ethnic and religious composition: all its inhabitants were now Greek Orthodox, apart from a few Jews and Armenians mostly concentrated in the towns of Herakleion and Chania.

The Cretan population continued to rise. According to the census of 1928 the total population of the island was 386,427 in contrast to 336,151 in 1913. The region of Chania had 111,513, the region of Rethymnon 68,180, the region of Herakleion 138,567 and the region of Lasithi 68,167. Of the smaller provincial units Pediada was the most populous with 32,813 inhabitants, and the least populous was Sphakia with 4,392.

4. The anti-dictatorship movement of Chania.

An important political episode took place in Chania in the summer of 1938. Various former politicians and army officers attempted to overthrow the dictatorship of Ioannis Metaxas and to restore democracy to the country. On the night of 28 July they took control of the radio-station of the town and broadcast a revolutionary declaration calling King George II and the armed forces to overthrow immediately the dictatorial regime. Among the key figures in this action were Aristomenis Mitsotakis, Manuel Voloudakis and General Mandakas. The movement of course was not isolated in its action. It was intended to be the first phase of a wider revolutionary movement whose ground had been prepared by anti-dictatorship elements in Athens, led by the then governor of the Bank of Greece Emmanuel Tsouderos, who later became prime minister of the Greek government-in-exile during the Nazi occupation of Greece in the Second World War.

The regime was alarmed but acted swiftly and efficiently. A strong naval force sailed down to Crete, while a squadron of seaplanes flew down to the island of Milos. Within a few hours the *putsch* had been crushed. Some of the ringleaders managed to escape to Cyprus and were condemned *in absentia* to death. Others, numbering about 60, were condemned to prison camps, island exile and other heavy sentences. The death sentence was not carried out.

5. The Battle of Crete

The last major event that remains for us to record in the long catalogue of Cretan history is the Battle of Crete, as the heroic resistance against the German invaders of the island came to be called. This battle, which took place during the last ten days of May 1941, was not just of local, but of far wider importance, and can be ranked as one of the major events of the Second World War. At the same time it was an important episode of Greek history, forming the dramatic conclusion to the Greek-Italian conflict. The battle began at dawn on 20 May and formally ended on the 29th, thus making the 29th of May (the day of the Fall of Constantinople to the Ottoman Turks) twice unlucky in the history of Hellenism.

Historians have not tired of ruminating on the details of the battle and seeking further evidence in the various archives, publishing documents and photographic records, debating problems which have yet been solved, laying the responsibility for mistakes and omissions in tactics and speculating on how things would have turned out if Crete's defences had been prepared earlier and more thoroughly. The literature on all these matters is abundant and the historian finds himself in a difficult position when faced with the task of evaluating the varied and frequently contradictory views and accounts. Here we shall leave these matters to the specialists and simply confine our account to a presentation of the main events.

Shortly before the occupation of Athens by the Germans, King George II and the Greek government under the leadership of Emmanuel Tsouderos, left for Crete (23 April 1941), the only remaining free Greek territory. The British, New Zealanders and Australians had undertaken to defend the island and were hastily transferred there from mainland Greece as the front collapsed in the face of the invading Germans. The British forces amounted to some 30,000 men. Their weapons were old and they were not equipped with modern anti-aircraft artillery fire. There were also Greek forces on the island: eight battalions of new recruits just transferred from Tripoli and Nafplion in the Peloponnese, untrained and unequipped. A more notable force was the Civil Militia School and the first grade of the Officer Training School, although again they were very insufficiently armed. There were no Cretan soldiers because they had been trapped in occupied Greece.

The defence of Crete had been neglected, perhaps because no one

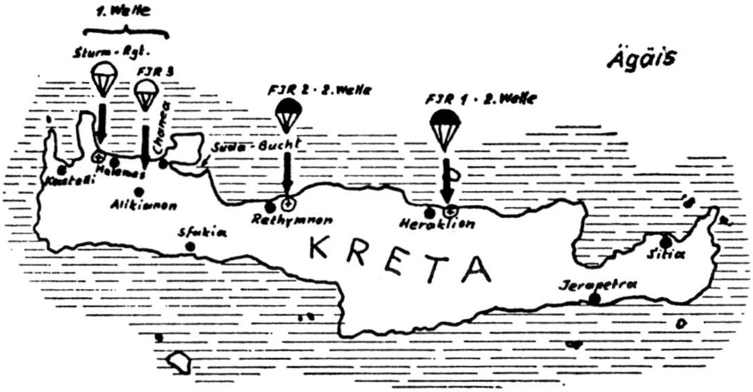

Figure 30
The main targets of the German parachutists (Franz Kurowski, *Der Kampf um Kreta,* Bonn 1965, 27).

really believed that Hitler would venture on such a bold campaign for its capture. However, the German leadership had already decided on its campaign and plan of action, to be named operation *Merkur.* It was to be based on the dropping of special brigades of parachutists onto the island. It was a scheme that reflected the unbridled ambition of Goering, the German commander of the Luftwaffe, and his second-in-command Student who had drawn up the plan and personally supervised its execution.

Preparations for the invasion began on 14 May with heavy air-raids on strategic positions of the island. The invasion itself started at dawn on 20 May 1941, with a relentless bombardment and the dropping of parachutists in the area of Chania. At midday on the same day further parachutists were dropped over Rethymnon and, shortly afterwards, Herakleion. The main objective of the invaders was the capture of the aerodrome at Maleme where they intended to land their aircraft with reinforcements and supplies.

The events in Crete were almost indescribable and provoked the admiration of the world. Unarmed civilians, men, women, the elderly and children, rushed spontaneously to fight a desperate and bloody struggle in defence of their homeland and freedom. The Allied forces and the local population all impressed the world with their unhoped-for and stubborn resistance against the most efficient and strongest war machine on earth. Crete was transformed into a living hell while one of the most terrible battles in history was waged. The Germans were compelled to expend vast efforts and supplies, and the cream of their forces, in order to take control of the island, which they managed to do within ten days, step by step. Their losses were staggering. Over 4,000 parachutists, the 'spearhead of the Nazi force' were killed, the 7th airborne division was virtually destroyed, and over 170 aircraft shot down. The supposedly invincible weapon of the parachutists took a heavy beating in Crete and it is interesting that since that date a like force has never been used again in such large military campaigns. Hitler himself admitted that 'Crete demonstrated that the great days of the parachutists are over'. And Winston Churchill noted in his memoirs that 'In Crete Goering won a Pyrrhic victory, because with the forces he wasted there he could easily have conquered Cyprus, Syria, Iraq or even Persia... He committed the foolish mistake of allowing these great opportunities to slip from his hands, sacrificing irreplaceable forces in a fatal struggle that was frequently carried out as hand to hand fighting'.

Crete bowed before the most awesome war machine that the world had known. On 27 May Chania and Rethymnon were captured. And on 30 May Herakleion fell in its turn. On that same day the last British defenders of Crete left Sphakia for the Middle East. The mopping up operations of the Germans ended on 31 May and the swastika was raised above the blood-drenched island. Along with Greece and the rest of mainland Europe, Crete now entered the grim darkness of the Nazi horror. Occupation began with its terrible reprisals and the indescribable barbarity of the occupier towards the civilian population, the first victim of the German firing squads being the village of Kandanos (2 July 1941). The fight for Cretan freedom bore a heavy price, with arrests, mass executions, concentration camps, the decimation of entire villages, and the frightful events that took place at Skine, Anogeia, Viannos and elsewhere.

Nevertheless, the rallying call for resistance had been sounded from the very first day of the invasion, and the acts of violence of the occupier could never bend the Cretan will to resist. A new period of self-sacrifice and valiant deeds, the period of the Nazi occupation and the national resistance in Crete, awaits its historian.

BIBLIOGRAPHY

GENERAL WORKS

DETORAKIS TH., Βιβλιογραφία της Κρητικής Ιστορίας, Παλίμψηστον 3, 1986, 161-237.

EKKEKAKIS G.P., Τα Κρητικά βιβλία. Σχεδίασμα Κρητικής Βιβλιογραφίας. Α'. 1499-1863. Β' 1864-1913. Rethymnon 1990, 1991.

FOUNTOUKAKIS K., Ιστορία της Κρήτης από των αρχαιοτάτων μέχρι των καθ' ημάς χρόνων, Athens 1903

KRIARIS P., Ιστορία της Κρήτης (Νέα) από των αρχαιοτάτων μέχρι των καθ' ημάς χρόνων, I - III, Athens , 1930 - 1937

MATTON R., La Crète au cours des siècles , Athènes 1955

— La Crète antique , Athens 1960

PANAYOTAKIS N., (ed.), Κρήτη. Ιστορία και πολιτισμός, I - II , Iraklion 1987 - 1988

PSILAKIS B., Ιστορία της Κρήτης I - III, Chania 1899 - 1909

STAVRAKIS N., Στατιστική του πληθυσμού της Κρήτης, μετά διαφόρων γεωγραφικών, ιστορικών, αρχαιολογικών, εκκλησιαστικών κλπ. ειδήσεων περί της νήσου, Athens 1890

TULARD J., Histoire de la Crète , Paris 1962 (Que sais-je ? 1018)

XANTHOUDIDIS ST., Επίτομος Ιστορία της Κρήτης , Athens 1909

GUIDES-VISITORS-MAPS

ALEXIU S., A Guide to the Minoan Palaces: Knossos, Phaistos, Mallia, Iraklion 1973.

BELON DU MANS P., Les Observations de plusieurs singularitez et choses memorables trouvées en Grèce..., Paris 1554

BOSCHINI MARCO, Il Regno tutto di Candia, Venice 1651 (Modena 1967)

BUONDELMONTI CHR., Descriptio Insule Crete et Liber Insularum, cap. XI : Creta. Édition critique par Marie-Anne van Spitael, Iraklion 1981

BOWMAN J., Crete , London 1978

CORONELLI P.M., Isolario del Atlante Veneto, Venice 1696

DE TOURNEFORT L.P., Relation d' un voyage du Levant... I , Paris 1717

GUANELLA H. , Kreta . Ein Reisenfürher, Zurich 1969
PASHLEY R., Travels in Crete, I-II , London 1937 (Amsterdam 1970)
POCOCKE R., A Description of the East and Some other Countries, I. London 1743
RATTI ANT., La cartografia di Creta, Πεπραγμένα Ε' Διεθνούς Κρητολ. Συνεδρίου, II, 330 - 337
RAULIN V., Description physique de l' île de Crète, Paris 1869
SAVARY M., Lettres sur la Grèce, Paris 1788
SIEBER F.W., Reise nach der Insel Kreta im griechischen Archipelagus im Jahre 1817..., Leipzig und Sorau 1823
SMITH M.L., The Great Island . A Study of Crete, London 1965
SPANAKIS ST., Κρήτη. Τουρισμός, ιστορία, αρχαιολογία. Α'. Ανατολική Κρήτη. Β'. Δυτική Κρήτη, Iraklion 1983[2]
SPEICH R., Kreta , Tübingen 1965
SPRATT T.A.B., Travels and Researches in Crete I -II , London 1865
STÜRZL E ., Kreta , die Insel im Herzen der Alten Welt, Vienna 1948
STYLIANOY ANDR., The Map of Crete and Cyprus in the Theatrum Orbis Terrarum of Abraham Ortelius, Antwerp 1570, Πεπραγμένα Γ' Διεθνούς Κρητολ. Συνεδρίου II, 291 - 314

NEOLITHIC CRETE

FAURE P., Αι εγχάρακτοι βραχογραφίαι του σπηλαίου Ασφένδου Σφακίων, Αμάλθεια 9, 1971, 277 - 283
HUTCHINSON R., Prehistoric Crete, Harmondsworth 1965
SAKELLARAKIS J., Νεολιθική Κρήτη, in the volume : Νεολιθική Ελλάς, Athens 1970 , 131 - 146
ZERVOS C., L'Art de la Crète néolithique et minoenne , Paris 1965

MINOAN CIVILISATION

1. General Works

ALEXIOU ST., Μινωικός πολιτισμός, Iraklion.
— Minoan Civilization (tranlated from the Greek by Cressida Ridley), Heraclion.
BOARDMAN J., Pre-classical: From Crete to Archaic Greece, Harmondsworth 1967
BRANIGAN K., The Foundations of Palatial Crete , London 1970
CADOGAN G., Palaces of Minoan Crete , Oxford 1976

EVANS A., The Palace of Minos at Knossos, I - IV , London 1921 - 1936
FAURE P., Fonctions des cavernes crétoises, Paris 1964
GLOTZ G., La Civilisation Egéenne , Paris 1952
GRAHAM J.W., The Palaces of Crete, Princeton Univ.Press 1962
HOEGLER R.G. - REVERDIN O., Kreta - Mutterland der Kultur Europas, Luzern 1960
HOOD S., The Home of the Heroes. The Aegean before the Greeks, London 1967
— The Minoan Crete in the Bronze Age, London 1971
HOOD S.-SMYTH D., Archeological Survey of Knossos Area, London 1981
HOOD S. - TAYLOR W., The Bronze Age Palace at Knossos, London 1981
HUXLEY C.L., Crete and the Luvians , Oxford 1961
KENNA V. E.G., Cretan Seals , Oxford 1960
LA ROSA V., « Festos » , Creta Antica. Cento anni di archeologia italiana, Rome 1984
LEVI DORO, Festos e la civiltà minoica, I -IV , Rome 1976 (= Incunabula graeca LX)
LUCE T.V., The End of Atlantis. New light on an Old Legend, Granada 1975
MARINATOS S. - HIRMER M., Kreta und das Mykenische Hellas, Munich 1959
MATT L. von - ALEXIOU ST.- PLATON N. - GUANELLA H., Ancient Crete, New York 1968.
MATZ FR., Le monde Egéen : Troie-Crète - Mycènes, Paris 1956
PALMER L.R., The Penultimate Palace of Knossos, Rome 1969
PELON O., Les Palais de Malia , Paris 1980
PENLEBURY J.D.S., Archaeology of Crete, London 1939
PLATON N., Crète. Archaeologia Mundi, Geneva 1966
ΠΛΑΤΩΝ Ν ., Ζάκρος. Τό νέον μινωικόν ανάκτορον, Athens 1971
POPHAM M., The Destruction of the Palace at Knossos, Göteborg 1970
RAISON J., Le Grand Palais de Cnossos, Paris 1969 (= Incunabula Graeca , XXXIV)
REVERDIN O. - HOEGLER R., La Crète, berceau de la civilisation européenne, Lucerne 1960
SAKELLARAKIS J. - SAPOUNA E., Αρχάνες, Athens 1991
SCHACHERMAYER F., Die minoische Kultur des alten Kreta, Stuttgart 1964
TZEDAKIS J. , Kastelli Chanion, Paris 1977 (= Incunabula Graeca LXVI)
VAN EFFENTERRE H ., Le Palais de Malia et la cité minoenne, I - II , Paris 1980 (=Incunabula Graeca LXXVI)

2. Minoan Religion and Mythology

ALEXIOU S., Η μινωική θεά μεθ' υψωμένων των χειρών, Κρητικά Χρονικά 13, 1958, 179 - 299

EVANS A., The earlier religion of Greece in the light of Cretan discoveries, London 1931

FAURE P., A la recherche du vrai Labyrinthe de Crète, Κρητικά Χρονικά 17, 1963, 315 - 326

MATZ F., Göttererscheinungen und Kultbild im minoischen Kreta, Wiesbaden 1958

NILSSON M.P., The Minoan- Mycenaean Religion and its survival in Greek Religion, Lund 1950

PEARSSON A., The Religion of Greece in Prehistoric Times, Berkeley and Los Angeles 1942

PICARD CH., Les religions préhelléniques (Crète et Mycènes) , Paris 1948

RUND I.M., Minoan Religion. A Bibliography , Oslo 1980

3. Minoan Language and Writing

BONNET E.L.- CHADWICK J.-VENTRIS M ., The Knossos Tablets. A Translation, London 1959

BRICE W.C., Inscriptions in the Minoan Linear script of Class A, Oxford 1961

CHADWICK J., The Decipherement of Linear B, New York 1960 (Cambridge 1967)

CHADWICK J.- KILLEN J.T.- OLIVIER J.P., The Knossos Tablets, 1971

CHAPOUTIER F., Les écritures minoennes au palais de Malia, Paris 1930

DUHOUX Y., L' écriture et le texte du Disque de Phaestos, Πεπραγμένα Δ' Διεθνούς Κρητολ. Συνεδρίου, I , 112 - 136

EVANS A., Scripta Minoa. The written documents of Minoan Crete with special reference to the Archives of Knossos, I - II , Oxford 1909

FAURE P., Observations sur le Disque de Phaistos, Κρητολογία 2,1976, 47- 64

GORDON C.H., New Light on the Minoan Language, Πεπραγμένα Δ' Διεθνούς Κρητολ. Συνεδρίου I, 205 - 209

PALMER L.R.- BOARDMAN J., On the Knossos Tablets, Oxford 1963

RAISON J.-POPE M., Index du Linéaire A, Rome 1971 (= Incunaula Graeca XLI)

VENTRIS M., The Language of the Minoan and Mycenaean Civilisations, London 1950

4. Public Life in Minoan Crete

FAURE P., La vie quotidienne en Crète au temps de Minos , Paris 1973

MARINATOS S., Θέατρα και θεάματα του μεσογειακού πολιτισμού, Ηώς (Αφιέρωμα στην Κρήτη) 1964, 30 - 35

WARREN P., Knossos and its foreign relations in the Early Bronze Age, Πεπραγμένα Δ' Διεθνούς Κρητολ. Συνεδρίου I, 628 - 637

THE POSTPALATIAL OR MYCENAEAN PERIOD

BOARDMAN J., Pre-classical: From Crete to Archaic Greece, Harmondsworth 1967

DESBOROUGH V., The Last Mycenaeans and their Successors, Oxford 1964

DUHOUX Y., L' Étéocretois , Amsterdam 1982

HALLAGER E.,The Destruction of the Mycenaean Palace at Knossos, Stockholm 1977

— The Mycenaean Palace at Knossos, Medelhavmusseet, Memoir I, Stockholm 1977

HOOD M.S.F., The Last Palace at Knossos and the Date of its Destruction, Studi Micenei ed Egeo-anatolici 2, 1967, 63 - 70

THE DORIAN PERIOD

BOARDMAN J., The Cretan Collection in Oxford. The Dictaean Cave and Iron Age, Oxford 1961

BOSSERT H.TH., Alt Kreta, Berlin 1937

BROCK J.K., Fortetsa. Early Greek Tombs near Knossos, Cambridge 1957

DEMARGNE P., La Crète dédalique.Histoire d' une Rennaissance, Paris 1947

FAURE P., Les sept inscriptions dites « Étéocrétoises » reconsidérées, Κρητικά Χρονικά 28 - 29 , 1988 - 1989, 94 - 109

GUARDUCCI M., Inscriptiones Creticae I - V , Rome 1935 - 1950

JENKINS R., Daedalica, Cambridge 1936

KIRSTEN E., Das dorische Kreta, Würzburg 1942

KITCHELL KENNETH FR., Topographica Cretica: Topoi of Classical Crete with testimonia, Layola University of Chicago 1977

KOHLER J. - ZIERBARTH E , Das Staatdrecht von Gortyn , Göttingen 1942

LE RIDER G. , Monnaies Crétoises, Athens 1966

LEVI DORO, Early Hellenic pottery of Crete, Princeton 1945 (Amsterdasm 1969)

MANNING ST.W., The Volcano of Thera and the Destruction of Minoan Crete, Κρητικά Χρονικά 27, 1987 , 59 - 85

MATTON R., La Crète antique, Athens 1960
MORROW G.R., Plato' s Cretan City, Princeton 1960
PLATAKIS EL., Το Ιδαίον Άντρον , Iraklion 1965
SAKELLARAKIS J., Ιδαίο Άντρο: Η μινωική και η ελληνική λατρεία, Κρητικά Χρονικά 28 - 29, 1988 - 1989 , 22 - 27
SVORONOS J., Numismatique de la Crète ancienne, Paris 1890
STAMBOLIDIS N. Ελεύθερνα, Rethymnon 1993
STRATARIDAKI A., The Historians of Ancient Crete: A Study in Regional Historiography, Κρητικά Χρονικά 28-29, 1988 - 1989, 137 - 193
TSIPOPOULOU M., Γεωμετρική καί Ανατολίζουσα κεραμεική της Ετεοκρητικής περιοχής, Athens 1987
VERBRUGGEN H., Sources Pertaining to the Cult of Zeus in Crete, Louvain 1979
— Le Zeus Crétois, Paris 1981
WILLETS R.F., Ancient Crete. Social History from Early Times until the Roman Occupation, London 1965
— Aristocratic Society in Ancient Crete , London 1965
— The Law Code of Gortyn. Edition with Introduction, Translation and a Commentary, Berlin 1967
— Everyday Life in Ancient Crete , London 1969
— Cretan Cults and Festivals , London 1962

HELLENISTIC PERIOD

BRULÉ P., La piratérie crétoise hellénistique, Paris 1978
HERROG R., Κρητικός Πόλεμος , Klio 2, 1902, 316 - 333
MICROGIANNAKIS EMM., Η Κρήτη κατά τους ελληνιστικούς χρόνους. Αι πολιτικαί ιδίᾳ σχέσεις της νήσου μετ' άλλων πόλεων ή κρατών, Athens 1967
PETROPOULOY ANG., Beitrage zur Wirtschafts-und Geselschaftsgeschichte Kretas in hellenistischen Zeit, Frankfurt -Bern 1985
SPYRIDAKIS ST., Ptolemaic Itanos and Hellenistic Crete, Berkeley 1970
VAN DER MJNSBRUGGE M., The Cretan Koinon , New York 1931
VAN EFFENTERRE H., La Crète et le monde grec de Platon à Polybe, Paris 1948

THE ROMAN PERIOD

PASSERINI A., La preparazione della guerra contro Creta, Athenaeum 14, 1936, 45 - 53

PERNIER L., Gortina, capitale della provincia Cretae et Cyrenarum, Atene e Roma 18, 1915, 49 - 68
SANDERS J.F., Roman Crete, Warminster 1982
SPYRIDAKIS ST., Crete and the Romans, Κρητολογία 9, 1979, 85 - 98

THE BYZANTINE PERIOD

AHRWEILER H., L'administration militaire de la Crète byzantine, Byzantion 31, 1961, 224 - 237
CHRISTERN J., Die Datierung von A.Titos in Gortys, Πεπραγμένα Γ' Διεθνούς Κρητολογικού Συνεδρίου , II, 37 f.
CHRISTIDES B., The Conquest of the Crete by Arabs (ca. 824). A turning point in the Struggle between Byzantium and Islam , Athens 1984
— The Raids of the Moslems of Crete in the Aegean Sea, Byzantion 51, 1981, 76 f.
GALLAS KL. - WESSEL KL. - BORBUDAKIS M., Byzantinisches Kreta, Munich 1983
GURUNI SP.A. - DONATI L., Creta Byzantina, Rome 1987.
DETORAKIS TH., Οι άγιοι της πρώτης 6υζαντινής περιόδου της Κρήτης και η σχετική προς αυτούς φιλολογία (διδ. διατριβή), Athens 1970
DI VITA A., Contributi alla conoscenza di Gortina bizantina, Πεπραγμένα Ε' Διεθνούς Κρητολογικού Συνεδρίου, II, 137 - 143
KONIDARIS G., Αι επισκοπαί της Κρήτης μέχρι του Ι' αιώνος, Κρητικά Χρονικά 7, 1953, 462 - 478
LAURENT V., Le statut de la Crète byzantine avant et après sa liberation du joug arabe, Πεπραγμένα Α' Διεθνούς Κρητολογικού Συνεδρίου, II, 382 - 396
MILES G., A provisional reconstruction of the genealogy of the Arab Amirs of Crete, Πεπραγμένα Α'. Διεθνούς Κρητολογικού Συνεδρίου, II, 59-73
— Byzantium and the Arabs: Relations in Crete and the Aegean area, Dumbarton Oaks Papers 18, 1964, 1 - 32
PETIT L., Saint Jean Xenos ou l' Ermite d' après son autobiographie, Analecta Bollandiana 42, 1924, 5 - 20
TOMADAKIS N., Η Αποστολική Εκκλησία της Κρήτης κατά τους αιώνας Η' - ΙΓ' και ο τίτλος του προκαθημένου αυτής, Επετηρίς Εταιρείας Βυζαντινων Σπουδών 24, 1954, 67 - 107
TSOUGARAKIS D., Byzantine Crete. From the 5th Century to the Venetian Conquest, Athens 1988
VOLANAKIS J., Τα παλαιοχριστιανικά μνημεία της Κρήτης, Κρητικά

Χρονικά 27, 1987, 235 - 261
XANTHOUDIDIS ST., Περί της Μητροπόλεως Κρήτης και του μητροπολιτικού ναού του Αγίου Τίτου κατά την β' βυζαντινήν περίοδον, Iraklion 1925 (1974[2])

THE PERIOD OF VENETIAN RULE

ALEXIOU ST., Το Κάστρο της Κρήτης και η ζωή του στον ΙΣΤ' και ΙΖ' αιώνα , Κρητικά Χρονικά 19, 1965, 146 - 178
BORSARI S., Il dominio veneziano a Creta nel XIII secolo, Naples 1963
BROWNING R., A note on the capture of Constantinople, Byzantion 22, 1952, 379 - 386
CORNELIUS FL., Creta Sacra, I - II , Venice 1755
DETORAKIS TH., Η πανώλης εν Κρήτῃ. Συμβολή είς τήν ιστορίαν των επιδημιών της νήσου, Επιστημονική Επετηρίς Φιλοσοφικής Σχολής Πανεπιστημίου Αθηνών 1970 - 71, 118 - 136
— Η αγγαρεία της θάλασσας στη βενετοκρατούμενη Κρήτη, Κρητολογία 16 -17, 1984, 103 -139
DIMACOPOULOS J., Italian renaissance in Crete , Architectural Review , No 960 (London , Febr. 1977) , 128 f.
ZACHARIADOU EL.A., Trade and Crusade. Venetian Crete and the Emirates of Menteshe and Aydin (1300 - 1415) , Venice 1984
ZVI ANKORI, Jews and the Jewish Community in the History of Medieval Crete, Πεπραγμένα Β' Διεθνούς Κρητολογικού Συνεδρίου III, 312 - 367
GASPARIS CHAR., Η γη και οι αγρότες στη μεσαιωνική Κρήτη (13ος - 14ος αι.) , I - III, Rethymnon 1986
GEANAKOPLOS D.J., The Library of the Cretan Humanist -Bishop Maximos Margunios, especially his collection of Latin books bequeathed to Mount Athos, Πεπραγμένα Β' Διεθνούς Κρητολογικού Συνεδρίου III , 75 - 91
GERLAND E., Kreta als venetianische Kolonie, München 1899
GEROLA G., Monumenti Veneti nell' isola di Creta, I -IV, Venice 1905 - 1932
GEROLA G. Topografia delle chiese della città di Candia, Bessarione 34, 1918, 99 - 100 , 239 - 281.
GEROLA G.-ΛΑΣΣΙΘΙΩΤΑΚΗΣ Κ., Τοπογραφικός κατάλογος των τοιχογραφημένων Εκκλησιών της Κρήτης, Iraklion 1961
MALTEZOU CHR., Η παρουσία της γυναίκας στις νοταριακές πράξεις της περόδου της βενετοκρατίας, Κρητολογία 16 - 19, 1983 - 1984 , 62 - 79

— Το παιδί στην κοινωνία της 6ενετοκρατούμενης Κρήτης, Κρητικά Χρονικά 27, 1987, 214 - 227

MANOUSSAKAS M.J., Les derniers défenseurs Crétois de Constantinople d' après les documents vénitiens, Akten des XI Internat. Byzantinisten-kongress, Munich 1960, 331 - 340

MILLER W., Kreta under Venetians (1204 - 1669) . Essays on Latin Orient, Cambridge 1921

NOIRET H., Documents inédits pour servir à l'histoire de la domination vénitienne en Crète, de 1380 à 1485 , Paris 1893

PANAYOTAKIS N, Ο ποιητής του « Ερωτοκρίτου » και άλλα 6ενετο-κρητικά μελετήματα, Iraklion 1989

— Η κρητική περίοδος της ζωής του Δομήνικου Θεοτοκόπουλου, Athens 1986

— Φραγκίσκος Λεονταρίτης, Κρητικός μουσικοσυνθέτης του δέκατου έκτου αιωνα. Μαρτυρίες για τη ζωή και το έργο του, Venice 1990

PAPADAKIS EMM., Μορφαί του λαϊκού πολιτισμού της Κρήτης του 15ου και 16ου αιώνος κατά τας γραμματειακάς πηγάς, Athens 1976

PUCHNER W., Ο ρόλος της μουσικής στο Κρητικό Θέατρο, Κρητικά Χρονικά 27, 1987, 193 - 213

RATTI - VIDULICH P., Duca di Candia (1313 - 1329), Venice 1965

— Duca di Candia. Quadernus Conciliorum (1340 - 1350), Venice 1976

SANTSCHI EL., Régestes desarrêts civils et des memoriaux (1363 -1399) des archives du Duc de Crète, Venice 1976

SCHREINER P., Die byzantinischen Kleinchroniken, I - II, Wien 1975, 1977.

SPANAKIS ST., Μνημεία Κρητικής Ιστορίας I - VI , Iraklion 1940 - 1976

TATAKIS B.N., Γεράσιμος Βλάχος ο Κρης (1605 / 7 - 1685), φιλόσοφος, θεολόγος, φιλόλογος, Venice 1973

THEOTOKIS SP., Αποφάσεις του Μείζονος Συμ6ουλίου της Βενετίας, I-II, Athens 1933

THIRIET FR., Candie, grande place marchande dans la première moitié du XVe siècle. Études sur la Romanie Gréco-vénitienne (Xe -XVe siècles), London 1977 (Variorum Reprints)

— Sui dissidi sorti il Commune di Venezia e i suoi feudatori di Creta nel trecento, Études sur la Romanie Gréco-vénitienne aux XIV - XV siècles, London 1977 (Variorum Reprints)

— La Romanie Vénitienne au Moyen Age. Le developpement et l' exloitation du domaine colonial vénitien (XIIe - XVe siècles), Paris 1975

TOMADAKIS N., Ο Ιωσήφ Βρυέννιος και η Κρήτη κατά τό 1400. Μελέτη φιλολογική και ιστορική, Athens 1947

TOPPING P., Co- existence of Greeks and Latins in Frankish Morea and Venetian Crete. Studies on Latin Greece (A.D. 1205 - 1715), London 1977 (Variorum Reprints)

XANTHOUDIDIS ST., Η Ενετοκρατία εν Κρήτῃ και οι κατὰ των Ενετών αγώνες των Κρητών , Athens 1939

— Χάνδαξ - Ηράκλειον. Ιστορικά σημειώματα, Iraklion 1964

Monuments

ALEXIOU ST., Το δουκικόν ανάκτορον του Χάνδακος , Κρητικά Χρονικά 14, 1960, 102 -108

CURUNI SP.A. - DONATI L., Creta Veneziana, Venezia 1988

DIMAKOPOULOS J., Η Lozza του Ρεθέμνου. Ένα αξιόλογο έργο αρχιτεκτονικής του Michelle Sammicheli στην Κρήτη, Πεπραγμένα Γ' Διεθνούς κρητολογικού Συνεδρίου, ΙΙ, 64 - 83

FATOUROU - HESYCHAKI K., Η Ρετόντα της Κρήτης. Η χρήσις ενός αρχιτεκτονικού θέματος του εις έπαυλιν της Κρητικής Αναγεννήσεως, Athens 1972

— Η κρητική Αναγένηση και τα ιταλικά πρότυπα της αρχιτεκτονικής της, Αριάδνη Α', 1983, 103 - 138

GEROLA G., Monumenti Veneti nell' isola di Creta, I - IV, Venice 1905 - 1932

UNIVERSITY OF CRETE, Βενετσιάνικα μνημεία του νομού Ρεθύμνου, Rethymnon 1980

SPANAKIS ST., Η ύδρευση του Ηρακλείου (828 - 1939), Iraklion 1981

STERIOTOU J., Οι βενετικές οχυρώσεις του Ρεθύμνου (1540 - 1646). Συμβολή στή φρουριακή αρχιτεκτονική του 16ου και 17ου αιώνα, Thessaloniki 1974

The Church of Crete

SETTON K.M., The papacy and the Levant, 1204 -1571. I. The Thirteenth and Fourteenth Centuries, Philadelphia 1976 (= The American Philosophical Cociety)

TSIRPANLIS Z., Το κληροδότημα του καρδιναλίου Βησσαρίωνος για τους φιλενωτικούς της βενετοκρατούμενης Κρήτης (1439 - 17ος αι.), Thessaloniki 1967

— « Κατάστιχο ἐκκλησιών και μοναστηριών του Κοινού » (1248-1548). Συμβολή στη μελέτη των σχέσεων πολιτείας και Εκκλησίας στη βενετοκρατούμενη Κρήτη , Jannina 1985

THIRIET FR., La situation réligieuse en Crète au début du XVe siècle, London 1977 (Variorumn Reprints)

— Églises, fidèles et clergés en Crète Vénitienne, Acts of 4th Intern. Cretol. Congr. II, 484 - 500

TOMADAKIS N., Ο Ιωσήφ Βρυέννιος και η Κρήτη κατά το 1400. Μελέτη ιστορική και φιλολογική, Athens 1947

— Οι ορθόδοξοι παπάδες επί ενετοκρατίας και η χειροτονία αυτών , Κρητικά Χρονικά 13, 1959, 39 - 72

— Πρωτοπαπάδες Κρήτης (1210 - 1669), Κρητολογία 4, 1977, 39 - 48

— La politica religiosa di Venezia a Creta verso i Cretesi ortodossi dal XIII al XV secolo, in: Venezia e il Levante fino al secolo XV, 2, Florence 1973, 783 - 800

Cretan Painting

CHATZIDAKIS M., Recherches sur le peintre Théophane le Crétois, Dumbarton Oaks Papers 23 - 24 , 1969 - 70 , 302 - 352

CHATZIDAKIS NANO , Icons of the Cretan School (15th - 16th Century), Athens 1983 (Benaki Museum)

EMBIRICOS AL., L' École crétoise , dernière phase de la peinture byzantine, Paris 1967

KALOKYRIS K., The Byzantine Wallpainting of Crete, New York 1973

KONSTANTOUDAKI M., Οι ζωγράφοι του Χάνδακος κατά το πρώτον ήμισυ του 16ου αιώνος οι μαρτυρούμενοι εκ των νοταριακών αρχείων, Θησαυρίσματα 10, 1973, 291 - 380

PALIOURAS ATH., Ο ζωγράφος Γεώργιος Κλόντζας (1540 - 1608) και αι μικρογραφίαι του κώδικος αυτού, Athens 1977

UNIVERSITY OF CRETE and BIKELAIA LIBRARY, Εικόνες της Κρητικής Τέχνης (Από τον Χάνδακα ώς την Μόσχα και την Αγία Πετρούπολη). Introduction Man.Chatzidakis, Iraklion 1993

Cretan Literature

ALEXIOU ST., Κρητική Ανθολογία (ΙΕ' - ΙΖ' αιώνες) , Iraklion 1969

– Βιτσέντζος Κορνάρος Ερωτόκριτος , Athens 1980 (1986 ^{2})

EMBIRIKOS AL., La Renaissance Crétoise (XVIe et XVIIe siècles). I. La Littérature, Paris 1960

HOLTON D.W. (ed.), Literature and society in Venetian Crete, Cambridge 1991

MANOUSSAKAS M.I., Η κρητική λογοτεχνία κατά την εποχή της βενετοκρατίας Thessalonike 1965

MARSHALL F.H., Old Testament Legends, from a Greek Poem on Genesis and Exodus by Georgios Choumnos, Cambridge 1925

MAYROGORDATO J., The Greek Drama in crete in the Seventeenth Century, Journal of Hellenic Studies 48, 1928, 75 - 96

— Three Cretan Plays : The Sacrifice of Abraham, Erophile, and Gyparis, also the Cretan Pastoral Poem The Fair Shepherdess, translated fron the Greek by F.H.Marshall, with an Introduction by,– Oxford - London 1929

— The Erotokritos, translated by – Oxford 1929

MORGAN G., Cretan Poetry. Sources and Inspiration, Κρητικά Χρονικά 14, 1960, 7 - 68 and 203 -270, 379 - 434

VAN GEMERT A.F., The Cretan Poet Marinos Falieros, Θησαυρίσματα 14, 1977, 7 -70

POLITIS L., Il teatro a Creta nei suoi rapporti con il teatro italiano del Rinascimento, e in particolare con la comedia veneziana . Venezia e l' Oriente fratardo Medioevo e Rinascimento, Firenze 1966 (= Variorum Reprints , 1975)

The Cretan War

BERNARDY A.A., Venezia e il Turco nella seconda metà del sec. XVII, Florence 1902

BRUSONI GIR., Historia dell' Ultima Guerra tra i Veneziani e Turchi nei regni di Candia e Dalmacia dal 1644 al 1671, Venice 1673

CHIONIDES CH., Αγγλικόν Υπόμνημα περί της πολιορκίας και πτώσεως του Χάνδακος, Κρητικά Χρονικά 3, 1949, 403 - 505

DETORAKIS TH., Ένα άγνωστο Γαλλικό Υπόμνημα του 1661 για την Κρήτη, Πεπραγμένα ΣΤ' Διεθνούς Κρητολογικού Συνεδρίου, II, 149 - 155

MORGAN GAR., English State Papers on the Siege of Candia, Κρητικά χρονικά 13, 1959, 311 - 318

PESTALOZZI A., Auf den Spuren von General Johann Rudolf Werdmüller in der Agäis (1664 - 1667), Zurich 1973.

ROMANIN S., Storia documentata di Venezia, III, Venice 1974 [2]

VOKOTOPOULOS C., Ιστορία του Νέου Ελληνισμού, III , Thessalonike 1968, 483 - 525

THE PERIOD OF THE OTTOMAN RULE (1669 - 1898)

1. The Early Turkish period (1669 - 1821)

CHIDIROGLOU P., Σημαίνοντες Τουρκοκρήτες , Κρητικά Χρονικά 24, 1972, 465 - 476

— Εξισλαμισμοί στην Κρήτη,Πεπραγμένα Δ' Διεθνούς Κρητολογικού Συνεδρίου, III, 336 - 350

FOURNARAKIS C.G., Τουρκοκρήτες , Chania 1929

LAOURDAS B., Η επανάστασις των Σφακιανών και ο Δασκαλογιάννης κατά τα έγγραφα του Τουρκικού Αρχείου Ηρακλείου, Κρητικά Χρονικά 1,1947, 275 - 290

PAPADOPETRAKIS GR., Ιστορία των Σφακίων, ήτοι μέρος της Κρητικής Ιστορίας, Athens 1888 (1971 ^{2})

SABATIER D., Les relations commerciales entre Marseilles et la Crète dans la première moitié du XVIII siècle, in: J. P.FILIPPINI etc., Dossiers sur le commerce français en Méditerranée Orientale au XVIII siècle, Paris 1976 (= P.U.F.) , 151 - 233

TRIANTAGYLLIDOU-BALADIÉ Y , Les conditions de commerce en Crète pendant les premières décennies de la domination ottomane, Πεπραγμένα Δ' Διεθνούς Κρητολογικού Συνεδρίου, III, 297 - 304

STAVRINIDES N., Μεταφράσεις τουρκικών ιστορικών εγγράφων αφορώντων εις την Ιστορίαν της Κρήτης, 1 - 5 , Iraklion 1975 - 1985

— Συμβολή εις την ιστορίαν των Σφακίων (1645 - 1770) , Κρητικά Χρονικά 9, 1956, 213 - 333

VAKALOPOULOS C., Ιστορία του Νέου Ελληνισμού, 4, Θεσσαλονίκη 1973, 88 f , passim

— Quelques informations statistiques sur la crète avant et après la revolution de 1821, πεπραγμένα Δ' Διεθνούς Κρητολογικού Συνεδρίου, III , 26 -30

2. The period of Cretan Uprisings (1821 - 1898)

The Uprising of 1821

KOKKINOS D., Η Ελληνική Επανάστασις , 1 - 6 , Athens 1967 - 1969

KRITOVOULIDIS C., Απομνημονεύματα του περί της αυτονομίας της Ελλάδος πολέμου των Κρητών , Athens 1859

REINACH A.J., La Question Crétoise, Paris 1910

TOMADAKIS N., Κρητικά Ιστορικά Έγγραφα 1821 - 1830 (Α'. 1821-1824) Athens 1974

— Βιβλιογραφία των Κρητικών Επαναστάσεων, Α'. 1821 -1830. Συμβολή πρώτη, Δελτίον της Ιστορικής και Εθνολογικής Εταιρείας της Ελλάδος 13, 1959, 26 - 32

— Τα εν Κρήτη πολιτεύματα (1821 -1824), Δελτίον της Ιστορικής και Εθνολογικής Εταιρείας της Ελλάδος 15, 1961, 3 - 51

TSOKOPOULOS G.B, Ιστορία των επαναστάσεων της Κρήτης 1820 - 1889, Athens

VAKALOPOULOS AP., Ιστορία του Νέου Ελληνισμού Ε'- ΣΤ', Thessaloniki 1980, 1982, passim

Egyptian Rule (1830 -1840)

PETROPOULOS J.A., Politics and Statecraft in the Kingdom of Greece, 1833 - 1843 , Princeton 1968

RASENT ZENAP ISMAT, Η Κρήτη υπό την αιγυπτιακήν εξουσίαν (1830 -1840), (Translated fron Arabian by Eug. Michailidis), Iraklion 1878

STAVRINOU MIRANTA, Η Αγγλική πολιτική και το Κρητικό Ζήτημα (1839 -1841) Athens 1986

The Uprising of 1841

ZAMBETAKIS EMM., Συμβολή εις την καλυτέραν γνώσιν της επαναστατικής περιόδου του 1841 εν Κρήτη, Κρητικά Χρονικά 10, 1956, 171 - 214

LAIOS G., Οι κατακτητικές βλέψεις του Μέττερνιχ επί της Κρήτης (1840 - 1848), Πεπραγμένα Β' Διεθνούς Κρητολογικού Συνεδρίου IV, 277 - 282

The Uprising of 1866 - 1869

ARNAKIS GEORGIADES G., American Consul in a Cretan War: William J. Stillman . Revised edition of « The Cretan Insurrection of 1866 -7 -8», Austin,Texas 1966

DONTA D., Greece and the Great Powers 1863 - 1875, Thessaloniki 1966

MAMALAKIS J.,Ο Αγώνας του 1866 -1869 για την ένωση της Κρήτης: Ι. Η επιβολή της ιδδέας. ΙΙ. Περίοδος του Μουσταφά πασά, Thessaloniki 1942, 1947

MARKOGLOU EMM., Το ενδιαφέρον του Αμερικανικού Λαού διά την Κρητικήν επανάστασιν 1866 - 1869, Athens 1970

PREVELAKIS EL., Η μεγάλη Κρητική Επανάσταση 1866 - 1869, Athens 1966

PREVELAKIS EL. and PLAGIANNAKOU - BEKIARI B., Η Κρητική Επανάσταση 1866 - 1869. Εκθέσεις των εν Κρήτη προξένων της Ελλάδος, I - II , Athens 1970

TOMADAKIS N., Συμβολή εις την βιβλιογραφίαν των Κρητικών Επανα-

στάσεων, Β'. Βιβλιογραφία της Επαναστάσεως 1866 - 1869, Επετηρίς της Εταιρείας Κρητικών Σπουδών 2, 1939, 198 - 238
TSIRIDANIS N., Η πολιτική και διπλωματική ιστορία της εν Κρήτη Εθνικής Επαναστάσεως 1866 - 1869, I -III , Athens 1950 - 1951
VENERIS TIM., Το Αρκάδι διά μέσου των αιώνων, Athens 1938

The Uprising of 1878

MATZAPETAKIS ST., Συμβολή εις την ιστορίαν της Κρήτης κατά την επανάστασιν του 1878, Iraklion 1904
PARLAMAS M., Πρωτόκολλον του Γενικού Αρχηγού των Ανατολικών επαρχιών της Κρήτης κατά την επανάστασιν του 1878, Κρητικά Χρονικά 8, 1954, 171 - 203

The period 1878 - 1898

CELAIDIS P., L'Administration Turque actuelle dans l 'île de Crète, Athens 1892
EDWARDS CH., Letters from Crete. Letters written during the Spring of 1886, London 1887
KOUNDOUROS M., Ιστορικαί και διπλωματικαί αποκαλύψεις, Athens 1921
LEKANIDIS J.J., Ημερολόγιον της απελευθερωτικής επαναστάσεως της Κρήτης 1895 - 1898, Chania 1963
SCALZOUNIS J., Ile de Crète.Organisation des tribunaux , Athens 1880
TOMADAKIS N., Συμβολή εις την βιβλιογραφίαν των Κρητικών Επαναστάσεων. Α'. Βιβλιογραφία αναφερομένη εις τα γεγονότα των ετών 1895, 1896, 1897 και 1898, Επετηρίς της Εταιρείας Κρητικών Σπουδών 1, 1938, 530 - 555, and 2,1939, 239 -244.
VENIZELOS EL., Η Κρητική Επανάστασις του 1889, Athens 1889

History of Church (1645 - 1898)

DETORAKIS TH., Ανέκδοτοι επισκοπικοί κατάλογοι της Κρήτης, Κρητολογία 4, 1977, 65 - 112
PSILAKIS N., Μοναστήρια καί ερημητήρια της Κρήτης, I - II , Iraklion 1992, 1993
TOMADAKIS N., Ιστορία της Εκκλησίας Κρήτης επί Τουρκοκρατίας (1645 -1898). Α'. Αι Πηγαί, Athens 1974

— Έλεγχος των εν Κρήτη αρχιερατευσάντων επί Τουρκοκρατίας, Επετηρίς της Εταιρείας Κρητικών Σπουδών, 3,1940,114 - 144

THE PERIOD OF AUTONOMY (1898 -1913)

BERARD V., Les affaires de Crète , Paris 1900

BORDEAUX P.E., L'occupation de Crète (1897 -1910). Notes et souvenirs, Thonon -les -Bains 1946

LOMBARD H., L'occupation Internationale de la Crète de 1900 à 1906, Paris 1908

PIKROS J., Η Κρητική Πολιτεία, in: Ιστορία του Ελληνικού Έθνους 14, 1977, 88 -159

PRINCE GEORGES DE GRECE , Affaires de Crète, Paris 1905

— Αναμνήσεις εκ Κρήτης (1898 -1906) , Athens 1959

SVOLOPOULOS C., Ο Ελευθέριος Βενιζέλος και η πολιτική κρίσις εις την αυτόνομον Κρήτην (1901 - 1906), Athens 1974

THE BATTLE OF CRETE (1941)

BUCKLEY CHR. Greece and Crete 1941, London 1977

CLARK A., The Fall of Crete, London 1962

HETHERINGTON J., Airborne invasion.The Story of the Battle of Crete, London 1974

KUROWSKI FR., Der Kampf um Kreta, Bonn 1965

SPENCER J.H., Battle of Crete, London 1976

STEWART I.M.G., The Struggle for Crete (20 May -1 June 1941), London 1966

THOMAS D.A., Crete 1941. The Battle at Sea, London 1972

INDEX

PICTURES - MAPS - PHOTOGRAPHS

1. Palace of Knossos - Western wing (Reconstruction by Piet de Jong - N. Platon) (See also, S. Logiadou-Platonos and N. Marinatos, Crete, Athens 1985, 89-90).

2. The famous Agia Triada Sarcophagus.

3. Drawn reconstruction of the west façade of the palace of Knossos (Sir Arthur Evans).

4. The throne room in the palace of Knossos.

6. The Serpent Goddess (Archaeological Museum, Herakleion)

5. The Prince with the Lilies. From a frieze fresco at Knossos.

7. The «Parisienne» . A famous fresco at Knossos (ca. 1500 B.C.) .

9. The famous Harvester Vase from the villa at Agia Triada.

8. Kamares ware *krater* (bowl) from the palace at Phaistos.

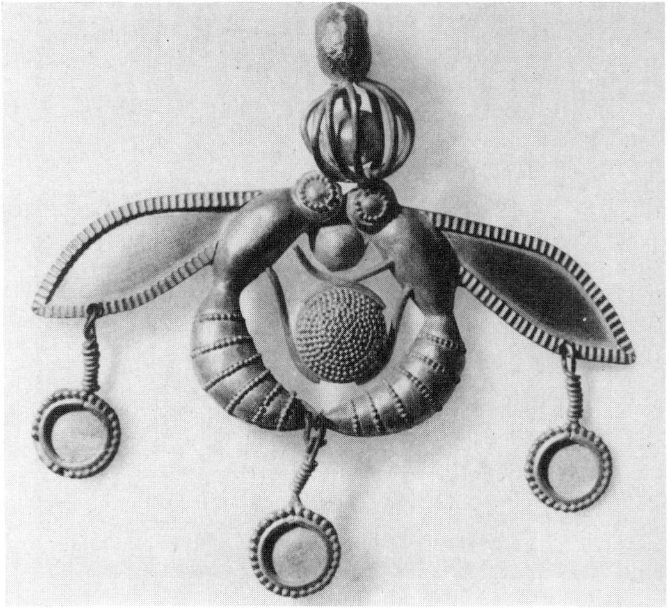

11. The famous gold pendant with bees on a honeycomb, a unique example of Minoan jewellery craftsmanship. From the site of Chrysolakkos, Mallia.

10. A votive vessel (*rhyton*) in the shape of a bull's head, from the small palace at Knossos.

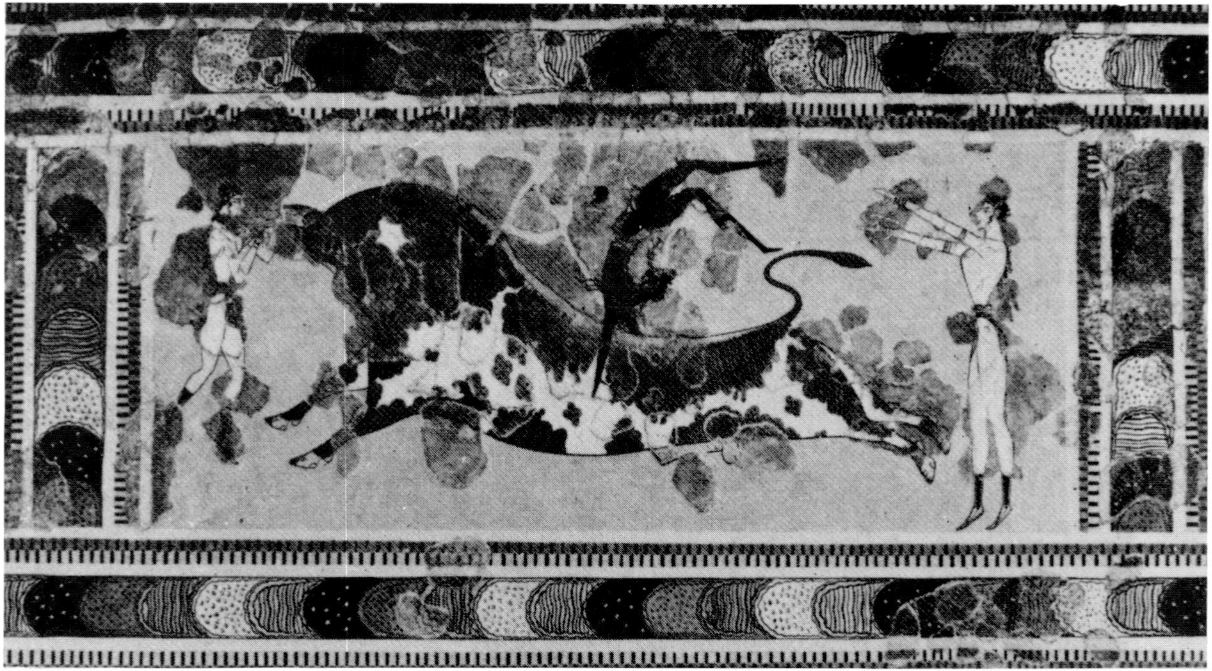

12. Bull vaulting. Fresco in the palace of Knossos.

13. An excellent rhyton of rock crystal, from the palace of Zakros (ca. 1500 - 1450 B.C.) .

14 . Clay tablets with Linear script. Right, Linear A from Agia Triada. Left, Linear B from Knossos (Marinatos-Hirmer, *Kriti kai Mykenaiki Ellas,* 116).

15. The Phaistos Disk.

16. The so-called 'Lady of Auxerre' (Louvre, Paris). It is a characteristic example of the Daidalic art style (R. Matton, *La Crète antique*, XXXI).

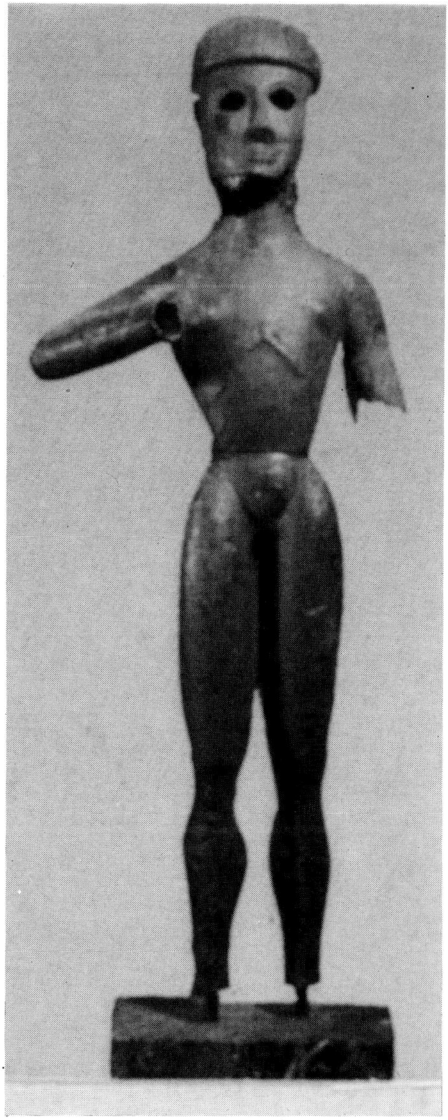

17. Bronze figurine from Dreros (G. Sakellarakis, *The Archaeological Museum of Herakleion: an illustrated guide,* p. 141).

18. The Asklepieion sanctuary at Levina at the time of excavating (1900), with Cretan gendarmes in traditional breeches.

19. The temple of Pythian Apollo at Gortyn, at the time of excavating (1900).

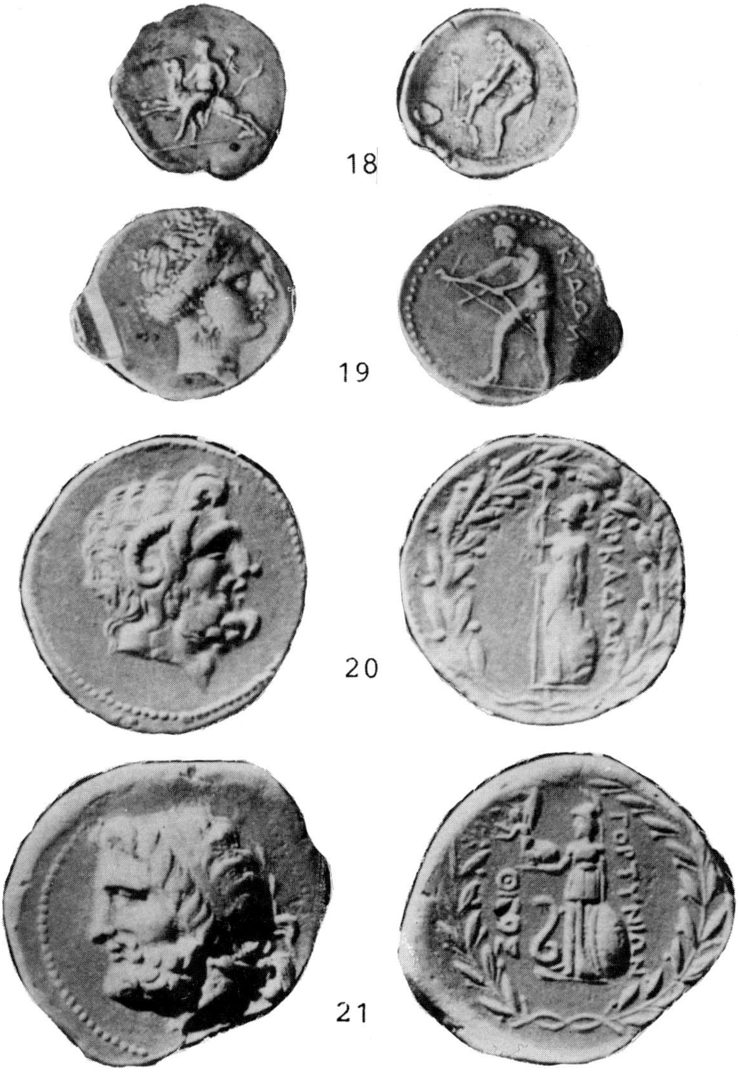

20 - 23 . Coins minted in Cretan cities: 18. Syvrita (350-300 B.C.) 19. Kydonia (350-300 B.C.) 20. Arkades (Ist century B.C. 21. Gortyn (Ist century B.C.)

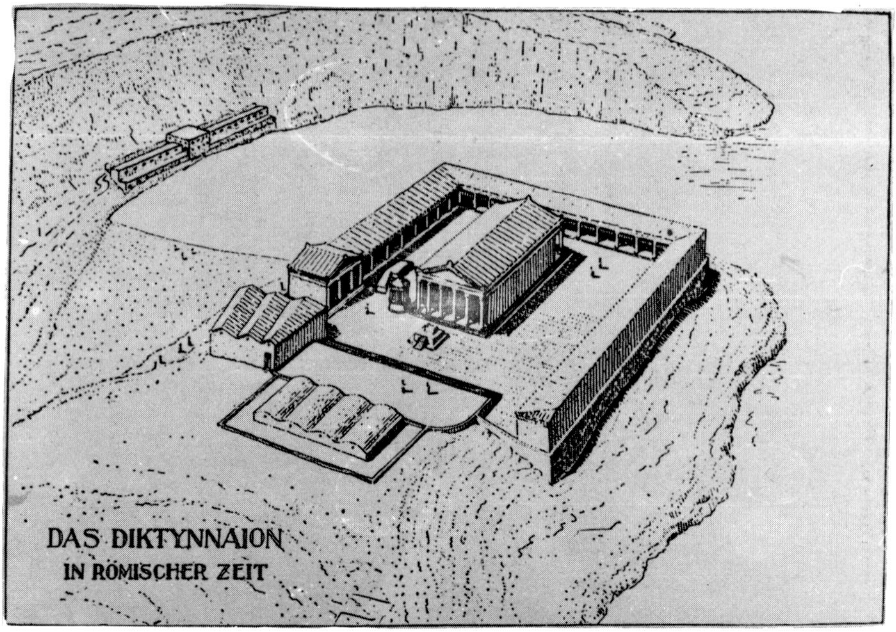

24. The Diktynnaion sanctuary at Menies (Kisamos), as it may have appeared in the 2nd century B.C. (drawn reconstruction by Fr. Matz, *Forschungen auf Kreta,* Berlin 1951).

25. Mosaic floor decoration from the Roman period, depicting a Satyr carrying off the nymph Amymone and her rescue by Poseidon. It is topped by a representation of a cock fight (Archaeological Museum, Chania).

26. A statue of Aphrodite in bath, from Gortyn, dating in the Roman period.
(G. Sakellarakis, *o.c.*, 138)

27. Mosaic decoration with peacocks and a vase on the floor of an early Christian basilica in Suyia (Selino) dated to the 6th-7th centuries A.D. (drawing by Ant. Orlandos, *Kritika Chronika* 7, 1953, figure 12).

28. Manuscript illustration from ms. 427 of the monastery of Great Lavra, Mount Athos (11th century). It depicts the martyrdom of the Ten Holy Martyrs of Crete (B. Laourdas, Paratiriseis eis ta encomia ton Agion Deka, *Kritika Chronika* 4, 1950, Plate II).

29. Nikephoros Phokas the Emperor .

30. The famous icon of the Virgin (Mesopantitissa), today in the church of Santa Maria della Salute in Venice :
Our prayers are unheard and my heart is broken,
for you have gone, my Lady, Virgin Mesopantitissa...
(From the Lament of Candax in the poem *The Cretan War* by Marinos Tzane Bounialis, p. 554, lines 23-24.) .

31. Rethymnon in the early 17th century. Painting by an unknown painter from Rethymnon (A. Nenedakis, Rethemnos. *Trianda aiones politeia,* Athens 1983, p. 17).

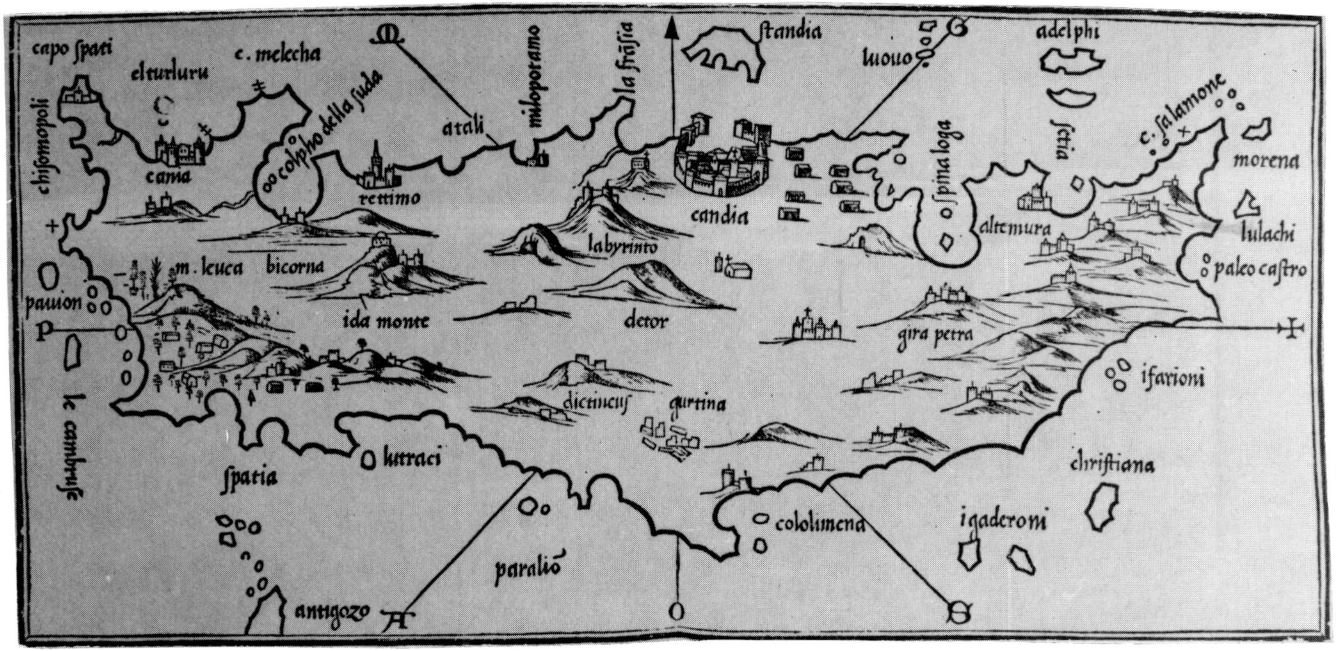

32. Map of Crete. Woodcut from the Isolario by Benedetto Bordone, II, LI, Venice 1528 (A. Stylianos, The Map of Crete and Cyprus, *Pepragmena* III, II, 29 5, plate 62a).

33. Icon of Theotokos « The Bramble », by Michael Damaskenos (16th century).

34. Christ (deesis). Painter Angelos (Hagia Moni in Viannos). 15th century.

MARE ADRIATICVM.
MARE CRETICVM.
CRETA
MARE MEDITERANEVM
C°. BVSO.
C°. SPADA.
C°. MELECCA.
CANEA
RETTIMO.
C°. CRIO.

35. Map of Crete, drawn by Fr. Basilicata , 16th century (Venice, Museum Correr, cod. 44)

36. Map of Crete, by the Cretan cartographer George Sideris or Kalapodas (1537- 1565).

37. The Venetian Club of Candia (1627).

38. The Morozini Fountain (1628), as it stands today.

39. The Venetian commemorative medallion for the Morozini Fountain. On the one side is depicted the commissioner of the work, with the inscription FRANC(ISCUS) MAUROC(ENUS) VEN(ETUS) CRETAE PROCONSUL. On the obverse side Zeus rides astride an eagle in the clouds, above a faithful miniature representation of the fountain, accompanied by the elegant wordplay GAUDET FLUMINE, NON FULMINE (Zeus joys in water and not in thunder). The date is MDCXXVIII (1628).

40. The large monastery of St. Catherine's of the Sinaits in Herakleion (photographed in 1900).

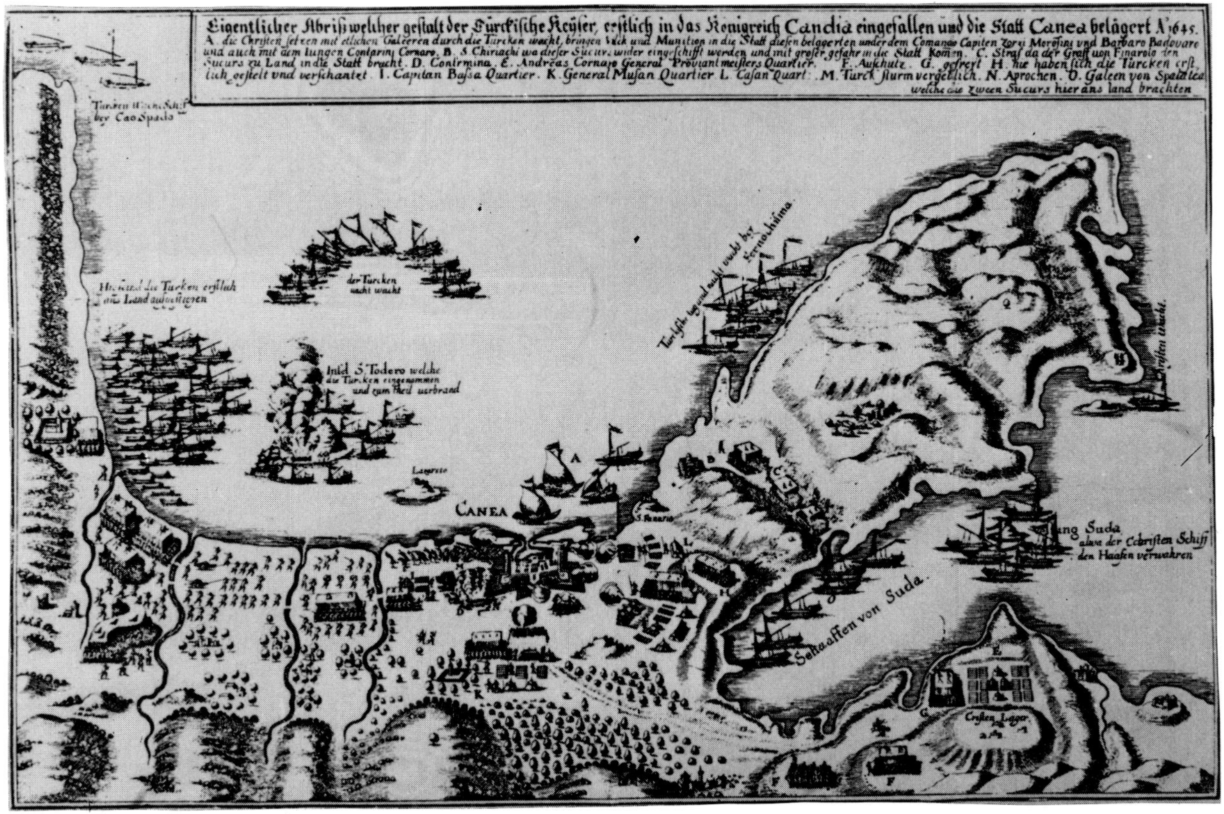

41. The Turkish landing at Chania and the siege of the fortified town (1645). German copperplate engraving of the period (Cartographic Monuments of Crete, III, 20).

42. The fortified city of Candia during the last years of the siege. From a military report of the period (1667?).

43. Rethymnon in 1699 drawn by Tournefort .

45. The Rethymnon-born Sultana Evmenia Vergitzi (1643-1715), the famous Rebya Gyulnus (Spring Rose-Water). Copperplate engraving by N. de Larmessin (= M. I. Manousakas, in *Kritika Chronika* 5, 1951, plate 15, picture 4).

44. Sphakian archer. From the book by C. Vecellio, Costumes anciens et modernes, Paris 1860, 406 (= N. Stavrinidis, in *Kritika Chronika* 9, 1955, Plate 5).

46. The cathedral of St. Titus in Herakleion, converted by the Turks to a mosque (Vizir çamii). Photograph taken in 1900.

47. The Catholic church of the Saviour in Herakleion, converted by the Turks to a mosque (Valide çamii), Photograph taken in 1900.

49. Daskaloyannis, the first to raise the flag of rebellion, and to die, for the cause of Cretan freedom.

48. The tombstone of Ferhat Pasha (Historical Museum of Crete, Herakleion).

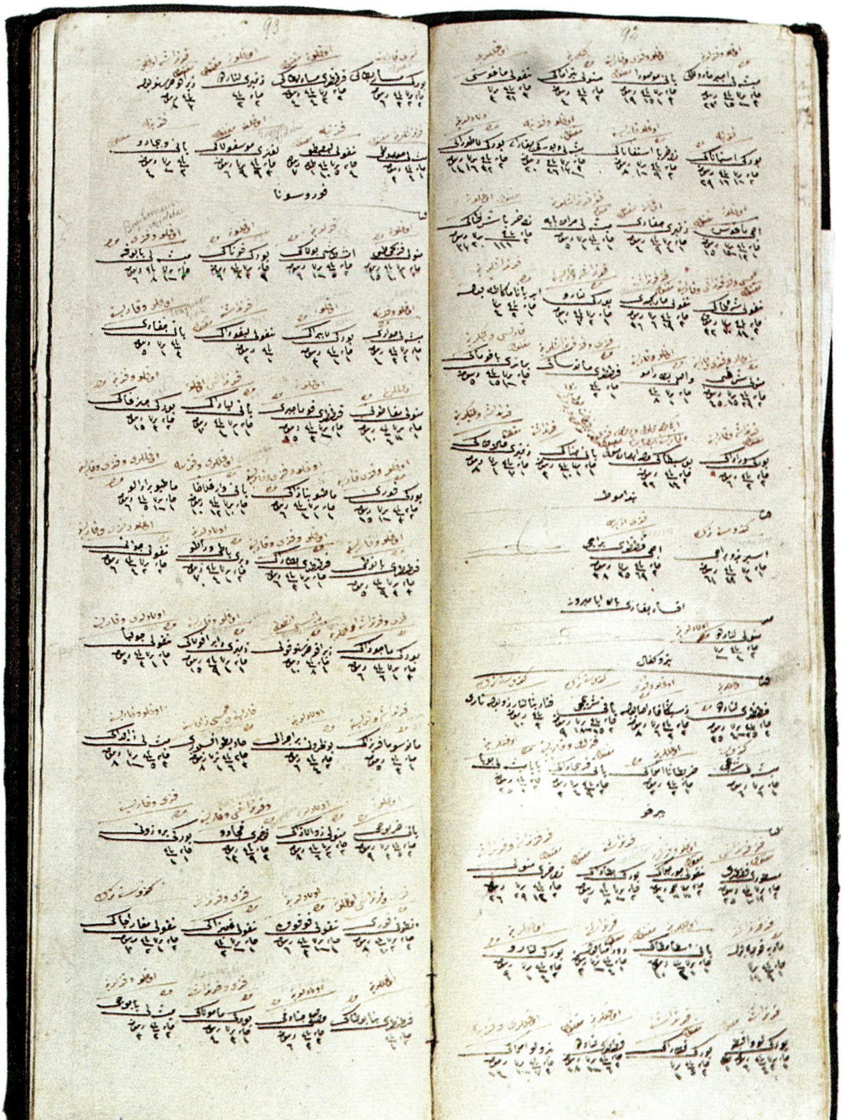

50. The Cod. 120 of the Turkish Archives of Herakleion, so-called « Codex of Sacrificies » , p. 92.

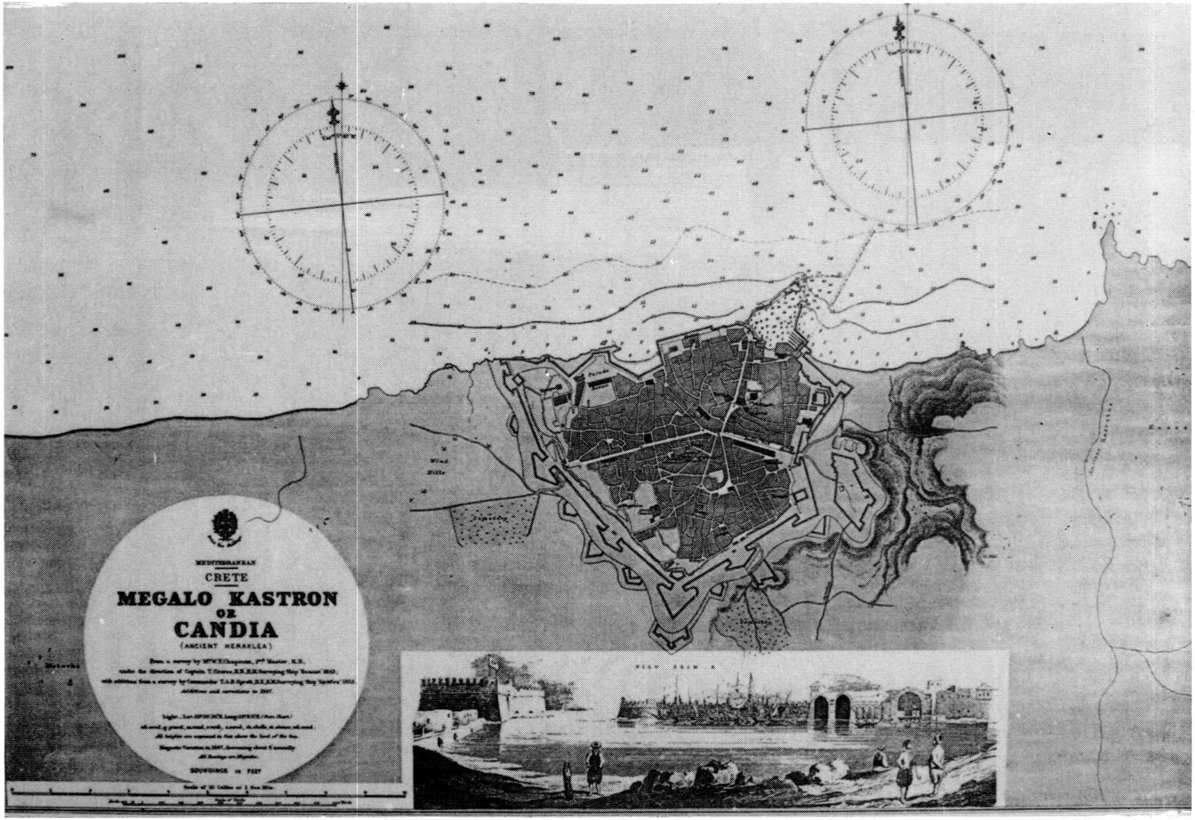

51. The Megalo Kastron (Fortified city of Candia) of Crete in 1843. Lithograph from the map of the British Admiral, surveyed by W. T. Chapman (= Cartographic Monuments of Crete, I, 30).

52. Lithograph depicting the explosion of Arkadi. Reproduced by kind permission of the Historical Museum of Crete (no. 624).

54. Hadji-Michalis Yannaris (1827-1916), leading figure of the Cretan struggle for freedom (1858-1898).

53. Michael Korakas (1787-1882), commander-in-chief of the Eastern provinces of the island, and leading figure of the Cretan rebellions (1821-1878).

56. Manousos Koundouros, organiser of the Political Action Committee.

55. Antonios Michelidakis, political figure of Herakleion, Chairman of the Cretan Assembly.

57. Lithograph of 1897, entitled: 'The resurrection of Crete'. From left to right the figures are the sultan Hamit, Ioannis Sphakianakis, chairman of the executive body of Crete, King George I of Greece, the czar of Russia, Queen Victoria, Crete, Felix Vor, Humbert and the people of Crete.

58. The Cretan Pantheon (1898). Reproduced by kind permission of the Historical Museum of Crete (no. 1064).

59. The executive body of Crete (1897-1898). In the middle of the first row sits the chairman Ioannis Sphakianakis. On his right is Eleftherios Venizelos, deputy for Chania, and on his left is Mylonoyannis, deputy of Sphakia. From left to right in the back row are Zacharakis (Rethymnon), Hatzidakis (Herakleion) and Yamalakis (Lasithi).

60. Prince George, High Commissioner of Crete and the admirals of the Great Powers photographed on the day of the handing over of power (9 December 1898). From the archive collection of I. D. Mourellos (Historical Museum of Crete).

61. Parade of British forces in Herakleion (1900).

62. The first Constituent Assembly of Crete. Photograph from the archive collection of I. D. Mourellos (Historical Museum of Crete).

64. Eleftherios Venizelos. Photograph taken in 1903.

63. Prince George, High Commissioner of Crete.

65. Popular demonstration at Chania in support of union with Greece (2 April 1905). Photograph from the archive collection of I. D. Mourellos.

66. The rebels of Therisos (1906). Photograph from the archive collection of I. D. Mourellos.

68.Alexander Zaimis, High Commissioner of Crete (1906-1908).

67. The lowering of the British Union Jack on the day of the departure of British forces from Herakleion (13 July 1909).

69. Senior and junior officers of the Cretan civil guard.

70. Cretan deputies, having been refused membership of the Greek parliament were held on the ships of the Great Powers (1911).

71. Photograph of the drop of the German parachutists on Crete.

72. Kalokerinou Avenue, Herakleion, after the Battle of Crete (1941).

74. British soldier sporting a Swastika flag as spoils of war. Photograph from the collection of the Historical Museum of Crete.

73. The destruction of Kandanos that marked the beginning of Nazi reprisals in Crete (2 June 1941). Photograph taken from the book by V. Mathiopoulos, *Ikones tis Katochis,* Athens 1980, p. 165.

75. British newspapers, containing news about the Battle of Crete. 'Crete News' was the first English language paper to be published in Crete (Chania).

THEOCHARIS DETORAKIS
HISTORY OF CRETE

ISBN 960 - 220 - 712 - 4

Printed in Iraklion of Crete
by "TYPOKRETA" S.A.
Indusrial Area of Iraklion
Tel. 229313 and 229357